CW01095978

INSOLVENT PARTNERSHIPS

INSOLVENT PARTNERSHIPS

Glen Davis MA (OXON)
of Middle Temple and Gray's Inn, Barrister

Michael Steiner MA (OXON)
Solicitor of the Supreme Court

Malcolm Cohen BSc (Hons), FCA, MSPI
Chartered Accountant and Licensed Insolvency Practitioner

JORDANS

1996

Published by
Jordan Publishing Limited
21 St Thomas Street
Bristol BS1 6JS

British Library Cataloguing-in-Publication Data
A catalogue record for this book is available from the British Library.

ISBN 0 85308 351 7

Typeset by Mendip Communications Limited, Frome, Somerset
Printed by Bookcraft (Bath) Limited, Midsomer Norton, Avon

FOREWORD

In *Re Marr* [1990] Ch 773 at 779H, Nicholls LJ referred to partners becoming 'enmeshed in the intricacies of the legislation relating to the winding up of insolvent partnerships'. This must be a frequent experience for those who are concerned with the problems of a partnership which is or may become insolvent.

When a partnership faces insolvency, all of the technical problems which can arise under the Insolvency Act 1986 – problems of liquidations, of administrations, of voluntary arrangements – may be encountered in the partnership context. These technical problems are compounded by unresolved issues which are intrinsic to the basic law of partnership itself. The Insolvent Partnerships Order 1994 contains a praiseworthy attempt to provide a comprehensive code. It still remains, however, to a large extent unexplored territory.

There is now a considerable industry devoted to publishing books about insolvency, but this is the first book to deal comprehensively with the insolvent partnership in the context of the Insolvent Partnerships Order 1994. It is, in my view, an authoritative guide benefiting from the different professional backgrounds of the three authors.

I have no doubt that it will be of great assistance to everyone who practises in this area, and I have no hesitation in recommending it to practitioners.

Michael Crystal QC
3–4 South Square
Gray's Inn

PREFACE

'A barrister, a solicitor and an accountant...' sounds like the lead-in to one of those jokes that come out with the scotch and chasers late at night at an ILA or SPI conference. In fact, we have found working on this book a valuable and enjoyable collaboration. We have drawn a great deal on our different backgrounds as we have tried to comprehend the sometimes opaque drafting of the Insolvent Partnerships Order, to identify the practical problems which it is likely to generate, and to anticipate how a court might deal with those issues.

In many respects, partnership law is undeveloped in England and Wales; it has been left behind by the rapid evolution of the law of private and public companies in the course of this century. It may be that the number of partnerships will decline and there will be a rush to incorporate offshore and obtain the benefits of limited liability that way. None the less, partnership remains a very common form of economic organisation, from the married couple who manage a pub or newsagency to the city accountants and solicitors with international practices and lists of partners running into the hundreds. Some of these will inevitably get into financial difficulties and we need a simple regime to ensure that those which can be rescued, are rescued and those which can't be rescued are liquidated economically so as to maximise the returns to creditors. Unfortunately, the approach of the Insolvent Partnerships Order 1994, which frequently treats a partnership as if it were a company, is likely to be far from straightforward to apply in practice. Many of the technical issues which arise have no easy solution, and it must always be borne in mind that individual partnerships differ from each other much more than companies do.

We are grateful to our respective colleagues who have been so generous with their time, ideas, comments and criticisms, particularly John Briggs, Robin Knowles, Mark Phillips, Robin Dicker and Antony Zacaroli at 3–4 South Square, Neil Griffiths and Michael Rutstein at Denton Hall and Paul Clark at BDO Stoy Hayward. However, the finished text is our own, and we bear the responsibility for any errors. We must thank Ceri Evans, for her patience as our editor, and Martin West of Jordans, whose idea this book originally was; if he had any regrets as he found himself negotiating the contract word by excruciating word with the three of us, he had the grace not to show it.

We must also record our thanks to Michael Crystal QC who has kindly found the time to write the Foreword.

We know how much time we have spent on this book at the expense of our families. We love them dearly, and hope that they will think that their forbearance has been worthwhile. It is to Deborah, Joshua and William, to Pat, Clare and Jamie, and to Shoshi, Talia, Benjamin and Yardenna, that this work is dedicated.

We have endeavoured to state the law as at 1 July 1996.

GLEN DAVIS
MICHAEL STEINER
MALCOLM COHEN
July 1996

CONTENTS

TABLE OF CASES

References are to paragraph numbers.

TABLE OF STATUTES

References are to paragraph numbers.

Italic text indicates that the reference is to a statutory provision as modified by the Insolvent Partnerships Order 1994 ('the Order').

TABLE OF STATUTORY INSTRUMENTS

Chapter 1

INTRODUCTION

1.1 BACKGROUND TO THE NEW LAW

In this book, we aim to provide a reasonably concise guide to the practical application of the Insolvent Partnerships Order 1994 ('the Order'), to be used in particular by insolvency practitioners and their legal advisers. For a number of reasons, this is not an entirely straightforward task.

Partnerships do not have a separate legal personality from their members; they are simply aggregates of the individuals or companies which comprise them and the name of a firm is merely a convenient collective noun for the members at a particular time.

Prior to 1986, insolvent companies were dealt with under the Companies Acts, and insolvent individuals under the Bankruptcy Acts. The Insolvency Act 1986 ('the Act') brought these two regimes together in one statute, but for the most part retains a clear demarcation between those sections relating to companies, and those relating to individuals. The Order operates by applying provisions of the Act to partnerships in a modified form. It does so by setting out in its articles various possible permutations for dealing with a partnership which is or may be insolvent, and then applying a modified version of relevant sections of the Act, as provided in the various Schedules to the Order[1].

Insolvency is very much a practical issue for both debtors and creditors. The law in this area ought to provide a straightforward framework for the orderly management of the insolvent estate and the fair treatment of creditors. Unfortunately, the Order is not only unwieldy to apply, but the drafting frequently gives rise to considerable conceptual uncertainty. Until a body of case-law has developed[2], it will not be possible to give any certain reading of how particular provisions would in practice be applied by the courts. We have tried to highlight some of these uncertainties in our text, and to provide a possible indication of what the answer might be if and when a case on the point is decided.

It is assumed that any reader of this book is reasonably familiar with the structure of the Act and the Insolvency Rules 1986, as amended ('the Rules'). For the most part, therefore, we do not dwell in detail on provisions of the Act or the Rules. However, it is not possible to approach the insolvent partnership without having at least a general appreciation of the legal context in which a solvent partnership operates. A concise overview is provided in **Chapter 2**.

The Order introduces for the first time the partnership voluntary arrangement ('PVA') (*Article 4*) and the partnership administration order (*Article 6*). However, we take as our starting point the premise that, where creditors are asked to consider alternatives to bankruptcy or liquidation, they will usually agree only if they perceive a potential commercial benefit to them; that is to say, there has to be at least the prospect that they will fare better out of a voluntary arrangement than in a liquidation. We therefore deal in detail in **Chapters 3**, **4** and **5** with the liquidation of a partnership, paying particular attention to the changes which the Order makes to the rules for the distribution of assets. Following the categories which apply under the Order, **Chapter 3** covers petitions by creditors, either without (*Article 7*) or with (*Article 8*) a concurrent petition against one or more members. **Chapter 4** covers petitions by members, either without a concurrent petition against one or more members (*Article 9*) or with concurrent petitions against all members (*Article 10*), and joint bankruptcy petitions by all the individual members (*Article 11*).

Chapter 5 deals with other provisions which apply under the Order in relation to insolvent partnerships. In particular, these involve the procedure for winding up an unregistered company which is itself a member of an insolvent partnership (*Article 12*), deposits on petitions (*Article 13*) and the powers given to a court under Article 14 to apply provisions of the Order when a petition is presented against a member of an insolvent partnership. Article 14 may prove extremely important in practice because it appears, for example, to give a court the discretion to apply the revised priorities for treatment of debts in Schedule 4 even where concurrent petitions have not initially been presented against the firm and one or more members.

In **Chapter 6**, we move on to consider the defensive manoeuvres which may be available to the members of an insolvent partnership. There will be many cases where individual partners will need to consider obtaining the protection of an interim order under Part VIII of the Act, so we begin by discussing individual voluntary arrangements ('IVAs'). This is partly because there will still be some cases where a proposal of interlocking IVAs by the members of a small partnership will be the most cost-efficient and effective solution, and partly to lay the foundations for the detailed treatment of the new PVA procedure in **Chapter 7**. Detailed consideration of the new partnership administration regime is to be found in **Chapter 8**.

The Order also applies certain parts of the Company Directors Disqualification Act 1986 to those who have been involved in an insolvent partnership; the procedure and some of the implications of this are considered in **Chapter 9**. Surprisingly, it appears that the penalty for misfeasantly managing a partnership may be prohibition from acting as a director of a limited company, but not from continuing to trade as a partner.

Finally, in **Chapter 10**, we take an overview of the various routes and permutations available in dealing with an insolvent partnership, and consider some of the tactical issues which are likely to arise in practice.

In this introductory chapter, we aim to set the Order in its legal context, by outlining briefly the main provisions of statute and common law which are relevant.

---

1 The Order is the second attempt to do this. It replaces the Insolvent Partnerships Order 1986 (which took the same approach).
2 There are as yet almost no reported cases under the Insolvent Partnerships Order 1986.

1.2 PARTNERSHIP LAW BEFORE 1890

The Partnership Act 1890[1] was the crucial watershed for the development of partnerships in English law, and it is now the single most important source for anyone considering partnership in a legal context. However, the Partnership Act codified a body of case-law and academic comment which had developed over several hundred years both in the Courts of Law (in which the partnership was treated as a matter of contract, often between merchants) and in the Courts of Equity (which dealt with the relationship of trust and conscience between the partners). With the passing of the Judicature Acts, which combined those two branches of the English law in 1875, it became possible for both strands to become entwined and given a substantially statutory form[2].

However, the Partnership Act not only did not set out to make new law, it expressly preserved the previous rules of equity or common law applicable to partnership, except so far as they are inconsistent with the Partnership Act itself[3]. It is frequently necessary to refer to pre-1890 decisions in order to understand the terms of the Partnership Act, and to fill in the gaps left by the statute. It is also worth noting that, as partnership is to a considerable extent contractual, questions relating to when a contract is made or broken, and when it can be rectified or set aside, fall to be dealt with on normal contractual principles.

1 Referred to in this book as 'the Partnership Act'.
2 The Partnership Law Amendment Act 1865 (usually known as Bovill's Act) was an earlier attempt to negate potential liability as a partner in four particular cases, today found in subsections 2(3)(b)–(e) of the Partnership Act 1890.
3 Partnership Act 1890, s 46.

1.3 THE PARTNERSHIP ACT 1890

By modern standards, the Partnership Act is relatively short, and deceptively clear. Its principal features are dealt with in Chapter 2.

However, it is worth noting that, while it offers a definitional framework for partnership, and sets out to regulate the relationships between partner and partner, the Partnership Act is in no sense a compulsory statutory code; the partners are always free to vary their mutual rights and obligations[1].

1 Partnership Act 1890, s 19.

1.4 THE LIMITED PARTNERSHIPS ACT 1907

The limited partnership (ie a partnership in which some partners are not fully liable for the debts of the firm) had become well known in continental Europe during the 19th century, but was not available under English law until the passage of the Limited Partnerships Act in 1907. In that year, Parliament also passed the Companies Act 1907, which introduced the private company; it is probably for that reason that limited partnerships have remained relatively uncommon in this jurisdiction.

The Limited Partnerships Act modifies the application of the Partnership Act, which continues to apply[1]. In a limited partnership, a distinction is drawn between the general partner(s), who are responsible for the debts and obligations of the firm, and the limited partner(s), who are merely investors[2]. A limited partner is precluded from participation in the management of the firm[3], and cannot withdraw his investment during the life of the firm without becoming liable for the firm's debts up to that amount[4]. A limited partnership must be registered with the Registrar of Companies[5].

It should be noted that no distinction is made in the Order between limited partnerships and general partnerships, but on the rare occasions when a limited partnership is encountered, special consideration will need to be given to the position of a limited partner.

1 Limited Partnerships Act 1907, s 7.
2 Ibid, s 4(2).
3 Ibid, s 6(1).
4 Ibid, s 4(3).
5 Ibid, ss 5, 8: the effect of non-registration is that the firm is treated as a general partnership and any limited partner as a general partner: see also the Limited Partnerships Rules 1907, SR&O 1907/1020, which provide for relevant forms.

1.5 THE BANKRUPTCY ACT 1914

Prior to 1986, it was generally the law of bankruptcy, and not the law of company liquidation, which applied to the winding up of an insolvent partnership. However, a firm with eight or more partners could be wound up as an unregistered company under the Companies Acts[1].

Partners could be bankrupted either individually or collectively. Where the partnership itself was made bankrupt in proceedings brought against the firm in the firm's name, it followed that each of the individual partners was bankrupt. Alternatively, bankruptcy proceedings might be brought against all the partners, or just one. Where an individual partner was adjudicated bankrupt in proceedings brought against him in his own name, this did not result in the bankruptcy of the partnership. However, the bankruptcy of the individual partner did in principle result in the dissolution of the partnership[2].

One of the most important features of the Bankruptcy Act 1914 was that it gave statutory force[3] to the long-established common-law rule[4] that the debts of the firm (the joint estate) were to be treated separately from the debts of each individual partner (the separate estates). The rule was that partnership (joint) creditors were to be paid out of the joint estate, and each individual's private creditors were to be paid out of that individual's (separate) estate. Only after the joint creditors were satisfied in full was any surplus to be distributed to pay the separate estate creditors. Similarly, any surplus on a separate estate was then to be applied to make up any deficiency on the joint estate.

Where the joint estate was *entirely* empty, the joint estate creditors were entitled to prove in the separate estates[5]. However, this did not apply if there was anything at all in the joint estate, no matter how little[6]. Even £1 in the partnership bank account would postpone the rights of joint estate creditors to claim against the separate estate of a partner until the creditors of that separate estate had been satisfied in full.

1 Eg see the Companies (Consolidation) Act 1908, s 286, Companies Act 1948, s 398(1)(c).
2 See the Partnership Act, s 33; however, this is subject to any agreement between the partners, and there is frequently a provision in the partnership deed excluding this rule; in practice, a re-constituted partnership of the remaining partners often seems to have continued using the firm's name, even without any such provision.
3 Bankruptcy Act 1914, ss 33(6), 63; replacing the Bankruptcy Act 1883, ss 40(3), 59.
4 Expressed in *Ex p Cook* (1728) 2 PW 500, *Ex p Elton* (1796) 3 Ves Jr 238: see also *Re Rudd & Son Ltd* [1984] Ch 237. Note that this common-law rule remains applicable in any case where provisions of the Order to the contrary do not apply.
5 *Re Carpenter* (1890) 7 Morr 270; *Re Budgett, Cooper v Adams* [1894] 2 Ch 557.
6 *Ex p Peake* (1814) 2 Rose 54; *Ex p Harris* (1816) 1 Madd 583; *Ex p Kennedy* (1852) 2 De G M & G 228.

1.6 THE CORK REPORT[1]

As part of its overall review of individual and corporate insolvency in 1982, the Cork Committee criticised the rule postponing joint estate creditors behind creditors of the separate estates as being neither logical nor fair, and recommended that it should be changed. It also recommended simplifying the procedure for commencing insolvency proceedings against a partnership.

1 *Insolvency Law and Practice – Report of the Review Committee* (HMSO Cmnd 8558, 1982 Ch 39).

1.7 THE INSOLVENCY ACT 1986

The Insolvency Act 1986 represents a legislative attempt to provide a comprehensive framework for both corporate[1] and individual[2] insolvency. The Act included some, but not all, of the reforms proposed in the Cork Report, including the introduction of rescue mechanisms for insolvent or near-insolvent entities, such as company and individual voluntary arrangements and administration for companies.

As practitioners will be well aware, the individual and corporate provisions of the Act largely mirror each other, but do not do so entirely[3]. Unregistered companies are nowadays wound up under Part V of the Act.

The Act did not address insolvent partnerships directly, but merely gave the Lord Chancellor power to make secondary legislation[4].

1 Parts I–VII of the Act.
2 Parts VIII–XI of the Act.
3 These differences sometimes become particularly significant when dealing with insolvent partnerships where the procedure is a hybrid of the two.
4 Insolvency Act 1986, s 420: note that the wording of this section expressly permits the application of provisions of the Act to insolvent partnerships with such modifications as may be specified; it is thought that this provides sufficient *vires* to enable the Act itself to be amended by the Order.

1.8   THE INSOLVENT PARTNERSHIPS ORDER 1986

The Insolvent Partnerships Order 1986 ('the 1986 Order')[1] was made pursuant to s 420 of the Act and came into force on 29 December 1986. From the outset, it was generally regarded as unnecessarily convoluted and complicated.

An insolvent partnership was wound up under the 1986 Order as an *unregistered company* under s 221 of the Act (in which case, claims for any shortfall on the partnership account might be brought against the partners as *contributories*, with the leave of the court[2]).

However, the would-be petitioning creditor was offered a number of alternatives:

(i)   winding up the insolvent partnership only[3];
(ii) winding up the insolvent partnership and/or presenting a petition against two or more members[4];
(iii) presenting bankruptcy petitions against one or more partners without seeking to wind up the partnership (in which case, a trustee in bankruptcy of one of the partners might subsequently seek to wind up the partnership);
(iv) presenting bankruptcy petitions against all the partners without seeking to wind up the partnership.

In addition, where all the members of a partnership were individuals, they could, if they all agreed, collectively petition for bankruptcy; in which case, their trustee in bankruptcy would wind up the partnership and administer the partnership property[5].

Corporate and individual members of partnerships were allowed to propose company voluntary arrangements ('CVAs') or individual voluntary arrangements ('IVAs') respectively, with partnership creditors becoming included within the class of individual creditors for purposes of the voluntary arrangements[6]. This gave rise to the practice of arranging IVAs for all the members of a partnership, usually with identical provision (at least in respect of partnership debts) and a common supervisor. However, this procedure was regarded as impracticable for large partnerships.

The 1986 Order did not adopt the Cork Report's proposal to change the treatment of creditors in the joint estate. Instead, the long-standing statutory and common-law rule[7] became embodied in art 10 of the 1986 Order.

The 1986 Order was revoked upon the coming into force of the Insolvent Partnerships Order 1994 ('the Order') on 1 December 1994[8]. However, it remains of some relevance because under the transitional provisions in the Order, the 1986 Order continues to apply where a winding-up or bankruptcy order had already been made under it[9], and, where insolvency proceedings were pending on 1 December 1994, the court has a discretion which Order to apply[10].

---

1 SI 1986/2142.
2 Insolvency Act 1986, s 228.
3 Insolvent Partnerships Order 1986, Part 2, art 7.

4 Ibid, Part 3, arts 8, 9.
5 Ibid, Part 4.
6 Ibid, art 11.
7 See para **1.5** above.
8 Insolvent Partnerships Order 1994, art 20.
9 Ibid, art 19(1).
10 Ibid, art 19(2): it is difficult to conceive of a compelling reason why the court would not apply the newer Order, but a separate estate creditor disadvantaged by the changes in priority under the Order might argue that the old regime should continue to apply.

1.9 OTHER SECONDARY LEGISLATION UNDER THE 1986 ORDER

The principal secondary legislation made under the Act is the Insolvency Rules 1986[1] ('the Rules') which provide the comprehensive procedural framework required to make the Act work in practice. Other relevant subordinate legislation includes the Insolvency Regulations 1994[2] ('the Regulations') and the Insolvency Fees Order 1986[3] ('the Fees Order'). These orders will be very familiar to most readers of this book, and no attempt is made to deal with them in detail[4].

The Rules, the Regulations and the Fees Order were applied to insolvent partnerships by art 5(1) of the 1986 Order. However, it should be noted that they were applied 'with the necessary modifications'.

1 SI 1986/1925, as amended.
2 SI 1994/2507 which revoked the Insolvency Regulations 1986, SI 1986/1994 ('the 1986 Regulations') from 24 October 1994, subject to transitional provisions.
3 SI 1986/2030.
4 The most comprehensive collection of primary and secondary legislation relating to insolvency is *Butterworths Insolvency Law Handbook* (3rd Edn, 1994), of which Glen Davis is the Assistant Editor.

1.10 THE INSOLVENT PARTNERSHIPS ORDER 1994

Although the defects in the 1986 Order have long been recognised, and amending legislation has long been promised, the Insolvent Partnerships Order 1994 ('the Order') is still a particularly unwieldy statutory instrument, and its drafting seems bound to give rise to conceptual uncertainty where there needs to be procedural precision.

The Order introduces three fundamental changes:

(i)   the partnership voluntary arrangement ('PVA')[1];
(ii) administration of a partnership[2];
(iii) the priority rules relating to joint and separate estates are reversed (implementing the recommendation of the Cork Report referred to above[3]).

The Order maintains the approach adopted by the 1986 Order. That is to say, it is essentially parasitic on the Act and the Company Directors Disqualification Act 1986 ('the CDDA'), but introduces modifications to that primary legislation in a number of Schedules. Unfortunately, there are a number of complicating factors which make the Order particularly difficult to assimilate:

(a) a given section of the Act may be modified differently under different scenarios contained in the Order;

(b) because only certain sections are contained in the respective Schedules, constant cross-reference to the Act is required;

(c) a partnership is treated as if it were a company (which it is not) and the assumption is made that equivalents will always be found for company terms and practices.

Under the Order, it is expressly stated that a creditor remains free to bring a bankruptcy petition (or, against a corporate partner, a winding-up petition) against one or more partners, without seeking to wind up the partnership[4]. In that event, either the partner(s) will pay the debt and seek a contribution from the other partners, or they will be made bankrupt or wound up, as appropriate. In the latter case, the insolvent partner's trustee or liquidator may subsequently wind up the partnership.

As in the 1986 Order, the Order offers the partnership creditor a number of different options:

(i) to wind up the partnership as an unregistered company without presenting any concurrent bankruptcy petition against a member[5];

(ii) to wind up the partnership and present one or more concurrent petitions against partners[6].

The Order also provides for scenarios where:

(i) a partner petitions for the partnership to be wound up, without also bringing a petition against another member[7];

(ii) a partner petitions for the partnership to be wound up, and also brings petitions against *all* other members[8];

(iii) there is a joint presentation of bankruptcy petitions by *all* the members of a partnership[9].

Where a court becomes aware that a winding-up or bankruptcy petition has been presented against a person who is a partner, the court has jurisdiction to apply 'any provisions' of the Order 'with any necessary modifications'[10], including giving directions as to how the joint estate of the partnership and the separate estate of any member are to be administered[11]. This could arise when a creditor has not commenced concurrent proceedings or when, for example, the existence of the partnership is only belatedly discovered. From the literal wording, it seems that the Act has been modified to give the court carte blanche to modify any provision of the Order in any way it can be persuaded is 'necessary' in the circumstances.

The procedural and tactical issues which arise under the various scenarios envisaged in the Order are obviously extremely complex and require very careful consideration in the circumstances of each case. However, some tactical questions do seem to recur, and these are discussed in general terms in Chapter 10.

Where a partnership is wound up as an unregistered company, certain of the provisions of the Company Directors Disqualification Act 1986 are applied in modified form by the Order[12].

The Order expressly does not prevent the presentation of a petition against an insolvent partnership under legislation other than the Act[13].

1 Insolvent Partnerships Order 1994, Part II, arts 4 and 5, Sch 1.
2 Ibid, Part III, art 6, Sch 2.
3 See para **1.6** above.
4 Insolvent Partnerships Order 1994, art 19(5).
5 Ibid, art 7 and Sch 3. See further para **3.2** below.
6 Ibid, art 8 and Sch 4. See further para **3.3** below.
7 Ibid, art 9 and Sch 5. See further para **4.2** below.
8 Ibid, art 10 and Schs 4 and 6. See further para **4.3** below.
9 Ibid, art 11 and Sch 7. See further para **4.4** below.
10 Sections 168(5A) and 303(2A) of the Insolvency Act 1986, as inserted by art 14(1) of the Order.
11 Sections 168(5B) and 303(2B) of the Insolvency Act 1986, as inserted by art 14(1) of the Order.
12 Insolvent Partnerships Order 1994, art 16 and Sch 8: see discussion in Chapter 9.
13 See para **1.14** below.

1.11 SUBORDINATE LEGISLATION APPLIED BY THE ORDER

A wider range of subordinate legislation is applied under the Order than was formerly applied under the 1986 Order. The list still includes the Rules, the Regulations and the Fees Order, but now includes, for example, the Administration of Insolvent Estates of Deceased Persons Order 1986, and the Cooperation of Insolvency Courts (Designation of Relevant Countries and Territories) Order 1986 which is now applied to insolvent partnerships under the Order[1].

However, this subordinate legislation is applied:

'with such modifications as the context requires for the purpose of giving effect to the provisions of the Act and of the Company Directors Disqualification Act 1986 which are applied by this Order.'[2]

In some cases, it appears to be obvious what slight changes must be made. However the subordinate legislation was often drafted to deal in detail with procedure relating to companies, which have very well-defined statutory characteristics. There are no such requirements imposed upon partnerships, which can vary enormously and may be relatively informal. There is therefore enormous scope for argument about what modifications are or are not required to apply such provisions to a particular insolvent partnership[3].

1 Insolvent Partnerships Order 1994, art 18(1) and Sch 10.
2 Ibid, art 18(1).
3 See further under 'Definitions', para **1.12** below.

1.12 DEFINITIONS

The list of definitions in s 436 of the Act is enlarged by the further set of definitions contained in art 2 of the Order[1]. Although many are self-evident, some are crucial to an understanding of the operation of the Order. The following, in particular, must always be borne in mind:

'the court'	in relation to an insolvent partnership, the court which has jurisdiction to wind up the partnership[2];
'corporate member'	an insolvent member which is a company;
'individual member'	an insolvent member who is an individual;
'insolvency order'	(a) in the case of an insolvent partnership or a corporate member, a winding-up order; and (b) in the case of an individual member, a bankruptcy order; .
'insolvency petition'	in the case of a petition presented to the court– (a) against a corporate member, a petition for its winding up by the court; (b) against an individual member, a petition for a bankruptcy order to be made against that individual, where the petition is presented in conjunction with a petition for the winding up of the partnership by the court as an unregistered company under the Act;
'insolvency proceedings'	any proceedings under the Act, the Order or the Rules;
'insolvent member'	a member of an insolvent partnership, against whom an insolvency petition is being or has been presented;
'member'	a member of a partnership and any person who is liable as a partner within the meaning of s 14 of the Partnership Act[3];
'officer'	in relation to an insolvent partnership– (a) a member; or (b) a person who has management or control of the partnership business[4].

In addition, the distinction between the joint and separate estates is paramount, so the following definitions will be particularly important in practice:

'joint debt'	a debt of an insolvent partnership in respect of which an order is made by virtue of Part IV or V of the Order[5];
'joint estate'	the partnership property of an insolvent partnership in respect of which an order is made by virtue of Part IV or V of the Order;
'separate debt'	a debt for which a member of a partnership is liable, other than a joint debt;
'separate estate'	the property of an insolvent member against whom an insolvency order has been made.

It is also important to note that the Order states that references to companies in the Act or the Company Directors Disqualification Act 1986 must be construed as references to insolvent partnerships[6], save that references to the Registrar of Companies are to be ignored (since partnerships other than limited partnerships need not be registered). References to shares become references to either:

(a) the right to share in the capital of a partnership[7]; or
(b) where the partnership has no capital, as the interest giving the right to share in profits or the liability to contribute to losses, debts or expenses[8].

Other expressions appropriate to companies are to be construed as references to the corresponding persons, officers, documents or organs appropriate to a partnership[9]. In some instances, this will be relatively straightforward; for example, a partnership deed may reasonably be regarded as the equivalent of the articles of a company. Other cases may not be nearly so obvious[10]; again, this provision seems likely to give rise to uncertainty and argument.

---

1 Insolvent Partnerships Order 1994, art 2(2).
2 Note: this may be different from the court which would have jurisdiction in respect of a bankruptcy petition against an individual partner.
3 In essence, actual members and those held out as members; this is likely to be particularly important in practice – see the detailed discussion in paras **2.11.2** and **2.11.3**.
4 Ie an employee of the partnership given management responsibility.
5 Ie which has been wound up on a creditor's petition (Part IV) or a member's petition (Part V).
6 Insolvent Partnerships Order 1994, art 3(2).
7 Ibid, art 3(3)(a).
8 Ibid, art 3(3)(b).
9 Ibid, art 3(4).
10 For instance, in the case of an informal trading partnership between three individuals, where is the 'registered office'? See, in this regard, Ord 81, r 3 of the Rules of the Supreme Court 1965.

1.13 TRANSITIONAL PROVISIONS

The Order came into force on 1 December 1994[1], and the 1986 Order was revoked from that date[2].

Where a winding-up or bankruptcy order had been made in relation to a partnership or an insolvent member of a partnership under the 1986 Order before 1 December 1994, the 1994 Order does not apply, and the law in force immediately before the Order came into force continues to have effect in respect of that insolvency[3]. It appears that this would not preclude the court from exercising its powers to apply the 1994 Order[4] when proceedings are commenced under the 1994 Order against a member of a partnership which had been wound up under the 1986 Order.

Where winding-up or bankruptcy proceedings were pending[5] on 1 December 1994, the court is given a choice under the 1994 Order whether those proceedings are to be continued in accordance with the newer Order[6] or whether to direct that they must be continued under the provisions of the former Order, in which case the law in force immediately before the 1994 Order came into force continues to have effect. It is thought that a court would normally prefer to apply the newer legislation[7].

1 Insolvent Partnerships Order 1994, art 1(1).
2 Ibid, art 20.
3 Ibid, art 19(1).
4 Under art 14(1) of the Order modifying ss 168 and 303 of the Insolvency Act 1986; eg to adjust priorities between joint and separate estates.
5 Ie a statutory or written demand had been served or a winding-up or bankruptcy petition had been presented: by art 19(3) of the Order.
6 Insolvent Partnerships Order 1994, art 19(2)(a).
7 This provision will of course become progressively redundant with the passage of time.

1.14 SUPPLEMENTAL PROVISIONS

The court may consolidate bankruptcy proceedings[1] against a number of partners irrespective of whether they were commenced under the Bankruptcy Act 1914, the Insolvency Act 1986, the Insolvent Partnerships Order 1986 or the Insolvent Partnerships Order 1994[2]. An application for consolidation may be made by the official receiver, any responsible insolvency practitioner, the trustee of the partnership or any other interested person[3] (which would include, for example, a creditor). If the court makes such an order for consolidation, it must make provision for the manner in which the consolidated proceedings are to be conducted[4]. It is thought that in such circumstances the court would usually prefer to apply the provisions of the 1994 Order, except where a separate estate creditor manages to persuade the court that the revised priorities between joint and separate estates in that Order would unfairly prejudice its position.

The Order does not prevent any partnership creditor or creditors from presenting a petition under the Act against one or more members of the partnership[5] liable for a partnership debt or debts without including the other members and without presenting a petition for the winding up of the partnership as an unregistered company[6]. A creditor is therefore not compelled to wind up a partnership for a partnership debt; however, when the court's attention is drawn to the fact that the subject of a petition is a member of an insolvent partnership, the court can apply the Order 'with any necessary modifications' to the future conduct of the insolvency proceedings against the individual partner[7], which may reduce any procedural advantages from taking the simpler route.

The Order also does not preclude a petition being presented against an insolvent partnership under:

(a) s 53 or s 54 of the Insurance Companies Act 1982[8];
(b) s 72(2)(d) of the Financial Services Act 1986[9];
(c) s 92 of the Banking Act 1987[10]; or
(d) any other enactment[11].

However, it should be noted that it is only when the court makes an order under s 72(1)(a) of the Financial Services Act 1986 or under s 92(1)(a) of the Banking Act 1987 that the court has the power to apply the provisions of the Order to the relevant winding-up proceedings[12]. In other windings up under the Insurance Companies Act 1982, the Financial Services Act 1986 or the Banking Act 1987, the Order will not apply unless a winding-up or bankruptcy petition is brought against a member and the partnership is insolvent[13]. In other cases, there is no jurisdiction to apply the Order. This means that the former rules about priorities[14] must in such circumstances continue to apply.

1 Under s 303(2B) of the Insolvency Act 1986, as inserted by art 14(2) of the Order.
2 Insolvent Partnerships Order 1994, art 19(6).
3 By s 303(2C) of the Insolvency Act 1986, as inserted by art 14(2) of the Order.
4 Insolvent Partnerships Order 1994, art 19(6).
5 See para **1.12** above and paras **2.11.2** and **2.11.3** below.
6 Insolvent Partnerships Order 1994, art 19(5): cf *Schooler v Customs & Excise Commissioners* [1995] 2 BCLC 610.
7 By ss 168(5A) and 303(2A) of the Insolvency Act 1986, introduced by art 14(1) and (2) of the Order respectively.
8 Insolvent Partnerships Order 1994, art 19(4)(a).
9 Ibid, art 19(4)(b).
10 Ibid, art 19(4)(c).
11 Ibid, art 19(4)(d).
12 By s 168(5C) of the Insolvency Act 1986, as inserted by art 14(1) of the Order, in what is thought to be a drafting oversight.
13 In which case, the court has power to apply the provisions of the Order under ss 168(5A) and 303(2A) of the Insolvency Act 1986, introduced by art 14(1) and (2) of the Order respectively.
14 See para **1.5** above.

1.15   FORMS

The Order specifies the forms which are to be used in and in connection with proceedings under the Order[1], whether in the High Court or in a county court. These forms may be used with such variations, if any, as the circumstances require[2]. A list of the forms may be found on page 341 below, and the forms themselves are reproduced on pp 343 to 395.

1 Insolvent Partnerships Order 1994, art 17 and Sch 9.
2 Ibid, art 17(2).

1.16   GENERAL APPROACH

We have not set out to produce an academic textbook. Our aim has been to combine a reasonably clear presentation of the Order with some sense of the practical, tactical and legal context. We are only too aware that this is secondary legislation in a complicated area which has yet to be interpreted by the courts.

Chapter 2

THE SOLVENT PARTNERSHIP

2.1 THE NATURE OF A PARTNERSHIP

2.1.1 Introduction

Partnerships stand at the crossroads of contract, agency and trusts. In order to deal with the practical problems which will arise in the context of an insolvent partnership, it is necessary to have some grasp of the nature of a partnership in English law, and of the rules which apply to the solvent partnership and govern relationships between partner and partner, and between partners and the rest of the community. This chapter sets out a brief (and somewhat simplified) account of those aspects which are usually of most significance in the context of the insolvent partnership.

2.1.2 What is a partnership?

A partnership has no separate existence from its members in English law. It is merely a formal relationship[1]. That relationship exists between a group of members (who may be individuals, or companies, or other organisations) for a period of time. Whereas a company is a separate entity from its officers or shareholders, a partnership is no more than the sum of its partners. In the case of a company, the directors may come and go, the shareholders may change, but the company itself carries on as a discrete entity. Partnership is not like that. When one partner leaves, that partnership ends and a different partnership may be left in place among those who remain. Similarly, when a new partner joins, a different partnership is constituted. There is no continuing 'firm' in that sense.

Of course, for day-to-day purposes and administrative convenience, it is often useful, or even necessary, to behave as if a partnership did have an existence independent of the partners. Partnership accounts are drawn up, the partnership is assessed for tax[2], and registration for VAT may be in the firm's name[3]. Partnerships appear to deal with tradesmen, employ staff, operate bank accounts, all in the name of the firm. Firms apparently sue and are sued[4]. While some trading partnerships may last only for the duration of a single venture, there are numerous instances of firms of solicitors and accountants which appear to have continued for decades, operating proudly under the same name. Nevertheless, it is important to bear in mind that this appearance of independent personality and continuity only masks the legal reality which is just the reverse: the firm's name is a mere expression, a convenient shorthand, and the firm has no existence as an independent entity[5].

---

1 Note that the position is different in other jurisdictions; in Scotland, for example, a partnership *does* have separate personality.

2 The relevant provision, first introduced in the Income Tax Act 1918, is nowadays contained in s 111 of the Income and Corporation Taxes Act 1988, as substituted by s 215(1) of the Finance Act 1994. Note that the tax regime is now changing to replace joint assessment of the firm with individual assessment of each partner on his share of profits; firms formed after 6 April 1994 are already subject to the new regime, while 'continuing' firms will move to individual assessment from tax year 1997/8. A business which has a cessation between 6 April 1994 and 5 April 1997 for tax purposes will be regarded as a 'new' business. Capital gains tax has always been assessed on partners separately (see s 59 of the Taxation of Chargeable Gains Act 1992), although the Inland Revenue has mollified the severity of this in the Statement of Practice *Capital Gains Tax: Partnerships* (D12) extended in 1979 (SP1/79) and 1989 (SP1/89).

3 Section 30(1) of the Value Added Tax Act 1983, as modified by the Finance (No 2) Act 1992, Sch 3, para 31.

4 In the High Court under Ord 81 of the Rules of the Supreme Court 1965; in the county court under Ord 5, r 9 of the County Court Rules 1981. This is discussed further below.

5 *Sadler v Whiteman* [1910] 1 KB 889; *Customs and Excise Commissioners v Glassborow* [1975] QB 465.

2.2 DEFINITION

For more than a century, the relationship which gives rise to partnership has been defined by statute. The definition is contained in s 1(1) of the Partnership Act 1890:

> 'Partnership is the relation which subsists between persons carrying on a business in common with a view of profit.'

2.2.1 *'The relation'*

Partnership is a particular relationship. Whether the relationship exists is a question of fact. If it exists, particular legal rules apply. The relationship between the partners is primarily a contractual one[1]. There may be an express agreement between the partners, contained in a partnership deed or evidenced by other documents. Often there is no formal documentation, but the terms of the agreement can be ascertained by inference, from the way the partnership has actually been conducted. The Partnership Act lays down a minimum legal framework for the relationship between the partners, but where all the partners consent, or where such consent is inferred from a course of dealing, the partners are free to depart from the terms of the Act and make whatever provision they choose to regulate their mutual affairs[2].

There is therefore no single 'relation' applicable to all partnerships. In each case, it is necessary to identify what, if any, relevant documents exist, in order to establish how the partners have chosen to regulate such matters as their internal decision-making, the apportionment of profits, liability to contribute for losses, etc. Even where there has been no express agreement, it will be necessary to inquire how the partnership's affairs have been conducted, in order to see whether there is any evidence of a course of conduct from which consent might be inferred.

1 *Pooley v Driver* (1876) 5 Ch D 458.

2 Partnership Act 1890, s 19.

2.2.2 'Between persons'

The 'persons' who may be in a partnership can be an individual, a company[1], or even another partnership[2], in any desired combination. This is necessarily subject to some considerations as to legal capacity. A company will not be able to enter a partnership unless this is permitted by its memorandum and articles of association[3] (which usually is the case). Minors[4] may be partners; they can become entitled to a share in profits, but in general they cannot become liable for debts[5]. It is generally thought that a person who is subject to a period of disqualification from acting as a director[6] *is* none the less able to act as a partner[7].

In principle, it is possible for a bankrupt to become, or continue as, a partner although there is a risk that a bankruptcy offence will be committed if the bankruptcy is not disclosed[8].

There are certain cases where statutory or other restrictions will affect who may be a member of a particular partnership. Thus a solicitor may not at present be in partnership with someone who is not a solicitor[9], while a practising barrister may not be in partnership at all[10]. A new partner can only be admitted to a partnership which is authorised to carry on deposit-taking business if the Bank of England raises no objection[11].

In wartime, it would not be possible for a resident of a hostile state to be a member of an English partnership.

---

1 'A body of persons corporate or unincorporate': s 5 of, and Sch 1 to, the Interpretation Act 1978.
2 See, for example, art 12 of the Order.
3 In *Newstead v Frost* [1980] 1 WLR 135, the phrase 'all kinds of financial … or other operations' in the relevant company's articles was held to be sufficient to permit carrying on business in partnership.
4 Ie a child under 18: s 1 of the Family Law Reform Act 1969.
5 *Re A and M* [1926] Ch 274; *Lovell and Christmas v Beauchamp* [1894] AC 607; a minor can repudiate the partnership until he turns 18, or for a reasonable period after that.
6 Under the Company Directors Disqualification Act 1986.
7 See, for example, comments of Harman J in *Re Chartmore Ltd* [1990] BCLC 673 at 675e, and in *Re Probe Data Systems (No 3)* [1991] BCC 428 at 434 D. It is suggested that this applies even where the punishment is imposed in respect of conduct arising from an *insolvent partnership*, because the definition of 'company' in s 22(2)(b) of the Company Directors Disqualification Act 1986 only applies to a company which may be wound up under Part V of the Act, and a *solvent partnership* does not fall within that definition. Note that subsidiary legislation cannot alter the meaning of provisions in an Act which it does not purport to modify (per Bingham MR in *Re Cupit* (unreported) Court of Appeal transcript, 7 April 1993). For further discussion of this point, see para **9.1**.
8 See s 360(1) of the Insolvency Act 1986.
9 Section 66(1) of the Courts and Legal Services Act 1990 repealed the provision in the Solicitors Act 1974 which made it illegal for solicitors to enter into partnership with non-solicitors, but this is still prohibited by r 7(6) of the Solicitors' Practice Rules 1990. Under that provision, a solicitor may only enter into partnership with another solicitor, a foreign lawyer or a recognised body (which is defined by r 18(2)(f) of the Solicitors' Practice Rules 1990 as a body corporate recognised under the Solicitors' Incorporated Practice Rules; ie a body corporate recognised by The Law Society as suitable to undertake provision of legal services. See the Solicitors' Incorporated Practice Rules 1988 and the Solicitors' Incorporated Practices Order 1991, SI 1991/2684).
10 See Code of Conduct of the Bar of England and Wales, para 207.
11 Banking Act 1987, ss 21(1), 22.

2.2.3 *'Carrying on a business'*

'Business' is not explicitly defined in the Partnership Act, although it includes every trade, occupation or profession[1]. Mere joint ownership of property is not sufficient[2]; what is required is some element of commercial activity. Not all the partners have to participate fully in the business activities; a 'sleeping partner' can be a partner, although note that mere receipt of profits is not enough to make him one[3].

1 Partnership Act 1890, s 45.
2 Ibid, s 2(1).
3 *Cox v Hickman* (1860) 8 HL Cas 268.

2.2.4 *'In common'*

Not every collaborative venture is a partnership. The companies operating on a building site will usually regulate their inter-relationships with a series of contracts for the sale of goods and the provision of services. If, on the other hand, they were to choose to work together on a particular site, pooling their resources, deducting all overheads from the receipts, and distributing any profit, that probably would constitute a partnership.

At the core of a partnership, there has to be a single business. Where the supposed partners are in fact carrying on *different* businesses, there is no partnership. One example of this is the 'share farming agreement', where a land owner supplies land and a working farmer carries out the physical farming operations[1], without a partnership being created. Similarly, an arrangement for a company to manage a property development for a developer does not necessarily create a partnership with the developer (even if payment is calculated as a share of profits)[2].

1 See *Lindley and Banks on Partnership* 17th Edn (Sweet & Maxwell, 1995) at para 5-19.
2 *Strathearn Gordon Associates Ltd v Commissioners of Customs and Excise* [1985] VATTR 79.

2.2.5 *'With a view to profit'*

The aim to be profit-making is fundamental to the existence of a partnership[1]. Charities, clubs and social associations, which are inherently *non*-profit-making, are incapable of constituting partnerships[2].

1 There is no definition of 'profit' in the Partnership Act. The courts approach profit as
   implying a comparison year-on-year, taking it as 'the amount of gain made by the business
   during the year' (per Fletcher Moulton LJ in *Re Spanish Prospecting Co Ltd* [1911] 1 Ch 92 at
   98–99). Simplistically, 'Profits consist of a sum arrived at by adding up the receipts of a
   business and by deducting all the expenses and losses, including depreciation and the like,
   incurred in carrying on the business' (per Atkinson J in *Rushden Heel Co Ltd v Keene* [1946] 2
   All ER 141 at 144). See also *Gresham Life Assurance Society v Styles* [1892] AC 309, *Whimster v
   IRC* [1926] SC 20; *Beauchamp v F W Woolworth Plc* [1990] 1 AC 478.
2 In one well-known case, for example, a railway preservation society was not a partnership by
   this test (*Goddard v Mills* (1929) *The Times*, 16 February).

2.2.6 *Sharing profits and sharing gross returns*

The Partnership Act sets out various rules to assist in determining whether a partnership does or does not exist[1]. The mere existence of common property does not of itself give rise to a partnership[2]. Similarly, the sharing of gross returns does not of itself create a partnership[3].

On the other hand, receiving a share of profits *is* 'prima facie evidence' that the recipient is a partner[4], but is not enough, by itself, to establish that fact. Others may also receive a share of profits, without becoming partners; for example, an employee of the partnership[5], a lender to the partnership[6], or a creditor who is being paid off by instalments[7].

---

1 Partnership Act 1890, s 2.
2 Ibid, s 2(1).
3 Ibid, s 2(2): this preserved a rule established in case-law prior to the Partnership Act.
4 Ibid, s 2(3).
5 Ibid, s 2(3)(b).
6 Ibid, s 2(3)(d).
7 Ibid, s 2(3)(a); note that if this were not the case, it would not be possible to have a PVA without the creditors thereby becoming partners!

2.3 LEGAL STATUS OF THE FIRM

A firm is not an independent entity in English law[1]. It is merely a convenient collective expression for the group of individual legal persons who are carrying on business together for profit[2].

For certain specific purposes, English law treats a firm as if it were a separate entity. One example of this is, of course, the insolvency regime under the Order, when a partnership is wound up as if it were an unregistered company.

However, in general, the acts of a firm are the acts of the partners, the rights of a firm are the rights of the partners, the obligations of a firm are the obligations of the partners[3] and, as there is no separate entity to hold property, the property 'of the firm' is in reality the common property of the partners[4]. Just as a man cannot make a contract with himself, a partner cannot be employed by his firm[5]. Similarly, a man cannot grant a lease to himself (or at least not one in which any covenants are enforceable)[6].

---

1 See the Partnership Act 1890, s 4(1): 'Persons who have entered into partnership with one another are for the purposes of this Act called collectively a firm, and the name under which their business is carried on is called the firm-name'.
2 See para **2.1**.
3 So one can refer to a joint debt of the partnership as the debt of one of the joint debtors: per Bingham MR in *Re Cupit* (unreported) Court of Appeal transcript, 7 April 1993; *Schooler v Customs & Excise* [1995] 2 BCLC 610, CA.
4 *Green v Hertzog* [1954] 1 WLR 1309.
5 See *Ellis v Joseph Ellis & Co* [1905] 1 KB 324.
6 See the decision of the House of Lords in *Rye v Rye* [1962] AC 49, and the judgment of Lord Evershed MR in the Court of Appeal [1961] Ch 70 at 78.

2.4   THE INTERNAL STATUS OF A PARTNER

2.4.1   *The provisions of the Partnership Act*

Under the Partnership Act, the starting point is equality; every partner is to share equally in capital, profits and losses[1], and every partner may take part in the management of the partnership[2]. Only a simple majority is required for decisions as to 'ordinary matters', but the consent of all existing partners is required for any change in the nature of the partnership business[3], or before a new partner is admitted[4].

However, the relevant provisions of the Partnership Act are expressly made to be subject to any agreement between the partners[5], so that in many cases the internal status and rights of a partner will be specified in some detail in the partnership deed. Nowadays, it is quite common for the day-to-day management of a large firm to be delegated to a small executive committee or even an individual partner.

1   Partnership Act 1890, s 24(1).
2   Ibid, s 24(5).
3   Ibid, s 24(8).
4   Ibid, s 24(7).
5   Ibid, s 24.

2.4.2   *The duty of good faith*

The relationship between partners is a *fiduciary* relationship. This means that every partner must conduct himself towards his co-partners with the utmost good faith, and that absolute trust is fundamental to the relationship[1]. Although this remains essentially an equitable duty, it is in part given statutory force in the Partnership Act. So partners are bound to render true accounts and full information to each other[2], and must account to the firm for any secret profit made from any use of the firm's name or any business connection or transaction concerning the partnership[3]. Similarly, a partner may not compete with his firm without the consent of the other partners; if he does so, he must again pay over to the firm any profits he has made[4].

1   *Blisset v Daniel* (1853) 10 Hare 493; *Helmore v Smith* (1886) 35 Ch D 436; *Cassels v Stewart* (1881) 6 App Cas 64.
2   Partnership Act 1890, s 28.
3   Ibid, s 29.
4   Ibid, s 30.

2.5   THE EXTERNAL STATUS OF A PARTNER

As far as interaction with the world outside the partnership is concerned, the relationship is one of agency, but an individual partner is both principal and agent. That he is an agent of his partners is explicit from s 5 of the Partnership Act, which provides:

'Every partner is an agent of the firm and his other partners for the purpose of the business of the partnership; and the acts of every partner who does any act for carrying on in the usual way business of the kind carried on by the firm of which he is a member bind the firm and his partners, unless the partner so acting has in fact no authority to act for the firm in the particular matter, and the person with whom he is dealing either knows that he has no authority, or does not know or believe him to be a partner.'

Thus the liability of a partner for the acts of his co-partners is the liability of a principal for the acts of his agent[1].

It is conventional to consider an agent's authority as being either:

(a) actual; or
(b) implied or usual; or
(c) ostensible[2].

Whether a partner has actual authority in a particular case is always a question of fact; the same is true of employees and other agents of a firm. The act of an agent within his actual authority binds the principal as a matter of the general law of agency; that proposition is also incorporated in the Partnership Act[3].

The scope of any partner's *actual* authority is a matter of choice for the partners. There may be decisions of the partnership, or express provision in the partnership deed, which seek to limit it. For example, a ceiling may be imposed on the value of trading contracts which may be made by individual partners without wider approval. A third party who has notice of such a limitation cannot enforce against the firm an agreement made in breach of the restriction[4].

In most cases, however, there will be no clear statement of the scope of a partner's actual authority, and it will be necessary to consider what is the *usual* authority in a particular business or profession. There are no hard-and-fast rules, and the scope of usual authority may well change over time[5].

---

1 *Cox v Hickman* (1860) 8 HL Cas 268.
2 *Ostensible* authority arises where there is a representation by the principal as to the authority possessed by the agent; if a third party relies on that representation and deals with the agent, the principal will be bound.
3 Partnership Act 1890, s 6.
4 Ibid, s 8.
5 In *United Bank of Kuwait v Hammoud and Others; City Trust Ltd and Another v Levy* [1988] 1 WLR 1051, Staughton LJ warned that old cases dealing with the usual authority of solicitors should be treated with caution; the question of usual authority requires contemporary expert evidence if the matter comes before a court.

2.6 DURATION OF PARTNERSHIPS

There is no requirement for a partnership to last for any minimum time, and no restriction on the maximum lifespan of a partnership.

2.6.1 Partnership at will

Where no fixed term has been agreed for a partnership, there will be a 'partnership at will', which can be brought to an end at any time by one partner giving notice to the others[1]. As usual under the Partnership Act, this is subject to the possible contrary agreement of the partners[2], so determining the partnership, for example, would require a majority vote, if that is what the partners have agreed.

---

1 Partnership Act 1890, s 26(1).
2 Ibid, s 32(c).

2.6.2   *Partnership for a fixed term*
Where a partnership is regulated by a well-drafted express agreement, this will usually specify the date on which the partnership is to commence, and make provision for its duration. This will give rise to a 'partnership for a fixed term'.

Greater difficulty arises when the agreement for a fixed term has to be implied from some term which is inconsistent with a partner having the right to terminate on notice[1].

After the expiry of its fixed term, a partnership continues, unless there is a further express agreement, on the same terms as before but as a partnership at will[2].

---

1 So the mere duration of a lease of fixed duration is not evidence either way as to the intended duration of a partnership: *Crawshay v Maule* (1818) 1 Swan 495.
2 Partnership Act 1890, s 27(1).

2.6.3   *Partnership for a single undertaking*
In some cases, a partnership will be entered into for a single joint venture or undertaking. The duration of such a partnership will usually be for as long as it takes to complete the venture[1].

---

1 *Reade v Bentley* (1858) 4 K&J 656, and see the Partnership Act 1890, s 32(b).

2.7   THE EFFECT OF CHANGE OF PARTNERS

Any change in the partners composing the firm destroys the identity of the firm[1]. The firm's name may continue to be used[2], but this is deceptive. Suppose that A, B and C are in partnership as 'A & Co'[3]; if C leaves and D and E 'join', there is now a partnership of A, B, D and E. Even if the new partnership still trades as 'A & Co'[4], it is important to grasp that this is a *different* partnership. While contractual provision can be made to regulate the rights and liabilities of outgoing and incoming partners[5], this is not inevitably done, and may in any case not be fully operative where a partnership subsequently becomes insolvent. The terms of the new partnership will depend, first, on the original terms of the old partnership (ie, whether it was a partnership for a fixed term with a provision that new partners might be admitted) and, secondly, on whether the new partners have agreed (either expressly or by implication) to be bound by that agreement. Alternatively, a new agreement may be drawn up for the new partnership, containing whatever terms the new partners wish to (or are able to) agree. Thus the new A & Co might be a partnership for a different term, between different partners, with different internal regulation and different limits on the actual authority of the members.

1 Per Lord Lindley in *Green v Hertzog* [1954] 1 WLR 1309. However, in *Sheppard and Cooper v TSB Bank* (1996) *The Times*, 26 February, CA, Sir John Balcombe said that a reference to 'the firm' in an undertaking must be taken to mean 'the partners for the time being of the firm, whenever the time arises'.
2 See para **2.10** below.
3 '& Co' is often seen in the title of a partnership, but has no formal significance.
4 Assuming compliance with formalities regarding the firm's name; see para **2.10**.
5 See paras **2.11.9** and **2.11.10** below.

2.8 FORMATION AND FORMALITIES

2.8.1 *The size of the firm*

Only partnerships of specified types are permitted to have more than 20 members[1]. The specified types include solicitors[2], accountants[3], members of a recognised stock exchange[4], surveyors, auctioneers and estate agents[5], actuaries[6], 'building designers' (ie architects and chartered surveyors)[7], loss adjusters[8], insurance brokers[9], town planners[10], chartered engineers[11], patent agents[12], and trade mark agents[13]. It will be noted that these are all categories of professional partnership, where in each case the members will be regulated by some professional organisation; there is generally a requirement that all or three-quarters of the members of the partnership are members of a specified professional body.

All other partnerships (including, therefore, all general trading partnerships) are restricted to a maximum size of 20 partners.

1 Companies Act 1985, s 716.
2 Ibid, s 716(2)(a).
3 Ibid, s 716(2)(b).
4 Ibid, s 716(2)(c).
5 Partnerships (Unrestricted Size) No 1 Regs 1968, SI 1968/1222.
6 Partnerships (Unrestricted Size) No 2 Regs 1970, SI 1970/835.
7 Partnerships (Unrestricted Size) No 4 Regs 1970 SI 1970/1319.
8 Partnerships (Unrestricted Size) No 5 Regs 1982, SI 1982/530.
9 Partnerships (Unrestricted Size) No 6 Reg 1990, SI 1990/1581.
10 Partnerships (Unrestricted Size) No 7 Regs 1990, SI 1990/1969.
11 Partnerships (Unrestricted Size) No 10 Regs 1992, SI 1992/1349.
12 Partnerships (Unrestricted Size) No 11 Regs 1994, SI 1994/644.
13 Partnerships (Unrestricted Size) No 11 Regs 1994, SI 1994/644.

2.8.2 *Creation of a partnership*

No specific formalities are required to create a partnership, but, because partnership is principally contractual, the usual rules about formation of a contract will apply. While it is preferable for the partnership agreement to be contained in a written document, agreement may be (and often is) oral. Where there has been a suitable course of dealing, the necessary agreement may be inferred[1].

1 *Dungate v Lee* [1967] 1 All ER 241.

2.8.3 Consideration

A partnership agreement must be supported by consideration. This may take
the form of a contribution of capital or skill to the enterprise, or may be
represented by the mutual obligations undertaken by the prospective partners.
Alternatively, the fact that a liability is incurred to a third party will constitute
sufficient detriment to furnish consideration[1]. In accordance with general
principles, the courts will not examine the adequacy of consideration for a
partnership agreement[2]. An incoming partner to a successful business may
have to purchase a share of the goodwill generated to date[3].

1 *The Herkimer* (1840) Stuart Adm 17; *Anderson's Case* (1877) Ch D 75.
2 *Dale v Hamilton* (1846) 5 Hare 369.
3 Note that s 54 of the National Health Service Act 1977 makes it an offence to require an
   incoming partner to an NHS medical practice to pay for goodwill.

2.9 THE PARTNERSHIP AGREEMENT

The first question to be asked of any partnership is whether there is a written
partnership agreement. (Where such an agreement exists, it is still often
executed in the form of a deed.) Given the contractual nature of partnership, it
is important to ascertain the terms of the agreement between the partners.

2.9.1 Default provisions in the Partnership Act

It is relatively common for even quite substantial partnerships to operate for
many years without any formal partnership agreement, or with a document
which is silent on some crucial aspect. In such cases, the Partnership Act
provides a basic regime. Some of the most important features are as follows:

(a) all partners share equally in capital and profits, and must contribute
     equally to losses[1];
(b) every partner may take part in the management of the partnership
     business[2];
(c) a simple majority is required for any decision on an ordinary matter
     connected with the partnership business[3];
(d) unanimity is required for any change in the nature of the partnership
     business[4];
(e) unanimity is required for the admission of a new partner[5];
(f) a partner cannot be expelled by the other partners[6];
(g) a partner is entitled to inspect the books of the partnership, and to receive
     accounts and full information concerning the partnership[7];
(h) there will be a partnership at will, which may be determined by any partner
     at any time[8];
(i) when a partner gives notice to end a partnership, the partnership is
     dissolved from the date specified in the notice, or from the date of
     communication of the notice where no such date is specified[9];
(j) a partnership for a single venture ends when the venture ends[10];

(k)   a partnership is automatically dissolved by the death of a partner[11];

(l)   a partnership is automatically dissolved by the bankruptcy of any partner[12];

(m)   if a partner charges his share of the partnership for his separate debt, the other partners have the option to dissolve the partnership[13];

(n)   on dissolution, the property of the firm is to be applied to pay the debts and liabilities of the firm with any surplus to be paid to the partners (after deduction of any debt from a partner to the firm)[14];

(o)   on dissolution, losses are paid[15]:

    (i)   out of profits; then (if necessary)

    (ii)   out of capital; then (if necessary)

    (iii)   by contributions from the partners[16];

(p)   on dissolution, assets are applied according to the following priorities[17]:

    (i)   in paying debts and liabilities to third parties;

    (ii)   in repaying partners for advances to the firm (as distinct from capital);

    (iii)   in paying out each partner's share in respect of capital[18];

    (iv)   in paying out each partner's share of profits[19].

---

1   Partnership Act 1890, s 24(1): thus when the Partnership Act refers to a 'partner', it means a full partner, and there is no room for a 'salaried partnership' which can only be the product of agreement (see para **2.11.4**).

2   Ibid, s 24(5): again, this refers to full partners. Without agreement, a 'salaried partner' or a person who is liable as a partner by estoppel under s 14 of the Partnership Act has no right to take part in the management of the partnership. Note that this contrasts with the wider definition of 'member' of a partnership under art 2(1) of the Order (see para **2.11.2**). The result is apparently that an individual may be liable as a member of an insolvent partnership, without having any right to participate in the management and decision-making of the partnership.

3   Ibid, s 24(8).

4   Ibid, s 24(8): note that this is thought to extend to anything fundamentally altering the partnership, for example a decision to sell the assets and goodwill of a partnership, to incorporate, to propose a partnership voluntary arrangement or to seek a partnership administration order.

5   Ibid, s 24(7).

6   Ibid, s 25.

7   Ibid, ss 24(9) and 28.

8   Ibid, s 26(1); notice must be given to all other partners.

9   Ibid, s 32.

10   Ibid, s 32(b).

11   Ibid, s 33(1).

12   Ibid, s 33(1): it would appear that this provision is limited to personal bankruptcy under English law, and does not extend either to foreign equivalents of bankruptcy, or to any form of corporate insolvency. There does not appear to be any reported decision on the point. However, as insolvency or winding up would apparently render a partner incapable of performing his part of the partnership contract, in such cases a partner can apply to the court for the partnership to be dissolved, either under s 35(b) or s 35(f) of the Partnership Act.

13   Ibid, s 33(2).

14   Ibid, s 39: the Partnership Act thus provides a regime for the orderly management of winding up the affairs of a solvent partnership. For those cases where this cannot be achieved co-operatively, s 39 also gives any partner the right to apply to the court to wind up the business and affairs of the firm. Note that in such circumstances the Order apparently would not apply (because the partnership was not insolvent) and it would not appear to be possible to apply s 221 of the Insolvency Act 1986 and wind up a solvent partnership as an

unregistered company (eg on the 'just and equitable' ground) because a partnership arguably does not, absent the provisions of the Order, fall within the definition of an unregistered company in s 220(1) of the 1986 Act.

15 Partnership Act 1890, s 44(a).
16 Ie equally under s 24(1) of the Partnership Act 1890, absent agreement to the contrary.
17 Partnership Act 1890, s 44(b).
18 Ie equally under s 24(1) of the Partnership Act 1890, absent agreement to the contrary.
19 Again, equally under s 24(1) of the Partnership Act 1890, absent agreement to the contrary.

2.9.2 Usual provisions in the partnership deed

Broadly speaking, the partners may include whatever terms they choose in the partnership agreement, which is customarily drafted in the form of a deed. Partners are expressly free to contract out of the statutory provisions of the Partnership Act[1]. Of course, a partnership agreement cannot vary or oust the jurisdiction of the court[2], it will not of itself be binding between the firm and a third party, and the usual rule that it is not possible to contract out of the insolvency regime will still apply. Note that a partnership agreement, no matter how comprehensive, is not regarded as exhaustively defining all the rights and obligations of the partners[3]. The detailed provisions will still fall to be supplemented by the Partnership Act and case-law. This is particularly true of the *fiduciary* obligations of partner towards partner.

In general, however, one would expect in a reasonably well-drafted partnership agreement to find the following subjects dealt with in adequate detail to provide a clear framework for conduct of the partnership business.

1 Partnership Act 1890, s 19, and see also ss 21, 24, 25, 26, 27(1), 32, 33, 42, 43 and 44.
2 Although it may include an arbitration clause.
3 *Smith v Jeyes* (1841) 4 Beav 503 at 505.

(a) The parties

The parties to the agreement should be specified. Where there are different categories of partner, the status should be defined and spelled out. In large partnerships, where there may be several classes of partner, it will often be convenient for the partners to be listed in one or more schedules. Note the distinction between a salaried partner and a mere employee[1]; the latter should not be a party to the agreement (or, conversely, the fact that an employee is a party to the agreement might indicate that that person is a 'salaried partner').

1 See para **2.11.4** below.

(b) The business

The nature of the business is fundamental to the partnership, and should be clearly defined. This is not least because it will be by reference to that business that each partner has capacity to bind the firm and his partners[1].

1 Partnership Act 1890, s 5.

(c)   *The place of business*

The place of business may be necessary to establish the nationality or domicile of a particular partnership, and the jurisdiction of a particular court. It will be the address where the books of the partnership are to be kept and may be inspected by a partner[1]. It will also be the address for service of a writ in the High Court[2].

1 Ibid, s 24(9).
2 Order 81, r 3(1)(b), (c) of the Rules of the Supreme Court 1965.

(d)   *Start date*

It is necessary to specify the date on which the partnership commenced, because that is the date from which the acts of a partner bind his co-partners. If no other date is specified, a partnership agreement will be taken to begin on the date (and at the time) of its actual execution[1]. It is possible for an earlier or later date to be specified, but in that case consideration must be given to when the partners actually begin to carry on business together.

1 *Morell v Studd & Millington* [1913] 2 Ch 648.

(e)   *Duration*

It is frequently preferable to specify a term in the partnership agreement, to prevent the partnership being merely a partnership at will[1]. This may be a specified term of years, or a term for the joint lives of the partners or some of them. Alternatively, it may suit the partners to have the partnership determinable by one, or a specified number, of the partners giving a specified period of notice.

1 See para **2.6.1**.

(f)   *Firm name*

It will usually be preferable to specify the name or names under which the business of the firm is to be carried on; the name of an established firm may well accrue considerable goodwill, and thus become an asset of the firm in its own right.

(g)   *Property and shares in property*

The property of the partnership should be listed, preferably in a schedule which can then be updated from time to time. If any property of a partner is to be used by the partnership, without becoming partnership property, this should also be specified in sufficient detail to avoid subsequent disputes.

There should be a clear record of the capital subscribed by each partner (in money terms), and of the proportions in which each partner is to share in the capital of the partnership on dissolution. If it is agreed that capital should pay interest, this must be the subject of specific provision.

In appropriate cases, provision should be made for intangible assets, such as trade marks, other intellectual property rights, and goodwill.

(h)   *Profits and losses*
The ratio in which profits and losses are to be apportioned should always be specified. In practice, this can vary from the Partnership Act starting point of equal shares to very complex formulae allocating profits according to age, seniority, or other criteria. There will frequently be provision to permit partners to draw from the partnership on account of profits, before the accounts for a trading period have been finalised. Note that undistributed profits will not be treated as added to capital unless there is specific provision to this effect.

(i)   *Management*
In many cases, the partnership agreement will contain specific provisions detailing how the business of the partnership is to be managed. Powers may be delegated to an individual partner or group of partners, or the senior partner may have a specified right of veto.

(j)   *Internal decision-making*
It will frequently be necessary to have detailed provision for the taking of decisions within the firm, particularly on those matters where the Partnership Act would otherwise require unanimity. In firms of any size, there will usually be provisions regulating the calling of meetings, their frequency, the form of notice required, what quorum is necessary, whether proxy votes are allowed, whether voting is to be by classes, the role of the chairman and so on.

It is possible for voting to be by simple majority of those attending a meeting, or of all partners, by number, or by value of capital contribution or profit share[1].

Unless the partners are content to live with the requirement for unanimous decision-making, it is necessary to make specific provision for taking fundamental decisions affecting the partnership. These will include, for example, the majority and the procedures required to:

(a)   introduce a new partner;
(b)   expel an existing one;
(c)   move premises;
(d)   change the firm's name;
(e)   permit sale of part of the partnership's business;
(f)   merge with another partnership;
(g)   propose a partnership voluntary arrangement;
(h)   petition for a partnership administration order;
(i)   dissolve the partnership.

---

1 Where there are only two partners, unanimity will be required for any decision: see *Lindley and Banks on Partnership* 17th Edn (Sweet & Maxwell, 1995) at para 10-84, p 205.

(k) *Authority, powers and duties of a partner*

A partner's obligation to act with the utmost good faith towards his partners is fundamental in partnership, and will always be implied. Such clauses are nonetheless found in many agreements. If the partners are to be obliged to devote themselves exclusively to the partnership, this will need to be set out, as will any restrictions on the authority of any partners or the partners in general. The agreement should deal with holiday entitlement, provisions for maternity leave or other sabbaticals, etc. Where an individual partner (or a partner holding a particular post) is to have special or exclusive powers or authority, this must be specified.

(l) *Retirement*

There is no right of retirement provided in the Partnership Act, but such a right may be conferred under the partnership agreement. This will generally require service of a written notice, and may be subject to restrictions or require the agreement of the other partners. Alternatively, it may be mandatory for partners to retire at a certain age, or in specified circumstances[1].

---

1 For instance, the loss of a necessary practising certificate or membership of a specified professional body.

(m) *Expulsion*

Detailed provision should be made for the circumstances in which a partner may be expelled. These will usually include: insolvency[1], mental or physical incapacity, misconduct, dishonesty, etc. Unless expulsion is to be automatic on the happening of a specified contingency, there is commonly some form of notice procedure, requiring the support of a specified number or majority of the partners[2].

---

1 In which case the operation of s 33(1) of the Partnership Act 1890, automatically dissolving a partnership on bankruptcy, will be excluded by implication. Note that it is usually desirable to define insolvency very widely. Arguably this should include, for example, consulting an insolvency practitioner to draft a proposal for an individual voluntary arrangement (IVA) (and it may be thought desirable explicitly to require a partner to notify his partners before he does so) to circumvent any complications which may arise from the operation of an interim order.

2 A power to expel must, of course, only be exercised *bona fide*, and an expulsion clause will always be construed particularly strictly.

(n) *Death*

Provision for the death of a partner must be included not only to avoid the automatic dissolution which would otherwise be mandated under the Partnership Act[1], but also to make any desired provision for a dead partner's dependants (for example, the continued payment of an annuity to a widow(er)).

---

1 Partnership Act 1890, s 33(1).

(o)   *Dissolution*

Although the reason it is desirable to include retirement or expulsion clauses is
to avoid the need for a dissolution of the partnership under the Partnership
Act, there may nonetheless be circumstances where the partners would prefer
to bring the partnership as a whole to an end. This might, for example, be a
precursor to incorporation, or it might be if the number of partners fell below a
certain number. There may be a general power to dissolve, or the power may
only be exercisable in specified cases; for instance, where the continued
involvement of a particular member is regarded as critical to the commercial
viability of the partnership, or if it is no longer possible to trade from a
particular location, or if the partnership makes a loss in any one year. Such
grounds for dissolution should be specified, and again procedural
requirements should be spelled out. Unless the partners wish to have a
partnership determinable at will by just one partner, it will be necessary to have
a procedure to validate a dissolution notice (eg by requiring a meeting to pass
the necessary resolution by a specified majority, or by requiring a notice to be
signed by a minimum number of partners).

(p)   *Mechanics for dealing with outgoing partners*

Technically, any change in the composition of the firm produces a dissolution
as a matter of law[1]. If the partnership agreement is silent as to what is to happen
in such circumstances, an outgoing partner could compel the winding up of
the partnership and the distribution of its assets[2]. In order to mitigate these
consequences, partnership agreements will frequently provide for the
remaining partners to acquire the outgoing partner's share in the partnership,
either by giving them the option to do so, or by the share vesting in them
automatically on the outgoing partner's departure[3]. In either case, provision
must also be made for the valuation of the relevant share, so that the financial
entitlement of the outgoing partner can be paid out to him (or, in a relevant
case, to his personal representative or trustee in bankruptcy[4]). It is also possible
(and not uncommon) for there to be provision for payment by instalments
(with or without interest) and for retention to cover relevant liabilities.
However, if the partnership is unable to satisfy the payments due to an outgoing
partner, this may precipitate insolvency proceedings against the partnership.

---

1 See para **2.7**.
2 Although it may be possible to force the outgoing partner to sell his share to the others; see
  Sobell v Boston [1985] 1 WLR 1587.
3 Referred to as 'automatic accruer'.
4 Or liquidator, etc. It appears that, as long as full value is paid, a *bona fide* agreement to
  purchase an insolvent partner's share in a partnership will be valid: *Borland's Trustee v Steel
  Bros & Co Ltd* [1901] 1 Ch 279.

(q)   *Indemnity to an outgoing partner*

A partner remains liable for partnership debts and obligations incurred prior
to his retirement[1] or expulsion. It is, however, common for the remaining
partners to indemnify an outgoing partner. Even where there is no express
indemnity, an indemnity will readily be implied[2].

1 Partnership Act 1890, s 17(2).
2 *Gray v Smith* (1889) 43 Ch D 208.

(r) *Mechanics for dealing with incoming partners*

The introduction of a new partner also technically gives rise to a new partnership. If, as will usually be the case, it is desired that the new partnership will continue on the same terms, there must be:

(i)   provision in the partnership agreement for new partners to be admitted, detailing, for example, any redistribution of the shares of the existing partners in capital and undistributed income (to which, prima facie, they remain entitled);

(ii) provision for the new partner to become bound by the terms of the agreement (by signing an accession schedule or a separate deed).

(s) *Restrictions on competition*

There will only be a restriction on the outgoing partner's right to set up in competition with his former partners if there is some express provision either in the partnership agreement or in some other contract (such as a termination contract). Such a provision will be valid only if it is reasonable and not excessive[1].

1 Although reference may be made to cases on *restraint of trade* between employer and employee, partners (other than those 'salaried partners' who *are* employees) are strictly speaking in a different category: see the Privy Council decision in *Bridge v Deacons* [1984] AC 705. Note that a restriction which might interfere with trade between Member States of the EU would potentially fall foul of art 85 of the EC Treaty: see *Gottfried Reuter v BASF AG* [1976] 2 CMLR D44 (76/743/EEC).

(t) *Books and accounts*

There will customarily be provision for the book-keeping of the partnership, and for the preparation of accounts on a regular basis[1]. This will usually specify who is to draw up the accounts, the relevant dates for accounting purposes, and any relevant matters concerning the basis on which accounts are to be drawn up (for instance, the treatment of work in progress, goodwill, and any extraordinary items). If the books are at any time to be kept somewhere other than at the partnership's place of business, or if access by partners is in any way to be restricted, there needs to be specific provision to supplant the rules in the Partnership Act[2].

1 Under the Partnerships and Unlimited Companies (Accounts) Regulations 1993, SI 1993/1820, a *corporate partnership* (ie one whose members are, broadly, all limited or unlimited companies) must prepare and lodge accounts with the Registrar of Companies.
2 Partnership Act 1890, s 24(9).

(u) *Bank account*

The partnership's bank will usually be named in the partnership agreement, together with any special provisions (for example, dealing with client accounts, etc). The authority of each partner, and any requirements for signing of cheques should be dealt with. Where money is to be borrowed, there should be specific terms dealing with who is entitled to borrow, what consent is required before partnership assets can be used as security, etc.

(v)   *Variation*
It is advisable to make specific provision for the manner (if any) in which a partnership agreement can be varied.

(w)   *Arbitration*
It is frequently thought desirable for disputes arising from partnership agreements to be dealt with by arbitration rather than in court. In such cases, there needs to be a specific term in the agreement to that effect.

(x)   *Law and jurisdiction*
In any partnership with an international aspect, the governing law and the country whose courts are to have jurisdiction (or, where there is an arbitration clause, the place of arbitration) should be specified in the agreement to avoid subsequent disputes and potential forum shopping.

2.10   THE FIRM'S NAME

2.10.1   *General requirements*
The name of a firm is merely a collective noun for the partners at the particular time when the name is used[1]. Any partnership may, without restriction, operate under the names of all the partners[2]. However, any additional wording (such as the conventional '& Co'), or anything less than the complete list of partners, brings the firm within the ambit of the Business Names Act 1985[3].

Most partnerships of any size will therefore be subject to potential restrictions on the name of the firm[4], because it will be more convenient to operate under a trading name, or perhaps the names of just two or three partners.

In general, it is not permitted to use words in a business name which suggest that the business is connected with Royalty, the Government, or certain types of organisation[5], without first obtaining written approval from the Department of Trade and Industry[6].

---

1 Partnership Act 1890, s 4(1).
2 Ie the individual names of individuals, the corporate names of any corporate members, together with a few 'permitted additions' such as forenames or initials, or the letter 's' at the end of a surname shared by two or more partners.
3 By s 1 of the Business Names Act 1985.
4 Under s 2 of the Business Names Act 1985.
5 See the Company and Business Names Regulations 1981, SI 1981/1685, as amended in 1982 (SI 1982/1653) and 1992 (SI 1992/1196).
6 This applies if, for example, one of the names to be included is 'King'.

2.10.2   *Specific restrictions*
Specific restrictions may apply to partnerships operating in particular industries. For example, only an authorised partnership with designated fixed capital of not less than £5 million may use a banking name[1].

1 Section 67 of the Banking Act 1987.

2.10.3 Disclosure

Of greater significance, where the Business Names Act applies, is that a partnership must disclose the name of each partner, and an address for service, on all business documents and by a notice prominently displayed at the firm's business premises[1]. A firm with more than 20 partners may instead maintain a list of all partners at its principal place of business[2].

1 Section 4(1)(a) of the Business Names Act 1985.
2 Section 4(3) of the Business Names Act 1985.

2.10.4 Default

Failure to comply with the Business Names Act requirements is an offence, and may also place the firm under a disability in civil proceedings[1].

1 A firm cannot enforce an action based on a contract made while it was in breach if the defendant can show either that he was unable to pursue an action against the partnership, or that he has suffered financial loss, because of the breach: s 5 of the Business Names Act 1985.

2.11 WHO IS A PARTNER?

2.11.1 The partners

The question of who is a partner will become of particular significance in the context of a partnership which is insolvent. It will determine, for example:

- who must take part in the decision-making process before a partnership voluntary arrangement may be proposed, or a partnership administration order may be applied for;
- whose bankruptcy may automatically dissolve the partnership;
- whose assets are at risk if a partnership is wound up.

These will be fundamental questions of fact for anyone seeking to advise in respect of a partnership insolvency. Almost the first step to be taken in such circumstances is to establish the identity, status and individual solvency of each individual partner.

As a matter of definition, the partners will be those individuals, partnerships and companies which are carrying on business together with a view to profit[1]. The first place to look will therefore be in the partnership agreement (where there is one), on the headed notepaper, or in the list displayed at the partnership's principal place of business. In a surprising number of cases, no detailed records are kept of when individuals have joined or left a partnership, and it will frequently be necessary to consider carefully the circumstances of anyone who appears to have less than full partnership rights.

1 For consideration of who can or cannot be a partner, see para **2.11.2** below.

2.11.2   The definition of 'member' in the Order

For the purposes of the Order, the term a 'member' of a partnership:

> 'means a member of a partnership and any person who is liable as a partner within the meaning of section 14 of the Partnership Act 1890'[1].

It thus introduces into the category of 'member' of an insolvent partnership, for the purposes of the Act as modified by the Order, a category of persons who are *not* members under the formal documents of the partnership, and do not acquire the rights of members under the Partnership Act.

---

1 Insolvent Partnerships Order 1994, art 2(1); this definition did not appear in the Insolvent Partnerships Order 1986.

2.11.3   Liability as a partner through 'holding out'

Section 14 of the Partnership Act, which is headed 'Persons liable by "holding out"' provides:

> '(1) Every one who by words spoken or written or by conduct represents himself, or who knowingly suffers himself to be represented, as a partner in a particular firm, is liable as a partner to any one who has on the faith of any such representation given credit to the firm, whether the representation has or has not been made or communicated to the person so giving credit by or with the knowledge of the apparent partner making the representation or suffering it to be made.'

Section 14(2) goes on to exclude from liability the estate of a dead partner where his name continues to be used as part of the firm name.

Before the Partnership Act, there was sometimes said to be a category of 'quasi partners': those who were not partners but were liable as if they were. The Partnership Act dealt with such liability in terms of the specific relationship established by 'holding out'. Those who are held out are not partners[1], but they share the (joint) liability of partners in one limited set of circumstances.

If A and B are partners, and C helps them to borrow money from a bank either by permitting them to tell the bank he is a partner or by doing so himself, C shares the liability of A and B to the bank[2]. However, as long as the partnership is solvent, he would not be liable to any of the other creditors of the partnership, unless similar representations had been made to them and relied on by them.

It has become relatively common for certain types of professional firm to reward employees of a certain seniority with the appearance of their name on the firm's notepaper in a list which appears to be of partners, or to confer titles such as 'junior partner', 'associate partner', etc. Such an individual is obviously 'held out'. However, that in itself is not enough to establish liability as a partner under the Partnership Act. A third party must:

(i)   be aware of the holding out;
(ii) extend credit to the firm;
(iii) do so *in reliance upon* the representation;

in order for the individual to become liable to that third party.

Unless these three matters of fact are established, the individual will not have become liable under the Partnership Act, and so will not be a 'member' for purposes of the Order. This is significant, not only because it is necessary to determine who are the members who must comply with the formalities of the Order, but because it appears that the dramatic consequence of being a member under the Order is that the individual's estate is available to satisfy any shortfall on the joint estate – in other words, where the partnership is insolvent, the person held out becomes liable to *all* the creditors of the partnership, not merely the specific creditor who originally relied upon the holding-out[3].

It has been suggested that the term 'given credit to the firm' should not be construed in a technical or restrictive sense, but should be taken as describing 'any transaction with the firm'[4]. However, given the extreme consequences which may arise in the context of a partnership insolvency, it is thought that a court would be more likely to treat the term strictly, and to require cogent evidence to satisfy itself that the necessary factual preconditions for liability exist.

An individual who has become a 'member' through holding out will apparently be entitled to vote at a meeting of members[5], but his vote is to be left out of account in determining whether any resolution has obtained a majority[6]. Such an individual seems effectively to have been disenfranchised under the Insolvency Rules 1986, even though his assets may be available to satisfy the firm's creditors. There must be many people who have been flattered by being granted 'junior partner' status, who do not realise just how weak their position may be if their firm becomes insolvent.

1 *Hudgell Yeates & Co v Watson* [1978] QB 451, 467; *Re C & M Ashberg* (1990) *The Times,* 17 July.
2 Prior to the Partnership Act 1890, C would have been liable on the basis of *estoppel*; that is, he would not have been permitted to deny that he was a partner.
3 See s 175A(5)(a) as introduced by Sch 4 to the Order: an insolvency practitioner is to claim for any joint estate shortfall against the separate estate of *each* member of the partnership.
4 *Lindley and Banks on Partnership* 17th Edn (Sweet & Maxwell, 1995) at para 5-52, p 98; in Australia, equivalent wording has been held to extend to the deposit of money with solicitors for investment: *Lynch v Stiff* [1943] 68 CLR 428.
5 Under r 1.18(2) of the Insolvency Rules 1986.
6 Insolvency Rules 1986, r 1.20(2).

2.11.4 The salaried partner

The status of the 'salaried partner' is closely related to that of the partner by holding out. It is important to note that the term may cover two quite different sets of circumstances:

(a) a person who is otherwise entitled to all the privileges of partnership may receive, instead of a pure profit-share, a regular fixed sum as a 'salary', either in place of, or on account of, his share of profits: such a person is a partner;

(b) a person who is an employee of the partnership and thus receives a salary (which may include a profit-related bonus), and does not otherwise have any or all of the rights of a partner, but is none the less held out as a partner; such a person is not a partner but may become liable under s 14 of the Partnership Act if a third party extends credit to the firm in reliance upon that holding-out.

For internal purposes, whether the individual is or is not a partner will depend on the facts in each case[1]. If the conclusion is that he is one of the group carrying on business and exposed to the relevant risks, in other words, receiving a share of profits when there are profits, the proper conclusion is that the individual *is* a partner. If, on the other hand, an individual receives a monthly salary regardless of the performance of the firm, and is not fully entitled to participate in the management of the firm, that individual is not, in the strict legal sense, a partner. This question often requires close analysis[2].

For external purposes (and of particular significance under the Order), if the individual has been styled a partner, the considerations set out in the preceding section apply; the key question is then whether an individual creditor has extended credit on the faith of such a representation.

The fact that a particular partner receives a specified or smaller share of profits is an aspect of the internal status of that partner; it does not diminish his liability to the creditors of the partnership. However, junior classes of partner, and salaried partners (who, as we have seen, may or may not technically be partners) are often given indemnities by the senior or 'full' partners to mitigate this liability. Where the firm is insolvent, however, it appears that any such indemnity will be subordinated to the claims of third-party creditors[3] and will often be worthless. On the other hand, where as a matter of fact the individual is not a partner, and has not become a member under the Order by holding out[4], the individual will not be liable to creditors of the firm *at all.*

Note that the same considerations will apparently apply to junior and salaried partners, and those who have been held out as partners, after the individual in question has left the firm.

---

1 *Stekel v Ellice* [1973] 1 WLR 191: see in particular per Megarry J at 199 G–H; *Burgess v O'Brien* [1966] ITR 164; *Briggs v Oates* [1990] ICR 473; *Casson Beckman & Partners v Papi* [1991] BCLC 299, CA; cf *United Bank of Kuwait v Hammoud* [1988] 1 WLR 1051. In *Horner v Hasted* [1995] STC 766, the tax-payer had been held out as a partner in a firm of accountants, but he could not legally have become a partner because he was not a member of a relevant professional body: after careful consideration of all the circumstances, he was held to be an employee.
2 It appears possible for a full partner to reduce his status, perhaps as a stage of 'semi-retirement': *Marsh v Stacey* (1963) 107 SJ 512, CA.
3 Because of the rule that a partner may not compete with his creditors: see *Ex p Collinge* (1863) 4 De G J & S 533 and modified s 175C(2) in Sch 4 to the Order.
4 Ie where it cannot be established that a creditor has extended credit on the faith of the representation that X is a partner; see above.

2.11.5   *The equity partner*

The term 'equity partner' is sometimes used to denote a partner who is entitled to a share in the partnership assets and capital, as opposed to a lesser category of 'junior partner' who is entitled only to a share of profits. The terms used for categories of partners (and non-partners) need to be considered carefully in each case. In some firms it will only be the equity partners who are technically partners, although there may be 'junior partners' who have become members for the purposes of the Order through holding-out[1].

1 See para **2.11.3** above.

2.11.6 Husband and wife

Partnerships between married couples are relatively common, but the court may be reluctant to infer the existence of such a partnership[1]. Where the marital and business relationships are closely intertwined, the failure of the marriage may put an end to the partnership[2]. Under such circumstances, the partners' rights in respect of the partnership may fall within the jurisdiction of the Family Division[3].

1 *Parrington v Parrington* [1951] WN 534; *Nixon v Nixon* [1969] 1 WLR 1676.
2 *Bothe v Amos* [1976] Fam 46.
3 Cf *Williams v Williams* [1976] Ch 278; *Bernard v Josephs* [1982] Ch 391.

2.11.7 Sub-partnership

There is a maxim which states 'my partner's partner is not (necessarily) my partner'. It is possible for a partner to agree to share his entitlement to partnership profits with a third party. Such an arrangement gives rise to a sub-partnership[1]. Partnership agreements may prohibit the creation of sub-partnerships, or require the consent of the other partners.

A sub-partnership exists independently of the main partnership (sometimes termed the head partnership), and the terms of the main partnership are not incorporated by implication into a sub-partnership[2]. The duration of main and sub-partnerships may be different.

It may also be the case that there can be a sub-partnership consisting solely of a sub-set of partners; this may be the correct analysis where a large partnership has a number of autonomous regional offices, for example, and allocates profit shares on that basis.

1 *Ex p Barrow* (1815) 2 Rose 255; *Bray v Fromont* (1821) 6 Madd 5; *Ex p Dodgson* (1830) Mont & Mac 445.
2 *Frost v Moulton* (1856) 21 Beav 596.

2.11.8 Group partnership

It is important to distinguish between sub-partnerships and group partnership. In a group partnership, two (or more) partnerships come together in partnership for a joint business venture. As there are no individual entities other than the two sets of partners[1], it follows that every partner in a constituent partnership is also a partner in the group partnership. The group partnership is thus subject to the usual restrictions as to size[2].

An insolvent group partnership is wound up in the same way as any other partnership under the Order, and an insolvent partnership which is a member of an insolvent group partnership is wound up as though it were a corporate member of the group partnership[3].

1 See para **2.1.2** above.
2 See para **2.8.1** above.
3 Insolvent Partnerships Order 1994, art 12; arts 8 and 10 apply.

2.11.9 *The incoming partner*

Because a firm consists of those members composing it from time to time, the admission of a new partner constitutes a legally different partnership[1]. An incoming partner does not, merely by being admitted, become liable to the firm's creditors for anything done before he joined[2]. Similarly, he does not inevitably become entitled to a share of profits from work previously undertaken by the old firm, and it appears that any work in progress will not automatically become an asset of the new firm[3].

The relationship between an incoming partner and the prior partnership will often be the subject of express agreement, establishing clearly any rights the incoming partner acquires in respect of previous work, and any obligations he takes on to contribute to outstanding liabilities[4]. It may, and frequently will, be a condition of entry that the new partner takes on existing liabilities. As a matter of contract law, this agreement affects the relationship between the newcomer and his partners, but does not of itself give any rights to third parties.

An incoming partner who is aware of a particular substantial contingent liability (eg pending litigation for professional negligence which, if successful, would exhaust the firm's professional indemnity insurance cover) may be given indemnities by the other partners in respect of that specific liability[5]. Once again, the value of such an indemnity depends on the solvency of the firm; where the firm is insolvent it appears that any such indemnity will be subordinated to the claims of third-party creditors[6] and will often therefore be worthless[7].

It is possible for the newly constituted firm to take on the debts of the old firm by *novation*, but only a creditor who is a party to such an agreement will be entitled to rely upon it[8]. Novation may be inferred, but whether there has been novation is a question of fact[9]; the key issue is the existence of agreement by the creditor.

1 See *Ex p Jackson* (1790) 1 Ves Jr 131.
2 Partnership Act 1890, s 17(1). Note that it is therefore often necessary to pay close attention to the precise moment when a firm incurred a liability, ie when a contract was made, or when a cause of action accrued. A cause of action for breach of contract accrues when the breach occurs. Where a professional partner *omits* to do something, there is a continuing obligation to remedy the omission until that is no longer possible: *Midland Bank Trust Co Ltd v Hett, Stubbs & Kemp* [1979] Ch 384, but cf *Bell v Peter Browne & Co* [1990] 2 QB 495. In tort, a cause of action accrues when the plaintiff suffers damage. A claim which is not brought within six years is normally statute barred, but the Latent Damage Act 1986 amended the Limitation Act 1980 so that a plaintiff has a further three years from the date he had the requisite

knowledge, subject to a maximum period of 15 years. One cannot entirely rule out the possibility that an act which occurred before a person became a partner may give rise to a liability which accrues during the period when that person is a partner.

3 *Robertson v Brent* [1972] NZLR 406.
4 There is no presumption that the new firm acquires liabilities of the existing firm, merely because it acquires the existing firm's assets: *Creasey v Breachwood Motors Ltd* [1992] BCC 638. It would appear that any agreement prescribing the extent of the incoming partner's liability will determine the extent of his contribution in the event that the partnership is wound up.
5 Note that it is the partners at the time of the original negligent act who will be liable for the original negligence, not those who are partners when the writ is served.
6 Because of the rule that a partner may not compete with his creditors: see *Ex p Collinge* (1863) 4 De G J & S 533 and modified s 175C(2) of the Insolvency Act 1986 in Sch 4 to the Order.
7 Where there are sufficient assets in the partnership, one would usually expect the indemnity to be dealt with in the course of the regular settlement of accounts between the partners. An unpaid partner in these circumstances otherwise has a claim against his co-partners which they will generally prefer to settle if they can.
8 Cf *British Homes Assurance Corporation Ltd v Paterson* [1902] 2 Ch 404.
9 See *Ex p Whitmore* (1838) 3 Deac 365; *Rolfe v Flower* (1865) LR 1 PC 27.

2.11.10 *The outgoing partner*

Under the Partnership Act, retirement does not end a partner's liability for partnership debts and obligations incurred before his retirement[1], unless there is an agreement between the retiring partner, the members of the firm as newly constituted and the creditors[2]. In the case of a partnership at will, the retirement of one partner will determine the partnership[3]. Even where the partnership agreement of the former partnership provides for continuation, technically a new firm is constituted of the remaining partners.

A retiring partner will be entitled to receive his share of the partnership capital and profits, and in return will release his interest in the partnership to the remaining partners. It is often impractical to deal with this by formal assignment[4], although written formalities will be necessary where the property includes land[5]. The remaining partners will usually require a retention to cover accrued tax and VAT etc, and perhaps also specific contingent claims.

The continuing partners usually provide an indemnity to the retiring partner against partnership debts and obligations[6]. Where a partnership is solvent, one would expect general trade creditors to be paid within a reasonably short time, so that those liabilities of a retiring partner will rapidly have become extinguished[7]. However, obligations such as those under the covenants in a lease[8] and contracts still to be executed, or latent claims (such as for professional negligence), will continue, subject to the limitation period[9].

The grant of indemnity by the remaining partners is said to render the retiring partner a *surety*[10] for the continuing obligations of the firm. If a creditor with notice of the arrangement deals with the continuing firm in a way which might prejudice the surety's rights, the effect is that the retiring partner will no longer be liable.

A retiring partner may also be liable for obligations incurred *after* retirement, either where he continues to be held out as a partner[11], or where a creditor continuing to deal with the firm has not been given notice of the change[12]. Such previous creditors must be given express notice; for future creditors, it is sufficient if a notice is published in the *London Gazette*[13]. This will only be necessary if the creditor in question actually knew that the retiring partner[14] was a partner; where the creditor did not know, the partner is not liable for debts contracted after the date of his retirement[15].

Where a retiring partner remains liable to creditors but relies upon the indemnity from his former co-partners, the value of such an indemnity again depends on the solvency of the firm; where the firm is insolvent it appears that any such indemnity will be subordinated to the claims of third-party creditors[16] and will often be worthless. In this context, it should be noted that s 74(2)(a)–(d) of the Act, which restrict the liability of a former member of a company[17] to contribute if that company is wound up, expressly do not apply to the winding up of an insolvent partnership[18].

---

1 Partnership Act 1890, s 17(2).
2 Ibid, s 17(3); agreement may be express or inferred as a fact by a course of dealing.
3 Ibid, s 26.
4 But there may be an obligation to provide a formal assignment should it become necessary.
5 Law of Property (Miscellaneous Provisions) Act 1991.
6 And even where such indemnity is not explicit, it may be implied: see *Gray v Smith* (1889) 43 Ch D 208.
7 Complicated questions may arise as to whether the debt from the old firm is extinguished. Where there is a single account between the firm and the creditor, a payment which is not referable to a specific item will, under the rule in *Clayton's Case*, be applied to the earliest item(s).
8 See *Hoby v Roebuck and Palmer* (1816) 7 Taunt 157; *Graham v Wichelo and Hull* (1832) 1 Cr & M 188.
9 The liability of a contributory is a specialty debt, payable when calls are made, for which the relevant limitation period is 12 years (Insolvency Act 1986, s 80 and Limitation Act 1980, s 8(1)).
10 *Oakeley v Pasheller* (1836) 4 Cl & F 207.
11 Under the Partnership Act 1890, s 14 – for example, when his name continues to appear on the notepaper.
12 Partnership Act 1890, s 36(1).
13 Ibid, s 36(2).
14 The same applies to dead or bankrupt partners.
15 Partnership Act 1890, s 36(3).
16 Because of the rule that a partner may not compete with his creditors: see *Ex p Collinge* (1863) 4 De G J & S 533 and modified s 175C(2) of the Insolvency Act 1986 in Sch 4 to the Order.
17 Including, usually, an unregistered company, by application of s 221(1) of the Insolvency Act 1986.
18 See s 221(6) of the Insolvency Act 1986, as modified by Schs 3, 4, 5 and 6 to the Order.

2.11.11 The insolvent partner

The bankruptcy of an individual partner automatically dissolves a partnership, in the absence of agreement to the contrary[1]. The liquidation of a corporate partner does not automatically lead to dissolution, but will almost certainly provide grounds that it is 'just and equitable' for the partnership to be dissolved[2]. The same will be true of other forms of corporate insolvency, such as administration, corporate voluntary arrangement, or the appointment of a provisional liquidator.

A bankrupt partner's share in the partnership vests in his trustee, along with any other assets he may have. Assets do not automatically vest in a liquidator, although where a company is being wound up by the court, the court can make an order to that effect[3]; however, the liquidator is under a duty to get in the assets of the insolvent estate. A trustee or liquidator is only entitled to receive any balance due to the insolvent partner, after partnership accounts have been settled.

Where the partnership itself is solvent, the fact that an individual partner becomes insolvent need not give rise to any proceedings under the Order. However, where the attention of the court is drawn to the fact that an individual against whom a bankruptcy petition has been presented[4], or a person against whom a winding-up petition has been presented[5], is a member of an insolvent partnership, the court may make an order applying any provisions of the Order (with 'any necessary modifications') to the future conduct of the insolvency proceedings. This order may deal with the administration of the joint estate of the partnership and the separate estate of any member. In these circumstances, therefore, it appears that the court has discretion to apply the changed priorities for claims under the Order[6] and permit the joint estate (ie partnership creditors) to claim alongside separate estate creditors in *any* separate estate.

It appears that an agreement for the remaining partners to acquire the share of an insolvent partner is valid, as long as full value is paid[7].

It also appears that where the insolvent partner was one of the trustee partners holding land for the partnership[8], that property does not vest in a trustee[9].

---

1 Partnership Act 1890, s 33(1).
2 Under s 35(f) of the Partnership Act 1890.
3 Insolvency Act 1986, s 145(1).
4 Ibid, s 303(2A), as inserted by art 14(2) of the Order.
5 Ibid, s 168(5A), as inserted by art 14(1) of the Order.
6 For example, s 175A(5) of the Insolvency Act 1986, as modified by Sch 4 to the Order.
7 *Borland's Trustee v Steel Bros & Co Ltd* [1901] 1 Ch 279; in the earlier case of *Wilson v Greenwood* (1818) 1 Swan 471, an option agreement entered into a few months before a partner's bankruptcy had been held void as a fraud on the contemporary bankruptcy laws.
8 See para **2.13.4** below.
9 See *Re Holliday* [1981] Ch 405 at 411.

2.11.12 The dead partner

When a partner dies, the partnership is dissolved in the absence of an agreement to the contrary[1]. The late partner's share in the partnership vests in his estate, and his personal representatives have no right to become involved in the partnership (unless the partners have agreed otherwise). The surviving partners conduct the winding up[2], and the amount due to the dead partner becomes a debt accruing at the date of death[3]. If the surviving partners continue to use the capital and assets of the firm without a final settlement of accounts with the dead partner's estate, the estate is entitled to share in the post-dissolution profits, or to interest on his share of the assets at 5 per cent[4].

As a matter of general principle, the dead partner's estate remains liable for partnership obligations incurred before his death[5], but not for liabilities incurred in respect of transactions which were entered into after death[6] (except for liabilities which necessarily arise in winding up the partnership). An act of acknowledgement by a surviving partner can revive a liability of the estate of a deceased partner where it would otherwise have become statute barred, just as it can revive the liability of a living partner.

Note that there is a long-standing equitable rule[7] that the estate of a dead partner has *several* liability for debts and obligations incurred while he was a partner[8], so that a separate action could always be maintained against his estate. However, a partnership creditor is not allowed to compete with the separate estate creditors, and so ranks behind them in priority for payment[9].

1 Partnership Act 1890, s 33(1).
2 Ibid, s 38.
3 Ibid, s 43.
4 Ibid, s 42(1), in the absence of any agreement to the contrary.
5 *Devaynes v Noble* (1816) 1 Mer 529.
6 *Bagel v Miller* [1903] 2 KB 212.
7 Recognised by the House of Lords in *Kendall v Hamilton* (1879) 4 App Cas 504.
8 Unlike a living partner, where liability in this regard is joint: see para **2.12.4** below.
9 This position has been preserved in the Partnership Act 1890, s 9.

2.12 RELATIONSHIPS WITH THIRD PARTIES

2.12.1 The agency principle
A partner deals with third parties as the agent of 'the firm and his other partners', so that any act for carrying on the firm's business in the usual way will bind the partnership[1]. What is expected by the clients of a particular type of firm may well change over time[2], so the question of what a firm's 'business' is, and what constitutes carrying it on 'in the usual way', will be questions of fact (and, if necessary, expert evidence) in any particular case.

1 Partnership Act 1890, s 5.
2 See, for example, Staughton LJ's comments about the changing role of solicitors in *United Bank of Kuwait v Hammoud and Others; City Trust Ltd and Another v Levy* [1988] 1 WLR 1051 at 1063F.

2.12.2 The notice principle
A partner will not bind his co-partners if he does not have authority and the third party involved either knows that the partner has no authority to act for the firm in the particular transaction, or does not know or believe that he is a partner[1]. Thus it is possible for a firm to place a specific limitation on the authority of a particular partner or partners (eg by restrictions in a bank mandate) and, by informing a relevant third party, prevent such a partner from binding the firm.

Conversely, because each partner is an agent, notice to one partner in relation to partnership affairs operates as notice to the firm; an exception to this is made where there is a fraud on the firm committed by or with the consent of a partner[2]. It is generally thought that constructive notice will not be enough, and only actual notice will suffice[3].

1 Partnership Act 1890, s 5.
2 Ibid, s 16.
3 See *Lacey v Hill* (1876) 4 Ch D 537, and *Lindley and Banks on Partnership* 17th Edn (Sweet & Maxwell, 1995) at para 12-25.

2.12.3 Ratification
Where a partner has acted without authority, his action may nonetheless subsequently be ratified by his co-partners; in that case, it will be as if he had had authority all along. The partners can only ratify an action of which they have actual knowledge[1].

---

1 *Lacey v Hill* (1876) 4 Ch D 537 (affirmed sub nom *Read v Bailey* (1877) 3 App Cas 94); *Marsh v Joseph* [1897] 1 Ch 213; *Hambro v Burnand* [1903] 2 KB 399.

2.12.4 Partnership contracts
A partner has a general power to bind his firm by contract; he contracts as agent[1], so each of the partners will be a party to the contract as principal. Similarly, if an employee or other agent of the firm is authorised to make a contract[2], and the contract is executed in the firm's name or in any other manner which shows an intention to bind the firm, the firm will be bound[3]. Liability for debts and other obligations is a joint liability of all the partners[4]. Technically, this means that there is only one obligation[5] for which all partners are responsible; settlement with one partner will therefore extinguish the claim[6].

---

1 Partnership Act 1890, s 5.
2 There are exceptions for deeds (see para **2.12.5** below) and negotiable instruments, where pre-existing rules of law were expressly preserved by the Partnership Act 1890, s 6.
3 Partnership Act 1890, s 6.
4 Ibid, s 9.
5 As opposed to *joint and several liability*, where each partner is separately liable; see below.
6 See para **2.16** below for the implications for actions against a partnership.

2.12.5 Obligations entered into by deed
Special rules apply to deeds which are entered into by partners[1]. A partner generally requires express authority to bind his partners by a deed; there is no implied authority to do so[2]. A partner will have express authority if he executes a deed for himself and his partner(s), in the presence of the other partner(s)[3].

Specific formalities are required to make a deed legally binding; in this, partners are in the same position as other agents[4]. The authority to execute a deed must itself be in a deed[5], ie a power of attorney. A specific form of words used to be required: *made by A by his agent B*[6]. Nowadays, the requirements for a valid deed have been relaxed by recent statutes. An individual who is a partner, and who has been given a power of attorney by his co-partners, may execute a deed in his own name, and it will bind all the partners[7]. There is no longer any requirement for a seal[8], or for a deed to authorise another person to *deliver* a deed on behalf of the signatory[9].

A deed is validly executed by an individual if it is signed by him in the presence of a witness[10], or by someone else 'at his direction and in his presence' in the presence of two witnesses who each attest the signature[11]; the partners can therefore apparently convene to direct one person to sign a deed on behalf of them all.

If a partner has executed a deed without authority, he will generally be bound himself, even though his co-partners are not[12]. If the transaction in question does not require a deed, the fact that the deed is ineffective will apparently not prevent the firm being bound by the transaction[13].

---

1 By s 6, the Partnership Act 1890 does not affect any general rule of law relating to the execution of deeds, which were treated as more serious than simple contracts as they required no consideration.

2 *Harrison v Jackson* (1797) 7 TR 207; *Steiglitz v Egginton* (1815) Holt NP 141; *Marchant v Morton, Down & Co* [1901] 2 KB 829. A partner does have implied authority to enter into a deed of release of a debt (*Hawkshaw v Parkins* (1819) 2 Swan 539) or a deed of arrangement (*Dudgeon v O'Connell* (1849) 12 Ir Eq 566).

3 *Ball v Dunsterville* 4 TR 313. Since 31 July 1990, the position would be regulated by s 1(3)(a)(ii) of the Law of Property (Miscellaneous Provisions) Act 1989, and two witnesses would need to be present and attest the signature: see below.

4 See *Bowstead and Reynolds on Agency* 16th Edn (Sweet & Maxwell, 1996) art 10 at 2-039 (p 58) et seq.

5 *Steiglitz v Egginton*, above.

6 See, for example, *Combe's Case* (1613) 9 Co 76b.

7 By s 7(1) of the Powers of Attorney Act 1971, as amended by Sch 1 to the Law of Property (Miscellaneous Provisions) Act 1989. The section came into force on 31 July 1990 by SI 1990/1175 but applies whenever the power of attorney was created (by s 7(4) of the Powers of Attorney Act 1971, as amended).

8 Law of Property (Miscellaneous Provisions) Act 1989, s 1(b).

9 Ibid, s 1(c).

10 Ibid, s 1(3)(a)(i).

11 Ibid, s 1(3)(a)(ii).

12 *Elliott v Davis* (1800) 2 Bos & Pul 338.

13 Eg *Marchant v Morton, Down & Co* above.

2.12.6 Other partnership liabilities

In respect of civil wrongs (eg torts such as negligence, where the firm is liable to the same extent as the partner whose act or omission caused the harm[1], or misapplication of money or property entrusted to the partnership, where the firm is liable to make good the loss[2]), every partner has *joint and several* liability[3].

---

1 Partnership Act 1890, s 11.

2 Ibid, s 11 which encapsulated the position under previous case-law. *Clayton's Case* (*Devaynes v Noble*) (1816) 1 Mer 572 is a well-known example; partners in a banking firm were all held liable when exchequer bills deposited with the firm had been sold by one of the partners.

3 Partnership Act 1890, s 12.

2.12.7 Breach of trust

If a partner who is a trustee improperly employs trust property in the partnership's business, the other partners do not become liable except where any partner has notice of the breach of trust, or where the trust property can be traced and is still in the possession or control of the partnership[1].

---

1 Partnership Act 1890, s 13.

2.13 PARTNERSHIP PROPERTY

2.13.1 *The joint and separate estates*

There is a fundamental and vital distinction between those assets which represent the introduced capital of the partnership or have been bought out of partnership profits, and those assets which continue to be held separately by the individual partners. The former is referred to as the 'joint estate' of the partners, while those assets which a partner holds outside the partnership are referred to as his 'separate estate'[1].

---

1 Note that where they appear in the Order these terms bear a more limited meaning: 'joint estate' is defined as 'the partnership property of an insolvent partnership in respect of which an order is made by virtue of Part IV or V of this order'; and 'separate estate' is defined as 'the property of an insolvent member against whom an insolvency order has been made'.

2.13.2 *Joint property*

All the partners hold the partnership's property jointly. Property which is brought into the firm, or which is bought on account of the firm, or for the purposes and in the course of the partnership's business, becomes *partnership property* which must be held and applied by the partners exclusively for the purposes of the partnership and in accordance with the partnership agreement[1]. Any property bought with the firm's money is deemed to have been bought for the firm, unless the contrary intention appears[2].

In the absence of a specific agreement, it is thus necessary to consider how the property was acquired, how it was paid for and how it has been treated (for example, how it was dealt with in the accounts and records of the partnership).

When a firm is dissolved, each partner is entitled to have all the partnership property applied in payment of the debts and liabilities of the firm, and any surplus applied to pay the balance due to the partners[3].

---

1 Partnership Act 1890, s 20(1).
2 Ibid, s 21.
3 Ibid, s 39.

2.13.3 *Separate property*

Each partner will also own separate property, which does not constitute part of the assets of the partnership[1]. The partners can of course agree that property will remain separate even where it is used for the partnership; for example, where one partner owns the building or the farm where the partnership operates[2]. For day-to-day purposes, the individual partner is free to deal with his own property without reference to his partners. However, if the joint estate is insolvent, the assets in the separate estate are available to satisfy the partnership's creditors.

If security in the form of an 'all monies' charge is given over part of a separate estate to a creditor who is also a creditor of the partnership (which may arise where, for example, the partnership's bank has also financed the purchase of an individual partner's home), the effect is that the partnership liabilities will be secured by that charge[3].

1 Although it may be applied in satisfaction of the individual's partnership liabilities in an insolvency.
2 These facts arise in numerous old cases, for example where coachmen used their own horses but operated a coach as a partnership: *Barton v Hanson* (1809) 2 Taunt 49.
3 If the charge is enforced against his property, the partner will have a right of indemnity against his partners. However, this is a subordinated right in an insolvency, because of the rule, referred to several times above, that a partner cannot compete with his creditors.

2.13.4   Real property

Under the Law of Property Act 1925, an interest in land cannot be transferred into more than four names[1]. This creates an obvious difficulty where a partnership of more than four partners wishes to acquire an interest in land as a partnership asset. Only four partners' names will go on the title deeds, and those who hold the legal title will hold it on trust for all the partners, who will jointly own the beneficial interest.

Whether the land or buildings used by a partnership are in fact owned by the partnership may be a difficult question to decide. Where the land is 'accessory' to a particular trade, and has been purchased for the purposes of a partnership business to which it is essential[2], or devised under a will together with the business[3], the land will constitute partnership property.

However, it is sometimes possible for land to be owned by all the partners as co-owners, and for it nonetheless not to be partnership property[4]. For example, where a freehold or a superior lease is held by a sub-set of partners in different proportions to their shares in the partnership, the likely inference is that the interest in land was not partnership property. That conclusion will have greater force where the title is held by partners together with non-partners. In such a case, it is not necessary to infer a lease to the partnership, when a mere licence would be sufficient.

Where a firm consists of four partners or less, and those partners co-own land, they cannot grant a lease of it to the firm, because that would involve contracting with themselves[5]. These difficulties are sometimes circumvented by structures where the property vests in a limited company (in which the partners are shareholders) or is held by a group of partners and their spouses.

Similarly, where one or more partners own land which is to be used by the partnership, they cannot grant a licence to the partnership, because they already have a right to go on their own land; there is merely a licence to the other partners (and, by extension, to any employees or visitors of the partnership) to come onto the land for partnership purposes[6].

1 Law of Property Act 1925, s 34(2); Trustee Act 1925, s 34(2). If more than four grantees are named in a conveyance, the conveyance takes effect as a conveyance to the first four named.
2 Eg where partners take the lease of a colliery to work it as partners; *Faraday v Wightwick* (1829) 1 R & M 45.
3 Eg *Jackson v Jackson* (1804) 9 Ves Jr 591.
4 See *Lindley and Banks on Partnership* 17th Edn (Sweet & Maxwell, 1995), at paras 18-24, 18-25.
5 *Rye v Rye* [1962] AC 496.
6 *Harrison-Broadley v Smith* [1964] 1 WLR 456.

2.13.5 The problem of partnership leases

A combination of the statutory restriction that restricts the number of individuals who can hold land to four members[1], and the particular requirements which must be satisfied before a partner can bind his co-partners by deed[2], can create a particular problem for the landlord of larger partnerships[3].

A periodic tenancy for a term not exceeding three years does not require a deed; it therefore appears that a partner contracting on behalf of the partnership, with authority to do so, would bind the whole partnership regarding the covenants in such a lease. The problem affects leases for three years or more.

Where a lease is held by four members of a larger partnership, it is generally regarded as good conveyancing practice to take separate covenants from the other partners, who will then stand as sureties for the four tenant partners. Alternatively, the other partners may become contractual tenants as additional signatories to the lease, in which case they will be bound by the covenants although not vested with any legal interest in the property. It should be borne in mind that changes in the membership of the partnership will need to be reflected in changes to the lease and any separate covenants.

Unless the requirements for formalities described above have been complied with[4], it appears that a partnership will not be bound by a lease entered into purportedly on its behalf. The landlord may think of his tenant as being the firm, but it is generally understood that the tenancy will only be held by those four partners named on the lease, as individuals. They hold it as trustees. A landlord who does not have the benefit of separate covenants from the other partners only has a right of action against those four trustees, who will in turn have a right of indemnity against their co-partners[5].

This is potentially of very great significance in the insolvency of a partnership, because it means that the landlord (who will often be the largest unsecured creditor involved) is at one remove from the assets of the partnership; as a matter of fine technical analysis, he will often not be a creditor of the firm at all[6]. Moreover, the rule that a partner may not compete with his creditors apparently means that the right to an indemnity is subordinated to the claims of other creditors[7].

---

1 See para **2.13.4** above.
2 See para **2.12.5** above.
3 Where a partnership has four partners or fewer, each partner can be named in the lease, and so no problem will arise unless partners leave or join without the lease being amended.
4 Paragraph **2.12.5**.
5 Under s 24(2) of the Partnership Act 1890.
6 For the purposes of a partnership voluntary arrangement, or the individual voluntary arrangement of a partner who is neither one of the tenants nor a separate covenantor, it appears that the landlord is not contractually a creditor of the partnership and is not one of the persons to be summoned to the creditors' meeting under s 3(3) of the Insolvency Act 1986 as modified by Sch 1 to the Order. The landlord therefore apparently cannot become entitled to vote under the Act. Unless all the other creditors agree that specific provision must be made to deal with the landlord (which may well be a commercial necessity if the partnership is to continue to operate from those premises), it seems that admission of the

landlord might well constitute a material irregularity under s 6(1)(b) of the Insolvency Act 1986 as modified by Sch 1 to the Order, and unfair prejudice to a dissentient creditor under modified s 6(1)(a).

7 See *Ex p Collinge* (1863) 4 De G J & S 533 and modified s 175C(2) in Sch 4; compare paras **2.11.4** and **2.11.10** above.

2.14 PARTNERSHIPS AND CHARGES

2.14.1 *Financing and partnership*

The primary source of working capital for most partnerships will be money provided by the partners, but there will frequently be circumstances in which the firm will want (or need) to raise additional finance. As with any business, lenders are likely to require security.

2.14.2 *Charging the individual partner's share*

The property of the firm is owned jointly by all the partners[1]. Each individual partner has an equitable beneficial interest in the share to which he is entitled[2]. This interest has been described as being in the nature of a future interest taking effect in possession on (and not before) the determination of the partnership[3].

As long as the partnership is solvent, the partner's share has a positive value, and may be charged to a lender. This is commonly encountered in practice, when a bank lends to an individual partner the money which he contributes to the partnership as his share of the partnership capital, upon a direction that when the partner retires or when the partnership is dissolved, the amount due to the bank is to be paid out to the bank. Such a provision is treated as an equitable charge. As a charge of a chose in action, it does not require registration under the Bills of Sale Acts[4].

1 See para **2.13.2**.
2 Whether by provision in a partnership deed (see para **2.9.2(g)**) or under the default provisions of equality in the Partnership Act 1890 (see para **2.9.1**).
3 See *Lindley and Banks on Partnership* 17th Edn (Sweet & Maxwell, 1995) at para 19-09.
4 See *In re Bainbridge, ex parte Fletcher* (1878) 8 Ch D 218.

2.14.3 *Status of a partnership*

In considering the extent to which the partnership, as opposed to individual members, can grant charges over the assets or enterprise of the firm, it is important to note that there are in general two regimes which will apply to the creation of charges. A charge created by a company will be subject to the registration requirements of s 395 of the Companies Act 1985[1]. On the other hand, a charge created by an individual sole trader over 'personal chattels'[2] will be subject to the Bills of Sale Acts[3]. (In addition, a charge over land will be subject to registration under the Land Registration Act 1925.)

Except where all the partners are themselves companies, it appears that a partnership is subject to the individual regime. That is to say, it will be able to grant charges of specific property, subject to compliance with the statutory requirements under the Bills of Sale Acts. Failure to comply means that the lender cannot rely on his security against a creditor who has obtained a judgment, or against a trustee in bankruptcy.

1 These provisions are incipiently amended by the Companies Act 1989, but the relevant sections are not yet in force.
2 The term 'personal chattels' as defined in s 4 of the Bills of Sale Act 1878 means 'goods, furniture and other articles capable of complete transfer by delivery, and (when separately assigned or charged) fixtures and growing crops, but shall not include chattel interests in real estate, nor fixtures (except trade machinery as herein-after defined), when assigned together with any interest in the land on which they grow, nor shares or interests in the stock, funds or securities of any government, or in the capital or property of incorporated or joint-stock companies, nor choses in action, nor any stock or produce upon any farm or lands which by virtue of any covenant or agreement or of the custom of the country ought not to be removed from any farm where the same are at the time of making or giving of such bill of sale'. By s 5 of the Bills of Sale Act (1878) Amendment Act 1882, a bill of sale in respect of after-acquired property is void except against the grantor.
3 Ie Bills of Sale Act 1878, Bills of Sale Act (1878) Amendment Act 1882. In *Welsh Development Agency v Exfinco* [1992] BCLC 148, Dillon LJ described this area (in a different context) as 'bedevilled by law that is now very out-of-date'.

2.14.4 Floating charges by partnerships

It is not thought possible for a partnership to grant an effective floating charge over chattels, because such a charge cannot comply with the Bills of Sale Acts as they have been interpreted by the courts[1]. This is because the Acts require the relevant chattels to be specified, which is inherently contrary to the nature of the usual floating charge which is given over a changing body of stock.

It has been suggested that a partnership could give a more limited floating charge, restricted to future property at the time when the charge is given[2], but the practical reality is that the validity of such a security would probably be too uncertain to be of value to a lender.

This means that the ubiquitous 'fixed and floating charge' is not available as an instrument of partnership finance.

1 See W J Gough, *Company Charges* 2nd Edn (Butterworths, 1996) at pp 52–55.
2 Which would not fall within the definition of 'personal chattels' in the statute: see Fitzpatrick, 'Why Not a Partnership Floating Charge?' [1971] JBL 18.

2.14.5 Fixed charges over book debts

A book debt due to a partnership is a *chose in action*. Choses in action are expressly excluded from the definition of 'personal chattels' under the Bills of Sale Act 1878[1], and so a charge over book debts is not void for lack of proper form under that legislation[2]. However, the position is nowadays governed by s 344 of the Insolvency Act 1986[3]. An individual (and, by extension, a partnership involving individual partners) can give a charge over present and future book debts, but such a charge is a 'general assignment' which must be registered under the Bills of Sale Act 1878 as if it were an absolute bill of sale. The result of non-compliance with that requirement is that the assignment is void against a trustee in bankruptcy as regards debts which were not paid before the presentation of the bankruptcy petition[4].

The ability to grant a charge over its book debts may be of particular significance for a partnership facing financial difficulties or seeking to recover from insolvency, because it may represent the only available source of finance. Although the position is not entirely clear, it is suggested that the preferable approach (at least where the firm consists of or includes individuals) is to regard the partnership as subject to the same regime as the individual partners[5]. Although a charge over book debts might not be void against a liquidator of the partnership, it would after all be void against the trustee in bankruptcy of a partner[6].

Section 344 of the Act does not affect an assignment of book debts due at the date of assignment from specified creditors[7]. Well-advised lenders will therefore ensure that they obtain successive assignments of book debts, detailed in a schedule, on a regular (often weekly) basis. For maximum comfort, and for the avoidance of doubt, these schedules are often themselves registered under the Bills of Sale Act 1878, if only on 'belt-and-braces' grounds.

1 See footnote 2 to para **2.14.3** above.
2 *Tailby v Official Receiver* (1888) 13 App Cas 523.
3 Substantially reproducing a provision first introduced as s 14 of the Bankruptcy and Deeds of Arrangement Act 1913, and subsequently appearing as s 43 of the Bankruptcy Act 1914.
4 Insolvency Act 1986, s 344(2).
5 Bearing in mind that it has no separate identity: see para **2.3**.
6 So that, where such a charge has been given, it is anticipated that an unsecured creditor would be likely to present a combined petition under art 8 of the Order: see para **3.3**.
7 Insolvency Act 1986, s 344(3)(b)(i).

2.14.6   *Fixed and floating charges by corporate partnerships*
Where a corporate partner grants a fixed and floating charge, the subject-matter of that charge will include the corporate partner's share of the partnership assets. In one Australian case, all the partners were corporations and each had given such a charge. When the charges crystallised, the receivers and managers of the companies were also appointed as receivers and managers of the partnership assets, and the court permitted rectification of the relevant debentures in respect of that dual function[1].

1 *Bailey v Manos Breeder Farms Pty Ltd* (1990) 8 ACLR 1119.

2.14.7   *Agricultural charges*
It seems to be accepted that an agricultural partnership can create an agricultural floating charge under the Agricultural Credits Act 1928, although by s 5(7) of that Act, it is only a 'farmer' who can create such a charge[1]. A bank generally takes such a charge together with a fixed charge over the interest of each partner in the land which consistutes the agricultural holding.

1 See eg *Barclays Bank Ltd v Beck* [1982] 2 QB 47.

2.15   THE DISSOLUTION OF SOLVENT PARTNERSHIPS

2.15.1   *'Technical' or 'general' dissolutions*
Because a firm has no independent existence, there will technically be a dissolution every time there is a change in membership; the firm after a retirement, for example, is a different firm[1]. In such circumstances, the business of the firm is intended to continue, and what is necessary is the

rearrangement of the rights of former and future partners – for example, by valuing and paying out a retiring partner's share[2]. Such a dissolution is often referred to as a 'technical dissolution'.

On the other hand, where the partners do not wish, or are unable, to continue the firm's business, there will need to be a full winding up of the firm's affairs (often referred to as a 'general dissolution'). This will involve bringing in and realising the partnership's assets, settling the partnership's liabilities with third parties[3], and then finalising the rights of partners between themselves. Note that where the partnership itself is solvent (either because joint assets exceed joint liabilities, or because sufficient additional funds are available from the partners), no insolvency procedures need to be invoked, although the court may become involved in settling any dispute which may arise.

---

1 *Hadlee v Commissioner of Inland Revenue* [1989] 2 NZLR 447.
2 See para **2.11.10** above.
3 Bearing in mind that *contingent* liabilities, such as latent claims for professional negligence, will remain alive until the expiry of the relevant limitation period, and will remain the liability of the partners notwithstanding any 'dissolution' of the firm.

2.15.2 Causes of dissolution

The dissolution of a partnership may arise in various ways:

(a) by rescission of the partnership agreement (for example, where there has been fraud or misrepresentation inducing entry into the agreement);

(b) by an innocent partner accepting a repudiatory breach of the partnership agreement by a co-partner[1];

(c) by agreement of the partners (as a variation of the terms of the partnership deed)[2];

(d) where a partnership at will is ended by a partner serving a notice[3];

(e) by expiry of a term fixed in the partnership agreement[4];

(f) if a partnership for a single adventure or undertaking, by the determination of that adventure or undertaking[5];

(g) by the death of a partner[6];

(h) by the bankruptcy of a partner[7];

(i) at the option of the other partners, if a partner suffers his share of the partnership property to be charged for his separate debt[8];

(j) if it becomes unlawful for the partnership to carry on the business of the firm[9];

(k) in circumstances specified in the partnership agreement[10].

---

1 *Hitchman v Crouch Butler Savage Associates* (1983) 80 LS Gaz 554; *Fulwell v Bragg* (1983) 127 Sol Jo 171.
2 Partnership Act 1890, s 19.
3 Ibid, ss 26(1), 32(c); see para **2.6.1** above.
4 Ibid, s 32(a).
5 Ibid, s 32(b).
6 Ibid, s 33(1), subject to contrary agreement (in which case, there is a still a technical dissolution); see para **2.11.12** above.
7 Ibid, s 33(1), subject to contrary agreement (in which case there is a still a technical dissolution); see para **2.11.11** above.
8 Ibid, s 33(2).

9 Ibid, s 34; examples would be a partnership with an illegal alien in wartime (as in *R v Knupfer* [1915] 2 KB 321) or a prohibited professional partnership (as in *Hudgell Yeates & Co v Watson* [1978] QB 451, where a solicitor forgot to renew his practising certificate).
10 See para **2.9.2(o)** above.

2.15.3 Dissolution by the court

The court has a discretion to order the dissolution of a partnership on the application of a partner in the following circumstances:

(a) when a partner becomes incapable, by reason of mental disorder, of managing and administering his property and affairs[1];
(b) when a partner becomes permanently incapable of performing his part of the partnership contract[2];
(c) when a partner has been guilty of conduct which is calculated to prejudicially affect the carrying on of the business[3];
(d) when a partner wilfully or persistently commits a breach of the partnership agreement, or so conducts himself in matters relating to the partnership business that it is not reasonably practicable for the other partners to carry on in partnership with him[4];
(e) when the partnership business can only be carried on at a loss[5];
(f) when the court thinks it just and equitable to do so[6].

The Chancery Division of the High Court has jurisdiction to deal with the dissolution of partnerships[7], but an action begun in another division will not necessarily be transferred[8]. It may be appropriate for the dissolution of a partnership between husband and wife to be dealt with in the Family Division. The county court has jurisdiction to deal with dissolution of a partnership where the assets do not exceed £30,000[9], or where such jurisdiction is extended by written agreement between the parties or their legal representatives[10].

When the court dissolves a partnership, the date of dissolution will usually be the date of the order[11], although the court may declare the partnership dissolved as from the service of a notice (or, in an appropriate case, the writ).

1 Mental Health Act 1983, s 96(1)(g).
2 Partnership Act 1890, s 35(b).
3 Ibid, s 35(c).
4 Ibid, s 35(d).
5 Ibid, s 35(e); cf *Jennings v Baddeley* (1856) 3 K&J 78, *Handyside v Campbell* [1901] 17 TLR 623.
6 Ibid, s 35(f).
7 Supreme Court Act 1981, s 61(1), Sch 1, para 1(f).
8 Ibid, ss 61(6), 65.
9 County Courts Act 1984, s 23(f).
10 Ibid, s 24 (as amended by the Courts and Legal Services Act 1990, Sch 18).
11 *Lyon v Tweddle* (1881) 17 Ch D 529.

2.15.4 Consequences of dissolution

Where a partnership is dissolved, the authority of each partner continues, but only as far as is necessary to wind up the partnership and complete any unfinished transactions[1]. Each partner continues to be under an obligation to act in absolute good faith towards his co-partners.

A technical dissolution will not generally affect employees' continuity of employment[2], but a general dissolution terminates employment contracts[3].

1 Partnership Act 1890, s 38.
2 Employment Protection (Consolidation) Act 1978, Sch 13, para 17; *Harold Fielding Ltd v Mansi* [1974] ICR 347; *Allen & Son v Coventry* [1980] ICR 9; *Jeetle v Elster* [1985] ICR 389.
3 *Tunstall v Condon* [1980] ICR 786; *Briggs v Oates* [1990] ICR 473.

2.15.5 Post-dissolution profits
In the case of a technical dissolution, the outgoing partner or his estate is entitled to be paid out his share of the partnership capital and profits. Until the accounts have been settled and payment has been made, his money continues to be employed in the partnership. In the absence of an agreement to the contrary[1], the outgoing partner or his estate is entitled to choose between receiving the share of the post-dissolution profits attributable to the use of his share of the assets, or receiving interest at 5 per cent per annum on the amount of his share of the assets[2].

Calculation of shares of profits in these circumstances is often far from straightforward; it has also been held that there is no entitlement to share in post-dissolution capital profits, as opposed to trading profits[3].

1 Eg an option in the partnership agreement for the continuing partners to purchase the interest of a deceased or outgoing partner, or an agreement to leave the capital in the partnership.
2 Partnership Act 1890, s 42(1).
3 *Barclays Bank Trust Co Ltd v Bluff* [1982] Ch 172.

2.15.6 Return of premiums on dissolution
Nowadays, it is rare to find that incoming partners have been asked to pay a premium (ie a 'joining fee', as opposed to an investment of capital) to a partnership. Where such a premium has been paid and the partnership is dissolved before the agreed term has expired, the court may order that all or part (usually proportionate to the unexpired portion of the term) of the premium be repaid, unless the payer's misconduct has brought about the dissolution, or the partnership has been dissolved by an agreement which does not provide for such repayment[1].

1 Partnership Act 1890, s 40 codifying the previous law; mere incompetence is not 'misconduct' in this context: *Brewer v Yorke* (1882) 46 LT 289.

2.15.7 Winding up the affairs of the partnership
In many cases, it will be possible for the affairs of a generally dissolved solvent partnership to be wound up amicably by the partners themselves, with the assistance of the firm's accountants as necessary. This will usually be the cheapest option, and maintains confidentiality regarding the partners' affairs. However, where that is not possible, any partner or his representatives may apply to the court[1] to wind up the business and affairs of the firm[2].

In an appropriate case, the court will appoint a receiver to supervise the winding up[3], although it will be wary of appointing a receiver over a professional practice, because of the harm that might do[4]. It appears that a receiver will not usually be appointed where there is only a technical dissolution[5]. One of the partners may be, and often is, appointed to act as receiver[6]. Once appointed, a receiver is an officer of the court; he is entitled to be paid remuneration and costs from the assets of the partnership, but has no rights against the partners personally[7].

1 See para **2.15.3** above.
2 Partnership Act 1890, s 39.
3 *Dixon v Dixon* [1904] 1 Ch 161; *Boehm v Goodall* [1911] 1 Ch 155; *Rosanove v O'Rourke* [1988] 1 QdR 171; *Choudhri v Palta* [1994] 1 BCLC 184, CA.
4 *Floyd v Cheney* [1970] Ch 602.
5 *Sobell v Boston* [1975] 1 WLR 1587.
6 Eg *Dixon v Dixon*, above; *Davy v Scarth* [1906] 1 Ch 55.
7 *Boehm v Goodall*, above.

2.15.8   Realisation of the partnership assets

On dissolution, every partner is entitled first to have the property of the partnership applied in payment of the debts and liabilities of the firm and, secondly, to have any surplus after such payment applied in paying the net balance due to each partner[1].

A partner can enforce these rights by seeking a court order for sale of the assets. Where it is no longer practical for the court to order the sale of the assets (eg because considerable time has passed, so that their market value has changed), the court may resolve a dispute (in a technical dissolution) by treating surviving partners as having purchased the assets at their book value at the date of dissolution[2].

The respective rights and obligations of each partner to share in profits and capital will usually be set out in the partnership agreement[3], although it may also be necessary to consider the partners' subsequent conduct. It will be recalled that, in the absence of express or implied agreement, all partners will share capital and profits equally, and must contribute equally to losses[4].

1 Partnership Act 1890, s 39.
2 *Latcham v Martin* (1984) 134 NLJ 745, PC.
3 See para **2.9.2** above.
4 Partnership Act 1890, s 24(1).

2.15.9   Priorities in a winding up under the Partnership Act

Section 44 of the Partnership Act provides two sets of rules for settling accounts between partners. These rules apply 'subject to any agreement'.

(a)   *Payment of losses*

Losses (including losses and deficiencies of capital) are to be paid in the following order[1]:

(1)   out of profits;
(2)   next, out of capital;
(3)   finally, if necessary, by the partners individually in the proportion in which they were entitled to share profits.

In other words, partners do not contribute until the assets of the partnership have been applied[2] and exhausted.

---

1 Partnership Act 1890, s 44(a).
2 Under the Partnership Act 1890, s 39.

(b)   *Application of assets*

The assets of the firm, and any necessary contributions of partners, are to be applied in the following order[1]:

(1)   in paying debts and liabilities to non-partners;
(2)   in repaying rateably advances from partners;
(3)   in paying to each partner rateably what is due from the firm to him in respect of capital;
(4)   in paying any residue in the proportion in which profits are divisible.

The term 'advances from partners' would include payments made by individual partners to third parties on behalf of the partnership, in respect of which the partner is entitled to an indemnity from his co-partners.

---

1 Partnership Act 1890, s 44(b).

2.15.10   The rule in Garner v Murray[1]

In *Garner v Murray*, it was held[2] that s 44 of the Partnership Act does not compel solvent partners to make up the deficiency when one partner was insolvent and therefore unable to contribute his share of lost capital. The effect is that the inevitable deficiency in capital will be borne in proportion to their capital contributions, because capital is redistributed rateably. (The position is different when the partnership is insolvent.)

---

1 [1904] 1 Ch 57.
2 At first instance.

2.15.11   Rights after a winding up

Once the dissolution and winding up of a solvent partnership have been completed, there is generally nothing to prevent each partner starting up a business of the same type in the same area.

However, it should be noted that, unless there has been settlement of all possible claims, partners will remain liable until all limitation periods have expired. In the event of a claim being brought against a partner, he retains his rights of contribution and indemnity against co-partners, subject to any contrary agreement reached in the course of the dissolution and winding up.

2.16   LITIGATION AGAINST A PARTNERSHIP[1]

2.16.1   Who may be sued?

A partnership can be sued (and may sue) in the firm's name[2], but this is purely a matter of administrative convenience. In the High Court, partners must acknowledge service in their own names, although the action continues in the name of the firm[3].

Note that the action is against those who were partners when the cause of action accrued; this includes partners who have retired or been expelled, and the personal estates of dead partners. Where such former partners have a right of indemnity as against their co-partners, that does not prevent them being defendants to an action brought by a third party. However, where the plaintiff knows[4] that there has been a dissolution through the departure of a partner, the writ or summons[5] must be served on every person whom it is sought to make liable in the action[6]. A plaintiff may face practical difficulties in obtaining a list of those who were partners at the date when the cause of action accrued; once proceedings have commenced, however, the plaintiff can serve a notice on the defendants requiring them to provide a list of the names and addresses of all those who were partners at the relevant time[7].

An incoming partner cannot be sued on a cause of action which arose before he joined, unless he has expressly or impliedly agreed with the plaintiff that he will be liable[8]. If the incoming partner has agreed with his partners to assume former liabilities, however, they may, in an appropriate case, join him as a third party.

Where the cause of action concerns a joint liability, it used to be the case that all those who were jointly liable needed to be joined as defendants[9]. That is no longer so, because a claim can no longer be defeated by the non-joinder of a party[10].

Similarly, it was formerly the case that judgment against one partner would bar any subsequent action against other partners for a joint liability[11]. That common law position was altered by s 3 of the Civil Liability (Contribution) Act 1978, which provides that judgment recovered against any person liable in respect of any debt or damage shall not be a bar to an action, or to the continuance of an action, against any other person who is (apart from any such bar) jointly liable with him in respect of the same debt or damage.

There is therefore no longer any procedural bar to a partnership creditor bringing a claim for a partnership debt against one particular partner, although it is still generally regarded as preferable to bring actions for partnership obligations against all the relevant partners, by issuing proceedings against the firm[12]. Where a firm appears to be insolvent but an individual partner is known to have sufficient assets to meet the judgment, it may nonetheless be more convenient to bring an action purely against that solvent partner, leaving it to him to pursue his remedies against his co-partners[13].

---

1 Note that although this section deals only with actions *against* partnerships, similar considerations arise in respect of actions *by* partnerships.

2 Rules of the Supreme Court 1965, Ord 81, r 1; County Court Rules 1981, Ord 5, r 9(1); note, however, that some practitioners none the less regard it as preferable to name every partner in the writ or summons.

3 Rules of the Supreme Court 1965, Ord 81, r 4(1).

4 It is not clear that this is limited to *actual* knowledge; 'knowing' normally includes knowledge of circumstances which ordinarily lead to the conclusion that the state of things exists: *National Bank of Australasia v Morris* [1892] AC 287. In the case of any large firm, it appears that a plaintiff would have at least constructive notice that there will have been successive changes in the composition of the firm over time.

5 Which may be issued in the firm's name: *Re Wenham* [1900] 2 QB 698.

6 Rules of the Supreme Court 1965, Ord 81, r 3(3); County Court Rules 1981, Ord 7, r 13(2).

7 Rules of the Supreme Court 1985, Ord 81, r 2(3); County Court Rules 1981, Ord 5, r 9(2) or (3). If the defendants do not comply, the court may order them to do so.

8 *Wilsford v Wood* (1794) 1 Esp 182; *Ord v Portal* (1812) 3 Camp 239; *Young v Hunter* (1812) 4 Taunt 582; *Vere v Ashby* (1829) 10 B&C 288.

9 Where all those who were jointly liable were not joined as defendants, a defendant could bring a plea of *abatement*, a medieval procedure to quash the writ as invalid. Pleas in abatement were abolished in 1883, and replaced by rules of court.

10 Rules of the Supreme Court 1965, Ord 15, rr 4(2), 6(1); County Court Rules 1981, Ord 5, r 4.

11 *Kendall v Hamilton* (1879) 4 App Cas 504.

12 Partnership Act 1890, s 23(1) provides that a writ of execution shall not issue against any partnership property except on a judgment against a firm; a creditor who obtains judgment against only one partner is therefore limited to enforcement only against that individual partner's separate assets. This is subject to the possibility of obtaining a charging order against the partner's interest in the partnership property and/or profits, under the Partnership Act 1890, s 23(2): for procedure in the High Court, see Rules of the Supreme Court 1965, Ord 81, r 10.

13 Which would be subordinated to claims of partnership creditors in an insolvency of the partnership.

2.16.2 *Judgment against a partnership*

Where a creditor obtains judgment in an action brought against a firm, he has a choice of whether to levy execution against any part of the joint estate of the partnership which is within the jurisdiction[1], or against the separate estate(s) of one or more partners if:

(a) the person acknowledged service of the writ as a partner[2];
(b) the person was served as a partner but failed to acknowledge service[3];
(c) the person admitted in his pleading that he is a partner[4];
(d) the person was adjudged to be a partner[5];
(e) or, where none of the above apply, where the court gives leave[6].

Particular rules apply to execution against a partner who was outside the jurisdiction when a writ was issued. Unless such a partner has acknowledged service of the writ as a partner, or been served with the writ as a partner[7], he will not be liable to have execution levied on his separate assets[8].

Where the plaintiff knew of a dissolution but has not served the proceedings on a former partner, that partner will not be liable to execution by the plaintiff[9]. However, note that he may still be liable to an action by his former co-partners under s 3 of the Civil Liability (Contribution) Act 1978[10].

---

1 Rules of the Supreme Court 1965, Ord 81, r 5(1).

2 Ibid, r 5(2)(a).

3 Ibid, r 5(2)(b).

4 Ibid, r 5(2)(c).

5 Ibid, r 5(2)(d).

6 Ibid, r 5(5); if necessary, there will be a separate trial as to the liability of the alleged partner.

7 Either within the jurisdiction, or outside the jurisdiction with the leave of the court under Rules of the Supreme Court 1965, Ord 11.

8 Rules of the Supreme Court 1965, Ord 81, r 3.

9 *Wigram v Cox & Co* [1894] 1 QB 792; despite the mandatory wording of Rules of the Supreme Court 1965, Ord 81, r 3(3), it does not appear that failure to serve a former

partner has any effect on the effectiveness of the proceedings against other partners, or the possibility of execution against assets of the firm.

10 See above: where an express indemnity has been given by the continuing partners to an outgoing partner, this would probably act as an estoppel barring an action for contribution.

2.16.3   *Insolvency proceedings against an individual partner*

A bankruptcy or winding-up petition may be brought against an individual partner in respect of a partnership debt without issuing such a petition against other partners, and without presenting a petition to wind up the partnership[1]. It appears that such a petition may also be presented against one who is a 'member' under the Order through holding out[2]. Where one partner facing a bankruptcy petition promised to discharge the debt by a series of post-dated cheques, a court has held that the creditor was still entitled to a bankruptcy order against a co-partner for the same debt[3].

1 Insolvent Partnerships Order 1994, art 19(5), and see *Schooler v Customs & Excise Commissioners* [1995] 2 BCLC 610 where the Court of Appeal upheld a bankruptcy order made against one partner for a partnership debt where the other partner had entered into an individual voluntary arrangement. The case was on art 15(3) of the 1986 Order, which is substantially reproduced in art 19(5) of the 1994 Order.
2 See para **2.11.3** above.
3 *In re a Bankrupt (No 622 of 1995)* (1996) *The Times*, 27 June.

2.17   PARTNERS AS 'ASSOCIATES' UNDER THE INSOLVENCY ACT 1986

Under s 435(3) of the Act, a partner is an 'associate' of any person with whom he is in partnership and of the husband or wife or a relative of any individual with whom he is in partnership. It is sometimes thought that the use of the phrase 'is in partnership' in the present tense means that once a person has retired from a partnership, or the firm has been dissolved, those concerned are no longer in partnership together.

It should be borne in mind that retiring from a partnership will not of itself mean that the retiree is discharged from liabilities he has incurred as a partner[1], although there may be an agreement to that effect with the creditors[2]. Similarly, after the dissolution of a partnership, rights and obligations of the partners continue notwithstanding the dissolution as far as may be necessary to wind up the affairs of the partnership[3]. It is therefore suggested that it is only when the relationship of obligation as a partner has finally been brought to an end that a partner ceases to be 'in partnership' for purposes of the Act. Until then, he is an associate.

1 Partnership Act 1890, s 17(2).
2 Ibid, s 17(3).
3 Ibid, s 38.

Chapter 3

LIQUIDATION ON CREDITORS' PETITIONS

3.1 INTRODUCTION

Insolvent partnerships are wound up as unregistered companies under Part V of the Act, but different considerations affect how the Act is modified, depending upon the precise approach which is chosen by the petitioner. The initial distinction is between:

(i) taking insolvency proceedings only against the partnership, without presenting a concurrent petition against any of the members[1]; and

(ii) taking insolvency proceedings against both the partnership and one or more of the members[2].

If a creditor takes the first path and then subsequently presents petitions against one or more members, it may be possible to persuade the court to apply the art 8 scheme under the powers provided by modified ss 168 and 303 of the Act[3]. Some of the tactical issues militating for one or other course are discussed in Chapter 10.

---

1 See art 7 of the Order applying the Act as modified in Sch 3.
2 See art 8 of the Order applying the Act as modified in Sch 4.
3 Subsections 168(5A)–(5C) and 303(2A)–(2C) inserted by art 14 of the Order.

3.2 WINDING UP WHERE NO CONCURRENT PETITION IS PRESENTED AGAINST MEMBER

3.2.1 *Applicability of Part V of the Act*[1]

Part V of the Act is headed 'Winding up of unregistered companies'. Under art 7(1) of the Order the provisions of Part V of the Act (subject to certain modifications[2]) apply in relation to the winding up of an insolvent partnership as if it were an unregistered company provided that:

(a) the petition is presented by a creditor, or a responsible insolvency practitioner[3] or the Secretary of State or any other person other than a member[4], and

(b) no insolvency petition is presented by the petitioner against a member or former member of that partnership in his capacity as such[5].

---

1 Insolvent Partnerships Order 1994, art 7.
2 See Parts I and II of Sch 3 to the Order.
3 'Responsible insolvency practitioner' is defined by art 2(1) of the Order as meaning: (a) in a winding up, the liquidator of an insolvent partnership or corporate member and (b) in bankruptcy, the trustee of the estate of an individual member, and in either case includes the Official Receiver when so acting.
4 The addition of 'any other person other than a member' was effected by the Insolvent Partnerships (Amendment) Order 1996, SI 1996/1308, to enable bodies such as the Bank of

England and the Securities and Investments Board to present a petition for the winding up of an insolvent partnership.

5 Where a concurrent insolvency petition is presented then art 8 applies (see below).

3.2.2 Winding up of unregistered companies[1]

Subject to two qualifications, any insolvent partnership may be wound up under the Act if it has, or at any time had, in England and Wales either:

(i)   a principal place of business; or
(ii) a place of business at which business is or has been carried on in the course of which the debt (or part of the debt) arose which forms the basis for the petition for winding up of the partnership[2].

The first qualification to the above rule is that an insolvent partnership may not be wound up under the Act if the business of the partnership has not been carried on in England and Wales[3] at any time in the period of three years ending with the day on which the winding-up petition is presented[4].

The second qualification concerns an insolvent partnership which has a principal place of business situated in Scotland or in Northern Ireland. In this situation, the court does not have jurisdiction to wind up such a partnership unless, in the former case, it had a principal place of business in England and Wales at any time in the period of one year, or, in the latter case, at any time in the period of three years, ending in each case with the day on which the winding-up petition is presented[5].

It is expressly provided that no insolvent partnership can be wound up under the Act voluntarily[6]. This does not of course prevent a partnership being 'wound up' under the provisions following a dissolution under the Partnership Act.

All the provisions of Part V are applied to insolvent partnerships with certain exceptions[7] and additions in a new s 221A (see para **3.2.3** below).

The circumstances in which an insolvent partnership may be wound up as an unregistered company are:

(a) if the partnership is dissolved, or ceases to carry on business, or is carrying on business only for the purpose of winding up its affairs;
(b) if the partnership is unable to pay its debts;
(c) if the court is of the opinion that it is just and equitable that the partnership should be wound up[8].

There is a prescribed form of affidavit verifying a petition for the winding up of an insolvent partnership under Part V of the Act[9].

---

1 Section 221 of the Insolvency Act 1986, as modified by the Order, Sch 3, Part I, para 3.
2 Ibid, s 221(2) (as modified).
3 In the case of *In the matter of SHV Senator Hanseatische Verwaltungsgesellschaft mbh (the Vice-Chancellor Sir Richard Scott)* (unreported, 14 June 1996) the Secretary of State for Trade and Industry had presented a petition for the compulsory winding up of a company incorporated in Germany and of a corporate body, which alleged it was an unincorporated partnership registered and organised under the laws of Germany, on the grounds that both should be wound up on the just and equitable ground pursuant to s 124(A) of the Companies Act 1985. It was alleged in the petition that both the company and the unincorporated partnership

were insolvent. It was contended by counsel for the unincorporated partnership that the court did not have jurisdiction to wind up an insolvent foreign partnership. The Vice-Chancellor concluded that there was an error in the Order that had not occurred to its draftsman and that he considered the Secretary of State would be well advised to amend the Order so as to remove the anomaly as soon as possible. He went on to hold, however, that the Order was irrelevant to the case, because he was satisfied that the unincorporated partnership could not be described as a partnership in the sense that the Order uses that term.

4   In the case of *In re a Debtor (No 784 of 1991)* [1992] 3 WLR 119, it was held that a debtor 'carries on business in England and Wales' so long as he or she owes trading debts, even though the debtor may have left the jurisdiction four years before a bankruptcy petition was presented.

5   Insolvency Act 1986, s 221(3) (as modified).

6   Ibid, s 221(4) (as modified).

7   Ibid, s 221(5) and (6) (as modified). The exceptions are ss 73(1), 74(2)(a)–(d), (3), 75–78, 83, 122, 123, 202, 203, 205 and 250.

8   Ibid, s 221(7) (as modified).

9   Ibid, s 221(8) (as modified) and Form 2, Sch 9 to the Order.

3.2.3   Petition to wind up insolvent partnership as unregistered company[1]

A petition in the prescribed form may be presented by:

(a)   the liquidator; or

(b)   the administrator of a corporate member or of a former corporate member of the partnership; or

(c)   the trustee of an individual (or former individual) member's estate; or

(d)   the supervisor of a voluntary arrangement approved under Part I of the Act in relation to a corporate member or the partnership, or under Part VIII of the Act in relation to an individual member, if the ground of the petition is one of the circumstances set out in s 221(7) of the Act (as modified by Sch 3) (ie if one of the circumstances set out in para **3.2.2** above is present[2]).

If the ground of the petition is that the partnership is unable to pay its debts and the petitioning insolvency practitioner (ie one of the persons entitled to present a petition under s 221A (as inserted by Sch 3)) is able to satisfy the court that an insolvency order has been made against the member whose liquidator or trustee he is, because of that member's inability to pay a joint debt, that order will, unless it is proved otherwise to the satisfaction of the court, be proof that the partnership is unable to pay its debts[3]. For example, a trustee in bankruptcy of a member of a partnership can allege that the partnership is unable to pay its debts if the bankrupt member was bankrupted on the grounds of his inability to pay a debt of the partnership.

There are provisions for the appointment of a provisional liquidator[4] and for such individual to be appointed liquidator if a winding-up order is made[5].

Where a winding-up petition is presented under s 221A(1) (as inserted), in the event of the partnership property being insufficient to satisfy the costs of the petitioner, the costs may be paid out of the assets of the insolvent estate of which the petitioner is the office holder, as part of the expenses of the relevant liquidation, administration, bankruptcy or voluntary arrangement. The order of priority will be the same as applies to expenses properly chargeable or incurred by the practitioner in getting in any of the assets of the member[6].

1 Section 221A of the Insolvency Act 1986, as inserted by the Order, Sch 3, Part I, para 3.
2 Ibid, s 221A(1) (as inserted).
3 Ibid, s 221A(3) (as inserted).
4 Ibid, s 221A(4) (as inserted).
5 Ibid, s 221A(5) (as inserted).
6 Ibid, s 221A(6) (as inserted).

3.2.4   *Inability to pay debts: unpaid creditor for £750 or more*[1]

An insolvent partnership is deemed (for the purposes of s 221 of the Act (as modified by Sch 3)) unable to pay its debts if there is a creditor, by assignment or otherwise, to whom the partnership is indebted in a sum exceeding £750 then due, and:

(a)   the creditor has served on the partnership, in the manner specified below, a written demand in the prescribed form requiring the partnership to pay the sum so due; and

(b)   the partnership has for three weeks after the service of the demand neglected to pay the sum or to secure or compound for it to the creditor's satisfaction[2].

Service of the demand referred to above is to be effected:

(a)   by leaving it at a principal place of business of the partnership in England and Wales; or

(b)   by leaving it at a place of business of the partnership in England and Wales at which business is carried on in the course of which the debt (or part of the debt) referred to in s 223(1) (as modified) arose; or

(c)   by delivering it to an officer[3] of the partnership; or

(d)   by otherwise serving it in such manner as the court may approve or direct[4].

Provision is made enabling the figure of £750 to be increased or reduced by regulations under s 417 of the Act[5].

1 Section 222 of the Insolvency Act 1986, as modified by the Order, Sch 3, Part I, para 4.
2 Insolvency Act 1986, s 221(1) (as modified).
3 'Officer' is defined by art 2(1) of the Order as (a) a member, or (b) a person who has management or control of the partnership business. It follows that such an individual need not himself be a partner.
4 Insolvency Act 1986, s 222(2) (as modified).
5 Ibid, s 222(3) (as modified).

3.2.5   *Inability to pay debts: debt remaining unsatisfied after action brought*[1]

There is a further test for when an unregistered company shall be deemed for the purposes of s 221 of the Act (as modified by Sch 3) to be unable to pay its debts, which does not have any equivalent in the case of a registered company. That test is modified in the case of an insolvent partnership to the effect that a partnership is deemed (for the purposes of s 221) unable to pay its debts if an action or other proceeding has been instituted against any member for any debt or demand due, or claimed to be due, from the partnership, or from him in his character of member, and:

(a) notice in writing of the institution of the action or proceeding has been served on the partnership in a specified manner; and

(b) the partnership has not within three weeks after service of the notice paid, secured or compounded for the debt or demand, or procured the action or proceedings to be stayed or sisted, or indemnified the defendant or defender to his reasonable satisfaction against the action or proceeding, and against all costs, damages and expenses to be incurred by him because of it[2].

The provisions for service of the notice are the same as for the service of the demand under s 222(2) of the Act (as modified), see para **3.2.4** above[3].

1 Section 223 of the Insolvency Act 1986, as modified by the Order, Sch 3, Part I, para 5.
2 Ibid, s 223(1) (as modified). The last scenario (the indemnification of the defendant by the partnership to his reasonable satisfaction) is an odd way of negating the deemed insolvency of the partnership but presumably the logic is that, unless the partnership does in some way protect or support the partner who is being pursued for what is alleged to be a partnership debt, it runs the risk of being deemed to be insolvent itself.
3 Ibid, s 223(2) (as modified).

3.2.6 *High Court and county court jurisdiction*[1]

The provisions relating to High Court and county court jurisdiction are applied to insolvent partnerships as if they were unregistered companies, subject to certain modifications and conditions[2].

The jurisdictional basis is the same as described in para **3.2.2** above, the net effect of which is that, subject to the qualification set out in that paragraph, the winding-up petition may be presented in the High Court or the appropriate county court under art 7 of the Order. Where there are no concurrent petitions against members this does not give rise to any problem, but if concurrent petitions are presented against members (see art 8) then one may find that whilst the petition against the partnership will be dealt with in the High Court, the bankruptcy petitions may have to be dealt with in the county court and, indeed, quite possibly several county courts, which may give rise to all sorts of procedural problems, with different courts dealing with the individual partners in different courts and on different dates.

1 Section 117 of the Insolvency Act 1986, as modified by the Order, Sch 3, Part II, para 6.
2 See Insolvency Act 1986, s 223(1) (as modified) and s 117(5) and (6) (as modified).

3.2.7 *Statement of affairs of insolvent partnership*[1]

The right of the Official Receiver following the making of a winding-up order against a company or the appointment of a provisional liquidator to require various persons to submit a statement in the prescribed form as to the affairs of the company is applied to an insolvent partnership by substituting 'the partnership' for 'the company' in the relevant section of the Act.

1 Section 131 of the Insolvency Act 1986, as modified by the Order, Sch 3, Part II, para 7.

3.2.8   *Public examination of officers of insolvent partnership*[1]

Section 133 of the Act, which deals with the public examination of officers of companies being wound up by the court, is applied to insolvent partnerships by substituting 'the partnership' for 'the company', thereby enabling the Official Receiver to apply for the public examination of officers of the partnership and other individuals.

---

1 Section 133 of the Insolvency Act 1986, as modified by the Order, Sch 3, Part II, para 8.

3.2.9   *Getting in partnership property*[1]

Where, by virtue of the Order, an insolvent partnership is being wound up, or a provisional liquidator of an insolvent partnership is appointed, the liquidator or the provisional liquidator of the partnership has the same rights in respect of getting in partnership property as if he were the liquidator or provisional liquidator of a company[2].

Any person who is or has been an officer of the partnership, or who is an executor or administrator of the estate of a deceased officer of the partnership, is required to deliver up to the office-holder, for the purposes of the exercise of the latter's functions under the Act and, where applicable, the Company Directors Disqualification Act 1986, possession of any partnership property which he holds for the purposes of the partnership[3]. The provisions of the Act relating to:

(a)   the powers of the court to require delivery up of assets of the partnership;
(b)   the immunity of the office-holder from liability except for negligence arising from loss or damage as a result of the seizure or disposal of part of property thought to be partnership property; and
(c)   the imposition of a lien on the property, or the proceeds of its sale, for such expenses as were incurred in connection with such seizure or disposal;

are applied to insolvent partnerships[3].

---

1 Section 234 of the Insolvency Act 1986, as modified by the Order, Sch 3, Part II, para 9.
2 Ibid, s 234(1) (as modified).
3 Ibid, s 234(2) (as modified).
4 Ibid, s 234(4) and (5) (as modified).

3.2.10   *Powers of liquidator*[1]

The powers of the liquidator of a partnership set out in Sch 4 to the Act (as modified) are split into those exercisable with sanction and those without, and mirror the corresponding provisions applicable to a liquidator in a compulsory winding up.

---

1 Schedule 4 to the Insolvency Act 1986, as modified by the Order, Sch 3, Part II, para 10.

3.3 WINDING UP WHERE CONCURRENT PETITION(S) PRESENTED AGAINST MEMBER(S)

3.3.1 *Applicability of relevant Parts of the Act* [1]

Subject to the modifications[2] that are specified in the Order, the provisions of Part V of the Act (other than ss 223 and 224) are applied by art 8 to the winding up of an insolvent partnership as an unregistered company on a creditor's petition where insolvency petitions are presented by the petitioner against the partnership and against one or more members or former members of the partnership in their capacity as such. Where there is no concurrent petition presented, art 7 will apply (see para **3.2** above).

Because under art 8 the possibility of a concurrent petition against a corporate member or a former corporate member of the insolvent partnership is envisaged, certain Parts of the Act are also applied (with modifications) to that situation, namely Part IV, Part VI, Part VII and Parts XII to XIX.

Similarly, since this article envisages the possibility of a concurrent petition against an individual member or individual members or former individual members of the insolvent partnership, certain Parts of the Act dealing with individual insolvency are also applied (with modifications)[3]. The relevant Parts which apply are Part IX (other than ss 269, 270, 287 and 297), and Parts X to XIX.

All the provisions applied by art 8 are further modified so that references to corporate or individual members include any former such member against whom an insolvency petition is being or has been presented by virtue of art 8.

---

1 Insolvent Partnerships Order 1994, art 8.
2 See Part I and Part II of Sch 4 to the Order.
3 See Part II of Sch 4 to the Order.

3.3.2 *Winding up of insolvent partnership as unregistered company* [1]

For the purposes of art 8, s 221 of the Act is modified in exactly the same way as for the purposes of art 7 (see para **3.2.2** above). All the comments made in that paragraph apply to a winding up of the partnership under art 8, except that the only circumstance in which an insolvent partnership may be wound up as an unregistered company under art 8 is that the partnership is unable to pay its debts[2] and the other two grounds set out in the modified s 221(7) for the purposes of art 7 do not apply.

Unless the contrary intention appears, a member of a partnership against whom an insolvency order has been made by virtue of art 8 is treated as a contributory for the purposes of the Act[3]. The reason for this provision is presumably that the separate estates of such members are available to satisfy any shortfall in the joint estate under ss 175A–175C of the Act. Any members against whom an insolvency order has not been made under art 8 will be treated as contributories.

1 Section 221 of the Insolvency Act 1986, as modified by the Order, Sch 4, Part I, para 3.
2 Ibid, s 221(8) (as modified).
3 Ibid, s 221(7) (as modified). The words 'unless the contrary intention appears' imply that the court can in its order provide that members against whom bankruptcy orders are made are to be treated as contributories.

3.3.3 Inability to pay debts: unpaid creditor for £750 or more[1]

An insolvent partnership is deemed unable to pay its debts if there is a creditor, by assignment or otherwise, to whom the partnership is indebted in a sum exceeding £750 then due, and:

(a) the creditor has served on the partnership, in the manner specified, by a written demand requiring the partnership to pay the sum so due[2];

(b) the creditor has also served on any one or more members or former members of the partnership liable to pay the sum so due (in the case of a corporate member, by leaving it at its registered office and in the case of an individual member, by serving it in accordance with the Rules) a demand, requiring that member or those members to pay the sums so due[2], and

(c) the partnership and its members have for three weeks after service of the demands, or the service of the last of them if served at different times, neglected to pay the sum or to secure or compound for it to the creditor's satisfaction[3].

As regards the method of service, the method is the same as prescribed under the modified s 222 under art 7 (see para **3.2.4** above)[4]. Provision is made enabling the figure of £750 to be increased or reduced[5].

1 Section 222 of the Insolvency Act 1986, as modified by the Order, Sch 4, Part I, para 4.
2 In Form 4, Sch 9 to the Order.
3 Insolvency Act 1986, s 222(1) (as modified).
4 Ibid, s 222(2) (as modified).
5 Ibid, s 222(3) (as modified).

3.3.4 High Court and county court jurisdiction[1]

The provisions of the Act relating to High Court and county court jurisdiction in relation to winding up of a company by the court and the presentation of a bankruptcy petition against an individual debtor are applied to insolvencies of partnerships, provided the same conditions as are imposed by Sch 3 to the Order are satisfied (see para **3.2.2** above[2]).

Subject to what follows, the court has jurisdiction to wind up a corporate member or former corporate member, or make a bankruptcy order against an individual member or former individual member, of a partnership against which a petition has been presented by virtue of art 8 if it has jurisdiction in respect of the partnership[3].

There are provisions relating to exclusion of the jurisdiction of certain county courts and the extent of winding-up jurisdiction[4].

1 Sections 117 and 265 of the Insolvency Act 1986, as modified by the Order, Sch 4, Part II, para 5.
2 Ibid, s 117(1)–(4) (as modified).
3 Ibid, s 117(5) (as modified). 'Court' does not include a district registry of the High Court: see s 117(6) (as modified).
4 Ibid, s 117(7) (as modified).

3.3.5 Circumstances in which a member of the insolvent partnership may be wound up or made bankrupt by the court[1]

A corporate member or former corporate member of a partnership may be wound up by the court under s 122 of the Act (as modified by Sch 4) if it is unable to pay its debts, but the other six grounds in s 122 of the Act are excluded.

Where a petition for the winding up of an insolvent partnership has been presented to the court under art 8, the petition against any individual member or former individual member of that partnership by virtue of the article must be in respect of one or more joint debts owed by the insolvent partnership, and the petitioning creditor or each of the petitioning creditors must be a person to whom the debt or (as the case may be) at least one of the debts is owed[2].

Subject to what follows, a creditor's petition may be presented to the court in respect of the joint debt or debts only if, at the time the petition is presented:

(a) the amount of the debt or the aggregate amount of the debts, is equal to or exceeds the bankruptcy level (ie £750 unless and until otherwise specified by the Secretary of State);

(b) the debt, or each of the debts, is for a liquidated sum payable to the petitioning creditor, or one or more of the petitioning creditors, immediately, and is unsecured;

(c) the debt, or each of the debts, is a debt for which the individual member or former member is liable and which he appears to be unable to pay; and

(d) there is no outstanding application to set aside a statutory demand served in respect of the debt or any of the debts[3].

1 Section 122 of the Insolvency Act 1986 (as modified) (corporate member); s 267 of the Insolvency Act 1986 (as modified) (individual member): both as modified by the Order, Sch 4, Part II, para 6.
2 Ibid, s 267(1) (as modified).
3 Ibid, s 267(2) (as modified).

3.3.6 Definition of inability of member to pay debts[1]

A corporate member or former member of an insolvent partnership is deemed unable to pay its debts if:

(a) there is a creditor, by assignment or otherwise, to whom the partnership is indebted in a sum exceeding £750 then due for which the member or former member is liable; and

(b) the creditor has served on that member or former member and the partnership in the specified manner, a written demand[2] requiring that member or former member and the partnership to pay the sum so due; and

(c)   the corporate member or former member and the partnership have, three
      weeks after the service of the demands, or the service of the last of them if
      served at different times, neglected to pay the sum or to secure or
      compound for it to the creditor's satisfaction[3].

Service of the demand is to be effected in the same manner as described in para
3.2.4 above[4]. The sum of £750 may be reduced or increased by the Secretary of
State by statutory instrument[5].

An individual member or former individual member will be deemed to be
unable to pay a joint debt for which he is liable if the debt is payable
immediately and the petitioning creditor to whom the insolvent partnership
owes the joint debt has served:

(a)   on the individual member or former individual member in accordance
      with the Rules a demand (known as 'the statutory demand')[6]; and
(b)   on the partnership in the specified manner a demand (known as 'the
      written demand')[7], requiring the member or former member and the
      partnership to pay the debt or to secure or compound for it to the
      creditor's satisfaction; and
(c)   at least three weeks have elapsed since the service of the demands, or the
      service of the last of them if served at different times; and
(d)   neither demand has been complied with nor the demand against the
      member set aside in accordance with the Rules.[8]

Service of the written demand referred to in (b) above is to be effected in the
same manner as described in para **3.2.4**[9].

The Court of Appeal has held in a case under the 1986 Order (but which would
have been decided the same way under the 1994 Order) that a bankruptcy
order can be made against one partner for a partnership debt[10].

---

1 Section 123 of the Insolvency Act 1986 (as modified) (corporate member); s 268 of the
   Insolvency Act 1986 (as modified) (individual member): both as modified by the Order,
   Sch 4, Part II, para 7.
2 In Form 4, Sch 9 to the Order.
3 Insolvency Act 1986, s 123(1) (as modified).
4 Ibid, s 123(2) (as modified).
5 Ibid, s 123(3) (as modified).
6 Form 4, Sch 9 to the Order.
7 Ibid.
8 Ibid, s 268(1) (as modified).
9 Ibid, s 268(2) (as modified).
10 *Schooler v Customs & Excise Commissioners* [1995] BCLC 610, CA, a case on art 15(3) of the
    1986 Order (which is substantially reproduced in art 19(5) of the Order).

3.3.7 Applications to wind up an insolvent partnership and to wind up or bankrupt an insolvent member[1]

There are prescribed forms of petition against a partnership[2], against a
corporate member or former corporate member[3] and against an individual
member or former individual member[4].

Each of the above-mentioned petitions may be presented by any creditor or creditors to whom the partnership and the member or former member in question is indebted in respect of a liquidated sum payable immediately[5].

Each must be presented to the same court and, except as the court otherwise permits or directs, on the same day and, except in the case of the petition against an individual member or former individual member, must be advertised[6].

At any time after presentation of the petition the petitioner may, with the leave of the court obtained on application and on such terms as the court thinks just, add other members or former members of the partnership as parties to the proceedings in relation to the insolvent partnership[7].

Each petition must contain particulars of other petitions being presented in relation to the partnership, identifying the partnership and members concerned[8].

The hearing of the petition against the partnership fixed by the court must be in advance of the hearing of any petition against an insolvent member[9]. It is understood that in the High Court the winding-up petition will be fixed for first hearing in the morning in the Wednesday list and the bankruptcy petition(s) in the afternoon of the same day before the same Bankruptcy Registrar[10]. On the day appointed for the hearing of the petition against the partnership, the petitioner must, before the commencement of the hearing, hand to the court a form duly completed headed 'Notice to court of progress on petitions presented'[11]. If there are adjournments, it seems highly desirable that the Registrar or district judge should deal with all petitions, particularly if one or more petitions become disputed.

Any member of the partnership or any person against whom a winding-up or bankruptcy petition has been presented in relation to the insolvent partnership is entitled to appear and to be heard on any petition for the winding up of the partnership[12].

A petitioner under ss 124 and 264 (as modified) may at the hearing withdraw the petition if:

(a) subject to what follows he withdraws at the same time every other petition which he presented under the relevant sections;
(b) he gave notice to the court at least three days before the date appointed for the hearing of the relevant petition of his intention to withdraw the petition[13].

A petitioner need not comply with the requirement to withdraw every other petition in the case of a petition against a member, if the court is satisfied on application made to it by the petitioner that, because of the difficulties in serving the petition or for any other reason, a continuance of that petition would be likely to prejudice or delay the proceedings on the petition which he has presented against the partnership or on any petition which he has presented against another insolvent member[14]. This provision is doubtless intended amongst other things to safeguard against the possibility that one or more partners may have disappeared or gone abroad, since, were it not for such a provision, it might be impossible for proceedings to be effective.

Where a petitioner gives notice that he intends to withdraw the petition, the court may, on such terms as it thinks just, substitute as petitioner, both in respect of the partnership and in respect of each insolvent member against whom a petition has been presented, any creditor of the partnership who in its opinion would have a right to present the petitions. If the court makes such a substitution the petitions in question will not be withdrawn. Substitution of a petitioner for this purpose will include a change of carriage of the petition in accordance with the Rules[15].

---

1 Sections 124 and 264 of the Insolvency Act 1986, as modified by the Order, Sch 4, Part II, para 8.
2 Form 5 in Sch 9 and the Insolvency Act 1986, s 124(1) (as modified).
3 Form 6 in Sch 9.
4 Form 7 in Sch 9.
5 See the Insolvency Act 1986, s 124(2) (as modified).
6 Form 8 in Sch 9 and the Insolvency Act 1986, s 124(3) (as modified).
7 Ibid, s 124(4) (as modified).
8 Ibid, s 125(5) (as modified).
9 Ibid, s 124(6) (as modified).
10 How the court will cope with a situation in which the winding-up petition is being dealt with in the High Court and there are, say, three concurrent bankruptcy petitions in different county courts remains to be seen.
11 Insolvency Act 1986, s 124(7) and Form 9 in Sch 9.
12 Ibid, s 124(8) (as modified).
13 Ibid, s 124(9) (as modified).
14 Ibid, s 124(10) (as modified).
15 Ibid, s 124(11) and (12) (as modified) and Insolvency Rules 1986, r 6.31.

3.3.8 Powers of court on hearing petitions against an insolvent partnership and its members[1]

(a) *Powers of the court*
On hearing a petition under s 124 of the Act (as modified by Sch 4) against an insolvent partnership or any of its insolvent members, the court may dismiss it, or adjourn the hearing conditionally or unconditionally or make any other order that it thinks fit. The court must not refuse to make a winding-up order against the partnership or a corporate member on the ground only that the partnership property or, as the case may be, the member's assets have been mortgaged to an amount equal to or in excess of that property or those assets, or that the partnership has no property or the member has no assets[2]. An order made on the hearing of such a petition may contain directions as to the future conduct of any insolvency proceedings in existence against any insolvent member in respect of whom an insolvency order has been made[3].

---

1 Sections 125 and 271 of the Insolvency Act 1986, as modified by the Order, Sch 4, Part II, para 9.
2 Ibid, s 125(1) (as modified).

3 Ibid, s 125(2) (as modified).

(b) *Hearing of petitions against members*[1]

A new s 125A is inserted into the Act by Sch 4 to the Order, setting out a series of options for the court on the hearing of a petition against members of a partnership.

The petitioner is required to draw the court's attention to the result of the hearing of the winding-up petition against the partnership and thereafter various other provisions apply[2]. If the court has neither made a winding-up order nor dismissed the winding-up petition against the partnership, it may adjourn the hearing of the petition against the member until either event has occurred[3].

Subject to what follows, if a winding-up order has been made against the partnership, the court may make a winding-up order against the corporate member in respect of which, or, as the case may be, a bankruptcy order against the individual member in respect of whom, the insolvency petition was presented[4]. However, if no insolvency order is made against any member within 28 days of the making of the winding-up order against the partnership, the proceedings against the partnership should be conducted as if the winding-up petition against the partnership had been presented by virtue of art 7 of the Order and the proceedings against any member should be conducted under the Act without the modifications[5] made by the Order.

If the court has dismissed the winding-up petition against the partnership, the court may dismiss the winding-up petition against the corporate member or, as the case may be, the bankruptcy petition against the individual member. However, if an insolvency order is made against a member, the proceedings against that member will be conducted under the Act without the modifications made by the Order[6].

The court may dismiss the petition against an insolvent member if it considers it just to do so because of a change in circumstances since the making of a winding-up order against the partnership[7]. This provision is clearly intended to deal with the situation which arose in a case prior to the coming into force of the Order where doubt had arisen as to whether bankruptcy orders had to be made against the individual partners of a partnership which had been ordered to be wound up, but where the debt on which the winding-up petition had been based had been paid in full prior to the hearing of the bankruptcy petitions[8].

The court may dismiss a petition against an insolvent member who is a limited partner. It may do so if such member lodges in court for the benefit of the creditors of the partnership sufficient money or security to the court's satisfaction to meet his liability for the debts and obligations of the partnership, or the member satisfies the court that he is no longer under any liability in respect of the debts and obligations of the partnership[9].

Nothing is to prejudice the power of the court, in accordance with the Rules, to authorise a creditor's petition to be amended by the omission of any creditor or debt and to be proceeded with as if things done for the purposes of those sections had been done only by or in relation to the remaining creditors or debts[10].

1 Section 125A of the Insolvency Act, as inserted by the Order, Sch 4, Part II, para 9.
2 Ibid, s 125A(1) (as inserted).
3 Ibid, s 125A(2) (as inserted).
4 Ibid, s 125A(3) (as inserted).
5 Ibid, s 125A(4) (as inserted) but subject to the modifications to ss 168 and 303 made by art 14.
6 Ibid, s 125A(5) (as inserted) but subject to the modifications to ss 168 and 303 made by art 14.
7 Ibid, s 125A(6) (as inserted).
8 *Re Marr (a Bankrupt)* [1990] Ch 773.
9 Ibid, s 125A(7) (as inserted).
10 Ibid, s 125A(8) (as inserted).

3.3.9 Statements of affairs[1]

Where the court:

(a) has made a winding up order; or
(b) has appointed a provisional liquidator in respect of an insolvent partnership or a corporate member of that partnership; or
(c) has made a bankruptcy order in respect of an individual member of that partnership;

the Official Receiver may require specified persons (including officers or former officers of the partnership) to make out and submit to him a statement as to the affairs of the partnership or member in a prescribed form[2]. The contents of the statement are identical to those applicable to companies (substituting 'partnership' for 'company'). The persons who may be required to make the statement are the same as those specified in the Act[3]. It will be remembered that 'officer' means not only a member, but also a person who has management or control of the partnership business[4].

The obligations to comply within 21 days, the ability of the Official Receiver to release an individual from his obligation and/or to extend the time-limit for compliance, and the penalty for default are all identical to the provisions contained in the Act[5].

1 Sections 131 and 288 of the Insolvency Act 1986, as modified by the Order, Sch 4, Part II, para 10.
2 Ibid, s 131(1) (as modified).
3 Ibid, s 131(2), (3) and (4) (as modified).
4 See art 2(1) of the Order.
5 Insolvency Act 1986, s 131(5)–(9) (as modified).

3.3.10 Public examination of officers of insolvent partnerships[1]

The provisions of the Act dealing with the public examination of officers of a company are applied to insolvent partnerships. The list of potential examinees, the obligation of the Official Receiver to make the application if so requested by a sufficient number of creditors, and the list of persons entitled to take part in the public examination are identical to the provisions relating to companies. It is further provided that the court may direct that the public examination of any person in relation to the affairs of an insolvent partnership can be combined with the public examination of that person under the Act in relation to his own affairs if an insolvency order has been made against him[2].

1 Section 133 of the Insolvency Act 1986, as modified by the Order, Sch 4, Part II, para 11.
2 Insolvency Act 1986, s 133(5) (as modified).

3.3.11 *Functions of Official Receiver relating to office of responsible insolvency practitioner*[1]

(a) *Status of Official Receiver*
Subject to what follows, where insolvency orders are made in respect of an insolvent partnership and one or more of its insolvent members by virtue of art 8 of the Order, the Official Receiver, by virtue of his office, becomes the responsible insolvency practitioner of (a) the partnership and (b) any insolvent member. He continues in office until another person becomes the responsible insolvency practitioner under the provisions of Part IV of the Act[2]. Furthermore, the Official Receiver is the responsible insolvency practitioner during any vacancy[3]. At any time when he is the responsible insolvency practitioner, the Official Receiver may summon a combined meeting of the creditors of the partnership and/or the creditors of such member, for the purpose of choosing a person to be a responsible insolvency practitioner in place of himself[4].

1 Sections 136, 293 and 294 of the Insolvency Act 1986, as modified by the Order, Sch 4, Part II, para 12.
2 Ibid, s 136(2) (as modified).
3 Ibid, s 136(3) (as modified).
4 Ibid, s 136(4) (as modified).

(b) *Duty of Official Receiver to summon meetings*[1]
Under the new s 136A inserted into the Act by Sch 4 to the Order, it is the duty of the Official Receiver as soon as practicable in the period of 12 weeks beginning with the day on which the insolvency order was made against the partnership to decide whether to exercise his power to summon a creditors' meeting. If he decides not to exercise that power, he must give notice of his decision before the end of that period to the court and to the creditors of the partnership and the creditors of any insolvent member against whom an insolvency order has been made[2]. Whether or not the Official Receiver has decided to exercise his power to summon a creditors' meeting, he must exercise it to summon a meeting if he is at any time requested to do so in accordance with the Rules by one-quarter (in value), of either:

(i) the partnership creditors; or
(ii) the creditors of any insolvent member against whom an insolvency order has been made.

Where such demand is made by the requisite percentage of creditors, the Official Receiver no longer has to exercise his own discretion[3].

Where the Official Receiver gives notice that he does not intend to call a meeting, such notice must contain an explanation of the creditor's power to require him to summon a combined meeting of the creditors of the partnership and of any insolvent member[4]. Where, however, the Official Receiver decides in pursuance of his own discretion to exercise his power to summon a meeting that meeting must be held in the period of four months beginning with the day on which the insolvency order was made against the partnership[5].

If, whether or not he has decided to exercise his power, the Official Receiver is requested by the requisite number of creditors to summon a meeting then he must hold such meeting in accordance with the Rules[6].

Where a meeting of the creditors of the partnership and of any insolvent member has been held and an insolvency order is subsequently made against a further insolvent member under art 8, any person chosen at that meeting to be the responsible insolvency practitioner in place of the Official Receiver will also be the responsible insolvency practitioner of the member against whom the subsequent order is made[7].

1 Section 136A of the Insolvency Act 1986, as inserted by the Order, Sch 4, Part II, para 12.
2 Ibid, s 136A(1) (as inserted).
3 Ibid, s 136A(1)(c) (as inserted).
4 Ibid, s 136A(2) (as inserted).
5 Ibid, s 136A(3) (as inserted).
6 Ibid, s 136A(4) (as inserted).
7 Ibid, s 136A(5) (as inserted). In this case the remaining provisions of s 136(1) and s 136A do not apply.

3.3.12 *Appointment of responsible insolvency practitioner by Secretary of State*[1]

(a) *Application by the Official Receiver to Secretary of State*
Where the court has made insolvency orders in respect of an insolvent partnership and one or more of its insolvent members by virtue of art 8 of the Order, the Official Receiver may, at any time when he is the responsible insolvency practitioner of the partnership and of any insolvent member, apply to the Secretary of State for the appointment of a person as responsible insolvency practitioner of both the partnership and of such members in his place (a 's 137 application'). If a meeting of creditors is held and no person is chosen to be the responsible insolvency practitioner as a result of that meeting, it is the duty of the Official Receiver to decide whether to refer the need for an appointment to the Secretary of State.

1 Sections 137, 295, 296 and 300 of the Insolvency Act 1986, as modified by the Order, Sch 4, Part II, para 13.

(b)   *Consequences of a s 137 application*[1]

Under s 137A, which is an entirely new section introduced by Sch 4 to the Order, where the Official Receiver makes an application under s 137(2) or on a reference made in pursuance of a decision under s 137(3), the Secretary of State must either make an appointment or decline to make one[2]. Where no appointment is made the Official Receiver continues to be the responsible insolvency practitioner of the partnership and its insolvent member or members but without prejudice to his power to make a further application or reference[3].

Where a responsible insolvency practitioner has been appointed by the Secretary of State and an insolvency order is subsequently made against a further insolvent member under art 8 of the Order, then the practitioner so appointed will also be the responsible insolvency practitioner of the member against whom the subsequent order is made[4]. Provision is made for notification to creditors of an appointment by the Secretary of State or of the responsible insolvency practitioner having become the responsible insolvency practitioner of a further insolvent member[5].

In the notification or the advertisement of appointment, the responsible insolvency practitioner must state whether he proposes to summon a combined meeting of the creditors of the insolvent partnership and of the insolvent member or members against whom insolvency orders have been made for the purposes of determining whether a creditors' committee should be established under s 141 (as modified). If he does not propose to summon such a meeting, he must set out the power of the creditors of the partnership and of the insolvent member or members requiring him to summon one[6]. Where a meeting has already been held, the responsible insolvency practitioner must state in the notice or advertisement whether a creditors' committee was established at that meeting. If such a committee was established he must state whether he proposes to appoint additional members. If a creditors' committee was not established, he must set out the power of the creditors to require him to summon a meeting for the purposes of determining whether a creditors' committee should be established[7].

---

1 Section 137A of the Insolvency Act 1986, as inserted by the Order, Sch 4, Part II, para 13.
2 Ibid, s 137A(1) (as inserted).
3 Ibid, s 137A(2) (as inserted).
4 Ibid, s 137A(3) (as inserted).
5 Ibid, s 137A(4) (as inserted).
6 Ibid, s 137A(5) (as inserted).
7 Ibid, s 137A(6) (as inserted).

3.3.13   *Rules applicable to meetings of creditors*[1]

The Order regulates meetings of three types:

(1)   separate meetings of the creditors of the partnership or any corporate member against which an insolvency order has been made;

(2)   combined meetings of the creditors of the partnership and the creditors of the insolvent member or members[2]; and

(3) separate meetings of the creditors of an individual member against whom
      a bankruptcy order has been made[3].

The provisions of the Rules relating to the requisitioning, summoning, holding
and conducting of creditors' meetings are applied with the necessary
modifications.

No provision is made for convening a separate meeting of the 'members' of the
partnership, who, for this purpose, are equivalent to the contributories of a
company.

Note that by virtue of these modifications, where there is a concurrent winding
up of a partnership and one or more bankruptcies of the individual partners,
there has to be a separate meeting of the creditors of the partnership but that
can be followed by combined meetings of the creditors of the partnership and
of the creditors of the insolvent member or members. Any combined meeting
of creditors should be conducted as if the creditors of the partnership and the
insolvent member or members were a single set of creditors[4].

As has already been noted, the major change made by the Order is to provide
that where there is a deficiency in the partnership estate, the liquidator of the
partnership is entitled to claim in the separate estates of the partners for the
deficiency in the partnership estate. It is not immediately clear how this affects
the right to vote at the first meetings of the creditors of the partnership and of
the insolvent member or members. It is suggested that the only practical course
is to permit creditors of the partnership to vote at the individual meetings of the
insolvent member or members in each case for the full amount of what the
creditor is owed by the partnership. Although it might, at first sight, appear to
be the more practical course to allow the liquidator of the insolvent partnership
to prove at the initial meeting and to vote in respect of the deficiency in the
partnership estate at the meetings of the creditors of each insolvent member, in
practice this does not seem possible. On the assumption that all the meetings
are taking place on the same day, the liquidator will not have been given
appropriate notice of the individual member's creditors' meetings since he will
only have been appointed a few hours before the meeting(s) actually take place
and he will not have been able to lodge a proof of debt. It is suggested that once
the first meetings have been held, as soon as the liquidator of the insolvent
partnership has notified his claim to the trustee in bankruptcy of the individual
member, the trustee should call upon the partnership creditors who may have
submitted proofs against the estates of the individual members to withdraw
their proofs of debt since, clearly, the trustee cannot admit their proofs for
dividend purposes as well as the proof of the liquidator of the insolvent
partnership for the deficiency in the partnership estate. There is a cardinal
principle of insolvency law that there should not be double proof in any
insolvency and this seems to be the only way of achieving that objective.

---

1 Section 139 of the Insolvency Act 1986, as modified by the Order, Sch 4, Part II, para 14.
2 Ibid, s 139(2) (as modified).
3 Ibid, s 139(3) (as modified).
4 Ibid, s 139(4) (as modified).

3.3.14 Appointment by the court following administration or voluntary arrangement[1]

Insolvency orders may be made in respect of an insolvent partnership and one or more of its insolvent members under art 8 of the Order immediately upon the discharge of either an administration order in respect of the partnership or at a time when there is a supervisor of voluntary arrangement approved in relation to the partnership. In such cases, the court may appoint as responsible insolvency practitioner the person who ceased on the discharge of the administration order to be the administrator or the person who is the supervisor at the time when the winding-up order against the partnership is made, as the case may be[2].

1 Section 140 of the Insolvency Act 1986, as modified by the Order, Sch 4, Part II, para 15.
2 Ibid, s 140(2) and (3) (as modified). Where the court makes an appointment under this section the Official Receiver does not become the responsible insolvency practitioner as otherwise provided for by s 136(2) (as modified), and has no duty under s 136A in respect of the summoning of creditors' meetings: see s 140(4) (as modified).

3.3.15 Creditors' committee[1]

(a) *Establishment of creditors' committee*

Where insolvency orders have been made in respect of an insolvent partnership and one or more of its insolvent members under art 8 of the Order, and a combined meeting of creditors has been summoned for the purpose of choosing a person to be the responsible insolvency practitioner of the partnership and of any such insolvent member or members, a creditors' meeting may establish a committee ('the creditors' committee') which will consist of the creditors of the partnership or creditors of any insolvent member against whom an insolvency order has been made, or both[2]. The responsible insolvency practitioner of the partnership and of its insolvent member or members may at any time, if he thinks fit, summon a combined general meeting of the creditors for the purpose of determining whether such a committee should be established and, if it is so determined, of establishing it. He must summon such a meeting if he is requested, in accordance with the Rules, to do so by one-tenth (in value) of either the partnership's creditors or the creditors of any insolvent member against whom the insolvency order has been made[3].

1 Sections 141, 301 and 302 of the Insolvency Act 1986, as modified by the Order, Sch 4, Part II, para 16.
2 Ibid, s 141(2) (as modified).
3 Ibid, s 141(3) (as modified).

(b) *Functions and membership of creditors' committee*[1]

A committee established under s 141 of the Act (as modified by Sch 4) will act as the liquidation committee for the partnership and for any corporate member against which an insolvency order has been made, and as the creditors' committee for any individual member against whom an insolvency order has been made. It will, as appropriate, exercise the functions conferred on liquidation and creditors' committees in winding up and bankruptcy by or under the Act[2]. The Rules relating to liquidation committees apply (with the necessary modifications and with exclusion of all references to contributories) to such a committee. There is no provision for representatives of the members to be appointed to a liquidation committee[3].

Where the responsible insolvency practitioner has been appointed in relation to a further member, the practitioner may appoint any creditor of that member (provided that he is duly qualified under the Rules to be a member of the committee) to be an additional member of any committee already established under s 141 (as modified), provided that the creditor concerned consents to act[4]. The court may also at any time on application by a creditor of the partnership or of an insolvent member against whom an insolvency order has been made, appoint the applicant an additional member of the committee. Such appointments are permissible even if by virtue of such an appointment the maximum number of members of the committee specified in the Rules is exceeded[5].

The creditors' committee is not able or required to carry out its functions at any time when the Official Receiver is the responsible insolvency practitioner of the partnership and of its insolvent member or members. In such a period, the functions of such a committee are vested in the Secretary of State except to the extent that the Rules otherwise provide[6].

In addition, where there is for the time being no creditors' committee and the responsible insolvency practitioner is a person other than the Official Receiver, the functions of such a committee are vested in the Secretary of State except to the extent that the Rules otherwise provide[7].

---

1 Section 141A of the Insolvency Act 1986, as inserted by the Order, Sch 4, Part II, para 16.
2 Ibid, s 141A(1) (as inserted).
3 Ibid, s 141A(2) (as inserted).
4 Ibid, s 141A(3) (as inserted).
5 Ibid, s 141A(4) and (5) (as inserted). The maximum number is currently five.
6 Ibid, s 141A(6) (as inserted).
7 Ibid, s 141A(7) (as inserted).

3.3.16 *General functions of responsible insolvency practitioner*[1]

The functions of the responsible insolvency practitioner are those which the Act provides are the functions of a liquidator of a registered company and of a trustee in bankruptcy. These are to secure the realisation of the assets and the distribution to the respective creditors and, if there is a surplus in the estate, the distribution to the persons entitled to such surplus[2]. Subject to any provisions of the Act, the practitioner is entitled in the carrying out of functions and in the management of the property and assets to use his own discretion[3]. If he is not the Official Receiver, it is his duty to furnish the Official Receiver with such information, and produce for the Official Receiver's inspection such books, papers and other records as the Official Receiver may reasonably require and to give him such other assistance as he may reasonably require for the purposes of carrying out his functions in relation to the winding up of the partnership and any corporate member or the bankruptcy of any individual member[4].

1 Sections 143, 168(4) and 305 of the Insolvency Act 1986, as modified by the Order, Sch 4, Part II, para 17.
2 Ibid, s 143(1) (as modified).
3 Ibid, s 143(2) (as modified).
4 Ibid, s 143(3) (as modified).

3.3.17 Duties to summon final meeting of creditors[1]

If it appears to the responsible insolvency practitioner (where such practitioner is not the Official Receiver[2]) that the winding up of the partnership or of any corporate member or the administration of any individual member's estate is, for practical purposes, complete, he is required to summon a final general meeting of the creditors of the partnership or the insolvent member or members, as the case may be, or a combined final general meeting of the creditors of the partnership and of the insolvent member or members, which:

(a) will, as appropriate, receive the practitioner's report for the winding up of the insolvent partnership or of any corporate member or for the administration of the estate of an individual member; and

(b) will determine whether the practitioner should have his release[3].

The practitioner may, if he thinks fit, at the same time as giving the notice summoning the final general meeting, give notice of any final distribution of the partnership property or the property of the insolvent member or members. If summoned for a date earlier than the notice of final distribution, the final general meeting must be adjourned (and, if necessary, further adjourned) until a date on which he is able to report to the meeting that the winding up of the partnership or of any corporate member, or the administration of an individual member's estate, is for practical purposes complete[4]. It is his duty to retain sufficient sums from the partnership property and the property of any such insolvent member to cover the expenses of summoning and holding any meeting required[5].

1 Sections 146 and 331 of the Insolvency Act 1986, as modified by the Order, Sch 4, Part II, para 18.
2 See para **3.3.21** for the position where the responsible insolvency practitioner is the Official Receiver.
3 Ibid, s 146(2) (as modified).
4 Ibid, s 146(3) (as modified).
5 Ibid, s 146(4) (as modified).

3.3.18 Power of court to stay proceedings[1]

The power of the court to stay a winding up applies to an insolvent partnership on the application of the persons as listed and subject to the terms and conditions as provided in the modified s 147 of the Act[2]. It is further provided that if, in the course of hearing an insolvency petition presented against a member of an insolvent partnership, the court is satisfied that an application has been or will be made in order to stay a winding up following a winding-up order, the court may adjourn the petition against the insolvent member, either conditionally or unconditionally[3].

Where the court makes an order staying proceedings it may, on hearing any insolvency petition presented against an insolvent member of the partnership, dismiss that petition. If an insolvency order has already been made by virtue of art 8 of the Order in relation to an insolvent member of the partnership, the court may make an order annulling or rescinding that insolvency order, or it may make any other order that it thinks fit[4].

The court may, before making any order under the modified section, require the Official Receiver to furnish to it a report with respect to any facts or matters which are in his opinion relevant to the application[5].

---

1 Section 147 of the Insolvency Act 1986, as modified by the Order, Sch 4, Part II, para 19.
2 Ibid, s 147(1) (as modified).
3 Ibid, s 147(2) (as modified).
4 Ibid, s 147(3) (as modified).
5 Ibid, s 147(4) (as modified).

3.3.19 *Supplementary powers of responsible insolvency practitioner*[1]

Where the court has made insolvency orders in respect of an insolvent partnership and one or more of its insolvent members under art 8 of the Order, the responsible insolvency practitioner of the partnership and of such member or members may at any time summon either separate or combined general meetings of:

(a) the creditors or contributories of the partnership; and
(b) the creditors or contributories of the member or members,

for the purposes of ascertaining their wishes[2].

It is the duty of the responsible insolvency practitioner to summon separate meetings at such times as the creditors of the partnership or of the member, as the case may be, or the contributories of any corporate member, by resolution (either at the meeting appointing the responsible insolvency practitioner or otherwise) may direct, or whenever requested in writing to do so by one-tenth (in value) of such creditors or contributories[3]. A similar duty is imposed to summon combined meetings at such times as the creditors of the partnership and of the member or members by resolution (either at the meeting appointing the responsible insolvency practitioner or otherwise) may direct, or whenever requested in writing to do so by one-tenth (in value) of such creditors[4].

The practitioner may apply to the court (in the prescribed manner) for directions in relation to any particular matter arising in the winding up of the insolvent partnership or in the winding up or bankruptcy of an insolvent member[5].

If any person is aggrieved by an act or decision of the responsible insolvency practitioner, that person may apply to the court which may confirm, reverse or modify the act or decision complained of and make such order in the case as it thinks just[6].

1 Sections 168, 303 and 314(7) of the Insolvency Act 1986, as modified by the Order, Sch 4, Part II, para 20.
2 Ibid, s 168(2) (as modified).
3 Ibid, s 168(3)(a) (as modified).
4 Ibid, s 168(3)(b) (as modified).
5 Ibid, s 168(4) and (5) (as modified).
6 Ibid, s 172(6) (as modified).
7 Ibid, s 172(7) (as modified).

3.3.20 *Removal etc, of responsible insolvency practitioner or provisional liquidator*[1]

The responsible practitioner or provisional liquidator may be removed from or vacate office in the following circumstances:

(a) subject to what follows, by an order of the court[2];
(b) if appointed by the Secretary of State he can only be removed from office by direction of the Secretary of State[3];
(c) if not the Official Receiver he must vacate office if he ceases to be a person who is qualified to act as an insolvency practitioner in relation to the insolvent partnership or any insolvent member of it against whom an insolvency order has been made[4];
(d) he may, with the leave of the court (or, if appointed by the Secretary of State, with leave of the court or the Secretary of State), resign his office by giving notice of his resignation to the court[5];
(e) where a final meeting has been held under s 146, the practitioner whose report was considered at the meeting shall vacate office as liquidator or as trustee, as the case may be, as soon as he has given notice to the court (and, in the case of a corporate member to the Registrar of Companies) that the meeting has been held and the decisions, if any of the meeting[6];
(f) he must vacate office as trustee of the estate of an individual member if the insolvency order against that member has been annulled[7].

1 Sections 172 and 198 of the Insolvency Act 1986, as modified by the Order, Sch 4, Part II, para 21.
2 Ibid, s 172(2) (as modified).
3 Ibid, s 172(3) (as modified).
4 Ibid, s 172(4) (as modified).
5 Ibid, s 172(5) (as modified).
6 Ibid, s 172(6) (as modified).
7 Ibid, s 172(7) (as modified).

3.3.21 *Release of responsible insolvency practitioner or of provisional liquidator*[1]

Where the Official Receiver ceases to be the responsible insolvency practitioner because of the appointment of some other person in his stead, the Official Receiver has his release with effect from the time at which he gives notice to the court that he has been replaced following the nomination of a successor by a combined general meeting of creditors of the partnership and of any insolvent member or members or an appointment by the Secretary of State. In the case where the successor has been appointed by the court, the release takes effect at such time as the court may determine[2].

If the Official Receiver while he is the responsible insolvency practitioner gives notice to the Secretary of State that the winding up of the partnership or of the corporate member or the administration of the estate of an individual member is for practical purposes complete, the release of the Official Receiver as liquidator or trustee (as the case may be) takes effect from such time as the Secretary of State may determine[3].

A person other than the Official Receiver who has ceased to be the responsible insolvency practitioner has his release as described in Table 1 below.

TABLE 1

Reason for Ceasing to be the Responsible Insolvency Practitioner	Time of Release
(a) Death	When notice is given to the court in accordance with the Rules that that person has ceased to hold office[4]
(b) Removal from office by the court or by the Secretary of State, or who has vacated office under s 172(4) of the Act (as modified)	As the Secretary of State may, on an application by such person, determine[5]
(c) Resignation	As may be directed by the court or, if he was appointed by the Secretary of State, at such time as may be directed by the court or the Secretary of State may, on application by such person, determine[6]
(d) Vacation of office under s 172(6) of the Act (as modified)	(i) If the final meeting referred to in s 172(6) (as modified) has resolved against such person's release, at such time as the Secretary of State, may, on an application by such person determine; and (ii) if that meeting has not so resolved, at the time at which such person vacated office[7]

A person who has ceased to hold office as a provisional liquidator has his release with effect from such time as the court may, on an application by him, determine[8].

Where a bankruptcy order in respect of an individual member is annulled, the responsible insolvency practitioner at the time of the annulment has his release with effect from such time as the court may determine[9].

The effect of the release of the responsible insolvency practitioner or provisional liquidator (including in both cases the Official Receiver when so acting), is to discharge him from all liability with effect from the time specified in ss 174 and 299 (as modified). Such release applies both to acts or omissions in the winding up of the insolvent partnership or of any corporate member or the administration of the estate of an individual member, as the case may be, and otherwise in relation to his conduct. Nothing in ss 174 and 299 (as modified) prevents the exercise, in relation to a person who has had his release under the section, of the court's powers under s 212 (summary remedy against directors, liquidators, etc) or s 304 (liability of trustee)[10].

---

1 Sections 174 and 299 of the Insolvency Act 1986, as modified by the Order, Sch 4, Part II, para 22.
2 Ibid, s 174(1) (as modified).
3 Ibid, s 174(2) (as modified).
4 Ibid, s 174(4)(a) (as modified).
5 Ibid, s 174(4)(b) (as modified).
6 Ibid, s 174(4)(c) (as modified).
7 Ibid, s 174(4) (as modified).
8 Ibid, s 174(5) (as modified).
9 Ibid, s 174(6) (as modified).
10 Ibid, s 174(7) (as modified).

3.3.22 *Priority of expenses and debts*[1]

(a) *Priority of expenses*

Section 175 of the Act (as modified by Sch 4) deals with the priority of expenses incurred by a responsible insolvency practitioner of an insolvent partnership and of any insolvent member of that partnership against whom an insolvency order has been made. The order of priority is as follows:

(a) the joint estate of the partnership is applicable in the first instance in payment of the joint expenses, and the separate estate of each insolvent member is applicable in the first instance in payment of the separate expenses relating to that member[2];

(b) where the joint estate is insufficient for the payment in full of the joint expenses, the unpaid balance must be apportioned equally between the separate estates of the insolvent members against whom insolvency orders have been made and shall form part of the expenses to be paid out of those estates[3];

(c) where any separate estate of an insolvent member is insufficient for the payment in full of the separate expenses to be paid out of that estate, the unpaid balance will form part of the expenses to be paid out of the joint estate[4];

(d) where, after transfer of any unpaid balance in accordance with (b) and (c) above, any estate is insufficient for the payment in full of the expenses to be paid out of that estate, the balance then remaining unpaid must be apportioned equally between the other estates[5];

(e) where, after an apportionment under (d) above, one or more estates are insufficient for the payment in full of the expenses to be paid out of those estates, the total of the unpaid balances must continue to be apportioned equally between the other estates until provision is made for the payment in full of the expenses or there is no estate available for the payment of the balance finally remaining unpaid, in which case it abates in equal proportions between all the estates[6].

In Appendix 1 some examples are set out of how these principles operate in practice.

Without prejudice to the above provisions, the responsible insolvency practitioner may, with the sanction of any creditors' committee established under s 141 (as modified) or with the leave of the court obtained on application:

(a) pay out of the joint estate as part of the expenses to be paid out of that estate any expenses incurred for any separate estate of an insolvent member; or

(b) pay out of any separate estate of an insolvent member any part of the expenses incurred for the joint estate which affects that separate estate[7].

The net effect of these provisions is to make sure, as far as possible, that when there is a deficiency the expenses incurred in the joint estate and in the separate estate rank pari passu, so that any deficiency is made up from the other estate or estates. Creditors of the separate estates could, in certain situations, be much worse off than under the law that existed prior to the Order. For example, where there is a substantial deficiency in paying the expenses of the administration of the joint estate, creditors of the separate estate may find some or all of the separate estates of the individual partners have to go towards satisfying that deficiency.

---

1 Sections 175 and 328 of the Insolvency Act 1986, as modified by the Order, Sch 4, Part II, para 23.
2 Ibid, s 175(2) (as modified).
3 Ibid, s 175(3) (as modified).
4 Ibid, s 175(4) (as modified).
5 Ibid, s 175(5) (as modified).
6 Ibid, s 175(6) (as modified).
7 Ibid, s 175(7) (as modified).

(b) *Priority of debts in joint estate*[1]

The new s 175A inserted into the Act by Sch 4 to the Order deals with the priority of debts in (as opposed to expenses of) the joint estate and is expressed to be subject, in the case of the liability of the estate of a deceased member, to the provisions of s 9 of the Partnership Act which provides that:

'Every partner in the firm is liable jointly with the other partners, and in Scotland severally also, for all debts and obligations of the firm incurred while he was a partner and after his death, his estate is also separately liable in a due course of administration for such debts and obligations, so far as they remain unsatisfied but subject in England or Ireland to the prior payment of his separate debts'.

After payment of expenses, the joint debts of the partnership must be paid out of its joint estate in the following order of priority:

(a) the preferential debts;
(b) the debts which are neither preferential debts nor postponed debts[2];
(c) interest under s 189 on the joint debts (other than postponed debts[2]);
(d) postponed debts[2];
(e) interest under s 189 on the postponed debts[3].

In the event of a surplus, the responsible insolvency practitioner has to adjust the rights among the members of the partnership as contributories and is required to distribute any surplus to the members according to their respective rights and interests in the surplus[4].

The preferential debts and the debts which are neither preferential nor postponed rank equally between themselves, and in each case if the joint estate is insufficient for meeting them, they abate in equal proportions between themselves[5]. Where the joint estate is insufficient for the payment of the joint debts as regards preferential debts and debts which are neither preferential nor postponed, the responsible insolvency practitioner must aggregate the value of those debts to the extent that they have not been satisfied or are not capable of being satisfied. The aggregate amount then ranks as a claim against the separate estate against each member of the partnership against whom an insolvency order has been made which:

(a) shall be a debt provable by the responsible insolvency practitioner in each such estate; and

(b) shall rank equally with the debts of the member referred to in s 175B(1) (b) of the Act (as inserted)[6].

It is to be noted, therefore, that the debt of a creditor of a partnership which cannot be satisfied out of the partnership estate now ranks as a debt ranking equally with the debts of the member as regards the separate estate. But such a debt is provable by the responsible insolvency practitioner and not by the creditor himself[7]. As has already been noted, art 8 of the Order applies only when the winding up of the insolvent partnership takes place concurrently with petitions presented against one or more members. Accordingly, it would seem that if two members of the partnership were to be made bankrupt and subsequently the partnership were to be wound up, the liquidator of the partnership would not be entitled to claim pari passu with the creditors of the individual member as, under art 9, there is no corresponding s 175A. However, as discussed in relation to art 14 (para **5.3** below), it may be that the court has the power to apply the provisions of Sch 4 to this situation also.

Section 175A contains further provisions for what is to happen where the joint estate is sufficient for the payment of the preferential debts and the debts which are neither preferential nor postponed, but is insufficient either to pay interest under s 189 of the Act on the joint debts (other than postponed debts), or to pay the postponed debts, or to pay the interest under s 189 of the Act on the postponed debts[8]. The deficiency is to be claimed from the other estates.

Where the responsible insolvency practitioner receives any distribution from the separate estate of a member in respect of interest on the joint debts or the postponed debts or interest on the postponed debts, that distribution becomes part of the joint estate and must be distributed in accordance with a presented order of priority[9].

---

1 Section 175A of the Insolvency Act 1986, as inserted by the Order, Sch 4, Part II, para 23.
2 Ibid, s 329.
3 Ibid, s 175A(2) (as inserted).
4 Ibid, s 175A(3) (as inserted).

5 Ibid, s 175A(4) (as inserted).
6 Ibid, s 175A(5) (as inserted).
7 Ibid, s 175A(5)(a) (as inserted).
8 Ibid, s 175A(6)–(8) (as inserted).
9 Ibid, s 175A(9) (as inserted).

(c) *Priority of debts in separate estate*[1]

A new s 175B is inserted into the Act by Sch 4 to the Order and deals with the priority of debts in separate estates.

The separate estate of each member of the partnership against whom an insolvency order has been made is applicable, after payment of expenses in accordance with payment of the separate debts of that member in the following order of priority:

(a) the preferential debts;
(b) the debts which are neither preferential debts nor postponed debts[2] (including any debts referred to in s 175A(5)(a) of the Act);
(c) interest under s 189 of the Act on the separate debts and under s 175A(6);
(d) the postponed debts of the member[2] (including any debt referred to in s 175A(7)(a)); and
(e) interest under s 189 on the postponed debts of the member[2] and under s 175A(8)[3].

The debts referred to in (a) and (b) above rank equally between themselves. In each case, if the estate is insufficient for meeting them, they abate in equal proportions between themselves[4].

Where the responsible insolvency practitioner receives any distribution from the joint estate or from the separate estate of another member of the partnership against whom an insolvency order has been made, that distribution shall become part of the separate estate and must be distributed in accordance with the order of priority set out above[5].

1 Section 175B of the Insolvency Act 1986, as inserted by the Order, Sch 4, Part II, para 23.
2 Ibid, s 329.
3 Ibid, s 175B(1) (as inserted).
4 Ibid, s 175B(2) (as inserted).
5 Ibid, s 175B(3) (as inserted).

(d) *Provisions generally applicable in the distribution of joint and separate estates*[1]

A new s 175C inserted into the Act by Sch 4 to the Order deals generally with applicable provisions.

Distinct accounts should be kept for the joint estate of the partnership and of the separate estate of each member of the partnership against whom an insolvency order has been made[2].

No member of the partnership may prove for a joint or separate debt in competition with the joint creditors, unless the debt has arisen:

(a) as a result of fraud; or
(b) in the ordinary course of business carried on separately from the partnership business[3].

By virtue of this provision, unless the obligation arises in the circumstances allowed for under the two exceptions, any rights which partners may have against each other for breaches of a partnership agreement will be deferred to claims of other creditors. As regards the position of a retired partner in relation to an indemnity which may have been given to him by the continuing partners of the partnership which subsequently becomes insolvent, see the discussion in para **2.11.10** above.

For the purposes of establishing the value of a debt provable in the separate estate where there is a deficiency in the joint estate because the joint estate is insufficient for the payment of the postponed joint debts, the value may be estimated by the responsible insolvency practitioner[4]. The trustee is allowed to estimate the value of any bankruptcy debt which, by reason of its being subject to any contingency or contingencies or for any other reason, does not bear a certain value and, where he makes an estimate, the amount provable in the bankruptcy is the amount of the estimate. Such an estimate is assumed to be capable of being challenged under s 303 (general control of trustee by court).

Interest under s 189 of the Act on preferential debts ranks equally with interest on debts which are neither preferential nor postponed[5] debts[6].

The provisions of ss 175A and 175B are without prejudice to any provision of the Act or of any other enactment concerning the ranking between themselves of postponed debts and interest thereon, but in the absence of any such provision they rank equally inter se[7].

If any two or more members of an insolvent partnership constitute a separate partnership, the creditors of such separate partnership are deemed to be a separate set of creditors and subject to the same statutory provisions as the separate creditors of any member of the insolvent partnership[8].

Where any surplus remains out of the administration of the estate of a separate partnership, the surplus must be distributed to the members or, where applicable, to the separate estates of the members of that partnership according to their respective rights and interest in it[9].

Special provision is made to preclude the Official Receiver, Secretary of State and/or a responsible insolvency practitioner from claiming remuneration or fees in relation to the transfer of surpluses from one estate to another, or to the distribution from a separate estate to the joint estate or to a distribution from the estate of a separate partnership to the separate estates of the members of that partnership[10].

---

1 Section 175C of the Insolvency Act 1986, as inserted by the Order, Sch 4, Part II, para 23.
2 Ibid, s 175C(1) (as inserted).
3 Ibid, s 175C(2) (as inserted).
4 Ibid, s 175C(3) (as inserted).
5 Ibid, s 329.
6 Ibid, s 175C(4) (as inserted).
7 Ibid, s 175C(5) (as inserted).
8 Ibid, s 175C(6) (as inserted).
9 Ibid, s 175C(7) (as inserted).
10 Ibid, s 175C(8) (as inserted).

3.3.23   Interest on debts[1]

Provision is made for interest to be paid in the order of priority laid down by ss 175A and 175B of the Act (as inserted by Sch 4 to the Order) on any debt proved in the winding up of an insolvent partnership or the winding up or bankruptcy of an insolvent member, including so much of any such debt as represents interest on the remainder[2]. Interest runs from the date of the winding-up order against the partnership or corporate member or from the date on which the bankruptcy order is made against any individual member[3]. The rate of interest is the same as provided for in the Act[4].

1 Sections 189 and 328 of the Insolvency Act 1986, as modified by the Order, Sch 4, Part II, para 24.
2 Ibid, s 189(1) (as modified).
3 Ibid, s 189(2) (as modified).
4 Ibid, s 189(3) (as modified).

3.3.24   False representations to creditors[1]

The provisions in the Act regarding false representations to creditors are applied to a situation where insolvency orders have been made against an insolvent partnership and any insolvent member or members by virtue of art 8 of the Order[2]. The provisions apply to any past or present officers of the partnership or a past or present officer (which for these purposes includes a shadow director) of a corporate member[3].

1 Sections 211 and 356 of the Insolvency Act 1986, as modified by the Order, Sch 4, Part II, para 25.
2 Ibid, s 211(1) (as modified).
3 Ibid, s 211(2) (as modified).

3.3.25   Appointment to office of responsible insolvency practitioner or provisional liquidator[1]

(a)   *Qualification for appointment*

Under the modified sections of the Act, no person may be appointed as responsible insolvency practitioner or provisional liquidator unless he is at the time of the appointment qualified to act as an insolvency practitioner both in relation to the insolvent partnership (and, in the case of appointment as provisional liquidator, to any corporate member) and in relation to the insolvent member or members[2].

Where a joint appointment is made, the appointment or nomination must declare whether any acts required which are authorised to be done by the practitioner or by the provisional liquidator are to be done by all or any one or more of the persons for the time being holding the office in question[3].

Any appointment takes effect only if that person accepts the appointment in accordance with the Rules but, subject thereto the appointment takes effect at the time specified in the certificate of appointment[4].

1 Sections 230, 231 and 292 of the Insolvency Act 1986, as modified by the Order, Sch 4, Part II, para 26.
2 Ibid, s 230(2) (as modified).
3 Ibid, s 230(3) (as modified).
4 Ibid, s 230(4) (as modified).

(b) *Conflicts of interest*[1]

Special provision is made for the situation which may well occur, where the responsible insolvency practitioner of an insolvent partnership being wound up by virtue of art 8 of the Order and one or more of its insolvent members forms the opinion at any time that there is a conflict of interest between his functions as liquidator of the partnership on the one hand and his functions as responsible insolvency practitioner of any insolvent member on the other, or between his functions as responsible insolvency practitioner of two or more insolvent members[2]. In such an event, the practitioner may apply to the court for directions. The court may, without prejudice to the generality of its power to give directions, appoint one or more insolvency practitioners either in place of the applicant or to act as responsible insolvency practitioner of both the partnership and its insolvent member or members or to act as joint responsible insolvency practitioner with the applicant[3].

1 Section 230A of the Insolvency Act 1986, as inserted by the Order, Sch 4, Part II, para 26.
2 Ibid, s 230A(1) (as inserted).
3 Ibid, s 230A(2) (as inserted).

3.3.26 *Getting in the partnership property*[1]

Where insolvency orders are made by virtue of art 8 of the Order in respect of an insolvent partnership and its insolvent member or members, or a provisional liquidator of an insolvent partnership and any of its corporate members is appointed, the liquidator or the provisional liquidator has the same rights in relation to getting in the property of the partnership as if he were the liquidator or provisional liquidator of a company (see para **3.2.9** above).

1 Section 234 of the Insolvency Act 1986, as modified by the Order, Sch 4, Part II, para 27.

3.3.27 *Definition of individual member's estate*[1]

The estate of an individual member of the partnership is defined so that the exempted items listed in s 283(2) of the Act (as modified) such as, for example, equipment which is not partnership property and which is necessary to the individual for use personally by him in his business, do not include any items which constitute partnership property.

1 Section 283 of the Insolvency Act 1986, as modified by the Order, Sch 4, Part II, para 29.

3.3.28 *Individual member: restrictions on dispositions of property*[1]

Where an individual member is adjudged bankrupt by virtue of art 8 of the Order, any disposition of property made by that member in the period[2] to which s 284 of the Act (as modified) applies is void except to the extent that it was made with the consent of the court, or was subsequently ratified by the court.[3] However a disposition of property is void notwithstanding that the property is not or as the case may be, would not be, comprised in the individual member's estate; but nothing in the modified s 284 affects any disposition made by a person or property held by him on trust for any other person other than a disposition made by an individual member of property held by him on trust for the partnership.[4]

1 Section 284 of the Insolvency Act 1986, as modified by the Order, Sch 4, Part II, para 29.
2 The period is defined as beginning with the day of the presentation of the petition for the bankruptcy order and ending with the vesting under Chapter IV of Part IX of the Act of the individual member's estate in a trustee: Insolvency Act 1986, s 284(3) (as modified).
3 Insolvency Act 1986, s 284(1) (as modified).
4 Ibid, s 284(6) (as modified).

3.3.29 *Powers of liquidator in a winding up*[1]

The powers of a liquidator in a winding up are the same as those under art 7 of the Order (see para **3.2.10** above).

1 Schedule 4 to the Insolvency Act 1986, as modified by the Order, Sch 4, Part II, para 30.

Chapter 4

LIQUIDATION ON MEMBER'S PETITION AND/OR JOINT BANKRUPTCY PETITIONS

4.1 INTRODUCTION

Insolvency proceedings initiated by the members of a partnership are dealt with in Part V of the Order, which is divided into three articles. Article 9 is headed 'Winding up of insolvent partnership as unregistered company on member's petition where no concurrent petition is presented against member'. This article should be read in conjunction with Schs 3 and 5 to the Order.

Article 10 is headed 'Winding up of insolvent partnership as unregistered company on member's petition where concurrent petitions presented against all members' and should be read in conjunction with Schs 4, 6 and 7 to the Order.

Article 11 is headed 'Insolvency proceedings not involving winding up of insolvent partnership as an unregistered company where individual members present joint bankruptcy petition' and should be read in conjunction with Sch 7 to the Order.

4.2 WINDING UP WHERE NO CONCURRENT PETITION IS PRESENTED AGAINST MEMBER

4.2.1 Applicability of relevant Parts of the Act[1]

Where a member petitions for the winding up of an insolvent partnership as an unregistered company, and no insolvency petition is presented by the petitioner against a member of that partnership in his capacity as such, the following provisions of the Act apply:

(a) ss 117 and 221, as modified by Sch 5 to the Order;
(b) other provisions of Part V of the Act, as modified by Part I of Sch 3 to the Order.

---

1 Insolvent Partnerships Order 1994, art 9.

4.2.2 High Court and county court jurisdiction[1]

The provisions relating to High Court and county court jurisdiction are applied to insolvent partnerships as if they were unregistered companies subject to certain modifications and conditions[2].

---

1 Section 117 of the Insolvency Act 1986, as modified by the Order, Sch 5, para 1.
2 Ibid, s 117 (as modified) and footnote 4 to para **3.2.2** above.

4.2.3   *Winding up of unregistered companies*[1]

The provisions of s 221 of the Act (as modified by Sch 5) mirror those in relation to a winding up under art 7 discussed in para **3.2.2** above[2].

---

1 Section 221 of the Insolvency Act 1986, as modified by the Order, Sch 5, para 2.
2 Ibid, s 221(1) (as modified) and footnote 4 to para **3.2.2** above.

4.2.4   *Who may present a petition*[1]

Under the new s 221A(1) inserted into the Act by Sch 5 to the Order, it is provided that a petition for winding up of an insolvent partnership may only be presented by any member of the partnership if the partnership consists of not less than eight members[2]. Provided that the conditions of s 221(7) (as modified) are satisfied, no leave is required of the court.

A petition for a winding up of an insolvent partnership may also be presented by any member of a partnership with seven or less members with the leave of the court (obtained on the petitioner's ex parte application) if the court is satisfied that:

(a)   the member has served on the partnership, by leaving at a principal place of business of the partnership in England and Wales, or by delivering to an officer of the partnership, or by otherwise serving in such manner as the court may approve or direct, a written demand[2] in respect of a joint debt or debts exceeding £750 then due from the partnership but paid by the member, other than out of partnership property;

(b)   the partnership has for three weeks after the service of the demand neglected to pay the sum or to secure or compound for it to the member's satisfaction; and

(c)   the member has obtained a judgment, decree or order of any court against the partnership for reimbursement to him of the amount of the joint debt or debts so paid and all reasonable steps (other than insolvency proceedings) have been taken by the member to enforce that judgment, decree or order.[3]

---

1 Section 221A of the Insolvency Act 1986, as inserted by the Order, Sch 5, para 2.
2 Ibid, s 221A(1) (as inserted) and Form 10 in Sch 9.
3 Ibid, s 221A(2) (as inserted).

4.3   WINDING UP WHERE CONCURRENT PETITIONS ARE PRESENTED AGAINST ALL MEMBERS

4.3.1   *Applicability of relevant Parts of the Act*[1]

Subject to the modifications that are specified in the Order, the following provisions of the Act apply in relation to the winding up of an insolvent partnership as an unregistered company on a member's petition where insolvency petitions are presented by the petitioner against the partnership and against all its members in their capacity as such:

(a)   ss 117, 124, 125, 221, 264, 265, 271 and 272[2]; and
(b)   ss 220 (as modified)[3], 225 and 227 to 229 in Part V.

Because under this article the possibility of a concurrent petition against a corporate member or a former corporate member of the insolvent partnership is envisaged, certain Parts of the Act are applied to that situation, namely Part IV, Part VI, Part VII and Parts XII–XIX.

Similarly, since this article envisages the possibility of a concurrent petition against an individual member or individual members or former individual members of the insolvent partnership, certain Parts of the Act dealing with individual insolvency are also applied, with modifications. The relevant Parts which are applied are Part IX (other than ss 273, 274, 287 and 297), and Parts X–XIX.

Certain of the provisions referred to above are modified in relation to the corporate or individual members of an insolvent partnership[4], save that the provisions on summary administration of a debtor's estate apply in relation to the individual members of insolvent partnerships[5].

1 Insolvent Partnerships Order 1994, art 10.
2 As modified by Sch 6 to the Order.
3 As modified by Part I of Sch 4 to the Order.
4 Under Part II of Sch 4 to the Order.
5 Under Sch 7 to the Order.

4.3.2 High Court and county court jurisdiction[1]

The provisions relating to High Court and county court jurisdiction are applied to insolvent partnerships as if they were unregistered companies, subject to certain conditions and modifications[2].

1 Sections 117 and 265 of the Insolvency Act 1986, as modified by the Order, Sch 6, para 1.
2 See s 117 (as modified) and footnote 4 to para **3.2.2**.

4.3.3 Applications to wind up insolvent partnership and to wind up or bankrupt insolvent members[1]

An application to the court by a member of an insolvent partnership under art 10 for the winding up of a partnership as an unregistered company and the winding up or bankruptcy, as the case may be, of all its members must be in a prescribed form[2].

Subject to what follows, a petition for the winding up of the partnership may only be presented by a member of the partnership on the grounds that the partnership is unable to pay its debts, and if:

(a) petitions are at the same time presented by that member for insolvency orders against every member of the partnership (including himself or itself); and

(b) each member is willing for an insolvency order to be made against him or it and the petition against him or it contains a statement to this effect[3].

If the court is satisfied, on application by any member of an insolvent partnership, that presentation of petitions against the partnership and every member of it would be impracticable, for example because of problems as to service because a partner has disappeared, the court may direct that the petitions be presented against the partnership and such member or members of it as are specified by the court[4].

The petitions:

(a) should all be presented to the same court and, except as the court otherwise permits or directs, on the same day; and
(b) (except in the case of a petition for the bankruptcy of an individual member) should be advertised[5].

Each petition presented under ss 124, 264 and 272 (as modified) must contain particulars of the other petitions being presented in relation to the partnership, identifying the partnership and members concerned[6]. The hearing of the petition against the partnership fixed by the court must be in advance of the hearing of the petitions against insolvent members[7].

On the day appointed for the hearing of the petition against the partnership, the petitioner must, before the commencement of the hearing, hand to the court a duly completed Notice to Court of Progress on Petitions Presented[8].

Any person against whom a winding-up or bankruptcy petition has been presented in relation to the insolvent partnership is entitled to appear and to be heard on any petition for the winding up of the partnership[9].

A petitioner under this section may at the hearing withdraw the petition if:

(a) subject to what follows he withdraws at the same time every other petition which he presented under this section;
(b) he gives notice to the court at least three days before the date appointed for the hearing of the relevant petition of his intention to withdraw the petition[10].

A petitioner under ss 124, 264 and 272 (as modified) may at the hearing withdraw the petition if:

(a) subject to what follows he withdraws at the same time every other petition which he presented under the relevant sections;
(b) he gave notice to the court at least three days before the date appointed for the hearing of the relevant petition of his intention to withdraw the petition[11].

A petitioner need not comply with the requirement to withdraw every other petition in the case of a petition against a member, if the court is satisfied on application made to it by the petitioner that, because of the difficulties in serving the petition or for any other reason, a continuance of that petition would be likely to prejudice or delay the proceedings on the petition which he has presented against the partnership or on any petition which he has presented against another insolvent member. This provision is doubtless intended amongst other things to safeguard against the possibility that one or more partners may have disappeared or gone abroad, since, were it not for such a provision, it might be impossible for proceedings to be effective.

1 Sections 124, 264 and 272 of the Insolvency Act 1986, as modified by the Order, Sch 6, para 2.
2 Ibid, s 124(1) (as modified). The prescribed forms are Form 11 (partnership), Form 12 (corporate member) and Form 13 (individual member).
3 Ibid, s 124(2) (as modified).
4 Ibid, s 124(3) (as modified).
5 Ibid, s 124(4) (as modified) and Form 8 in Sch 9.
6 Ibid, s 124(5) (as modified).
7 Ibid, s 124(6) (as modified).
8 Ibid, s 124(7) (as modified) and Form 9 in Sch 9.
9 Ibid, s 124(8) (as modified).
10 Ibid, s 124(9) (as modified).
11 Ibid, s 124(10) (as modified).

4.3.4 Powers of court on the hearing of petitions against insolvent partnership and members[1]

(a) *Powers of the court*
Subject to the provisions of s 125A of the Act (as inserted by Sch 6 to the Order), the powers of the court are identical to those which apply to a petition under art 8 of the Order (see para **3.3.8** above).

1 Sections 125 and 271 of the Insolvency Act 1986, as modified by the Order, Sch 6, para 3.

(b) *Hearing of petitions against members[1]*
The wording of s 125A of the Act (as inserted by Sch 6 to the Order), is identical to s 125A in Sch 4 (see para **3.3.8** above), but since art 10 covers only a petition brought by a member there is no provision corresponding to s 125A(8).

1 Section 125A of the Insolvency Act 1986, as inserted by the Order, Sch 6, para 3.

4.3.5 Winding up of unregistered company[1]
The provisions of s 221 of the Act (as modified by Sch 6 to the Order) mirror those in relation to a winding-up petition under art 7 discussed in para **3.2.2** above.

To the extent that they are applicable to the winding up of a company by the court in England and Wales on a member's petition, all the provisions of the Act and the Companies Acts in relation to winding up apply to the winding up of an insolvent partnership as an unregistered company[2]:

(a) with the exceptions[3] and additions mentioned in the modified subsections (5)–(8) of s 221; and
(b) with the modifications described in paras **3.3.3** to **3.3.29** above[4].

Unless the contrary intention appears, members of the partnership against whom insolvency orders are made under art 10 are not treated as contributories for the purposes of the Act[5].

The circumstances in which an insolvent partnership may be wound up as an unregistered company are that the partnership is unable to pay its debts[6].

Every petition for the winding up of an insolvent partnership under Part V of the Act has to be verified by a prescribed form of affidavit[7].

---

1 Section 221 of the Insolvency Act 1986, as modified by the Order, Sch 6, para 4.
2 Ibid, ss 221(1)–(4).
3 Ibid, s 221(5)(a) and (6) (as modified). The exceptions are ss 73(1), 74(2)(a)–(d) and (3), 75–78, 83, 124(2) and (3), 154, 202, 203, 205 and 250, all of which do not apply.
4 Ibid, s 221(5)(b) (as modified).
5 Ibid, s 221(7) (as modified). The reason members are not treated as contributories is that under these circumstances their assets are already available directly to creditors. Former partners are, it seems, to be treated as contributories and do not have the protection which a past member of a company would have had under s 74(2)(a)–(d) of the Act.
6 Ibid, s 221(8) (as modified).
7 Ibid, s 221(9) (as modified) and Form 2 in Sch 9 to the Order.

4.4 JOINT BANKRUPTCY PETITION PRESENTED BY INDIVIDUAL MEMBERS WITHOUT WINDING UP THE PARTNERSHIP AS AN UNREGISTERED COMPANY

4.4.1 *Presentation of joint bankruptcy petition*[1]

Subject to para **4.4.3** below, a joint bankruptcy petition may be presented to the court by virtue of art 11 of the Order by all the members of an insolvent partnership in their capacity as such, provided that all the members are individuals and none of them is a limited partner[2].

A petition may not be presented by the members of an insolvent partnership which is an authorised institution or former authorised institution within the meaning of the Banking Act 1987[3].

The petition must be in a prescribed form and must contain requests that the trustee should wind up the partnership business and administer the partnership property without the partnership being wound up as an unregistered company under Part V of the Act[4].

The petition must be accompanied by an affidavit made by the member who signs the petition, showing that all the members are individual members (and that none of them is a limited partner) and concur in the presentation of the petition, or contain a statement that all the members are individual members and be signed by all the members[5].

On presentation of the petition, the court may make orders for the bankruptcy of the members and the winding up of the partnership business and administration of its property[6].

---

1 Section 264 of the Insolvency Act 1986, as modified by the Order, Sch 7, para 2.
2 Ibid, s 264(1) (as modified).
3 Ibid, s 264(2) (as modified).
4 Ibid, s 264(3) (as modified) and Form 14 in Sch 9 to the Order.
5 Ibid, s 264(4) (as modified) and Form 15 in Sch 9 to the Order.
6 Ibid, s 264(5) (as modified) and Form 16 in Sch 9 to the Order.

4.4.2   Conditions to be satisfied in respect of members[1]

A joint bankruptcy petition can be presented to the High Court (other than to a district registry) under art 11 of the Order if the partnership has, or at any time had, a principal place of business in England and Wales or to a county court in England and Wales if the partnership has, or at any time had, a principal place of business within the insolvency district of that court[2]. There is the usual limitation that the business must have been carried on in England and Wales in the period of three years ending with the day on which the joint bankruptcy petition is presented[3].

1 Section 265 of the Insolvency Act 1986, as modified by the Order, Sch 7, para 3.
2 Ibid, s 265(1) (as modified).
3 Ibid, s 265(2) (as modified) and footnote 4 to para **3.2.2** above.

4.4.3   Other preliminary conditions[1]

If the court is satisfied, on application by any member of an insolvent partnership, that the presentation of the petition by all the members of the partnership would be impracticable, the court may direct that the petition be presented by such member or members as are specified by the court[2]. Once again, this provision is aimed at permitting a winding up where some partner has disappeared or will not respond to a request by the other members of the partnership to join in the presentation of the petition. It remains to be seen whether the court will construe the word 'impracticable' as allowing the court to allow presentation of the petition where, for example, one member of the partnership refuses to agree to the presentation of the petition.

A joint bankruptcy petition must not be withdrawn without the leave of the court[3]. The general powers of the court relating to bankruptcy petitions are extended to a joint bankruptcy petition[4].

1 Section 266 of the Insolvency Act 1986, as modified by the Order, Sch 7, para 4.
2 Ibid, s 266(1) (as modified).
3 Ibid, s 266(2) (as modified).
4 Ibid, s 266(3) (as modified).

4.4.4   Grounds for joint bankruptcy petition[1]

A joint bankruptcy petition may be presented to the court by the members of the partnership only on the grounds that the partnership is unable to pay its debts[2].

The petition must be accompanied by a statement of each member's affairs in a presented form[3] and by a statement of the affairs of the partnership in a presented form[4] sworn by one or more members of the partnership. The statements of affairs in both cases should contain particulars of the member's or, as the case may be, partnership's creditors, debts and other liabilities and of their assets and such other information as is required by the relevant form.

1 Section 272 of the Insolvency Act 1986, as modified by the Order, Sch 7, para 5.
2 Ibid.
3 Form 17 in Sch 9 to the Order.
4 Form 18 in Sch 9 to the Order.

4.4.5   Summary administration[1]

The court is required, if it appears to it appropriate to do so, to issue a certificate for the summary administration of any member's estate where it appears to the court:

(a) that the aggregate amount of the unsecured joint debts of the partnership and unsecured separate debts of the member concerned is less than the small bankruptcy level prescribed for the purposes of s 273 of the Act (as that section applies apart from the Order); and

(b) within the period of five years ending with the presentation of a joint bankruptcy petition, the member concerned has neither been adjudged bankrupt nor made a composition with his creditors in satisfaction of his debts or a scheme of arrangement of his affairs[2].

The court may at any time revoke a certificate if it appears to it that, on any grounds existing at the time the certificate was issued, the certificate ought not to have been issued[3].

1 Section 275 of the Insolvency Act 1986, as modified by the Order, Sch 7, para 6.
2 Ibid, s 275(1) and (2) (as modified).
3 Ibid, s 275(3) (as modified).

4.4.6   Definition of member's estate[1]

The estate of an individual member of the partnership is defined in s 283 of the Act (as modified by Sch 7) so as to make it clear that the exempted items listed in s 283(2) such as, for example, equipment which is not partnership property and which is necessary to the individual for use personally by him in his business, are not included in the definition of what constitutes partnership property.

1 Section 283 of the Insolvency Act 1986, as modified by the Order, Sch 7, para 7.

4.4.7   Restrictions on dispositions of property[1]

Where an individual member is adjudged bankrupt by virtue of art 10 of the Order, any disposition of property made by that member in the period to which s 284 of the Act (as modified by Sch 7) applies is void except to the extent that it is or was made with the consent of the court, or is or was subsequently ratified by the court. Although under s 284 of the Act a disposition of property is to be held void notwithstanding that the property is not or, as the case may be, would not be, comprised in the individual member's estate, nothing in s 284 affects any disposition made by a person of property held by him on trust for any other person other than a disposition made by an individual member of property held by him on trust for the partnership.

1 Section 284 of the Insolvency Act 1986, as modified by the Order, Sch 7, para 8.

4.4.8   Public examination of member[1]

Where orders have been made against the members of an insolvent partnership on a joint bankruptcy petition, the Official Receiver may, at any time before the discharge of any such member, apply to the court for the public examination of that member[2].

Unless the court otherwise orders, the Official Receiver must make an application if notice requiring him to do so is given to him, in accordance with the Rules, by one of the creditors of the member concerned with the concurrence of not less than one half in value of those creditors (including the creditor giving notice)[3].

On such an application, the court must direct that a public examination of the member is to be held on a day appointed by the court; the member must attend on that day and be publicly examined as to his affairs and dealings in property and as to those of the partnership[4].

The persons entitled to take part in the public examination questioning the member concerning these matters are:

(a) the Official Receiver;
(b) the trustee of the member's estate, if his appointment has taken effect;
(c) any person who has been appointed as special manager of the member's estate or business or of the partnership property or business;
(d) any creditor of the member who has tendered a proof in the bankruptcy[5].

On such an application the court may direct that the public examination of a member under this provision be combined with the public examination of any other person[6]. This enables all the public examinations of the partners to be held together where that is expedient. However, it is usually preferable that the public examination is held separately.

Failure to attend on such public examination without reasonable excuse renders the member concerned guilty of contempt of court and liable to be punished accordingly, in addition to any other punishment to which he might be subject[7].

---

1 Section 290 of the Insolvency Act 1986, as modified by the Order, Sch 7, para 9.
2 Ibid, s 290(1) (as modified).
3 Ibid, s 290(2) (as modified).
4 Ibid, s 290(3) (as modified).
5 Ibid, s 290(4) (as modified).
6 Ibid, s 290(5) (as modified).
7 Ibid, s 290(6) (as modified).

4.4.9 Power to appoint trustee[1]

(a) *General*

The power to appoint a person as both trustee of the estates of the members of the insolvent partnership against whom orders have been made on a joint bankruptcy petition and as trustee of the partnership is exercisable:

(a) by a combined general meeting of the creditors of the members and of the creditors of the partnership;
(b) under ss 295(2), 296(2) or 300(3) of the Act (as modified by Sch 7) by the Secretary of State[2].

If a combined general meeting of the creditors of the members and of the creditors of the partnership is held, problems may arise as to what claims should be admitted for voting purposes. It is suggested that creditors of the partnership should be regarded as being entitled to vote in that capacity but not to be allowed to vote in relation to claims arising out of partnership debts in the individual bankruptcies. More difficult is the position of claims of retired partners, partners who have acted as guarantors (for example in relation to mortgages of partnership property), and salaried partners who were given an indemnity by the partnership. Possibly the best course of action in relation to persons in this position is to view them as contingent creditors; but in view of the unlikelihood of there being any distribution to such a class (since this class will essentially be deferred to other creditors of the partnership), the right course of action may be to value the claims of this class of creditors for voting purposes at some kind of nominal figure such as £1.

Any appointee must at the time of his appointment be qualified to act as an insolvency practitioner both in relation to the partnership and to each of the members[3].

Any power to appoint a person as trustee includes a power to appoint two or more persons as joint trustees; but such an appointment must make provision as to the circumstances in which the trustees must act together and the circumstances in which one or more of them may act for the other[4].

The appointment of any person as trustee of the member's estate and of the partnership takes effect only if that person accepts the appointment in accordance with the Rules. Subject to this, the appointment of any person as trustee takes effect at the time specified in his certificate of appointment[5].

Section 292 (as modified) is without prejudice to the provisions of Chapter III of the Act under which the Official Receiver is, under certain circumstances, to be the trustee of the members' estates and of the partnership[6].

---

1 Section 292 of the Insolvency Act 1986, as modified by the Order, Sch 7, para 10.
2 Ibid, s 292(1) (as modified).
3 Ibid, s 292(2) (as modified).
4 Ibid, s 292(3) (as modified).
5 Ibid, s 292(4) (as modified).
6 Ibid, s 292(5) (as modified).

(b)   *Conflicts of interest*[1]

The new s 292A inserted into the Act by Sch 7 to the Order repeats verbatim the provisions of the new s 230A inserted by Sch 4 to the Order (see para **3.3.25** above) and allows the trustee of the members' estates and of the partnership to apply to the court for directions where he considers a conflict of interest exists. It gives the court a wide discretion including the power to appoint a co-trustee or trustees.

---

1 Section 292A of the Insolvency Act 1986, as inserted by the Order, Sch 7, para 10.

4.4.10 Summoning of meeting to appoint trustee[1]

The same modifications to ss 293 and 294 of the Act in relation to the summoning of a meeting to appoint a trustee apply as where a petition has been presented under art 8 of the Order (see para **3.3.11** above). In summary, where orders are made under art 11 the Official Receiver, by virtue of his office, becomes the trustee of the estates of the members and the trustee of the partnership and will continue in office until another person becomes trustee under the provisions of the Act as modified by the Order[2]. The Official Receiver has a 12-week period, beginning with the day on which the first order was made under art 11, in which to decide whether to call a meeting of creditors to appoint a trustee in his place and to call such a meeting if this is requested by creditors of not less than one-quarter in value of the creditors of any member against whom an insolvency order has been made or of the partnership's creditors[3].

1 Sections 293 and 294 of the Insolvency Act 1986, as modified by the Order, Sch 7, para 11.
2 Ibid, ss 293(1) and (2) (as modified).
3 Ibid, s 293(3) and (4) and see the detailed provisions in ss 293(5)–(8) (as modified).

4.4.11 Failure of meeting to appoint trustee[1]

Where a meeting of creditors summoned under s 293 of the Act (as modified) is held but no appointment of a person as trustee is made, it is the duty of the Official Receiver to decide whether to refer the need for an appointment to the Secretary of State[2]. On a reference made in pursuance of that decision, the Secretary of State shall either make an appointment or decline to make one[3].

If the Official Receiver decides not to refer the need for an appointment to the Secretary of State or, on such a reference the Secretary of State declines to make an appointment, the Official Receiver shall give notice of his decision or, as the case may be, of the Secretary of State's decision to the court[4].

1 Section 295 of the Insolvency Act 1986, as modified by the Order, Sch 7, para 12.
2 Ibid, s 295(1) (as modified)
3 Ibid, s 295(2) (as modified)
4 Ibid, s 295(3) (as modified)

4.4.12 Appointment of trustee by Secretary of State[1]

In summary, the Official Receiver is allowed to apply to the Secretary of State at any time when the Official Receiver is the trustee of the members' estates and of the partnership for the appointment of a person as trustee in place of the Official Receiver[2], s 296 being modified in the same way as where the petition has been presented under art 8 (see para **3.3.12** above). The Secretary of State has a discretion either to make the appointment or decline to make it[3]. If the appointment is made, various consequences follow[4].

1 Section 296 of the Insolvency Act 1986, as modified by the Order, Sch 7, para 13.
2 Ibid, s 296(1) (as modified).
3 Ibid, s 296(2) (as modified).
4 Ibid, ss 296(3)–(7) (as modified).

4.4.13 *Rules applicable to meetings of creditors*[1]

Where the court has made an order under art 11 of the Order then, subject to what follows, the Rules relating to the procedural requirements concerning meetings on the bankruptcy of an individual apply with necessary modifications to the holding of separate meetings for the creditors of each member and the holding of combined meetings of the creditors of the partnership and the creditors of the members[2].

Any combined meeting of creditors must be conducted as if the creditors of the members and of the partnership were a single set of creditors[3].

Where a combined meeting of creditors is held there will, once again, arise the problem of how to deal with claims of creditors who, prima facie, have claims for a partnership debt both against the partnership and against individual partners. There is a long-established rule against a double proof in respect of one debt for the protection of other creditors[4]. It is suggested that the approach should be the one advocated in para **4.4.9** above, namely that creditors of the partnership should not be regarded for this purpose as creditors also of the individual members in respect of a partnership debt. In addition, claims of retired partners, partners who have acted as guarantors of partnership obligations and salaried partners who have claims against the partnership under indemnities given to them, should all be regarded as contingent creditors of the partnership; but the value of their claims, for voting purposes at least, may well be nominal.

---

1 Section 297 of the Insolvency Act 1986, as modified by the Order, Sch 7, para 14.
2 Ibid, ss 297(1) and (2) (as modified).
3 Ibid, s 297(3) (as modified).
4 See *Re Oriental Commercial Bank, ex parte European Bank* (1871) 7 Ch App 99.

4.4.14 *Removal of trustee; vacation of office*[1]

The trustee of the estates of the members and of the partnership may be removed from office only by an order of the court[2] with the following exceptions:

(a) if the trustee was appointed by the Secretary of State, he may be removed by direction of the Secretary of State[3];

(b) the trustee (not being the Official Receiver) must vacate office if he ceases to be a person who is for the time being qualified to act as an insolvency practitioner in relation to any member or to the partnership[4];

(c) the trustee may, with the leave of the court (or, if appointed by the Secretary of State, with the leave of the court or the Secretary of State), resign his office by giving notice of his resignation to the court[5].

Subject to what follows any removal from or vacation of office relates to all offices held in the proceedings by virtue of art 11[6].

The trustee must vacate office on giving notice to the court that a final meeting had been held under s 331 (as modified) (final meeting of creditors of insolvent partnership or of members) and of the decision, if any, at that meeting[7].

The trustee shall vacate office as trustee of a member if the order made by virtue of art 11 in relation to that member is annulled[8].

---

1 Section 298 of the Insolvency Act 1986, as modified by the Order, Sch 7, para 15.
2 Ibid, s 298(1) (as modified).
3 Ibid, s 298(2) (as modified).
4 Ibid, s 298(3) (as modified).
5 Ibid, s 298(4) (as modified).
6 Ibid, s 298(5) (as modified).
7 Ibid, s 298(6) (as modified).
8 Ibid, s 298(7) (as modified).

4.4.15 *Release of trustee*[1]

The modifications made to s 299 of the Act by Sch 7 to the Order mirror the modifications which apply where a partnership is being wound up under the provisions of art 8 (see para **3.3.21** above).

Where the Official Receiver ceases to be the responsible insolvency practitioner because of the appointment of some other person in his stead following the nomination of a successor by a combined general meeting of creditors of the partnership and of any insolvent member or members or an appointment by the Secretary of State, the Official Receiver has his release with effect from the time at which he gives notice to the court that he has been replaced. In the case where the successor has been appointed by the court, the release takes effect at such time as the court may determine[2].

If the Official Receiver, while he is the responsible insolvency practitioner, gives notice to the Secretary of State that the winding up of the partnership or of the corporate member or the administration of the estate of an individual member is for practical purposes complete, the release of the Official Receiver as liquidator or trustee, as the case may be, takes effect from such time as the Secretary of State may determine[3].

A person other than the Official Receiver who has ceased to be the responsible insolvency practitioner has his release as described in Table 2 below.

TABLE 2

Reason for Ceasing to be the Responsible Insolvency Practitioner	Time of Release
(a) Death	When notice is given to the court in accordance with the Rules that that person has ceased to hold office[4]
(b) Removal from office by the court or by the Secretary of State, or who has vacated office under s 298(3) of the Act (as modified)	As the Secretary of State may, on an application by such person, determine[5]
(c) Resignation	As may be directed by the court or, if he was appointed by the Secretary of State, at such time as may be directed by the court or the Secretary of State may, on application by such person, determine[6]
(d) Vacation of office under s 298(6) of the Act (as modified)	(i) If the final meeting referred to in s 298(6) (as modified) has resolved against such person's release, at such time as the Secretary of State, may, on an application by such person determine; and (ii) if that meeting has not so resolved, at the time at which such person vacated office[7]

Where a bankruptcy order in respect of an individual member is annulled, the responsible insolvency practitioner at the time of the annulment has his release with effect from such time as the court may determine[8].

The effect of the release of the responsible insolvency practitioner or provisional liquidator (including in both cases the Official Receiver when so acting) is with effect from the time specified in s 299 (as modified) to discharge him from all liability. Such release applies both to acts or omissions in the winding up of the insolvent partnership or of any corporate member or the administration of the estate of an individual member, as the case may be, and otherwise in relation to his conduct. Nothing in the section prevents the exercise, in relation to a person who has had his release under the section, of the court's powers under s 304 (liability of trustee)[9].

---

1 Section 299 of the Insolvency Act 1986, as modified by the Order, Sch 7, para 16.
2 Ibid, s 299(1) (as modified).
3 Ibid, s 299(2) (as modified).
4 Ibid, s 299(3)(a) (as modified).
5 Ibid, s 299(3)(b) (as modified).
6 Ibid, s 299(3)(c) (as modified).
7 Ibid, s 299(3)(d) (as modified).
8 Ibid, s 299(4) (as modified).
9 Ibid, s 299(5) (as modified).

4.4.16 *Vacancy in office of trustee*[1]

Section 300 of the Act (as modified by Sch 7) applies where the appointment of any person as trustee of a member's estate and of the partnership fails to take effect or, such an appointment having taken effect, there is otherwise a vacancy in the office of trustee[2].

The Official Receiver may refer the need for an appointment to the Secretary of State and will be trustee until the vacancy is filled[3]. On such a reference, the Secretary of State must either make an appointment or decline to make one[4]. If he declines to make an appointment the Official Receiver will continue to be trustee, but without prejudice to his power to make a further reference[5].

References to a vacancy include a case where it is necessary, in relation to any property which is or may be comprised in members' estates, to revive the trusteeship of that estate after the holding of the final meeting summoned under s 331 (as modified) or the giving by the Official Receiver of notice under s 299(2) (as modified) of the Act[6].

1 Section 300 of the Insolvency Act 1986, as modified by the Order, Sch 7, para 17.
2 Ibid, s 300(1) (as modified).
3 Ibid, s 300(2) (as modified).
4 Ibid, s 300(3) (as modified).
5 Ibid, s 300(4) (as modified).
6 Ibid, s 300(5) (as modified).

4.4.17 *Creditors' committee*[1]

(a) *General*
Section 301 is modified by Sch 7 to the Order so as to provide that, subject to what follows, a combined general meeting of the creditors of the members and of the partnership, whether summoned under the preceding provisions of Chapter III of the Act or otherwise, may establish a committee (known as 'the creditors' committee') to exercise the functions conferred on it by or under the Act[2]. However, such a meeting will not establish a creditors' committee, or confer any functions on such a committee, at any time when the Official Receiver is the trustee, except in connection with an appointment made by that meeting of a person to be trustee instead of the Official Receiver[3].

1 Section 301 of the Insolvency Act 1986, as modified by the Order, Sch 7, para 18.
2 Ibid, s 301(1) (as modified).
3 Ibid, s 301(2) (as modified).

(b) *Functions and membership of creditors' committee.*
The new s 301A inserted into the Act by Sch 7 to the Order contains provisions identical to those applied to petitions under art 8 of the Order (see para **3.3.15** above).

A committee established under s 301 (as modified) will act as the liquidation committee for the partnership and for any corporate member against which an insolvency order has been made, and as the creditors' committee for any individual member against whom an insolvency order has been made. It will, as appropriate, exercise the functions conferred on liquidation and creditors' committees in winding up and bankruptcy by or under the Act[2]. The Rules relating to liquidation committees are to apply (with the necessary modifications and with exclusion of all references to contributories) to such a committee. There is no provision for representatives of the members to be appointed to a liquidation committee[3].

Where the responsible insolvency practitioner has been appointed in relation to a further member, the practitioner may appoint any creditor of that member (provided that he is duly qualified under the Rules to be a member of the committee) to be an additional member of any committee already established under s 301, provided that the creditor concerned consents to act[4]. The court may also at any time on application by a creditor of the partnership or of an insolvent member against whom an insolvency order has been made, appoint the applicant an additional member of the committee. Such appointments are permissible even if by virtue of such an appointment the maximum number of members of the committee specified in the Rules is exceeded[5].

---

1 Section 301A of the Insolvency Act 1986, as inserted by the Order, Sch 7, para 18.
2 Ibid, s 301A(1) (as inserted).
3 Ibid, s 301A(2) (as inserted).
4 Ibid, s 301A(3) (as inserted).
5 Ibid, s 301A(4) and (5) (as inserted). The current maximum number is five.

4.4.18 General functions and powers of trustees[1]

Section 305 of the Act (as modified by Sch 7) contains provisions identical to those applied to the appointment of a trustee following an order made on a contemporary petition in the circumstances envisaged by art 8 of the Order (see para **3.3.16** above). The functions of the responsible insolvency practitioner of an insolvent partnership and of its insolvent member or members against which an insolvency order has been made by virtue of art 10 are those which the Act provides are the functions of a liquidator of a registered company and of a trustee in bankruptcy. These functions are to secure the realisation of the assets and the distribution to the respective creditors and, if there is a surplus in the estate, distribution to the persons entitled to such surplus[2]. Subject to any provisions of the Act, the practitioner is entitled in the carrying out of functions and in the management of the property and assets to use his own discretion[3]. It is his duty (if he is not the Official Receiver) to furnish the Official Receiver with such information, and produce for the Official Receiver's inspection such books, papers and other records as the Official Receiver may reasonably require and to give him such other assistance as he may reasonably require for the purposes of carrying out his functions in relation to the winding up of the partnership and any corporate member or the bankruptcy of any individual member[4].

The modified section provides that the official name of the trustee in his capacity as trustee of a member shall be 'the trustee of the estate of ...., a bankrupt' (inserting the name of the member concerned)[5] and as trustee of the partnership shall be 'the trustee of ...., a partnership'[6]. In relation to the particular member, the trustee can be referred to as 'the trustee in bankruptcy' of the particular member[7].

1 Section 305 of the Insolvency Act 1986, as modified by the Order, Sch 7, para 19.
2 Ibid, s 305(1) (as modified).
3 Ibid, s 305(3) (as modified).
4 Ibid, s 305(4) (as modified).
5 Ibid, s 305(5) (as modified).
6 Ibid, s 305(6) (as modified).
7 Ibid, s 305(5) (as modified).

4.4.19   *Obligations to surrender control to trustee*[1]

When an order has been made under art 11 of the Order and a trustee has been appointed, any person who is or has been an officer of the partnership in question, or who is an executor or administrator of the estate of a deceased officer of the partnership, must deliver up to the trustee of the partnership possession of any partnership property which he holds for the purposes of the partnership[2].

Each member must deliver up to the trustee possession of any property, books, papers or other records of which he has possession or control and of which the trustee is required to take possession without prejudice to the general duties of the members as bankrupt under s 333 of the Act[3].

The duty to deliver up extends to the Official Receiver, a person who has ceased to be trustee of a member's estate, a person who has been the administrator of the partnership or supervisor of a voluntary arrangement approved in relation to the partnership or under Part I, and a person who has been the supervisor of an IVA approved in relation to a member under Part VIII[4].

This duty also extends to bankers or agents of the member or the partnership or to any other person who holds any property to the account of, or for, a member of the partnership, unless he is by law entitled to retain as against the member, the partnership or the trustee the property in question[5].

Failure without reasonable excuse to comply with the obligations under s 312 (as modified) renders the person concerned guilty of a contempt of court and liable to be punished accordingly, in addition to any other punishment to which he may be subject[6].

1 Section 312 of the Insolvency Act 1986, as modified by the Order, Sch 7, para 20.
2 Ibid, s 312(1) and (2) (as modified).
3 Ibid, s 312(3) (as modified).
4 Ibid, s 312(4) (as modified).
5 Ibid, s 312(5) (as modified).
6 Ibid, s 312(6) (as modified).

4.4.20   *Priority of expenses and debts*[1]

(a)   *Priority of expenses*

As regards the priority of expenses where a partnership is being wound up under art 11 of the Order, s 328 of the Act is modified to exactly the same effect as the modifications to s 175 in the case of a partnership being wound up under art 8 (see para **3.3.22** above).

Modified s 328 of the Act deals with the priority of expenses incurred by a responsible insolvency practitioner of an insolvent partnership and of any insolvent member of that partnership against whom an insolvency order has been made. The order of priority is as follows:

(a) the joint estate of the partnership is applicable in the first instance in payment of the joint expenses and the separate estate of each insolvent member is applicable in the first instance in payment of the separate expenses relating to that member[2];

(b) where the joint estate is insufficient for the payment in full of the joint expenses, the unpaid balance must be apportioned equally between the separate estates of the insolvent members against whom insolvency orders have been made and shall form part of the expenses to be paid out of those estates[3];

(c) where any separate estate of an insolvent member is insufficient for the payment in full of the separate expenses to be paid out of that estate, the unpaid balance must form part of the expenses to be paid out of the joint estate[4];

(d) where, after transfer of any unpaid balance in accordance with (b) and (c) above, any estate is insufficient for the payment in full of the expenses to be paid out of that estate, the balance then remaining unpaid must be apportioned equally between the other estates[5];

(e) where, after an apportionment under (d) above, one or more estates are insufficient for the payment in full of the expenses to be paid out of those estates, the total of the unpaid balances must continue to be apportioned equally between the other estates until provision is made for the payment in full of the expenses or there is no estate available for the payment of the balance finally remaining unpaid, in which case it abates in equal proportions between all the estates[6].

In Appendix 1, some examples are set out of how these principles operate in practice.

Without prejudice to the above provisions, the responsible insolvency practitioner may, with the sanction of any creditors' committee established under s 301 of the Act (as modified) or with the leave of the court obtained on application:

(a) pay out of the joint estate as part of the expenses to be paid out of that estate, any expenses incurred for any separate estate of an insolvent member; or

(b) pay out of any separate estate of an insolvent member any part of the expenses incurred for the joint estate which affects that separate estate.[7]

The net effect of these provisions is to make sure, as far as possible, that when there is a deficiency, the expenses incurred in the joint estate and in the separate estate rank pari passu so that any deficiency is made up from the other estate or estates. Creditors of the separate estates could in certain situations be much worse off than under the law that existed prior to the Order. For example, where there is a substantial deficiency in paying the expenses of the administration of the joint estate, creditors of the separate estate may find some or all of the separate estates of the individual partners have to go towards satisfying that deficiency.

---

1 Section 328 of the Insolvency Act 1986, as modified by the Order, Sch 7, para 21.
2 Ibid, s 328(2) (as modified).
3 Ibid, s 328(3) (as modified).
4 Ibid, s 328(4) (as modified).
5 Ibid, s 328(5) (as modified).
6 Ibid, s 328(6) (as modified).
7 Ibid, s 328(7) (as modified).

(b)   *Priority of debts in joint estate*[1]

The provisions concerning priority of debts in the joint estate introduced by the new s 328A inserted into the Act by Sch 7 to the Order mirror exactly provisions modifying s 175 in the case of a petition brought under art 8 of the Order (see para **3.3.22** above).

New s 328A deals with the priority of debts in (as opposed to expenses of) the joint estate and is expressed to be subject, in the case of the liability of the estate of a deceased member, to the provisions of s 9 of the Partnership Act which provides that:

> 'Every partner in the firm is liable jointly with the other partners, and in Scotland severally also, for all debts and obligations of the firm incurred while he was a partner and after his death, his estate is also separately liable in a due course of administration for such debts and obligations, so far as they remain unsatisfied but subject in England or Ireland to the prior payment of his separate debts.'

After payment of expenses the joint debts of the partnership shall be paid out of its joint estate in the following order of priority:

(a)   the preferential debts;
(b)   the debts which are neither preferential debts nor postponed debts[2];
(c)   interest under s 328D on the joint debts (other than postponed debts[2]);
(d)   postponed debts[2];
(e)   interest under s 328D on the postponed debts[3].

In the event of a surplus, the responsible insolvency practitioner must adjust the rights among the members of the partnership as contributories and is required to distribute any surplus to the members according to their respective rights and interests in the surplus[4].

The preferential debts and the debts which are neither preferential nor postponed rank equally between themselves, and in each case if the joint estate is insufficient for meeting them, they abate in equal proportions between themselves[5]. Where the joint estate is insufficient for the payment of the joint debts as regards preferential debts and debts which are neither preferential nor postponed, the responsible insolvency practitioner must aggregate the value of those debts to the extent that they have not been satisfied or are not capable of being satisfied. The aggregate amount then ranks as a claim against the separate estate against each member of the partnership against whom an insolvency order has been made which:

(a) shall be a debt provable by the responsible insolvency practitioner in each such estate; and

(b) shall rank equally with the debts of the member referred to in s 328B(1) (b)[6].

It is to be noted therefore that the debt of a creditor of a partnership which cannot be satisfied out of the partnership estate now ranks as a debt ranking equally with the debts of the member as regards the separate estate. But such a debt is provable by the responsible insolvency practitioner and not by the creditor himself[7]. As has already been noted, art 10 applies only when the winding up of the insolvent partnership takes place concurrently with petitions presented against one or more members. Accordingly, it would seem that if two members of the partnership were to be made bankrupt and, subsequently, the partnership were to be wound up, the liquidator of the partnership would not be entitled to claim pari passu with the creditors of the individual member as there is no corresponding s 328A under art 9. However, as discussed in relation to art 14 (see para **5.3**) it may be that the court has the power to apply the provisions of Sch 2 to this situation also.

Section 328A contains further provisions for what is to happen where the joint estate is sufficient for the payment of the preferential debts and the debts which are neither preferential nor postponed, but is insufficient either to pay interest under s 328D on the joint debts (other than postponed debts), or to pay the postponed debts, or to pay the interest under s 328D on the postponed debts[8]. The deficiency is to be claimed from the other estates.

Where the responsible insolvency practitioner receives any distribution from the separate estate of a member in respect of interest on the joint debts or the postponed debts or interest on the postponed debts, that distribution shall become part of the joint estate and shall be distributed in accordance with a prescribed order of priority[9].

---

1 Section 328A of the Insolvency Act 1986, as inserted by the Order, Sch 7, para 21.
2 Ibid, s 329.
3 Ibid, s 328A(2) (as inserted).
4 Ibid, s 328A(3) (as inserted).
5 Ibid, s 328A(4) (as inserted).
6 Ibid, s 328A(5) (as inserted).
7 Ibid, s 328A(5)(a) (as inserted).
8 Ibid, s 328A(6)–(8) (as inserted).
9 Ibid, s 328A(9) (as inserted).

(c) *Priority of debts in separate estate*[1]

The provisions of the new s 328B inserted into the Act by Sch 7 to the Order mirror the modifications made to s 175 in the case of a petition presented under art 8 of the Order (see para **3.3.22** above).

The separate estate of each member of the partnership against whom an insolvency order has been made shall be applicable, after payment of expenses, in accordance with payment of the separate debts of that member in the following order of priority:

(a)   the preferential debts;
(b)   the debts which are neither preferential debts nor postponed debts[2] (including any debts referred to in s 328A(5)(a));
(c)   interest under s 328D on the separate debts and under s 328A(6);
(d)   the postponed debts of the member[2] (including any debt referred to in s 328A(7)(a)); and
(e)   interest under s 328D on the postponed debts of the member[2] and under s 328A(8)[3].

The debts referred to in (a) and (b) above rank equally between themselves; in each case, if the estate is insufficient to meet the debts, they abate in equal proportions between themselves[4].

Where the responsible insolvency practitioner receives any distribution from the joint estate or from the separate estate of another member of the partnership against whom an insolvency order has been made, that distribution becomes part of the separate estate and must be distributed in accordance with the order of priority set out above[5].

1   Section 328B of the Insolvency Act 1986, as inserted by the Order, Sch 7, para 21.
2   Ibid, s 328.
3   Ibid, s 328B(1) (as inserted).
4   Ibid, s 328B(2) (as inserted).
5   Ibid, s 328B(3) (as inserted).

(d)   *Provisions generally applicable in distribution of joint and separate estates*[1]
The provisions of the new s 328C inserted into the Act by Sch 7 to the Order mirror the modifications made to s 175 in the case of a petition presented under art 8 of the Order (see para **3.3.22** above).

It is provided that distinct accounts should be kept for the joint estate partnership and of the separate estate of each member of the partnership against whom an insolvency order has been made[2].

No member of the partnership may prove for a joint or separate debt in competition with the joint creditors, unless the debt has arisen:

(a)   as a result of fraud; or
(b)   in the ordinary course of business carried on separately from the partnership business[3].

By virtue of this provision, unless the obligation arises in the circumstances allowed for under the two exceptions, any rights which partners may have against each other for breaches of a partnership agreement will be deferred to claims of other creditors. As regards the position of a retired partner in relation to an indemnity which may have been given to him by the continuing partners of the partnership which subsequently becomes insolvent, see the discussion in para **2.11.10** above.

For the purposes of establishing the value of a debt provable in the separate estate where there is a deficiency in the joint estate under the above provisions because the joint estate is insufficient for the payment of the postponed joint debts, the value may be estimated by the responsible insolvency practitioner[4]. The trustee is allowed to estimate the value of any bankruptcy debt which, by reason of its being subject to any contingency or contingencies or for any other reason, does not bear a certain value and, where he so makes an estimate, the amount provable in the bankruptcy is the amount of the estimate. Such an estimate is assumed to be capable of being challenged under s 303 (general control of trustee by court).

Interest under s 328D on preferential debts ranks equally with interest on debts which are neither preferential nor postponed[5] debts[6].

The provisions of ss 328A and 328D are without prejudice to any provision of the Act or of any other enactment concerning the ranking between themselves of postponed debts and interest thereon, but in the absence of any such provision they rank equally inter se[7].

If any two or more members of an insolvent partnership constitute a separate partnership the creditors of such separate partnership are deemed to be a separate set of creditors and subject to the same statutory provisions as the separate creditors of any member of the insolvent partnership[8].

Where any surplus remains out of the administration of the estate of a separate partnership, the surplus will be distributed to the members or, where applicable, to the separate estates of the members of that partnership according to their respective rights and interest in it[9].

Special provision is made so as to preclude the Official Receiver, Secretary of State and/or a responsible insolvency practitioner from claiming remuneration or fees in relation to the transfer of surpluses from one estate to another, or to the distribution from a separate estate to the joint estate or to a distribution from the estate of a separate partnership to the separate estates of the members of that partnership[10].

---

1 Section 328C of the Insolvency Act 1986, as inserted by the Order, Sch 7, para 21.
2 Ibid, s 328C(1) (as inserted).
3 Ibid, s 328C(2) (as inserted).
4 Ibid, s 328C(3) (as inserted).
5 Ibid, s 329.
6 Ibid, s 328C(4) (as inserted).
7 Ibid, s 328C(5) (as inserted).
8 Ibid, s 328C(6) (as inserted).
9 Ibid, s 328C(7) (as inserted).
10 Ibid, s 328C(8) (as inserted).

(e)	*Interest on debts*[1]

The new s 328D inserted into the Act by Sch 7 to the Order mirrors the modifications made to s 189 in the case of a petition presented under art 8 of the Order (see para **3.3.23** above).

Provision is made for interest to be paid in the order of priority laid down by ss 328A and 328D on any debt proved in the winding up of an insolvent partnership or the winding up or bankruptcy of an insolvent member, including so much of any such debt as represents interest on the remainder[2]. Interest runs from the date of the winding-up order against the partnership or corporate member or from the date on which the bankruptcy order is made against any individual member[3]. The rate of interest is the same as provided for in the Act[4].

1 Section 328D of the Insolvency Act 1986, as inserted by the Order, Sch 7, para 21.
2 Ibid, s 328D(1) (as inserted).
3 Ibid, s 328D(2) (as inserted).
4 Ibid, s 328D(3) (as inserted).

4.4.21 Final meeting[1]

The provisions of s 331 of the Act (as modified by Sch 7) mirror the modifications made to the same section in the case of a petition presented under art 8 (see para **3.3.17** above).

If it appears to the responsible insolvency practitioner (where such practitioner is not the Official Receiver) that the winding up of the partnership or of any corporate member or the administration of any individual member's estate is, for practical purposes, complete, he is required to summon a final general meeting of the creditors of the partnership or the insolvent member or members, as the case may be, or a combined final general meeting of the creditors of the partnership and of the insolvent member or members, which:

(a) will, as appropriate, receive the practitioner's report for the winding up of the insolvent partnership or of any corporate member, or the administration of the estate of an individual member; and

(b) will determine whether the practitioner should have his release[2].

The practitioner may, if he thinks fit, at the same time as giving the notice summoning the final general meeting, give notice of any final distribution of the partnership property or the property of the insolvent member or members. If summoned for an earlier date, the general meeting must be adjourned (and, if necessary, further adjourned) until a date on which he is able to report to the meeting that the winding up of the partnership or of any corporate member, or the administration of an individual member's estate is, for practical purposes, complete[3]. It is his duty to retain sufficient sums from the partnership property and the property of any such insolvent member to cover the expenses of summoning and holding any meeting required[4].

1 Section 331 of the Insolvency Act 1986, as modified by the Order, Sch 7, para 22.
2 Ibid, s 331(2) (as modified).
3 Ibid, s 331(3) (as modified).
4 Ibid, s 331(4) (as modified).

4.4.22 The 'relevant date'[1]

When an order has been made in respect of an insolvent partnership under art 11 of the Order, references in Sch 6 to the Order to 'the relevant date' (being the date which determines the existence and the amount of a preferential debt) are to the date on which the order under art 11 was made.

1 Section 387 of the Insolvency Act 1986, as modified by the Order, Sch 7, para 23.

Chapter 5

PROVISIONS APPLYING IN INSOLVENCY PROCEEDINGS

5.1 WINDING UP OF AN UNREGISTERED COMPANY WHICH IS A MEMBER OF AN INSOLVENT PARTNERSHIP[1]

Where an insolvent partnership or other body which may be wound up under Part V of the Act as an unregistered company is itself a member of an insolvent partnership 'being so wound up', arts 8 and 10 of the Order apply in relation to the latter insolvent partnership as though the former body were a corporate member of that partnership. It will be remembered that art 8 deals with the winding up of an insolvent partnership as an unregistered company on a creditor's petition where concurrent petitions have been presented against one or more members, and art 10 deals with the winding up of an insolvent partnership as an unregistered company on a member's petition where concurrent petitions have been presented against all members. Presumably therefore, the expression in art 12 'being so wound up' refers to a situation where a petition has been presented against the member but no order has yet been made thereon, as otherwise the requirements for concurrent presentation under arts 8 and 10 could not be satisfied.

---

1 Insolvent Partnerships Order 1994, art 12.

5.2 DEPOSIT ON PETITIONS[1]

Section 414 of the Act provides for the mechanism of making fees orders in company insolvency proceedings and s 415 in individual insolvency proceedings in England and Wales. Under orders made under these sections, it is provided that a petitioner must deposit a sum on presentation of a winding-up or bankruptcy petition. Article 13 of the Order provides that where concurrent petitions are presented by virtue of either art 8 or art 10 of the Order, the only fee to be deposited in respect of the petition is that payable on a petition for winding up the partnership and that should be treated as a deposit in respect of the member or members and production of evidence as to the sum deposited on presentation of the petition for winding up the partnership will suffice for the filing in court of an insolvency petition against an insolvent member.

---

1 Insolvent Partnerships Order 1994, art 13.

5.3 SUPPLEMENTAL POWERS OF COURT

5.3.1 *Power of the court to apply the Order with any necessary modifications*[1]
It is clearly foreseeable that occasions may arise where, after a winding-up petition has been presented to the court against any person (including an insolvent partnership or other body which may be wound up under Part V of

the Act as an unregistered company), it may be discovered that the person in question is a member of an insolvent partnership. Under the provisions of s 168(5A) of the Act, the court is permitted in this situation to make an order as to the future conduct of the insolvency proceedings and any such order may apply any provisions of the Order with any necessary modifications. The power given to the court is clearly far reaching and it remains to be seen how precisely the courts will approach problems which arise out of the ignorance of the petitioner that the subject of the petition, whether an individual or a company, is a member of an insolvent partnership.

It may well be that the court is empowered under art 14 of the Order to apply the provisions of Sch 4 to the Order notwithstanding the fact that the winding-up petition and the bankruptcy petition were not presented concurrently. The major difference between the provisions of Sch 3 and Sch 4 is the provision concerning the treatment of creditors of the insolvent partnership, whereby they are to rank pari passu for any deficiency in the separate estates of the individual members. It seems quite illogical that such creditors should be in a preferential position where the petitions are presented concurrently, but disadvantaged where the petitions are presented, say, two or three months apart; but if this was the intention, it is odd that the article does not make the position clear.

---

1 Section 168(5A) of the Insolvency Act 1986, as inserted by art 14 of the Order.

5.3.2 Application for and provisions in an order under s 168(5A)[1]

The power of the court to make an order as to the future conduct of the proceedings under s 168(5A) of the Act can be made or given on the application of the Official Receiver, any responsible insolvency practitioner, the trustee of the partnership or any other interested person. It also may include provisions as to the administration of the joint estate of the partnership and, in particular, how it and the separate estate of any member are to be administered.

---

1 Section 168(5B) of the Insolvency Act 1986, as inserted by art 14 of the Order.

5.3.3 Where an order is made under the Financial Services Act 1986 or the Banking Act 1987[1]

Where the court makes an order under s 72(1)(a) of the Financial Services Act 1986 or s 92(1)(a) of the Banking Act 1987 for the winding up of an insolvent partnership, the court is given the power to make an order as to the future conduct of the winding-up proceedings and such order may apply any provisions of the Order with any necessary modifications. The point has already been made that if a winding-up order is made only on the just and equitable grounds, then the provisions of the Order do not apply at all. On the assumption that an Order has been made on the basis that the partnership is insolvent then art 7 will apply, since it is not possible under the legislation mentioned above to present a petition against a person in his capacity as a member of a partnership except under art 7. Once again, the point discussed in para **5.3.1** arises, namely whether the court is entitled under this provision to apply the provisions of Sch 4 so as to ensure that the creditors of the partnership rank pari passu with the creditors of the individual member where there is a deficiency in the partnership estate.

1 Section 168(5C) of the Insolvency Act 1986, as inserted by art 14 of the Order.

5.3.4 The general control of the trustee by the court [1]

Article 14(2) of the Order supplements s 303 of the Act in relation to individual insolvency in precisely the same manner as art 14(1) supplements s 168 in relation to winding up of unregistered companies and allows the court to make orders applying any provisions of the Order with any necessary modifications. The new subsection (2B) provides that where a bankruptcy petition has been presented against more than one individual and at some time after the petition has been presented (whether under the Order or not), the attention of the court is then drawn to the fact that the person in question is a member of an insolvent partnership, the court may give such directions for consolidating the proceedings, or any of them, as it thinks just.

1 Sections 303(2A)–(2C) of the Insolvency Act 1986, as inserted by art 14 of the Order.

5.4 MEANING OF 'ACT AS INSOLVENCY PRACTITIONER'[1]

Section 388 of the Act is headed 'Meaning of "act as insolvency practitioner"'. The basis of the statutory requirement that every insolvency practitioner should be professionally qualified is the protection of creditors. Section 389 of the Act makes it an offence for a person to act as an insolvency practitioner in relation to a specific company or an individual at a time when he is not qualified to do so. Article 15 of the Order makes the necessary amendments to s 388(2) so as to define when a person acts as an insolvency practitioner in relation to an insolvent partnership. Those circumstances are described as when acting:

(a) as the liquidator, provisional liquidator or administrator of the partnership; or
(b) as trustee of the partnership under art 11 of the Order; or
(c) as the supervisor of a voluntary arrangement approved in relation to the partnership under Part I of the Act.

1 Insolvent Partnerships Order 1994, art 15.

Chapter 6

INDIVIDUAL VOLUNTARY ARRANGEMENTS FOR PARTNERS

6.1 INTRODUCTION

When a firm is facing the prospect of insolvency, the partners will wish to consider whether there is any possibility of escape. The Order has introduced two new insolvency regimes for partnerships, the partnership administration order[1] and the partnership voluntary arrangement ('PVA')[2].

An individual partner can, however, still propose an individual voluntary arrangement ('IVA') under Part VIII of the Act either as an individual acting alone or as one of a group of partners acting together. In the latter case, there will be a series of individual IVAs (often referred to as 'interlocking IVAs') the terms of which will substantially mirror each other, although there may need to be specific provision in the case of a particular partner who has particular separate assets or liabilities[3]. Similarly, a corporate partner can still propose a company voluntary arrangement ('CVA') under Part I of the Act[4].

Once an insolvency order[5] has been made against a partnership *and* an insolvent member, any reference to creditors of the member in Part I or Part VIII of the Act is treated as including a reference to creditors of the partnership[6].

---

1 See Chapter 8.
2 See Chapter 7.
3 For example, partners who are lessees on a lease which does not bind the partnership, and partners who have given personal guarantees to partnership creditors, will have separate estate liabilities in respect of those creditors, who may not feature as creditors of other separate estates.
4 This right is expressly preserved by art 5(2) of the Order.
5 Ie a winding-up order in respect of an insolvent corporate member, or a bankruptcy order in respect of an individual member, by art 2(1) of the Order.
6 Article 5(1) of the Order. If the provision was intended to clarify the treatment of debts for which the debtor is jointly liable, then it was not, strictly speaking, necessary. The joint debt of a partner is 'a debt owed by him' for the purposes of s 267(1) of the Act and for the IVA regime: see the opinion of Sir Thomas Bingham MR in *Re Cupit (A Bankrupt)* (unreported) Court of Appeal Transcript, 7 April 1993 and that of Nourse LJ in *Schooler v Customs and Excise Commissioners* [1995] 2 BCLC 610 (a case under the 1986 Order).

6.2 THE CHOICE OF PVA OR IVA

For larger partnerships, or those where the affairs of the firm and the partners are complex, the PVA is likely to be attractive as the cheapest route. On the other hand, where the partnership is relatively small[1], interlocking IVAs may still be the appropriate solution.

It should be borne in mind that while it appears to be the case that a PVA will protect an individual partner's estate from the claims of *partnership* creditors, it will not protect that estate from any separate estate creditor[2]. Furthermore, because the PVA regime is modelled on company rather than individual voluntary arrangements, there is no interim order protection prior to the PVA coming into force.

Similarly, it is not yet clear whether a partnership administration order will protect the individual partners from litigation and bankruptcy petitions by joint estate creditors, and it is at least arguable that it does not protect in the latter instance[3].

If only for safety's sake, some partners will still therefore be forced to contemplate IVA proposals in addition to making a PVA proposal, solely to obtain the protection of an interim order. Notwithstanding the additional complexity and cost, it is thought that prudent advisers will generally apply a 'belt-and-braces' approach[4].

Where agreement cannot be reached on a PVA or on interlocking IVAs, or where a single partner with some assets has been 'picked off' by a creditor who obtains a judgment or serves a statutory demand for an undisputed debt, a partner may have to consider whether to propose his or its own voluntary arrangement, regardless of the course adopted by the other partners. Generally, however, it will be thought tactically preferable and economically advantageous to deal with all the partners together.

---

1 Practical experience suggests that once the partnership exceeds five members, the complexities begin to become overwhelming.
2 Who would not need to be notified of the meeting, and so would not become bound by the result.
3 There has been at least one instance of a deputy registrar making bankruptcy orders against two partners where the partnership was in administration and the petitions were based on an (undisputed) partnership debt, but the debtors were unrepresented and the decision was made without full argument.
4 Corporate partners, of course, cannot enjoy the same protection, although there may be instances where appropriate protection can be obtained through an administration of the company which is a partner.

6.3   BASIC PROCEDURE[1]

When the practitioner learns at an initial interview that the debtor in question is a member of a partnership, questions will inevitably be raised. If it is at all possible, the insolvency practitioner will want to see any partnership agreement and accounts as early as possible and find out what steps, if any, are being taken by the other partners.

The general philosophy of interlocking IVAs, just as for a PVA, implies that all the partners will instruct the same insolvency practitioner(s) and that they will be able to agree on a common approach to their creditors.

It is important when dealing with a number of partners to be clear from the outset that there is a specific retainer from each individual who may be proposing an IVA[2]. Conflicts may arise, in which case the individuals concerned must be offered the opportunity to seek separate independent advice.

Consideration should be given at an early stage to any retired partners and any others who may be liable if the partnership is wound up[3]. If interlocking IVAs are to be proposed, the net should normally be thrown as wide as possible.

1 It is assumed that the reader is generally familiar with voluntary arrangement procedures, and with Part I and Part VIII of the Act and the relevant Rules. For more detailed information concerning individual voluntary arrangements, see Lawson *Individual Voluntary Arrangements*, 2nd Edn (Jordans, 1996).

2 Under rr 1.2 and 5.2 of the Insolvency Rules 1986, it is the debtor who prepares the proposal for a voluntary arrangement, but in practice almost all proposals are drafted by the nominee under a contract to advise the debtor.

3 It is important to investigate the position of anyone who may have been held out as a partner, and the status of any 'junior' or 'salaried' partners.

6.4 BASIC APPROACH TO JOINT AND SEPARATE ESTATES

An IVA proposal obviously needs to be commercially attractive to creditors, and the proposer will want to minimise the possibility of a challenge in the courts by a creditor on the grounds that the proposal is 'unfairly prejudicial'[1].

For both reasons, it is suggested that the paradigm model to be adopted in drafting an IVA proposal is the procedure under art 8 of the Order, which deals with the situation when concurrent petitions are presented against both the firm and the individual members. In such a case, a liquidator of the firm proves for any shortfall in each separate estate, ranking equally with the separate estate creditors. Another implication of the art 8 regime is that the assets of all those who would be 'members' (ie including any associate or salaried partners who would be liable to a single creditor under s 14 of the Partnership Act) would be available to partnership creditors.

1 Ie, under s 6(1)(a) of the Insolvency Act 1986, as modified by Sch 1 to the Order.

6.5 SEPARATE ESTATE CREDITORS

It is quite often the case that liabilities of individual partners which have arisen in the context of the partnership will, nonetheless, fall to be treated as separate estate claims when IVAs are being drawn up. Obvious examples are the claim of a landlord against those partners named in the lease or who have given individual covenants, and claims against individual partners who have given personal guarantees in support of the partnership's borrowings.

6.6 CLAIMS BETWEEN PARTNERS

Applying the art 8 regime, no partner would be allowed to compete with the joint creditors unless the debt had arisen through fraud or in the ordinary course of a business apart from the partnership business[1]. It is suggested that this approach[2] should similarly be used in constructing an IVA proposal. This means that the claims of partners with lease or guarantee liabilities to be indemnified by co-partners would also have to be treated as subordinated.

Where there is a shortfall on the joint estate and the partnership is insolvent overall, it will generally be possible to ignore the claims of partners entirely.

1 See s 175C(2) of the Insolvency Act 1986, as inserted by Sch 4 to the Order.
2 Which accords with the common-law position outside the Order.

6.7   JURISDICTION

There must be a bona fide intention on the part of the partner to make a proposal to his creditors[1]; it would be an abuse of the process of the court to present an application solely to gain the protection of an interim order.

An application for an interim order must be made to the court in which the individual would be entitled to present his own bankruptcy petition[2]. If the partner has resided or carried on business in the London insolvency district for the greater part of the previous six months (or for a longer period in those six months than anywhere else), the appropriate court will be the High Court[3]. A debtor who is not resident in England and Wales (such as, perhaps, a partner who is manning an overseas office) also applies in the High Court[4]. Otherwise, an application is made in the relevant county court, which will usually be the county court for the insolvency district where the individual partner's principal place of business is situated[5].

Where a partnership has a number of different offices, it would obviously be convenient to make all the applications for interim orders in the same court; but, unfortunately, it seems that that will not often be possible[6]. When bankruptcy proceedings are pending in a county court, a High Court judge can order them to be transferred into the High Court[7] upon the application of a person appearing to the court to have an interest in the proceedings[8], so even if the process has to be initiated by applications in various locations, it should sometimes be possible to bring them all together under one roof for administrative convenience.

1 See s 253(1) of the Insolvency Act 1986.
2 Insolvency Rules 1986, r 5.5A(1).
3 Ibid, r 6.40(1)(a).
4 Ibid, r 6.40(1)(b).
5 See r 6.40(2).
6 Without a change in the Rules.
7 Insolvency Rules 1986, r 7.11(4).
8 Ibid, r 7.11(5)(c).

6.8   THE PROTECTION OF AN INTERIM ORDER

Once an application for an interim order has been made, a court may stay any action, execution or other legal process against the debtor or his property[1].

When an interim order is in force, no bankruptcy petition may be presented or proceeded with against the individual concerned; proceedings, execution or other legal process may only be commenced or continued against the individual or his property with the leave of the court[2].

The precise scope of the statutory stay under an interim order in the context of a partnership is at present uncertain. It obviously protects the separate estate of the partner concerned, but does it prevent legal process against the property in the joint estate? As a matter of strict analysis, it should, because it is part of the individual partner's property, albeit part which he holds jointly with others. It is also thought that the statutory stay would be wide enough to preclude a winding-up petition against the partnership pending a decision on the IVA proposal[3].

Conversely, there is no connection between one partner and another partner's separate estate, so it appears that the interim order obtained by partner A would not prevent execution of a judgment (or the presentation of a winding-up or bankruptcy petition) against the separate property of partner B, who might be an unsuccessful applicant or someone who has not applied for an interim order.

---

1 Insolvency Act 1986, s 254(1).
2 Ibid, s 252(2).
3 See the opinion of Sir Thomes Bingham MR in *Re Cupit* (unreported) Court of Appeal transcript, 7 April 1993; there was no formal decision in that case.

6.9 THE PROPOSAL

Each proposal must provide a short explanation of why an IVA is desirable and give reasons why creditors might be expected to agree.

The proposal must contain the following details[1]:

(a) the following matters, so far as within the debtor's immediate knowledge:
    (i) his assets, with an estimate of their respective values;
    (ii) the extent, if any, to which the assets are charged in favour of creditors;
    (iii) the extent, if any, to which particular assets are to be excluded from the voluntary arrangement;
(b) particulars of any property, other than assets of the debtor himself, which is proposed to be included in the arrangement, the source of such property and the terms on which it is to be made available for inclusion;
(c) the nature and amount of the debtor's liabilities (so far as within his immediate knowledge), the manner in which they are proposed to be met, modified, postponed or otherwise dealt with by means of the arrangement and (in particular):
    (i) how it is proposed to deal with preferential creditors[2] and creditors who are, or claim to be, secured;
    (ii) how associates of the creditor (being creditors of his) are proposed to be treated under the arrangement[3]; and
    (iii) whether there are circumstances which would give rise to the possibility of claims in respect of transactions at an undervalue[4], preferences[5] or extortionate credit transactions[6];
    and, where such circumstances are present, whether, and if so how, it is proposed under the voluntary arrangement to make provision for wholly or partly indemnifying the insolvent estate in respect of such claims;

(d) whether any, and if so what, guarantees have been given of the debtor's debts by other persons, specifying which, if any, of the guarantors are associates of his;

(e) the proposed duration of the voluntary arrangement;

(f) the proposed dates of distributions to creditors, with estimates of their amounts;

(g) the amount proposed to be paid to the nominee (as such) by way of remuneration and expenses;

(h) the manner in which it is proposed that the supervisor of the arrangement should be remunerated and his expenses defrayed;

(j) whether, for the purposes of the arrangement, any guarantees are to be offered by any persons other than the debtor and, if so, whether any security is to be given or sought;

(k) the manner in which funds held for the purposes of the arrangement are to be banked, invested or otherwise dealt with pending distribution to creditors;

(l) the manner in which funds held for the purpose of payment to creditors, and not so paid on the termination of the arrangement, are to be dealt with;

(m) the manner in which the partnership business is proposed to be conducted during the course of the arrangement[7];

(n) details of any further credit facilities which it is intended to arrange for the debtor (including for the partnership, and how the debts so arising are to be paid);

(o) the functions which are to be undertaken by the supervisor of the arrangement;

(p) the name, address and qualification of the person proposed as supervisor of the voluntary arrangement, and confirmation that he, so far as the debtor is aware, is qualified to act as an insolvency practitioner in relation to him.

In addition, the proposal which forms part of a set of *interlocking* proposals will need to deal in detail with the interrelationship of the separate individual's proposals, and the extent to which they are mutually interdependent.

It should be borne in mind that the debtor commits an offence, punishable by imprisonment or a fine or both, if he makes any false representation or commits any other fraud for the purpose of obtaining the approval of his creditors to a proposal for a voluntary arrangement[8].

An application to the court for an interim order must be accompanied by an affidavit setting out the following[9]:

(a) the reasons for making the application;

(b) particulars of any execution or other legal process which, to the debtor's knowledge, has been commenced against him;

(c) that he is able to petition for his own bankruptcy[10];

(d) that no previous application for an interim order has been made by or in respect of the debtor in the period of 12 months ending with the date of the affidavit; and

(e) that the nominee under the proposal (naming him) is a person who is qualified to act as an insolvency practitioner in relation to the debtor, and is willing to act in relation to the proposal.

It is likely that any set of interlocking IVAs will need to be customised to fit the particular circumstances. Careful consideration will need to be given, in particular, to the question of whether each IVA is conditional upon all the other IVAs being accepted by the creditors. It may be necessary to 'ring-fence' the IVA of a partner who has particularly problematic private affairs.

---

1 Required under Insolvency Rules 1986, r 5.3(2).
2 Defined in s 258(7) of the Insolvency Act 1986.
3 It is suggested that it will generally be necessary to provide that any claim in respect of an indemnity arising out of the partnership is to be treated as a subordinated claim and only paid a dividend once all costs and expenses have been met and all other creditors have been paid out in full.
4 Under s 339 of the Insolvency Act 1986.
5 Ibid, s 340.
6 Ibid, s 343.
7 In anything beyond the simplest arrangements, it would be sensible to include a business plan and cash-flow forecast.
8 Insolvency Rules 1986, r 5.30.
9 Specified in Insolvency Rules 1986, r 5.5(1).
10 Or, where relevant, that he is an undischarged bankrupt.

6.10   THE NOMINEE

As with any IVA, the nominee reports to the court on the proposal[1]. It will usually be desirable for the same insolvency practitioner(s) to act as nominee and, subsequently, as supervisor in respect of an interlocking set of proposals. However, it must once again be borne in mind that there may be conflicts between the individual partners.

---

1 It should be noted that the court has a discretion whether or not to grant an interim order under s 255(2) of the Act. Experience until recently has been that many registrars and district judges give proposals only the most cursory of regulatory supervision on the basis that it is preferable for creditors to be given an opportunity to consider even the weakest proposals. However, there has recently been some suggestion, in London at least, that registrars intend to take a more interventionist approach and have been prepared to express a view on 'boiler plate' paragraphs in standard form IVA proposals. In particular, it has been suggested that there will be less tolerance for clauses which purport to oust the jurisdiction of the court and clauses which provide wide exclusion of liability for the insolvency practitioner involved and his firm.

6.11   THE CONCERTINA ORDER

Most insolvency practitioners will prefer to submit their report at the first hearing for an application for an interim order which will permit the court to make a 'concertina' order which combines:

(i) a 14-day interim order; with

(ii) an order extending the interim order to a date seven weeks after the date of the proposed meeting to consider the proposal, directing that meeting to be summoned for a date about three weeks after that hearing[1].

Wherever this is possible, it will of course save time and costs. However, where proposals for interlocking IVAs are being linked to a PVA under the Order, or in other circumstances where the affairs of the partners and the partnership are particularly complex, it may simply not be possible to prepare all the necessary paperwork for the initial application. In addition, it would probably be preferable to attend, in order to explain a complex set of proposals to the registrar or district judge. In such circumstances the two-stage procedure will be appropriate[2].

---

1 A concertina order may be made without attendance where:

  (1) the papers are in order;
  (2) the nominee's signed consent to act includes notice of a waiver of the application or a consent by the nominee to the making of an interim order without attendance;
  (3) the nominee's report has been delivered to the court;
  (4) the nominee's report complies with s 256(1) of the Insolvency Act 1986 and r 5.10(2) and (3) of the Insolvency Rules 1986;
  (5) the nominee's report proposes a date for the meeting not less than 14 and no more than 28 days after the date of the hearing.

However, it will not normally be appropriate to grant an order without attendance where a bankruptcy petition is pending or where a bankruptcy order has been made. See the *Practice Direction (bankruptcy: individual voluntary arrangements: orders without attendance) (No 1 of 1991)* [1992] 1 WLR 120.

2 Ie, where the application for the interim order is made followed by the submission by the nominee of his report to the court two days before the expiry of the interim order.

6.12   THE CREDITORS

6.12.1   Notices to creditors

A nominee must summon to the IVA meeting every creditor of the debtor whose name and address he is aware of[1]. The notices must be sent out at least 14 clear days before the day fixed for the meeting[2]. It appears that the courts will treat these rules strictly; if a creditor does not receive notice in accordance with the Insolvency Rules, he will not become entitled to vote[3] and so will not be bound by an IVA[4] even if it is passed by a majority at the meeting.

As the whole point of the IVA procedure is that there is a statutory mechanism for binding-in dissentient creditors, it is obviously vital to ensure that all creditors receive notice, but particular classes of creditors require careful consideration.

---

1 Section 257(2) of the Insolvency Act 1986.
2 Insolvency Rules 1986, r 5.13(2) and see *Mytre Investments v Reynolds (No 2)* [1996] BPIR 464.
3 Under Insolvency Rules, r 5.17.
4 Under s 260(2)(b) of the Insolvency Act 1986.

6.12.2   Partnership creditors

Each creditor of the partnership should be sent notice of, and admitted to vote in, every individual partner's respective IVA.

6.12.3   Separate estate creditors

Each creditor of a particular partner's separate estate should be sent notice of, and admitted to vote in, that partner's particular IVA.

6.12.4   Unascertained creditors

Where the amount of a creditor's claim is not settled at the date of the meeting, because it is *unliquidated* (as in a claim for damages) or because it is *unascertained* (as in a claim for future rent or for some other contingent liability), the creditor will only become allowed to vote under the Rules[1] where the chairman agrees to put an estimated minimum value upon the vote for the purpose of voting. No actual agreement with the creditor is required; the chairman merely needs to express his willingness to put, and to put, an estimated minimum value on the debt[2]. However, the chairman must make a bona fide attempt to value the creditor's claim[3]. A contingent claim may be valued by multiplying the amount likely to be claimed by a percentage which reflects a reasonable estimate of the probability of the contingency occurring.

A creditor for an unascertained amount who stays away from the IVA meeting will none the less be bound by the result[4], even where no agreed minimum value has been put on his vote, because r 5.17(3) only applies to persons present or represented at the meeting.

---

1   Under Insolvency Rules 1986, r 5.17(3).
2   *Doorbar v Alltime Securities* [1995] BCC 1149, CA.
3   *Re Cranley Mansions* [1994] 1 WLR 1610; *Doorbar v Alltime Securities* [1994] BCC 994.
4   *Beverley Group v McClue* [1995] BCC 751.

6.12.5   Secured creditors

An IVA proposal may not interfere with the rights of a secured creditor to enforce his security except with that creditor's agreement.

6.12.6   Landlords and other continuing liabilities

Where a partnership has more than four partners and there is a formal lease for more than three years, the landlord of the property occupied by the firm will generally only have separate estate claims against the four individuals whose names appear on the lease and any other partners who may have given personal covenants or guarantees. The landlord may have claims for unpaid rent and service charges which have already accrued, and will have prospective claims for future rent and dilapidations. Claims for future rent will be defeasible[1], in that if the lease is forfeited they will not arise, and therefore they would need to be valued by the chairman of an IVA meeting on the basis of the probability of that happening[2].

Although an IVA may bind a landlord as a creditor, it will not affect his proprietary rights, such as the right to forfeit a lease[3]. However, the basis of interlocking IVAs will often be that regular payments will be made to creditors from the firm's continued trading, and the firm will need somewhere to trade from. In such a case, there may need to be a provision that, as long as the firm continues to occupy the premises in question, the rent will be paid in full, but if the premises are vacated at a later stage, the landlord will be entitled to rank for a dividend. Such a provision has been approved by the court[4], and the fact that there was a differentiation between the landlord and other creditors with prospective future claims was not regarded as unfairly prejudicial. There may need to be provision for other creditors to be paid in full as an expense of the firm continuing.

1 Ie they may not happen.
2 *Doorbar v Alltime Securities* [1995] BCC 1149, CA.
3 *Re Mohammed Naeem (A Bankrupt) (No 18 of 1988)* [1990] 1 WLR 48; *Doorbar v Alltime Securities* (above).
4 *Re Cancol Ltd* [1996] 1 All ER 37.

6.13   THE MEETING

Technically, there needs to be a separate meeting for each separate IVA, which must be called to start between 10.00am and 4.00pm on a business day[1] at a venue which has regard to the convenience of the creditors[2].

There have been a number of successful interlocking IVAs since 1986, and the practice of at least some insolvency practitioners has been to call all the meetings for the same place at the same time and to run them effectively as one large meeting.

Where the major creditors of the partnership have the predominant votes in each IVA, having one large meeting may appear to be the most convenient way to deal with the practicalities. However, it should be remembered that each IVA is distinct, embodying a composition or scheme of arrangement of that individual's affairs. The chairman of each meeting is obliged to report the votes of that meeting separately to the court[3], and it appears likely to be the case that there will be some different separate estate creditors in each. Failure to account properly for the votes in each separate meeting would be a material irregularity.

1 Insolvency Rules 1986, r 5.14(2).
2 Ibid, r 5.14(1).
3 Under s 259(1) of the Insolvency Act 1986 and r 5.22 of the Insolvency Rules 1986.

6.14   VOTING AT THE MEETING

In order to be passed at an IVA meeting, a resolution must satisfy two tests:

(i)   a resolution for an IVA or for a modification to a proposal must achieve a majority in excess of 75 per cent[1] of those present in person or by proxy and voting; any other resolution must achieve a majority in excess of 50 per cent[2];

(ii) any resolution must also achieve the support of at least 50 per cent in value of the creditors[3], leaving out for this purpose the votes of associates of the debtor[4]. It should be borne in mind that a person is an associate of any person with whom he is in partnership[5], and of any person whom he employs or by whom he is employed[6].

1 Insolvency Rules 1986, r 5.18(1).
2 Ibid, r 5.18(2).
3 Ibid, r 5.18(4).
4 Ibid, r 5.18(4)(c).
5 Insolvency Act 1986, s 435(3).
6 Ibid, s 435(4).

6.15 THE EFFECT OF APPROVAL

Where a meeting of creditors summoned under s 257 of the Act has approved a voluntary arrangement, it takes effect as if it had been made by the debtor at the meeting[1], and binds every person who had notice of the meeting in accordance with the Rules and was entitled to vote at it[2]. The interim order remains in force for 28 days after the result of the meeting[3], which is the time within which any challenge must be brought[4].

1 Insolvency Act 1986, s 260(2)(a).
2 Ibid, s 260(2)(b).
3 Ibid, s 260(4).
4 Ibid, s 262(3); this is subject to the court's jurisdiction to extend time under s 376 of the Act.

6.16 THE POSSIBILITY OF CHALLENGE

It is possible for the proposer of an IVA, a creditor who was entitled to vote at the meeting or the nominee of the proposal to challenge the decision of an IVA meeting[1]. Challenges may be brought on the grounds either:

(a) that the voluntary arrangement unfairly prejudices a creditor of the debtor[2]; or
(b) that there has been some material irregularity at or in relation to the meeting[3].

In the context of an IVA, 'prejudice' is taken to refer to the rights of the creditor being adversely affected, and 'unfair' to refer to such treatment being different to the treatment of other creditors[4]. An 'irregularity' is a departure from the Rules[5] in connection with the proposal or the meeting, which will be 'material' if it can be shown that the irregularity in question would or might have affected the outcome of the meeting[6].

There is also a right of appeal under the Rules against a decision by the chairman of an IVA meeting on a voting question[7], in which case the chairman is not personally liable for any costs[8].

1 Insolvency Act 1986, s 262(2); a challenge may also be brought by the Official Receiver or a trustee in bankruptcy when the proposer is an undischarged bankrupt.
2 Ibid, 262(1)(a).
3 Ibid, s 262(1)(b).
4 In *Re Primlaks (UK) Ltd (No 2)* [1990] BCLC 234, a CVA proposed to pay trade creditors ahead of loan or bank creditors. Harman J apparently accepted the principle that different classes of creditor could be treated differently, and said that in his view it was not unfairly prejudicial as long as other creditors of the same 'type' were treated the same. In *Re Cancol Ltd* [1996]

1 All ER 37, Knox J said it was not unfairly prejudicial to distinguish in a CVA between creditors for future debts (such as a landlord) whose assets were to be used to earn the profits envisaged in the voluntary arrangement and who were to be paid in full, and other creditors for future debts whose assets were not to be so used, who would merely receive a dividend.
5 *Re a Debtor (No 222 of 1990), ex parte Bank of Ireland* [1992] BCLC 137.
6 Examples of material irregularities would include:
    (a) misconduct by the chairman at the meeting: *Ex parte Bank of Ireland* (above);
    (b) provision of false or misleading information in a proposal for a voluntary arrangement: *Re a Debtor (No 87 of 1993)(No 2)* [1996] BPIR 64;
    (c) refusal to recognise that a landlord's right of distress constitutes him a secured creditor: *Peck v Craighead* [1995] 1 BCLC 337;
    (d) failure to put a proper value on an unascertained creditor's vote: *Re Cranley Mansions* [1994] 1 WLR 1610.
7 Insolvency Rules 1986, rr 5.17(7), 5.18(7).
8 Ibid, r 5.17(9). If an application combines an appeal under the Rules with a complaint of material irregularity, the court may order the chairman to bear part of the costs (*Ex parte Bank of Ireland (No 2)* [1992] BCLC 233), but where the chairman has acted in complete good faith and there has been no culpable conduct on his part, the court will not, in its discretion, do so (*Re Cranley Mansions* (above)).

6.17 THE TERMS OF A VOLUNTARY ARRANGEMENT

Once a voluntary arrangement has taken effect, the nominee under the proposal (who in the real world is of course usually the insolvency practitioner who drafted the proposal, or another member of that practitioner's firm) becomes the supervisor of the voluntary arrangement[1], subject to the control of the court upon the application of anyone dissatisfied by his acts, omissions or decisions[2], and empowered to make his own application to the court for directions if he needs to[3].

However, it should be borne in mind that the voluntary arrangement regime provides only for light regulation by the courts. A supervisor is not an officer of the court, and he does not have statutory powers for the day-to-day management of an IVA. The supervisor's powers will only be those conferred under the arrangement, and it is therefore important to ensure in drafting a proposal that adequate provision is made. One elegant way to do this is to provide, where appropriate, that the supervisor is to have all the powers which a liquidator of the partnership would have if the partnership were to be wound up under art 8 of the Order.

1 By s 263(2) of the Insolvency Act 1986.
2 Ibid, s 263(3).
3 Ibid, s 263(4).

6.18 PROPERTY IN A VOLUNTARY ARRANGEMENT

A voluntary arrangement transforms the rights of creditors to sue the debtor for his debts into respective rights to prove for a dividend according to the IVA's scheme for distribution.

An arrangement may provide for assets to vest in the supervisor at the outset, in which case the debtor must do everything that is required for putting the supervisor into possession of those assets[1]. Interlocking IVAs by partners will often be put forward on the premise that by avoiding bankruptcy the partnership will be able to generate profits, and there will therefore be provision for periodic payments to be received. In addition, it is usual to provide for windfalls to be paid over to the supervisor[2].

Subject to the precise drafting of a particular arrangement, assets held by the supervisor of a voluntary arrangement will be held on trust for the creditors bound by that arrangement and according to its terms[3]. The effect of that trust is that those creditors remain entitled to those assets notwithstanding a bankruptcy order on a petition brought by a creditor not bound by an IVA[4]. Conversely, where a default by the subject of the IVA leads to a bankruptcy order[5], the terms of the voluntary arrangement cease to apply, the creditors are released, and any assets become part of the bankrupt's estate[6].

In the context of an insolvent partnership, it would appear that the same principles would apply where a subsequent creditor wound up the firm after the partners had entered interlocking IVAs. A more complicated question would arise if there was a default by one partner leading to his bankruptcy on a petition for default. Any joint estate property (or relevant contributions of assets) would have vested in the supervisor for the benefit of partnership creditors. The drafting of interlocking IVAs should make that clear and cater for such an eventuality. There may be instances where the role of particular partners is crucial, so that their non-participation will undermine the entire interlocking IVA structure, but in many cases it is thought that the creditors will want the other IVAs to continue.

---

1 Insolvency Rules 1986, r 5.21.
2 What used to be called the 'football pools' clause, and is nowadays referred to as the 'lottery clause'.
3 Cf *Re Leisure Study Group Ltd* [1994] 2 BCLC 65.
4 *In re Bradley-Hole (A Bankrupt)* [1995] 1 WLR 1097.
5 Eg following a petition by the supervisor or an arrangement creditor under s 264(1)(c) of the Insolvency Act 1986.
6 *Davis v Martin-Sklan, Re Hussein* [1995] BCC 1122. In *Doorbar v Alltime Securities* [1995] BCC 1149, Peter Gibson LJ proceeded on the basis that the law was as stated in this paragraph, but noted that *Re McKeen* and *Re Bradley-Hole* might need reconsideration on a future occasion.

6.19   THE PARTNERSHIP IN THE CONTEXT OF INTERLOCKING IVAs

Partners may propose to their creditors a 'bullet' solution, in which debts are released in return for a single agreed dividend or the proceeds of realisation of specified assets[1]. Such a scheme of interlocking IVAs will be of relatively short duration, and complex technical questions about the constitution of the partnership are unlikely to arise once the 'members' and their assets have been identified.

However, where it is intended that the firm will continue for some period with individual partners in IVAs in order to generate periodic payments, it is necessary to address the interrelationship between the voluntary arrangements and the partnership. Where there is no formal partnership deed regulating the relationship between the partners, it is suggested that it would be sensible to put one in place, and it may be necessary to incorporate aspects of it in the proposals, either by reference or, preferably, directly.

1 This type of voluntary arrangement, which is quite common where CVAs are concerned, is comparatively rare in the context of IVAs.

6.20 PUBLICITY

One of the reasons for professionals to arrange their businesses as partnerships has been the greater privacy that resulted from the lack of a requirement to file public accounts[1], and many partners are accustomed to being extremely discreet about their own and their clients' affairs.

This predisposition usually becomes even more intense if a firm gets into financial difficulties. The viability of a professional partnership will inevitably depend on retaining the goodwill of clients who can be expected to go elsewhere if they learn that their advisers may be insolvent, which can compound the difficulty of effecting a rescue.

Unfortunately, the interlocking IVA procedure is quite a public process. There will generally need to be a relatively high level of disclosure to creditors, to persuade them that they would not do better by winding up the partnership and bankrupting the partners. There may need to be protracted negotiations with key creditors, during which time details may leak out.

The chairman of a meeting called to consider a proposal for a voluntary arrangement must file a report in court within four days of the meeting[2], and immediately after that he must notify everyone who was sent notice of the meeting of the result[3], and he must register with the Secretary of State brief details of the voluntary arrangement, including the debtor's name and address and the court where the chairman's report is filed[4]. The Register of Individual Voluntary Arrangements is open to inspection by the public[5], and it is understood that credit reference agencies incorporate information from it in their reports.

Partners will often prefer to try to deal with their major creditors outside of a voluntary arrangement process, and where there are only two or three creditors involved (for example, the bank and the landlord) this might well be successful in many cases, with the added benefit of confidentiality.

1 However, there have been recent moves by some of the largest accountancy firms to publish accounts as a precursor to seeking incorporation off-shore in order to obtain the protection of limited liability.
2 Insolvency Rules 1986, r 5.22(3).
3 Ibid, r 5.22(4).
4 Ibid, r 5.24(1).
5 Ibid, r 5.23(2).

Chapter 7

PARTNERSHIP VOLUNTARY ARRANGEMENTS

7.1 INTRODUCTION

The voluntary arrangement of a partnership is one of the innovations introduced by the Order to enable a single vehicle to deal with joint estate creditors and joint assets. A partnership voluntary arrangement ('PVA') is modelled on the company voluntary arrangement ('CVA') regime in Part I of the Act, rather than the individual voluntary arrangement ('IVA') regime in Part VIII. While it is true that many provisions of the two regimes and of the Rules are identical[1], there are key differences between company and individual procedures. In particular, the present lack of an interim order under the CVA (and, therefore, the PVA) model may well have a significant bearing on how often PVAs are used in practice. Moreover, it may not be possible to deal effectively within a PVA with separate estate claims arising out of the partnership's affairs[2].

1 For example, Insolvency Rules 1986, rr 1.17 and 5.17 on voting at meetings.
2 Such as the claim of a landlord against an individual partner named on a lease, or a claim
  against an individual partner as a guarantor of the firm's or another partner's liabilities.

7.2 MODIFICATION AND APPLICATION OF THE ACT AND THE RULES

Article 4 of the Order applies Part I of the Act (as modified by Sch 1 to the Order) to an insolvent partnership. In addition, the Order[1] applies the following further provisions of the Act to an insolvent partnership insofar as they would apply to a CVA:

(a) s 233 in Part IV of the Act, which enables the supervisor of a voluntary arrangement to obtain supplies of gas, water, electricity and other utilities from a public supplier;
(b) Part VII (with the exception of s 250), which provides for definitions of certain relevant terms. These must, however, be read with art 3 of the Order, which provides that references to companies in provisions of the Act applied by the Order are to be read as references to insolvent partnerships[2] and expressions appropriate to companies are to be construed as references to the 'corresponding' persons, documents, officers or organs appropriate to a partnership;
(c) Part XII, which deals with preferential debts[3] and the 'relevant date'[4]. For purposes of a PVA, preferential debts are those set out in Sch 6 to the Act[5], and the relevant date for determining the existence and amount of a preferential debt will be the date of the making of a partnership administration order or, where no such order has been made, the date of the approval of the PVA[6];

(d) Part XIII, which defines 'act as insolvency practitioner' and deals with insolvency practitioners and their qualifications;

(e) ss 411, 413, 414 and 419 in Part XV, which provide for the making of company insolvency rules[7], for the establishment of the Insolvency Rules Committee[8], for the payment of fees and the making of relevant subordinate legislation[9] and for the making of regulations relating to insolvency practitioners, etc[10];

(f) Parts XVI–XIX including provisions against debt avoidance and criminal offences. Of particular significance is the definition of 'associate' which is set out in s 435 of the Act, which includes the provision that partners are associates[11], as are husbands, wives or relatives[12], and employers and employees[13].

---

1 Insolvent Partnerships Order 1994, art 4(2), (3).
2 Ibid, art 3(2).
3 Insolvency Act 1986, s 386.
4 Ibid, s 387.
5 Ie money due to the Inland Revenue for income tax deducted at source; VAT, car tax, betting and gaming duties, beer duty, lottery duty; social security and pension scheme contributions; remuneration of employees; levies on coal and steel production.
6 Insolvency Act 1986, s 387(2).
7 Ibid, s 411, contained in the Rules; rr 1.1–1.30 will apply to a PVA.
8 Ibid, s 413.
9 Ibid, s 414.
10 The Insolvency Practitioners Regulations 1990, SI 1990/439, as amended by the Insolvency Practitioners (Amendment) Regulations 1993, SI 1993/221, therefore apply in the context of a PVA.
11 Insolvency Act 1986, s 435(3).
12 Ibid, s 435(2); the term 'relative' in this context includes: brother, sister, uncle, aunt, nephew, niece, lineal ancestor, lineal descendant, half-blood, step- and adoptive relationships, illegitimate children (s 435(8)); the husband or wife of a relative is an associate (s 435(2)); the husband, wife or relative of a person's partner is an associate (s 435(3)); a reference to husband or wife includes a reference to a former husband or wife (s 435(8)).
13 Ibid, s 435(4).

7.3 PARTNERSHIPS TO WHICH THE PVA PROCEDURE APPLIES

The Order, and thus the PVA procedure, applies to any partnership which the courts in England and Wales have jurisdiction to wind up[1]; generally speaking, that means any insolvent partnership which has carried on business in England and Wales within the previous three years[2], and which either has, or at any time has had, a principal place of business in England and Wales[3].

A partnership which has a principal place of business in Scotland may not be wound up under the Order unless it had a principal place of business in England and Wales within the period of one year ending on the day on which a winding-up petition is presented[4].

A partnership which has a principal place of business in Northern Ireland may not be wound up under the Order unless it had a principal place of business in England and Wales within the period of three years ending on the day on which a winding-up petition is presented[5].

The Order also applies to a partnership whose principal place of business is outside England and Wales, so long as it has, or at any time has had, a place of business in England and Wales where the business in the course of which the debt (or part of a debt) which forms the basis of a winding-up petition arose.

It is not clear whether actual presentation of a petition is necessary to found jurisdiction in the case of a partnership which does not have its principal place of business in England and Wales. The phrase 'a principal place of business' in this context appears to envisage that a partnership may have more than one, and many professional partnerships do have a number of substantial offices in different countries.

The phrase 'carry on' a business has generated a substantial body of case-law, but has yet to be defined by the court in this context. However, the well-established general principle appears to be that an individual (and, therefore, a partnership) continues to carry on a business until all the debts are paid and all other obligations which have arisen (such as liability for tax) have been performed[6].

---

1 Insolvent Partnerships Order 1994, art 1(2)(a).
2 See s 221(2) of the Insolvency Act 1986, as modified by Schs 3, 4, 5, 6 to the Order.
3 Section 221(1) of the Act, as modified by Schs 3, 4, 5, 6 to the Order.
4 Section 221(3)(a) of the Act, as modified by Schs 3, 4, 5, 6 to the Order.
5 Section 221(3)(b) of the Act, as modified by Schs 3, 4, 5, 6 to the Order.
6 *Re Dagnall* [1896] 2 QB 407; *Re Worsley* 17 TLR 122; *Theophile v Solicitor-General* [1950] AC 186; *Bird v IRC* [1962] 1 WLR 686; *Re a Debtor (No 784 of 1991)* [1992] Ch 554.

7.4 WHO CAN PRESENT A PVA PROPOSAL?

A PVA proposal is one which provides for some person ('the nominee') to act in relation to a voluntary arrangement (a composition in satisfaction of the debts of the partnership or a scheme of arrangement of its affairs) either as trustee or otherwise for the purpose of supervising its implementation. As with IVAs and CVAs, the nominee must be a person who is qualified to act as an insolvency practitioner in relation to the insolvent partnership[1].

Where a partnership administration order is in force, a proposal may be presented by the administrator of the partnership[2].

Where the partnership is being wound up as an unregistered company (ie under arts 7, 8, 9 or 10 of the Order), a proposal may be presented by the liquidator of the partnership[3].

Where the individual members of the partnership have presented a joint bankruptcy petition under art 11 of the Order, a proposal may be presented by the trustee of the partnership.

Where no administration order is in force, the partnership is not being wound up and the partners have not presented a joint bankruptcy petition, a proposal may be presented by the members of the partnership.

1 Section 1(2) of the Insolvency Act 1986, as modified by Sch 1 to the Order.
2 Section 1(3)(a) of the Insolvency Act 1986, as modified by Sch 1 to the Order.
3 Section 1(3)(b) of the Insolvency Act 1986, as modified by Sch 1 to the Order.

7.5 AUTHORITY FOR PRESENTATION

It is unlikely that a court would regard partners as having authority to present a PVA proposal without there having been a relevant resolution passed by the partnership[1]. Once a resolution has been passed, if the internal requirements of the partnership for any necessary majority have been satisfied, it is likely that a court would take that as sufficient authorisation for a sub-group of one or more partners to instruct professionals and present a PVA proposal[2].

Because until recently a PVA was not possible, it is unlikely that there will be any provision in the relevant partnership deed specifying the necessary majority vote for partners to authorise the making of a PVA proposal. That being so, it is likely that the default provision in the Partnership Act will apply, requiring the consent of all existing partners to a change in the nature of the partnership business[3].

One difficulty which may arise is that the definition of 'member' for the purposes of the Order is a wide one, including anyone who is liable as a partner within s 14 of the Partnership Act; ie a non-partner who has been held out as a partner to a creditor who has, in reliance upon that holding out extended credit to the firm[4]. The consequences of being held to be a 'member' may be dramatic, because in the context of an insolvent partnership it appears that all the assets of the member will be available to all partnership creditors, whereas while the partnership is solvent only the creditor who actually relied would have a claim[5]. It follows that anyone who thinks that he might be able to defend a claim that he was held out as a partner within s 14 of the Partnership Act (and thereby incurred liability rendering him a 'member') should not take any step which would appear to concede the point. Where a partnership has a number of 'salaried partners' who might be 'members', it therefore may not be possible to obtain their consent. However, as the Partnership Act only requires actual partners to consent, it is thought that that would be sufficient in practice[6].

Insolvency practitioners who are approached by individual partners who are contemplating a PVA or seeking general advice in the context of the partnership being insolvent will need to raise at a very early stage the questions of authority and internal decision-making. This is not only because these questions will be directly relevant to whether a PVA proposal would attract sufficient support of the members to be viable, but also because a partner only has authority to bind the firm and his partners for carrying on in the usual way business of the kind carried on by his firm[7]. Quite simply, the partner may not have the authority to enter into a contract for the professional services of the insolvency practitioner on his firm's behalf!

1 Cf *Re Instrumentation Electrical Services Ltd* [1988] BCLC 550.
2 Cf *Re Equitycorp International plc* [1989] BCLC 597.
3 Partnership Act 1890, s 24(8).
4 See para **2.11.3** above.

5 And whereas in a solvent partnership the partner liable under s 14 of the Partnership Act 1890 may have an effective right of indemnity against the true partners, in an insolvent partnership that claim appears to be subordinated behind the creditors and likely to be worthless.

6 But note that this point has yet to be decided.

7 See Partnership Act 1890, s 5.

7.6 INSTRUCTING THE INSOLVENCY PRACTITIONER

According to the Rules, the partners must prepare a proposal for the intended nominee on which he will be able to make a report to the court[1]. In reality, there will usually be a contract between the firm and the insolvency practitioner's firm to advise on the possibility of an IVA. It is important to establish clearly at the outset exactly who is instructing the insolvency practitioner, and to identify any conflicts of interest which may arise.

1 Insolvency Rules 1986, r 1.2. In the context of a CVA, the proposal is made by the directors. Many partnerships require all significant management decisions to be taken by a meeting of partners and, in such a case, it appears that the proposal would have to be put forward by all the partners. Even where large partnerships have an executive committee to deal with day-to-day administration, it would be rare to find that they had been delegated authority to take so fundamental a step as the presentation of a PVA proposal. It is therefore thought that it will normally be the case that it will be all the partners who will put forward a PVA proposal, although day-to-day liaison with the nominee will frequently be dealt with by just one or two partners.

Given the requirements of good faith between partners, and the risks if a proposal turns out not to have the support of the partners, it would be preferable even where the matter is to be dealt with by a sub-group of partners for there first to have been a full meeting of the partnership to approve this course. Such a meeting must, of course, be put in a position to make a properly informed decision.

7.7 CONTENTS OF THE PROPOSAL

Under r 1.3, the proposal must provide a short explanation of why, in the partners' opinion, a PVA is desirable, and why the partnership's creditors may be expected to concur with such an arrangement. This will usually be because the creditors will prospectively do better out of the PVA than if the partnership is wound up.

A number of other matters must be stated or dealt with in the proposal[1]:

(a) so far as within the partners' knowledge:
  (i) the assets of the partnership, with estimated valuations;
  (ii) the extent, if any, to which assets are charged to creditors;
  (iii) the extent, if any, to which assets are to be excluded from the PVA;
(b) particulars of any property, other than the joint assets of the partnership, which is proposed to be included in the arrangement, the source of such property and the terms on which it is to be made available for inclusion[2];
(c) the nature and amount of the partnership's liabilities (so far as within the partners' immediate knowledge), the manner in which they are proposed to be met, modified, postponed or otherwise dealt with by way of the arrangement, and (in particular):
  (i) how it is proposed to deal with preferential creditors[3] and creditors who are, or claim to be, secured;

(ii) how persons connected with the partnership[4] (being creditors) are proposed to be treated under the arrangement; and

(iii) whether there are, to the partners' knowledge, any circumstances giving rise to the possibility, in the event that the partnership should be wound up as an unregistered company, of claims under:
- s 238 (transactions at an undervalue);
- s 239 (preferences);
- s 244 (extortionate credit transactions);
- s 245 (floating charges invalid);

and, where any such circumstances are present, whether, and if so how, it is proposed under the PVA to make provision for wholly or partly indemnifying the partnership in respect of such claims;

(d) whether any, and if so what, guarantees have been given of the partnership's debts by other persons, specifying which, if any, of the guarantors are persons connected with the partnership[5];

(e) the proposed duration of the PVA;

(f) the proposed dates of distributions to creditors, with estimates of their amounts;

(g) the amount proposed to be paid to the nominee (as such) by way of remuneration and expenses;

(h) the manner in which it is proposed that the supervisor of the arrangement should be remunerated and his expenses defrayed;

(j) whether, for the purposes of the arrangement, any guarantees are to be offered by partners, or other persons and, if so, whether any security is to be given or sought;

(k) the manner in which funds held for the purposes of the arrangement are to be banked, invested or otherwise dealt with pending distribution to creditors;

(l) the manner in which funds held for the purpose of payment to creditors and not so paid on the termination of the arrangement, are to be dealt with;

(m) the manner in which the business of the firm is proposed to be conducted during the course of the arrangement;

(n) details of any further credit facilities which it is intended to arrange for the partnership, and how the debts so arising are to be paid;

(o) the functions which are to be undertaken by the supervisor of the arrangement; and

(p) the name, address and qualification of the person proposed as supervisor of the PVA, and confirmation that he is, so far as the directors are aware, qualified to act as an insolvency practitioner in relation to the partnership.

The partners' proposal may be amended at any time up to the delivery by the nominee of his report to the court under s 2(2) of the Act (as modified) (see below), with the agreement in writing of the nominee[6].

---

1 Insolvency Rules 1986, r 1.3(2).

2 While this is a matter for the commercial judgement of the partners as to what will be the minimum acceptable to creditors, it should be remembered that in the event that the partnership is wound up with concurrent petitions against one or more members, *all* the assets of those members would be available to satisfy a shortfall on the joint estate.

3 As defined in s 4(7) of the Insolvency Act 1986, as modified by Sch 1 to the Order; ie by reference to s 386 of the Act which is applied by art 4(2) of the Order – see para **7.2** above.
4 A person is 'connected with' a partnership if he is an associate of any partner; see s 249 of the Act and para **7.2** above and footnotes 11 to 13 to that paragraph.
5 See footnote 4 above.
6 Insolvency Rules 1986, r 1.3(3).

7.8 NOTICE TO THE INTENDED NOMINEE

The partners must give the intended nominee written notice of their proposal, which must be delivered with a copy of the proposal to the nominee or to a person authorised to take delivery of documents for him. If the nominee agrees to act, a copy of the notice is endorsed to the effect that it has been received by him on a specified date, and that copy of the notice returned to the partners.

7.9 STATEMENT OF AFFAIRS

Within seven days of delivery of the proposal to the nominee, the partners must deliver a statement of affairs to him[1]. The nominee can allow them a longer period of time. The statement of affairs must comprise the following particulars[2]:

(a) a list of the partnership's assets, divided into appropriate categories, with estimated values assigned to each category;
(b) in the case of any property on which a claim against the company is wholly or partly secured, particulars of the claim and its amount, and of how and when the security was created;
(c) the names and addresses of the partnership's preferential creditors[3] with the amounts of their respective claims;
(d) the names and addresses of the partnership's unsecured creditors, with the amounts of their respective claims;
(e) particulars of any debts owed by or to the partnership to or by persons connected with it;
(f) the names and addresses of the partnership's members, together with their respective rights to share in the partnership capital (or, where a partnership does not have partnership capital, the proportions in which each partner would share in profits or be liable to contribute to losses, or would be obliged to contribute to the debts or expenses of the partnership in the event of a winding up)[4];
(g) such other particulars as the nominee may require in writing for the purposes of his report to the court on the proposal.

Two or more partners must certify that the statement is correct to the best of their knowledge and belief[5].

The partners must give the nominee access to the partnership's accounts and records[6], and he can require further information from the partners[7], including further and better particulars of why the partnership is insolvent[8], and details of any partner or officer who has been involved with any other company or partnership which has become insolvent[9], or who has become bankrupt or entered a voluntary arrangement[10], within the previous two years.

Any past or present member or officer of a partnership who makes a false representation or commits any other fraud for the purpose of obtaining the approval of the members or creditors of a partnership of a proposal for a PVA commits an offence and is liable to a fine or imprisonment or both[11].

---

1 Insolvency Rules 1986, r 1.5(1).
2 Ibid, r 1.5(2).
3 As defined in s 4(7) of the Insolvency Act 1986, as modified by Sch 1 to the Order; ie by reference to s 386 of the Act which is applied by art 4(2) of the Order – see (e) at para **7.2** above.
4 The reference in r 1.5(3)(f) of the Insolvency Rules 1986 to 'respective shareholdings' must be modified in accordance with art 3(3) of the Order. Where no proportions have been agreed between the partners, s 24(1) of the Partnership Act 1890 provides for profits and losses to be shared equally.
5 Insolvency Rules 1986, r 1.5(4).
6 Ibid, r 1.6(3).
7 Under r 1.6.
8 Ibid, r 1.6(1)(a).
9 Ibid, r 1.6(2)(a).
10 Ibid, r 1.6(2)(b).
11 Ibid, r 1.30.

7.10   THE REPORT TO THE COURT

Once a copy of the notice of the proposal has been endorsed by the nominee, the PVA clock is started[1]; the nominee then has 28 days within which to submit his report to the court[2], stating whether in his opinion meetings of the members of the partnership and of partnership creditors should be held to consider the proposal[3]. The report must be accompanied by a copy of the proposal with any amendments[4] and the statement of affairs[5].

The nominee must consider whether or not it is worth calling meetings of creditors and members of the partnership. If he thinks it is, he includes in his report the date, time and place on which he proposes that the meetings shall be held, and he must then annexe his comments on the proposal to his report. If he does not think it is worth putting the proposal to meetings, he must give his reasons with his report[6]. Where the nominee has formed the view that it would not be possible to obtain the requisite level of support by the members of the partnership, he would have to tell the court that, in his opinion, it would not be worth calling the meetings.

The nominee's report is a public document. It is open to inspection by any member of the partnership[7] and by any creditor, at all reasonable times on any business day[8], and a copy must be sent to the partnership[9].

At this stage, the court's role is usually purely administrative. However, if the nominee fails to make the required report, the person intending to make the proposal (which must include the members of the partnership acting as a body) may apply to the court which can direct the replacement of the nominee by another insolvency practitioner[10].

---

1 Insolvency Rules 1986, r 1.4(3).
2 Although the court may extend time.
3 Section 2(2) of the Insolvency Act 1986, as modified by Sch 1 to the Order.

4 Insolvency Rules 1986, r 1.7(1)(a).
5 Ibid, r 1.7(1)(b).
6 Ibid, r 1.7(2).
7 Given its wide meaning – ie including any person who has been held out as a partner and become liable through a creditor extending credit to the partnership in reliance upon that holding out.
8 Insolvency Rules 1986, r 1.7(3).
9 Ibid, r 1.7(4).
10 Section 2(5) of the Insolvency Act 1986, as modified by Sch 1 to the Order.

7.11 PROPOSALS BY A LIQUIDATOR, ADMINISTRATOR OR TRUSTEE

Where a liquidator, administrator or trustee[1] is making the PVA proposal, and is also the nominee under the proposal, he simply prepares a proposal and calls meetings of the members and creditors of the partnership, without making a report to the court[2]. The proposal must include all the matters which the partners would be required to include in a proposal by them[3], and any other matters which the insolvency practitioner considers appropriate for ensuring that members and creditors are able to reach an informed decision on the proposal[4].

If the partnership is in administration, the administrator must include the names and addresses of all preferential creditors of the partnership, with the amounts of their respective claims[5].

If the partnership is being wound up, the liquidator must give notice of the proposal to the Official Receiver[6].

However, where a liquidator, administrator or trustee is making the PVA proposal and a different insolvency practitioner is the nominee under the proposal, notice is given by the responsible insolvency practitioner to the intended nominee and the PVA proposal is prepared by him in the same manner that would be required of the partners if they were making the proposal[7]. In that case, the nominee must report to the court as set out in para **7.10**, and the procedure is very similar to that for a proposal by the partners.

In this instance, if the partnership is being wound up, the liquidator must send a copy of the proposal to the Official Receiver, together with the name and address of the nominee[8].

1 Although Chapters 3 and 4 of the Insolvency Rules 1986 only refer to administrators or liquidators of companies, s 1(3)(c) of the Insolvency Act 1986, as modified by Sch 1 to the Order, introduces into the class of 'responsible insolvency practitioners' who may propose a PVA the trustee of the partnership under art 11 of the Order. The effect of art 18(1) of the Order, which applies subordinate legislation 'with such modifications as the context requires for giving effect to the provisions of the Act ... which are applied by this Order', must be to apply Chapters 3 and 4 equally to a relevant trustee.
2 Section 3(2) of the Insolvency Act 1986, as modified by Sch 1 to the Order.
3 Insolvency Rules 1986 r 1.10(1)(a); ie under r 1.3 (see para **7.7** above).
4 Ibid, r 1.10(1)(b): non-discosure of information which is within the insolvency practitioner's knowledge would be a 'material irregularity'.
5 Ibid, r 1.10(1)(a).

7.12 SUMMONING OF MEETINGS: CREDITORS

The nominee must summon to the creditors' meeting every creditor of the partnership of whose claim and address he is aware[1]. It is fundamental to the statutory scheme that all the creditors are entitled to be given notice of the meeting, and it is in the interests of an insolvent partnership that as many creditors as possible are brought within the PVA.

Who is a creditor for these purposes? It is suggested that the only sensible approach is to embrace within the term anyone who would be able to prove in a liquidation of the partnership for a debt or liability[2]. For the purposes of winding up a partnership, it is immaterial whether the debt or liability is present or future, whether it is certain or contingent, or whether its amount is fixed or liquidated, or is capable of being ascertained by fixed rules or as a matter of opinion, or whether it sounds only in damages[3].

However, it should be noted that there may be significant creditors who would not be able to prove in a liquidation of the partnership, because they only have claims against the separate estates of individual partners. An example would be a landlord of property used by the partnership who only has claims against four lessee partners and any other separate covenantors[4]. A person who is not a *partnership* creditor is not entitled to attend the meeting of creditors within the Rules.

Former partners may have a contingent right of indemnity against the present partnership if they pay off a creditor to whom they are liable from the time when they were full partners. It therefore appears that they should receive notice of the creditors' meeting[5]. The same would apply to other guarantors of partnership liabilities who are not partners.

1 Section 3(3) of the Insolvency Act 1986, as modified by Sch 1 to the Order; Insolvency Rules
    1986, r 1.11(1)(a).
2 The absence of any statutory definition of 'creditor' in Part I of the Act, the wide definition
    of 'debt' and 'provable debt' in the winding up of companies (and partnerships), and the
    express inclusion of contingent or prospective creditors in ss 9 and 124 of the Act (cf s 9 of
    the Insolvency Act as modified by Sch 2) has led some commentators to suggest that the term
    'creditor' in the context of CVAs should be given a narrow meaning, excluding contingent or
    prospective creditors: see Goode, *Principles of Corporate Insolvency Law* (Sweet & Maxwell,
    1990) p 31; Sealy and Milman, *Annotated Guide to the Insolvency Legislation* 4th Edn (CCH,
    1994) p 28. This ignores the commercial imperative for a PVA to include as comprehensive a
    class of creditors as possible, in accordance with its statutory purpose.
       In *Re FMS Financial Management Services Ltd* (1989) 5 BCC 191, individuals with damages
    claims had been left out of a CVA, but Hoffmann J was prepared to modify the scheme after
    it had been approved to permit them to prove.
3 Insolvency Rules 1986, rr 12.3, 13.12(3); an order for costs is a debt; *Tottenham Hotspur plc v
    Edennote plc* [1994] BCC 681.
4 See para **2.13.5**.
5 One advantage of including former partners within the scheme is that it appears that it is
    thereby possible to modify the rights of other creditors against them, as parties to the
    'statutory contract' embodied in a PVA. This has yet to be tested.

7.13 SUMMONING OF MEETINGS: MEMBERS

The nominee must summon to the partnership meeting all persons who are, to the best of his belief, members of the partnership[1]. This means that a nominee will need to consider the individual circumstances of each person who has been held out as a member of the partnership, and to consider whether or not in his view he believes that a creditor has extended credit to the firm in reliance upon that person having been held out. It is suggested that, in the absence of specific evidence being put forward by a creditor that he has relied, it would be reasonable for an insolvency practitioner to conclude that a person has not become a member solely by being included on the notepaper, but careful consideration will have to be given to the facts in each case. On occasion, it may be necessary to enquire of creditors who might have relied whether in fact they regard themselves as having done so, and invite them to put forward any evidence in support of their contention.

It appears that a retired partner is no longer a partner for day-to-day purposes, and so (at least where formalities have been completed) should not be given notice of the members' meeting[2]. However, a retired partner may have been held out to creditors as a partner, for example if his name continued to appear on the notepaper. In such a case, consideration must be given as to whether there has been the necesary reliance by a creditor so that the retired partner is, nevertheless, a member under art 2 of the Order, in which case he must be sent notice.

---

1 See para **7.5**.
2 Unless he was a partner within the previous two years and the nominee thinks it would be of assistance for him to attend (see para **7.14**).

7.14 OFFICERS

In the case of a CVA, directors of the company must also be given 14 days' notice to attend the meetings of creditors and of members[1] (which in that context refers, of course, to the shareholders). The purpose is to ensure that the management of the company is present to answer any questions which may arise. In the context of an insolvent partnership, partners will already be given notice of the members' meeting, but it appears that those partners who have filled the equivalent role to directors (ie have taken part in the day-to-day management of the firm, or constituted an executive or management committee) must be given separate notice of the creditors' meeting.

The officers of the partnership include the members and any person who has management or control of the partnership business. This would include, for example, a full-time administrator or finance director employed by a firm of solicitors. If the nominee thinks that the presence of such a person is required at the meetings, he must give them 14 days' notice to attend. The same applies to any person who has been a member or officer of the partnership in the two years immediately preceding the date of the notice[2].

In the case of a CVA meeting, the chairman always has the power to exclude any present or former director or officer from the whole or part of a meeting[3];

this power surely cannot extend to exclusion of a partner from the members' meeting to consider a PVA, and must sensibly be read as limited to a power to exclude former members and officers who are not members in that context.

---

1 Insolvency Rules 1986, r 1.16(1)(a).
2 Ibid, r 1.16(1)(b); however, the Rules do not provide any sanction for non-attendance.
3 Ibid, r 1.16(2).

7.15 TIMING

The meetings must be held not less than 14 and not more than 28 days from the date when the nominee's report is filed in court[1]. If the nominee is the liquidator, administrator or trustee of the partnership, he must give at least 14 days' notice of the meetings[2].

Notices must be sent out 14 clear days before the day of the meeting to all creditors and all members of the partnership[3].

Both the creditors' meeting and the members' meeting must be called to commence between 10.00 am and 4.00 pm on a business day[4], and the person summoning the meeting[5] must have regard primarily to the convenience of the creditors in fixing the venue[6].

The meetings must be held on the same day and in the same place. The creditors' meeting must start first[7]; it may be adjourned and need not have concluded its business before the members' meeting. If it seems likely that there will be protracted negotiation about modifications, it is possible to hold one combined meeting[8] if the chairman thinks fit.

If, on the day of the meetings, approval is not forthcoming from both creditors and members, the chairman may adjourn the meetings for not more than 14 days[9]. The chairman must adjourn if there is a resolution passed to that effect[10]. A meeting may only be adjourned if the other meeting is also adjourned to the same business day[11]. Even if there are further adjournments, the final adjournment must not be to a date later than 14 days after the date of the original meetings[12]. If following a final adjournment the proposal has still not been agreed by both meetings, it is deemed to have been rejected[13].

---

1 Insolvency Rules 1986, r 1.9(1).
2 Ibid, r 1.11(1).
3 Ibid, r 1.9(2); *Mytre Investments v Reynolds (No 2)* [1996] BPIR 464, Blackburne J: the judge held that it is not open to the court to disregard the terms of r 5.13(2) (the case arose from an IVA, but r 1.9(2) is in the same terms) and abridge time.
4 Ibid, r 1.13(2).
5 Usually the nominee, although at this point in the Rules he becomes referred to as 'the convener'.
6 Insolvency Rules 1986, r 1.13(1).
7 Ibid, r 1.13(3).
8 Ibid, r 1.21(1), and see r 1.14(1).
9 Ibid, r 1.21(2); if the proposal is by the members of the partnership, the nominee must give notice of the adjournment forthwith to the court.

10 Ibid.
11 Ibid, r 1.21(4).
12 Ibid, r 1.21; it may be possible for a court to extend time under Rules of the Supreme Court 1965, Ord 3, r 5 or County Court Rules 1981, Ord 13, r 4 applied by r 7.51 to insolvency proceedings in the High Court and the county court respectively.
13 Ibid, r 1.21(6).

7.16 CHAIRMAN

The nominee must act as the chairman of both meetings[1], unless he is unable to attend, in which case he may nominate either another insolvency practitioner, or an employee of the nominee's firm who is experienced in insolvency matters, to act as chairman in his place[2].

1 Insolvency Rules 1986, r 1.14(1).
2 Ibid, r 1.14(2).

7.17 THE MEETINGS

The members' meeting and the creditors' meeting or, where appropriate, a combined meeting, must be conducted in accordance with the Rules[1].

As with the meetings called in respect of a CVA, the meetings:

(a) may approve modifications to the proposal[2];
(b) may modify the proposal so that there is a change of nominee (although the new nominee must similarly be a person qualified to act as an insolvency practitioner in relation to the insolvent partnership)[3];
(c) may not approve any proposal or modification which would affect the rights of a secured creditor of the partnership to enforce his security, except with the concurrence of the creditor concerned[4];
(d) may not approve any proposal or modification which would modify the priority of any preferential debt of the partnership, or provide for one preferential debt to receive a smaller dividend than another preferential debt, except with the concurrence of the creditor concerned[5].

1 Section 4(5) of the Insolvency Act 1986, as modified by Sch 1 to the Order.
2 Ibid, s 4(1) (as modified).
3 Ibid, s 4(2) (as modified).
4 Ibid, s 4(3) (as modified).
5 Ibid, s 4(4) (as modified).

7.18 VOTING AT THE MEETINGS

7.18.1 *Entitlement to vote*
Entitlement to vote at the meetings is particularly significant, because:

(a) if it is approved by the meetings, the PVA will bind every person who, in accordance with the Rules, had notice of and was entitled to vote at the meeting[1];

(b) those entitled to vote at either of the meetings are the principal class who are entitled to apply to the court with a complaint that there has been some material irregularity at or in relation to either of the meetings, or that the PVA is unfairly prejudicial[2].

1 Insolvency Act 1986, s 5(2)(b) as modified by Sch 1 to the Order.
2 Ibid, s 6(2)(a) (as modified).

7.18.2 Members

Members of the partnership vote at the members' meeting in accordance with their voting rights in the partnership[1]. Where the respective votes of partners are set out in a partnership deed, these votes will therefore apply at the members' meeting. Where there is no such deed, or the deed is silent, partners vote in the proportion of their rights to share in capital and profits. In the absence of any express or implied agreement, the rule under the Partnership Act is equality[2].

One of the distinguishing characteristics of 'salaried partners' or 'junior partners' in large partnerships is often that they do not have any right to take part in the management of the partnership, and there is quite frequently a provision that they do not have any rights to vote[3]. Where such an individual is a 'member' of an insolvent partnership[4], they will have no vote at the members' meeting because they would have no right to vote in the partnership generally.

Under r 1.18(2), where a member has no voting rights, he is nevertheless entitled to vote either for or against the proposal or any modification of it (but not, apparently, for any other resolution at the members' meeting). However, any such vote is left out of account in determining whether any resolution has achieved the required majority[5]. The only effect of being entitled to vote appears to be that the member is able to make an application to the court in respect of unfair prejudice or material irregularity.

1 Insolvency Rules 1986, r 1.18 as modified in the circumstances of a partnership.
2 Partnership Act 1890, s 24(1).
3 Even in the absence of any such express provision, it appears that this would be so.
4 Within the definition in art 2 of the Order (see para **7.5**).
5 Insolvency Rules 1986, r 1.20(2).

7.18.3 Unascertained creditors[1]

Where the amount of a creditor's claim is not settled at the date of the meeting, because it is *unliquidated* (as in a claim for damages) or because it is *unascertained* (as in a claim for future rent or for some other contingent liability), the creditor will only become allowed to vote under the Rules[2] where the chairman agrees to put an estimated minimum value upon the vote for the purpose of voting. No actual agreement with the creditor is required; the chairman merely needs to express his willingness to put, and to put, an estimated minimum value on the debt[3]. However, the chairman must make a bona fide attempt to value the creditor's claim[4]. A contingent claim may be valued by multiplying the amount likely to be claimed by a percentage which reflects a reasonable estimate of the probability of the contingency occurring.

If the nominee is of the view (on the facts before him) that the contingency is virtually certain to occur, the multiplier will be '1'; in other words, the claim will be valued at its full amount. Where the contingency is very unlikely to occur, the multiplier will be a very small fraction, and so there may still be occasions when it is appropriate to value the claim of a contingent creditor at a nominal level (eg £1).

A creditor for an unascertained amount who stays away from the PVA meeting will nonetheless be bound by the result[5], even where no agreed minimum value has been put on his vote.

---

1   See para **7.12**.
2   Under r 1.17(3).
3   *Doorbar v Alltime Securities* [1995] BCC 1149, CA.
4   *Re Cranley Mansions* [1994] 1 WLR 1610; *Doorbar v Alltime Securities* [1994] BCC 994.
5   *Beverley Group v McClue* [1995] BCC 751. Knox J said that the prohibition on voting under r 1.17(3) only makes sense in relation to a creditor who is physically in a position to vote – ie, by being present or represented at the meeting. He said those who do not attend in person or by proxy are liable to be bound by s 5(2) of the Act, if they had notice and became 'entitled to vote'. This can be seen as a purposive decision, preventing the unascertained creditor from producing by non-co-operation the effect that he is not bound by a voluntary arrangement.

7.18.4   *Retired partners*

Although a retired partner should have been sent notice of the creditors' meeting, he is only a creditor insofar as, if he pays partnership creditors, he will have a right of indemnity. As a matter of principle, it would be strange if a retired partner was permitted to compete with the joint creditors in a winding up of the partnership[1] and as a matter of commercial reality, it is unlikely that creditors asked to vote upon a PVA would usually regard that as acceptable. On the other hand, where a retired partner is making assets available in a PVA, the creditors may be prepared to relinquish other claims against him.

If a retired partner has already paid creditors, it is suggested that his claim should be admitted in that amount, but it may well have to be subordinated to the claims of the other creditors unless the majority are prepared to agree to some other treatment[2]. If the retired partner has not paid creditors, his claim is merely contingent; in order to prevent double-counting, it is suggested that the correct course would be to admit the claim in a nominal sum of £1.

---

1   See modified s 175C(2) of the Insolvency Act 1986 in Sch 4 to the Order.
2   It is suggested that, so long as all creditors apart from any retired partners, are treated equally, such a course would not be open to challenge by a dissentient creditor on grounds of unfair prejudice. Similarly, equivalent treatment to all retired partners should preclude the possibility of a challenge from one retired partner that he has been unfairly prejudiced.

7.18.5   *Majorities at the creditors' meeting*

In order to be passed, a resolution at the creditors' meeting must satisfy both the following tests:

(a) a resolution to approve any proposal or modification must achieve a majority in excess of 75 per cent of the creditors present in person or by proxy and voting on the resolution[1]. Other resolutions need only achieve a majority in excess of 50 per cent[2];

(b) to be 'valid', a resolution must achieve the support of at least 50 per cent of the creditors, leaving out anyone to whom notice of the meeting was not sent[3], and anyone whom the chairman believes to be connected with the partnership[4].

In either case, the chairman will leave out:

(i) the claim of a creditor who has not given written notice of his claim to the convener of the meeting or to the chairman either before or at the meeting[5];

(ii) the secured part of a creditor's claim[6];

(iii) a claim on or secured by a bill of exchange or promissory note, unless the creditor is prepared to treat the liability to him of every person liable antecedently to the partnership on the bill or note as security, and to deduct the value of such security from the value of the claim for voting purposes[7].

---

1 Insolvency Rules 1986, r 1.19(1).
2 Ibid, r 1.19(2).
3 Ibid, r 1.19(4)(a).
4 A person is 'connected with' a partnership if he is an associate of any partner; see s 249 of the Act and (f) at para **7.2** above. The chairman is entitled to rely on the information provided by the partnership in forming his view: r 1.19(5).
5 Insolvency Rules 1986, r 1.19(3)(a).
6 Ibid, r 1.19(3)(b); *Calor Gas v Piercy* [1995] BCC 69.
7 Ibid, r 1.19(3)(c).

7.18.6   *Disputed votes*

The creditors' meeting is not the place to go into lengthy debates about the status of a debt[1]. Where objections are raised as to the nature or amount of a creditor's claim which the chairman is not able to resolve upon a brief inquiry, he must mark the vote as objected to and allow the creditor to vote, subject to his vote being subsequently declared invalid if the objection is sustained[2].

---

1 Cf *Re a Debtor (No 222 of 1990) ex parte Bank of Ireland* [1992] BCLC 137.
2 Insolvency Rules 1986, r 5.17(6).

7.18.7   *Majorities at the members' meeting*

If there is a partnership deed provision which deals expressly with voting at PVA meetings, that provision will determine the majority which is required at the members' meeting. It is thought that a provision specifying the majority which is required for a fundamental change in the partnership business would similarly apply. In the absence of such a provision, a resolution is passed at the members' meeting if it achieves the support of more than 50 per cent in value of the members present in person or by proxy and voting[1].

The 'value' ascribed to each member's vote is determined by reference to the partnership agreement[2]. As set out above[3], where there is no partnership deed, or the deed is silent, partners vote in the proportion of their rights to share in capital and profits. In the absence of any express or implied agreement, the rule under the Partnership Act is equality[4].

1 Insolvency Rules 1986, r 1.20(1).
2 Ibid.
3 See para **7.18.1**.
4 Partnership Act 1890, s 24(1).

7.19 REPORT OF RESULT

Within four days of the meetings being held, the chairman must report the results to the court[1]. The chairman's report must:

(a) state whether the proposal was approved or rejected and, if approved, with what, if any, modifications[2];
(b) set out all resolutions and the decision on each one[3];
(c) list the creditors and the members of the partnership present or represented at each meeting with their respective values and how they voted on each resolution[4];
(d) include any further information which the chairman thinks it appropriate to make known to the court[5].

Immediately after reporting to the court, the chairman must give notice of the result of the meetings to everyone who was sent notice of the meetings[6]. This is normally done by circulating a copy of the same chairman's report filed in court.

1 Section 4(6) of the Insolvency Act 1986, as modified by Sch 1 to the Order; Insolvency Rules 1986, r 1.24(3).
2 Insolvency Rules 1986, r 1.24(2)(a).
3 Ibid, r 1.24(2)(b).
4 Ibid, r 1.24(2)(c).
5 Ibid, r 1.24(2)(d).
6 Section 4(6) of the Insolvency Act 1986, as modified by Sch 1 to the Order; Insolvency Rules 1986; r 1.24(4).

7.20 APPROVAL OF A PVA

If both the creditors' meeting and the members' meeting approve a proposal (either unmodified, or with the same modifications), it takes effect as if it had been made by the members at the creditors' meeting, and binds every person who in accordance with the Rules had notice of, and was entitled to vote at, the that creditors' meeting[1].

Once a PVA has been approved, the nominee (or his substitute) becomes the supervisor of the arrangement[2]. The members (or, where the partnership is being wound up or is in administration or is subject to an order under art 11 of the Order, the relevant responsible insolvency practitioner) must immediately do all that is required to put the supervisor in possession of the assets included in the arrangement.

If the partnership is being wound up, or is in administration, or if an order under art 11 of the Order has been made, the approval of a PVA gives the court discretion to:

(a) discharge the administration order[3] or stay all proceedings in the winding up or in the bankruptcy proceedings under art 11[4], including any related insolvency proceedings against a member of the partnership; and/or

(b) give directions for facilitating the implementation of the PVA with respect to the administration order, the winding up or the bankruptcy proceedings under art 11, and any related insolvency proceedings against a member of the partnership[5].

However, while the court can give directions immediately, it must not make any order to discharge an administration order or stay proceedings in a winding up or in bankruptcy proceedings under art 11 (including any related insolvency proceedings against a member of the partnership) for 28 days after the chairman has reported to the court[6], to allow time for any appeal against the chairman's decision or allegation of unfair prejudice or material irregularity to be brought before the court. Where such an application is made, the court may not make an order to discharge an administration or stay insolvency proceedings until the application has been determined and the time for any appeal has passed[7].

---

1 Section 5(2) of the Insolvency Act 1986, as modified by Sch 1 to the Order.
2 Ibid, s 7(2) (as modified).
3 Ibid, s 5(3)(a)(ii) (as modified).
4 Ibid, s 5(3)(a)(i) (as modified).
5 Ibid, s 5(3)(b) (as modified).
6 Ibid, s 5(4)(a) (as modified).
7 Ibid, s 5(4)(b) (as modified).

7.21 THE POSSIBILITY OF CHALLENGE

Just as in the case of an IVA[1], it is possible to challenge the decision to approve a PVA within 28 days of the date of the chairman's report to the court[2] on the grounds either:

(a) that the voluntary arrangement unfairly prejudices a creditor of the debtor[3]; or

(b) that there has been some material irregularity at or in relation to either of the meetings[4].

Those entitled to apply are:

(i) a person who in accordance with the Rules was entitled to vote at either of the meetings – ie members and creditors who received notice, subject to the points regarding creditors for unliquidated and unascertained amounts (see above)[5];

(ii)   the original nominee and any replacement[6];

(iii) if the partnership was being wound up, the liquidator[7];

(iv)   if the partnership was in administration, the administrator[8];

(v)   if the partners had presented a joint bankruptcy petition under art 11 of the Order, the trustee[9].

As in the context of an IVA, 'prejudice' in relation to a PVA meeting is taken to refer to the rights of the creditor being adversely affected, and 'unfair' to refer to such treatment being different to the treatment of other creditors[10]. An 'irregularity' is a departure from the Rules[11] in connection with the proposal or the meeting, which will be 'material' if it can be shown that the irregularity in question would or might have affected the outcome of the meeting.[12]. Unless an irregularity at or in relation to a meeting is held by a court to be material, it does not invalidate an approval of a PVA[13]. A challenge must be brought within 28 days beginning with the day on which the results of both the meeting of creditors and the meeting of members have been reported to the court[14].

There is also a right of appeal under the Rules against a decision by the chairman of a PVA meeting of creditors on a voting question[15]; in which case the chairman is not personally liable for any costs[16]. The appeal must be made within 28 days beginning with the day on which the decisions of both meetings have been reported to the court[17].

---

1   See para **6.16** above.

2   Section 6(3) of the Insolvency Act 1986, as modified by Sch 1 to the Order.

3   Ibid, s 6(1)(a) (as modified).

4   Ibid, s 6(1)(b) (as modified).

5   Ibid, s 6(2)(a) (as modified).

6   Ibid, s 6(2)(b) (as modified).

7   Ibid, s 6(2)(c) (as modified).

8   Ibid.

9   Ibid.

10 In *Re Primlaks (UK) Ltd (No 2)* [1990] BCLC 234, a company voluntary arrangement proposed to pay trade creditors ahead of loan or bank creditors. Harman J apparently accepted the principle that different classes of creditor could be treated differently, and said that in his view it was not unfairly prejudicial as long as other creditors of the same 'type' were treated the same.

In *Re Cancol Ltd* [1996] 1 All ER 37, Knox J said it was not unfairly prejudicial to distinguish in a company voluntary arrangement between creditors for future debts (such as a landlord) whose assets were to be used to earn the profits envisaged in the voluntary arrangement and who were to be paid in full, and other creditors for future debts whose assets were not to be so used, who would merely receive a dividend.

11 *Re a Debtor (No 222 of 1990), ex parte Bank of Ireland* [1992] BCLC 137.

12 Examples of material irregularities would include:

   (a) misconduct by the chairman at the meeting: *Ex parte Bank of Ireland* (above);

   (b) provision of false or misleading information in a proposal for a voluntary arrangement: *Re a Debtor (No 87 of 1993) (No 2)* [1996] BPIR 64;

   (c) refusal to recognise that a landlord's right of distress constitutes him a secured creditor: *Peck v Craighead* [1995] 1 BCLC 337;

   (d) failure to put a proper value on an unascertained creditor's vote: *Re Cranley Mansions* [1994] 1 WLR 1610.

13 Section 6(7) of the Insolvency Act 1986, as modified by Sch 1 to the Order.

14 Ibid, s 6(3), as modified by Sch 1 to the Order.

15 Insolvency Rules 1986, rr 1.17(7), 1.19(7).
16 Ibid, r 1.17(9). If an application combines an appeal under the Rules with a complaint of material irregularity, the court may order the chairman to bear part of the costs (*Ex parte Bank of Ireland (No 2)* [1992] BCLC 233), but where the chairman has acted in complete good faith and there has been no culpable conduct on his part, the court will not, in its discretion, do so *Re Cranley Mansions* (above)).
17 Insolvency Rules 1986, r 1.17(8).

7.22 POWERS OF A COURT ON A CHALLENGE

Where the court considers that an allegation of material irregularity or unfair prejudice has been made out, it has a discretion:

(a) whether to revoke or suspend the approvals given by the meetings[1];
(b) whether to direct further meetings to consider a revised proposal[2];
(c) whether (if there has been material irregularity) to direct a further meeting of members or creditors to reconsider the original proposal[3];
(d) whether, if it has decided to revoke or suspend approvals of a PVA, and/or to direct a further meeting, to give any supplemental directions.

If on an appeal the chairman's decision is reversed or varied, the court may order another meeting to be summoned, or make such other order as it thinks just[4], but only if it considers that the matter is such as to give rise to unfair prejudice or a material irregularity.

1 Section 6(4)(a) of the Insolvency Act 1986, as modified by Sch 1 to the Order.
2 Ibid, s 6(4)(b) (as modified).
3 Ibid.
4 Insolvency Rules 1986, r 1.17(7).

7.23 DISCHARGING THE FEES AND EXPENSES OF A FORMER INSOLVENCY PRACTITIONER

Where the partnership was being wound up or in administration at the time a PVA was approved, the supervisor must, upon taking possession of the assets, discharge any balance which is due to the liquidator or administrator by way of remuneration or on account of fees, costs, charges and expenses[1]. Alternatively, the supervisor must give the responsible insolvency practitioner a written undertaking to discharge his fees and expenses out of the first realisation of such assets[2] and the liquidator or administrator has a charge on the assets included in the voluntary arrangement until his fees and expenses have been paid (subject only to the costs of realisation by the supervisor)[3].

The relevant Rules do not include any reference to the trustee of a partnership where the partners have presented a joint bankruptcy petition under art 11 of the Order (which obviously does not arise in the original company context), but it is thought that that would be a necessary modification required by the context and imposed by art 18(1) of the Order. It is therefore thought that such a trustee should be treated in the same fashion as a liquidator or administrator.

1 Insolvency Rules 1986, r 1.23(2).
2 Ibid, r 1.23(3).
3 Ibid, r 1.23(4).

7.24 POWERS AND OBLIGATIONS OF THE SUPERVISOR

The supervisor of a PVA will only have those powers which are expressly incorporated in the terms of the proposal.

Where the proposal requires him to carry on trade, or to realise assets on behalf of the firm, or otherwise to administer funds, he is obliged to keep accounts and records, including records of all receipts and payments of money[1].

At least every 12 months from the date of his appointment, the supervisor must prepare an abstract of receipts and payments and send it, with his comments on the progress and efficacy of the arrangement, to:

(a) the court[2];
(b) all the creditors of the partnership bound by the arrangement[3];
(c) the members bound by the arrangement[4].

The Secretary of State has the same powers to require production of, and to order the auditing of, a supervisor's accounts and records in respect of a PVA as would be the case in respect of a CVA[5].

1 Insolvency Rules 1986, r 1.26.
2 Ibid, r 1.26(2)(a).
3 Ibid, r 1.26(2)(d).
4 Ibid, r 1.26(2)(e); it is thought that there is no need to send a separate report to the firm (eg at its principal place of business) under r 1.26(2)(c) because the partners are the firm. Note that the court can dispense with the report to members of a company, but it is doubted that this would be considered appropriate for a partnership.
5 Ie under r 1.27.

7.25 JURISDICTION OF THE COURT

The supervisor may apply to the court for directions in respect of any matter arising under the voluntary arrangement[1]. It is common to give a supervisor the same powers to admit or reject the proof of a creditor which he would have if he were the liquidator of the partnership.

As in other voluntary arrangements, any creditor or anyone else who is dissatisfied with any act, omission or decision of the supervisor of a PVA may apply to the court, which can confirm, reverse or modify any act or decision, give the supervisor directions or make such other order as it thinks fit[2].

The court also has jurisdiction to appoint a substitute or additional supervisor when it is expedient to do so[3].

Opinions are divided on whether the court has jurisdiction to vary a voluntary arrangement once it is in place. The better view is that it can, but it is preferable for there to be provision in the terms of the arrangement for the supervisor to call a further meeting of creditors to approve any variations which may be required by changes in circumstances. Commercially, this is common sense, but it remains to be seen whether a court would regard a dissentient creditor as bound by the decision of a further meeting as they would be bound by the statutory scheme if a proposal achieved a majority of 75 per cent or more at the original meeting of creditors[4].

1 Section 7(4)(a) of the Insolvency Act 1986, as modified by Sch 1 to the Order.
2 Ibid, s 7(3) (as modified).
3 Ibid, s 7(5) (as modified).
4 Cf Hoffmann J's decision in *Re FMS Financial Management Services Ltd* (1989) 5 BCC 191, which appears to be based on an inherent jurisdiction of the court. However, it should be noted that the courts have been reluctant to permit creditors to vary schemes of arrangement under s 425 of the Companies Act 1985 by provision in a relevant scheme: *Devi v People's Bank of Northern India Ltd* [1938] 4 All ER 337, PC; cf *Re Eastmond Pty Ltd* (1972) 4 ACLR 801, *Re Telford Inns Pty Ltd* (1985) 3 ACLR 660, *Re Leamon Consolidated (Vic) Pty Ltd* (1985) 10 ACLR 263.

7.26 CREDITORS' COMMITTEE

There is no formal requirement to establish a creditors' committee in respect of a PVA, but it is often desirable to constitute one. Where a creditors' committee is in existence because the partnership is in administration immediately before the PVA, it would probably be appropriate to provide in the proposal for that committee to continue in the PVA.

A creditors' committee in a PVA may operate any procedural arrangements which can be agreed, but the arrangements must be contained, either expressly or by reference, in the proposal or modifications of the proposal. In practice, it is convenient to take advantage of the Rules relating to creditors' committees in liquidation or in administration, and it is generally preferable to annexe these to the proposal in full for the benefit of those creditors who do not have access to them.

7.27 SUPERVISION AND TRADING

A supervisor, unlike an administrator, will not usually expect to become involved with the day-to-day management of the partnership. The precise nature of the supervisor's role will vary from PVA to PVA, and is a matter for negotiation between the supervisor, the creditors and the members of the partnership, at the stage when the proposal is being formulated.

Unless the proposal envisages merely an orderly winding down of the partnership's affairs, most PVAs (particularly those of professional partnerships) will involve some element of continued trading. At the very least, this should help to maximise the realisation of assets, as the value of any existing work-in-progress will be protected, and the collection of book debts will be made easier. It must be made clear in the proposal that it is the firm which is continuing to trade, not the supervisor, and a supervisor must be very careful that he does not incur personal liability.

Consideration needs to be given at the outset to what powers the supervisor is to have to control the firm, or to intervene in its affairs if the need arises. At one extreme, the supervisor may merely be given the power to petition to wind up the partnership on defined events of default; at the other, he may have at his option all the powers of an administrator under modified Sch 1 to the Act[1]. It is often commercially sensible to provide that a decision to petition for winding up is to be taken by the creditors' committee (where there is one) or by a meeting of creditors, so that revisions to the PVA can be considered as an alternative. Unlike individual voluntary arrangements, a partnership may propose PVAs as often as it wishes, and need not wait a year between proposals.

Typically, a PVA proposal will give the supervisor the power to regulate the internal affairs of a firm; for example, to approve the taking on of new partners (or employees). Equally, it may be a condition of a PVA that partners may not retire[2] during its duration. It is preferable for all these powers to be set out in detail in the proposal so that they can be reviewed by creditors in advance, and everyone understands from the outset where they stand.

---

1 In Sch 2 to the Order.
2 Except perhaps for reasons of ill health.

7.28   FINANCE

If the PVA envisages the continued trading of the partnership or some restructuring, there will be a requirement for working capital. However, it is likely that, by the time a partnership comes to realise that it must propose a PVA, its overdraft will be at its limit, and all the available security will already have been deployed. As the partnership gets into cash-flow difficulties, the likelihood is that the incidence of bad debts will be rising, and the level of work-in-progress may well be falling.

Before a lender can be persuaded to advance funds, it will need to be satisfied that the prospects for a rescue are realistic, but this may not become clear for some time. The creditors will need to be convinced at the outset that the money is available to service the projected requirements of the PVA.

In practice, it is unlikely that a trading PVA will be approved without the support of a bank. It may be that the partnership's bankers can be persuaded not to enforce security as long as agreed financial targets and cash-flow forecasts are met. Where the book debts of a partnership have not already been given as security, the creditors may as part of the proposal be prepared to allow them to be used as security for a continued overdraft or term loan.

7.29   COMPLETION OF THE ARRANGEMENT

The duration of the PVA should be specified in the proposal. Not more than 28 days[1] after the final completion of the PVA, the supervisor must send to all the creditors of the partnership who are bound by the arrangement, to all the members, and to the court[2] a notice that the PVA has been fully implemented[3], together with a report including a summary of his receipts and payments and explaining any difference in the actual implementation as compared with the proposal approved by the meetings of creditors and members[4].

---

1 Which may be extended by the court upon the application of the supervisor: r 1.29(4).
2 Insolvency Rules 1986, r 1.29(3).
3 Ibid, r 1.29(1).
4 Ibid, r 1.29(2).

Chapter 8

PARTNERSHIP ADMINISTRATION ORDERS

8.1 INTRODUCTION

The introduction of the administration procedure in respect of an insolvent partnership is the second main innovation introduced by the Order[1]. A partnership administration order is closely modelled on the regime under Part II of the Act but, as with a PVA, partnerships generate complex technical problems when those procedures are applied in practice.

---

1 Administration orders in respect of companies are only 10 years old, having been recommended by the Cork Committee, introduced in the Insolvency Act 1985 (which never came into force) and consolidated into Part II of the Insolvency Act 1986 ('the Act') which came into force on 29 December 1986. They were used on a number of notable occasions during the recession of the early 1990s, and they have become a key element in the development of the so-called 'rescue culture'. Although a great deal of practical experience has been gained, there have been relatively few administrations compared with the number of company insolvencies, and the procedure has been criticised for being unnecessarily expensive and time-consuming.

8.2 MODIFICATION AND APPLICATION OF THE ACT AND THE RULES

Article 6 of the Order applies Part II of the Act, as modified by Sch 2 to the Order, to an insolvent partnership. In addition, the Order[1] applies the following further provisions of the Act to an insolvent partnership insofar as they would apply to the administration of a company:

(a) s 212 in Part IV of the Act, so that the administrator of a partnership who has been guilty of misfeasance is subject to a summary remedy if the partnership is subsequently wound up;

(b) Part VI, thereby including the provisions of the Act which deal with: the administrator's qualifications (s 230); supplies of gas, water, electricity and telecommunications by a public supplier (s 233); powers to get in the partnership's property (s 234); the duty to co-operate with an administrator (s 235); powers to inquire into the dealings of an insolvent partnership (s 236); powers to overturn antecedent transactions (ss 238–245); unenforceability of a lien on the books and records of a partnership as against an administrator (s 246);

(c) Part VII (with the exception of s 250[2]), which provides for definitions of certain relevant terms. These must, however, be read with art 3 of the Order, which provides that references to companies in provisions of the Act applied by the Order are to be read as references to insolvent partnerships[3] and expressions appropriate to companies are to be construed as references to the 'corresponding' persons, documents, officers or organs appropriate to a partnership;

(d) Part XIII, which defines 'act as insolvency practitioner' and deals with insolvency practitioners and their qualifications[4];

(e) ss 411, 413, 414 and 419 in Part XV, which provide for the making of company insolvency rules[5], for the establishment of the Insolvency Rules Committee[6], for the payment of fees and the making of relevant subordinate legislation[7] and for the making of regulations relating to insolvency practitioners, etc[8];

(f) Parts XVI–XIX including provisions against debt avoidance and criminal offences. Of particular significance is the definition of 'associate' which is set out in s 435 of the Act, which includes the provision that partners are associates[9], as are husbands, wives or relatives[10], and employers and employees[11].

---

1 Insolvent Partnerships Order 1994, art 6(2), (3).
2 Insolvency Act 1986, s 250, which defines 'member' of a company, is excluded because a 'member' of an insolvent partnership is defined in art 2(1) of the Order.
3 Insolvent Partnerships Order 1994, art 3(2).
4 But note that s 388(2A) is added by art 15 of the Order, and provides that a person acts as an insolvency practitioner in relation to an insolvent partnership by acting, inter alia, as its administrator.
5 Insolvency Act 1986, s 411, contained in the Rules; rr 1.1–1.30 will apply to a PVA.
6 Ibid, s 413.
7 Ibid, s 414.
8 The Insolvency Practitioners Regulations 1990, SI 1990/439, as amended by the Insolvency Practitioners (Amendment) Regulations 1993, SI 1993/221, therefore apply in the context of a PVA.
9 Insolvency Act 1986, s 435(3).
10 Ibid, s 435(2); the term 'relative' in this context includes: brother, sister, uncle, aunt, nephew, niece, lineal ancestor, lineal descendant, half-blood, step- and adoptive relationships, illegitimate children (s 435(8)); the husband or wife of a relative is an associate (s 435(2)); the husband, wife or relative of a person's partner is an associate (s 435(3)); a reference to husband or wife includes a reference to a former husband or wife (s 435(8)).
11 Ibid, s 435(4).

8.3 PARTNERSHIPS TO WHICH THE PARTNERSHIP ADMINISTRATION PROCEDURE APPLIES

The Order, and thus the partnership administration procedure, applies to any partnership which the courts in England and Wales have jurisdiction to wind up[1]; generally speaking, that means any insolvent partnership which has carried on business in England and Wales within the previous three years[2], and which either has or at any time had a principal place of business in England and Wales[3].

A partnership which has a principal place of business in Scotland may not be wound up under the Order unless it had a principal place of business in England and Wales within the period of one year ending on the day on which a winding-up petition is presented[4].

A partnership which has a principal place of business in Northern Ireland may not be wound up under the Order unless it had a principal place of business in

England and Wales within the period of three years ending on the day on which a winding-up petition is presented[5].

The Order also applies to a partnership whose principal place of business is outside England and Wales, so long as it has at any time had a place of business in England and Wales where the business was carried on in the course of which the debt (or part of the debt) which forms the basis of a winding-up petition arose.

It is not clear whether actual presentation of a petition is necessary to found jurisdiction in the case of a partnership which does not have its principal place of business in England and Wales. The phrase 'a principal place of business' in this context appears to envisage that a partnership may have more than one, and many professional partnerships do have a number of substantial offices in different countries.

The phrase 'carry on' a business has generated a substantial body of case-law, but has yet to be defined by the court in this context. However, the well-established general principle appears to be that an individual (and therefore, a partnership) continues to carry on a business until all the debts are paid and all other obligations which have arisen (such as liability for tax) have been performed[6].

---

1 Insolvent Partnerships Order 1994, art 1(2)(a).
2 See s 221(2) of the Inbsolvency Act 1986, as modified by Schs 3, 4, 5, 6 to the Order.
3 Ibid, s 221(1) (as modified by Schs 3, 4, 5, 6).
4 Ibid, s 221(3)(a) (as modified by Schs 3, 4, 5, 6).
5 Ibid, s 221(3)(b) (as modified by Schs 3, 4, 5, 6).
6 *Re Dagnall* [1896] 2 QB 407; *Re Worsley* 17 TLR 122; *Theophile v Solicitor-General* [1950] AC 186; *Bird v IRC* [1962] 1 WLR 686; *Re a Debtor (No 784 of 1991)* [1992] Ch 554.

8.4 JURISDICTION OF THE COURT

8.4.1 *Circumstances in which the court may make an order*

The court may not make an administration order if:

(a) an order has been made for the partnership to be wound up as an unregistered company[1];

(b) an order has been made under art 11 of the Order for the bankruptcy of the individual members of an insolvent partnership and the winding up of the partnership business and administration of its property[2];

(c) the partnership is an insurance company within the meaning of the Insurance Companies Act 1982[3];

(d) the partnership is an authorised institution or a former authorised institution within the meaning of the Banking Act 1987[4];

(e) an agricultural receiver has been appointed[5] unless the person on whose behalf the receiver was appointed consents to the making of the partnership administration order[6] or the security by virtue of which the receiver was appointed is impeachable under Part VI of the Act[7].

In any other case, the court may grant an administration order if:

(a) it is satisfied that the partnership is unable to pay its debts[8]; and

(b) it considers that the making of the order would be likely to achieve one of the three statutory purposes[9].

The court has a complete discretion whether or not to grant an order[10], and may take into account in weighing the views of creditors that secured creditors do not stand to lose as much as unsecured creditors[11]. If proposals are unlikely to be approved by the creditors, that is a factor which would weigh strongly against an order[12].

---

1 Section 8(4) of the Insolvency Act 1986, as modified by Sch 2 to the Order; ie under arts 7, 8, 9 or 10 of the Order.
2 Ibid, s 8(4) (as modified).
3 Ibid, s 8(4)(a) (as modified).
4 Ibid, s 8(4)(b) (as modified). Administration orders are made in respect of present and former authorised institutions under the Banking Act 1987 by virtue of the Banks (Administration Proceedings) Order 1989, SI 1989/1276. That order modifies the provisions of the Act to apply the administration regime to banks and add the Bank of England to those who may petition for their administration. However, the Banks (Administration Proceedings) Order only applies to institutions 'which are companies within the meaning of section 735 of the Companies Act 1985', ie a company formed and registered under the Companies Act 1985 or previous legislation (s 735(1)(a)). In the case of a partnership, the Act is not amended. It therefore appears that, although a partnership is within the definition of an 'institution' (see Banking Act 1987, s 106(1)) and may therefore apply to become authorised under s 8 of the Banking Act, there is no jurisdiction to appoint an administrator in respect of an insolvent partnership which is or has been an authorised institution.
5 Ie a receiver appointed pursuant to a fixed and floating charge over farming stock and other agricultural assets under the Agricultural Credits Act 1928. Such a charge is quite a common feature of farming partnerships.
6 Section 9(3)(a) of the Insolvency Act 1986, as modified by Sch 2 to the Order.
7 Ibid, s 9(3)(b) (as modified); see para **8.2** above.
8 Ibid, s 8(1)(a) (as modified): note that whereas the equivalent test for a company is whether the company 'is or is likely to become unable to pay its debts', it is only the present state of the partnership which is relevant.
9 Ibid, s 8(1)(b) (as modified); see para **8.4.3** below.
10 *Re Consumer and Industrial Press Ltd* (1988) 4 BCC 68.
11 *Re Imperial Motors (UK) Ltd* (1989) 5 BCC 214.
12 *Re Arrows Ltd (No 3)* [1992] BCC 131.

8.4.2 Unable to pay its debts

The partnership is 'deemed unable to pay its debts'[1] if:

(a) the partnership has neglected to pay or secure or compound an undisputed and due debt of more than £750 in respect of which a statutory demand has been served on the partnership[2]; or

(b) an action or other proceeding[3] has been instituted against a member in respect of a partnership debt, and notice has been served on the partnership, but the partnership has not within three weeks of the notice either:
    (i) paid, secured or compounded for the debt or demand; or
    (ii) procured that the action or proceeding be stayed; or
    (iii) indemnified the defendant to his reasonable satisfaction against the action or proceeding and against all costs, damages and expenses[4]; or

(c) execution or other process has been issued on a judgment, decree or order against the partnership or any member in respect of a partnership debt and is returned unsatisfied[5];
(d) it is otherwise proved to the satisfaction of the court that the partnership is unable to pay its debts as they fall due[6];
(e) it is proved to the satisfaction of the court that the value of the partnership's assets is less than the amount of its liabilities, taking into account its contingent and prospective liabilities.

1 Within the meaning of ss 222, 223 or 224 of the Insolvency Act 1986.
2 Insolvency Act 1986, s 222.
3 Which, arguably, includes a bankruptcy petition: see per Rattee J in *Re a Debtor No 13A10 of 1994* [1996] BCC 57 at 65G.
4 Insolvency Act 1986, s 223.
5 Ibid, s 224(1)(a); note that this applies in England and Wales, and ss 224(1)(b) and (c) make equivalent provision for Scotland and Northern Ireland respectively.
6 Ibid, s 224(1)(d).

8.4.3 The three statutory purposes

A partnership administration order may be made for one or more of the following three purposes:

(a) the survival of the whole or any part of the undertaking of the partnership as a going concern[1];
(b) the approval of a PVA[2];
(c) a more advantageous realisation of the partnership property than would be effected on a winding up[3].

1 Section 8(3)(a) of the Insolvency Act 1986, as modified by Sch 2 to the Order.
2 Ibid, s 8(3)(b) (as modified): note that the achievement of interlocking IVAs, or IVAs of some of the partners, would not satisfy this purpose.
3 Ibid, s 8(3)(c) (as modified).

8.4.4 'Likely to achieve'

The court must form the view that there is a real prospect that one or more of the statutory purposes might be achieved[1]. The court will consider separately whether each proposed purpose satisfies this test[2]. Once the court has satisfied itself that it has jurisdiction, it then considers how likely the achievement of each specified statutory purpose is, as part of the exercise of its discretion whether to make the order[3].

1 *Re Harris Simons Construction Ltd* [1989] 1 WLR 368; *Re Primlaks (UK) Ltd* [1989] BCLC 734; *Re SCL Building Services Ltd* [1990] BCLC 98; *Re Rowbotham Baxter Ltd* [1990] BCLC 397; *Re Chelmsford City Football Club (1980) Ltd* [1991] BCC 133.
2 *Re SCL Building Services Ltd* (above).
3 *Re Harris Simons Construction Ltd* (above); *Re Primlaks (UK) Ltd* (above).

8.4.5 The survival of the undertaking of the partnership

Whereas s 8(3)(a) of the Act requires the survival of the company, there is no such requirement in respect of a partnership. The word 'undertaking' is not defined in the Act or the Order, but under other legislation it has been held to denote the business or enterprise undertaken by a company[1]. It appears that the condition would be satisfied in respect of a partnership if it could be shown that a sub-group of partners (for example, in one of a number of offices) would have a reasonable prospect of carrying on a solvent business[2].

---

1 *Baytrust Holdings v IRC* [1971] 1 WLR 1333, on s 55(1)(c)(i) of the Finance Act 1927.
2 Cf *Re Rowbotham Baxter Ltd* (above).

8.4.6 Partnership voluntary arrangement
See Chapter 7.

8.4.7 More advantageous realisation
There are a number of reasons why an administration might result in a more advantageous realisation of the partnership's assets than a winding up. A trading partnership will be able to continue in business (although it is not clear how far this would apply to a professional partnership where goodwill and clients might evaporate upon the making of an administration order). It is usually easier to persuade debtors to pay in full in an administration. An administrator may be able to deal with a partnership as a going concern, whereas a liquidator would not have the same power to deal with charged assets and would only be able to sell on a 'break up'. The partners are likely to be more motivated in an administration than in a winding up, when they might well face bankruptcy.

In an administration, funds would not need to be paid into the insolvency services account and would not be diminished by ad valorem fees; it is not thought that this practical aspect of more advantageous realisation would be a legitimate foundation for the making of an administration order. However, it may well be part of the basis on which a PVA is preferred by creditors to a liquidation.

8.5 WHO CAN PRESENT A PETITION FOR A PARTNERSHIP ADMINISTRATION ORDER?

8.5.1 Entitlement to present a petition
A petition[1] may be presented by either:

(a) the members of the insolvent partnership in their capacity as such[2]; or
(b) a creditor or creditors (including any contingent or prospective creditor or creditors)[3]; or
(c) the supervisor of a PVA[4];

and a petition may be presented by a creditor or creditors with the members.

---

1 Which must be in Form 1 in Sch 9 to the Order: see para **1.15** and the Form at p 343 in Appendix 2.
2 Section 9(1) of the Insolvency Act 1986, as modified by Sch 2 to the Order.
3 Ibid.
4 Section 7(4)(b) of the Insolvency Act 1986, as modified by Sch 1 to the Order.

8.5.2 The members
In order for a petition to be presented by 'the members', it appears that it would be sufficient for a decision to be taken by the partnership authorising

representative partners to present a petition in the name of the firm[1]. Such a decision will need to achieve whatever majority is specified in the partnership deed (if any). It was not possible until the Order came into force for a partnership to go into administration, so it is unlikely that there will be any provision in most partnership deeds specifying the necessary majority vote for partners to authorise the presentation of an administration petition. That being so, it is likely that the default provision in the Partnership Act will apply, requiring the consent of all existing partners to a change in the nature of the partnership business[2].

One difficulty which may arise is that the definition of 'member' for the purposes of the Order is a wide one, including anyone who is liable as a partner within s 14 of the Partnership Act; ie a non-partner who has been held out as a partner to a creditor who has, in reliance upon that holding out extended credit to the firm[3]. The consequences of being held to be a 'member' may be dramatic, because in the context of an insolvent partnership it appears that all the assets of the member will be available to all partnership creditors, whereas while the partnership is solvent only the creditor who actually relied would have a claim[4]. It would therefore be unwise for anyone who might be found to be a 'member' through holding out to take any step which could appear to concede the point, and where a partnership has a number of 'salaried partners' who might be 'members', it may not be possible to obtain their consent. However, as the Partnership Act only requires actual partners to consent, it is thought that that would be sufficient in practice[5].

---

1 Cf *Re Equitycorp International plc* [1989] BCLC 597.
2 Partnership Act 1890, s 24(8).
3 See para **2.11.3**.
4 And whereas in a solvent partnership the partner liable under s 14 of the Partnership Act 1890 may have an effective right of indemnity against the true partners, in an insolvent partnership that claim appears to be subordinated behind the creditors and likely to be worthless.
5 But note that this point has yet to be decided.

8.5.3 *The creditors*
The class of creditors entitled to present an administration petition against a partnership is wide. However, it does not include those creditors (such as, in certain cases, the landlord of a partnership) who may have a claim only in the separate estates of certain partners.

Experience has shown that in practice it is rare for creditors to present administration petitions in respect of companies, because they do not normally have sufficient information to do so, and perhaps because administration is regarded as a defensive tactic to produce a breathing space for a company in financial difficulties, rather than an offensive tactic by creditors[1]. However, presentation of a petition by a creditor would be one solution for those situations where a number of partners see the need for an administration but are unable to secure the requisite majority or unanimous vote for a petition to be presented by the members.

---

1 In the absence of a fixed and floating charge over the whole assets of a business, secured creditors may prefer administration as a means of obtaining a better realisation.

8.6 AFFIDAVIT IN SUPPORT OF THE PETITION

An affidavit must be prepared and sworn in support of the petition for an administration order[1].

(a) If the petition is to be presented by the members, the affidavit must be sworn by one of the partners, stating himself to make it on behalf of the members[2]. A solicitor (unless one of the members) cannot swear the affidavit in this instance.

(b) If the petition is to be presented by creditors (which includes the situation when a joint petition is presented by creditors and members), the affidavit must be made by a person acting under the authority of them all, whether or not one of their number[3]. In this case a solicitor *can* swear the affidavit so long as he is instructed by all parties. The affidavit must state:
  (i) the nature of the deponent's authority;
  (ii) the means of his knowledge of the matters to which the affidavit relates.

(c) If the petition is presented by the supervisor of a PVA, the petition is treated as if it were by the members of the partnership, and the affidavit must be sworn by one of the members[4].

---

1 Insolvency Rules 1986, r 2.1(1).
2 Ibid, r 2.1(2) (as modified).
3 Ibid, r 2.1(3).
4 Ibid, r 2.1(4).

8.7 THE CONTENTS OF THE AFFIDAVIT

The affidavit which is sworn in support of an administration petition must:

(a) state the deponent's belief that the partnership is, or is likely to become, unable to pay its debts and the grounds of that belief[1];

(b) state which of the statutory purposes is expected to be achieved by the making of an administration order[2];

(c) provide a statement of the partnership's financial position, specifying (to the best of the deponent's belief) assets and liabilities, including contingent and prospective liabilities;

(d) provide details of any security known or believed to be held by creditors of the partnership[3];

(e) if a petition for winding up the partnership has been presented, give details in the affidavit so far as these are within the knowledge of the deponent[4];

(f) state any other matters (within the knowledge or belief of the deponent) which, in the opinion of those intending to present the petition, will assist the court in deciding whether to make the order[5];

(e) either state that a report has been prepared under r 2.2, or, if there is no report under r 2.2, explain why[6].

There must be exhibited to the affidavit:

(a) a copy of the petition[7];
(b) written consent by the proposed administrator to accept appointment if an administration order is made[8]; and
(c) if a report has been prepared under r 2.2, a copy of it[9].

---

1 Insolvency Rules 1986, r 2.3(1)(a).
2 Ibid, r 2.3(1)(b).
3 Ibid, r 2.3(3); this rule also requires details of any powers to appoint, and any appointment of, an administrative receiver. This may be applicable where a partnership comprises companies, but where it is comprised of individuals, there cannot be an administrative receiver within the meaning of s 29(2) of the Act.
4 Ibid, r 2.3(4).
5 Ibid, r 2.3(5).
6 Ibid, r 2.3(6)
7 Ibid, r 2.4(6)(a).
8 Ibid, r 2.4(6)(b).
9 Ibid, r 2.4(6)(c).

8.8   THE 2.2 REPORT

Rule 2.2 provides for the preparation of a report by the proposed administrator of the partnership, or by some other independent person with sufficient knowledge of the partnership's affairs, to the effect that the appointment of an administrator for the partnership is 'expedient'. Such a report must specify the statutory purposes which an administration order may achieve[1]. The report is optional under the Rules, but in practice the '2.2 Report' is regarded as a valuable safeguard in assisting the court to see whether an application for an administration has a sound basis[2] and a court would be very unlikely to make an order without such a report being available[3] except perhaps in an entirely straightforward case[4].

In January 1994, Sir Donald Nicholls V-C issued a Practice Statement to clarify the purpose of the r 2.2 Report, which, in many instances, had become elaborate and expensive. He stressed that the costs of obtaining an administration order should not put the process out of the reach of smaller companies, and the same must apply to partnerships. He said:

'The extent of the necessary investigation and the amount of material to be provided to the court must be a matter for the judgment of the person who prepares the report and will vary from case to case. However, in the normal case, what the court needs is a concise assessment of the company's situation and of the prospects of an administration order achieving one or more of the statutory purposes. The latter will normally include an explanation of the availability of any finance required during the administration.

Every endeavour should be made to avoid disproportionate investigation and expense. In some cases a brief investigation and report will be all that is required. Where the court has insufficient material on which to base its decision, but the proposed administrator is in court, he may offer to supplement the material by giving oral evidence. In such a case he should subsequently provide a supplemental report covering the matters on which oral evidence was given so that this can be placed on the court file.'

Insolvent Partnerships

1 Insolvency Rules 1986, r 2.2(3).
2 *Practice Statement (Administration Orders: Reports)* [1994] 1 WLR 160.
3 *Re Newport County Association Football Club Ltd* [1987] BCC 635; *Re W F Fearman Ltd* (1988) 4 BCC 139; *Re Shearing & Loader Ltd* [1991] BCLC 764.
4 *Practice Statement* (above).

8.9   THE PETITION

If the petition is presented by the members of the partnership, it must state the name of the partnership and its address for service (which is the principal place of business of the partnership within the jurisdiction)[1].

If the petition is presented by one creditor, the petition must state his name and address for service[2]. If it is presented by more than one creditor, it must name each creditor, but from and after presentation it is treated as if it was the petition of only one of them, who must be nominated as petitioning on behalf of himself and other creditors, and his address for service must be specified[3].

The petition must specify the name and address of the proposed administrator, and it must state that, to the best of the petitioner's knowledge and belief, the person is qualified to act as an insolvency practitioner in relation to the partnership[4].

The petition and the affidavit are filed in court with sufficient copies to serve every necessary party[5]. Once the petition has been filed, it is the duty of the petitioner to notify the court in writing of any winding-up petition presented against the partnership, as soon as he becomes aware of it[6].

Once the petition has been presented, it may not be withdrawn except with the leave of the court[7].

1 Insolvency Rules 1986, r 2.4(1); cf Rules of the Supreme Court 1965, Ord 81, r 3(1)(b).
2 Ibid, r 2.4(2).
3 Ibid, r 2.4(4).
4 Ibid, r 2.4(5).
5 Ibid, r 2.5.
6 Ibid, r 2.5(4).
7 Section 9(2)(b) of the Insolvency Act 1986, as modified by Sch 2 to the Order.

8.10   THE EFFECT OF AN APPLICATION FOR A PARTNERSHIP ADMINISTRATION ORDER

From the moment a petition for an administration order is presented[1] until the Order sought has been made or the petition has been dismissed, a statutory moratorium is imposed which prevents the partnership being wound up or a joint bankruptcy petition being presented by the partners[2], and forbids the enforcement of security over the partnership's property without the leave of the court[3]. The terms of this moratorium are almost identical to the moratorium which comes into force when an administration order is made, which is discussed in detail below[4].

1 Where an agricultural receiver has been appointed, the period does not begin until the person by or on whose behalf the receiver was appointed has consented to the making of an administration order: s 10(3) of the Insolvency Act 1986, as modified by Sch 2 to the Order.
2 Under art 11 of the Order.
3 Section 10 of the Insolvency Act 1986, as modified by Sch 2 to the Order.
4 See para **8.19**.

8.11 SERVICE AND NOTICE OF THE PETITION

The petition, the affidavit and exhibits[1] must be served, not less than five days before the day fixed for the hearing[2]:

(a) on the proposed administrator[3];
(b) if a petition to wind up the partnership is pending, upon the petitioner[4];
(c) if a provisional liquidator has been appointed in respect of the partnership, upon him[5];
(d) if the petition is presented by creditors, upon the partnership[6].

The Rules also provide for service on an administrative receiver and on any person who is or may be entitled to appoint an administrative receiver[7]. This apparently will not arise if the members of a partnership are all individuals because individuals cannot grant a floating charge over their assets[8] and therefore cannot be subject to an administrative receiver within the meaning of s 29(2) of the Act. It may arise in the rarer circumstance where a partnership consists of companies (ie some forms of joint venture).

The documents may be served by sending them by first class post[9] or by delivery:

(a) to the partnership at its principal place of business within the jurisdiction[10] or if that is not practicable, to its last known principal place of business in England and Wales[11];
(b) to any other person at his proper address[12], which is any address he has previously notified for service or, failing that, his usual or last known address[13].

Service of the affidavit must be verified by affidavit, specifying the date and manner of service, which must be filed in court not less than one clear day before the hearing[14].

In addition, the petitioner must give notice of the petition forthwith:

(a) to any person who has appointed, or is or may be entitled to appoint, an agricultural receiver of the partnership[15];
(b) to any sheriff or other officer who to his knowledge is charged with an execution or other legal process against the partnership or its property;
(c) to any person who to his knowledge has distrained against the partnership or its property.

1 Insolvency Rules 1986, r 2.6(1).
2 Ibid, r 2.7(1).
3 Ibid, r 2.6(2)(d).
4 Ibid, r 2.6(2)(c).
5 Ibid.

6 Ibid, r 2.6(3).
7 Ibid, r 2.6(2)(a), (b).
8 Because such a charge is inconsistent with the requirement for defined assets to be charged under the Bills of Sale Act 1878, and possibly on the policy ground that an individual cannot dispose of all his assets, because that would be akin to slavery.
9 Insolvency Rules 1986, r 2.7(5).
10 Ibid, 2.7(2)(a) as modified; cf Rules of the Supreme Court 1965, Ord 81, r 3.
11 Insolvency Rules 1986, r 2.7(3).
12 Ibid, r 2.7(2)(b).
13 Ibid, r 2.7(4).
14 Ibid, r 2.8.
15 Section 9(2)(a) of the Insolvency Act 1986, as modified by Sch 2 to the Order.

8.12 THE POWER TO ABRIDGE TIME

In an appropriate case, the court has the power to abridge the period of five clear days specified in the Rules[1] and will hear an urgent application ex parte where it is satisfied that this is justified in all the circumstances[2].

1 Insolvency Rules 1986, r 12.9; *Re a Company No 00175 of 1987* (1987) 3 BCC 124; *Re Gallidoro Trawlers Ltd* [1991] BCLC 411.
2 *Re Cavco Floors Ltd* [1990] BCC 589; *Re Shearing & Loader Ltd* [1991] BCC 232; *Re Gallidoro Trawlers Ltd* (above); *Re Chancery plc* [1991] BCC 171 where, in a banking case, the application was heard in camera.

8.13 THE HEARING

It is important to ensure that all relevant information is put before the court[1]. The judge is to consider the proposal critically and, if necessary, the court will take further time for consideration even in an urgent case[2].

The following persons are entitled to be heard[3]:

(a) the petitioner;
(b) the members of the partnership[4];
(c) any person who has presented a petition for the winding up of the partnership;
(d) the proposed administrator.

The Rules also provide for attendance by an administrative receiver and by any person who is or may be entitled to appoint an administrative receiver[5]. Once again, this will not arise where the partners are individuals[6]. In addition, the court can permit any other person who appears to have an interest justifying his appearance to appear or be represented at the hearing[7]. That category might, for example, include retired partners, and creditors of individual partners[8]. If the court makes an administration order, the costs of the petitioner and of any person appearing whose costs are allowed by the court are payable as an expense of the administration[9].

On hearing the petition, the court may grant an administration order, or dismiss the petition, or adjourn the hearing with or without conditions[10], or make an interim order or any other order it thinks fit[11]. Generally, in considering how to exercise its discretion, the court will want to weigh up the interests of secured creditors, unsecured creditors and the members[12]. It will not make an order which would unfairly prejudice individual creditors or groups of creditors[13], or where it is clear that the statutory purposes would not be achieved because of opposition by the creditors[14]. In the context of an insolvent partnership, the court may well have to consider the position of creditors of individual partners who are not creditors of the partnership itself[15]. The court will be particularly concerned to know how it is proposed to fund the administration[16].

Where one of the causes for the partnership getting into financial difficulties is deadlock between the partners, it will be particularly important to reassure the court that those difficulties have been overcome. If that is not the case, it seems a court would be unlikely to make an administration order for the purpose of the continuation of the whole of the partnership's undertaking as a going concern[17].

---

1 *Re Sharps of Truro Ltd* [1990] BCC 94; *Astor Chemical Ltd v Synthetic Technology Ltd* [1990] BCC 97.

2 *Cornhill Insurance plc v Cornhill Financial Services Ltd* [1992] BCC 818.

3 Insolvency Rules 1986, r 2.9(1).

4 Partners and others who are members under the Order are obviously in a different position from the members of a company, who will often not be heard by a court where the company is plainly insolvent; cf *Re Chelmsford City Football Club (1980) Ltd* [1991] BCC 133.

5 Insolvency Rules 1986, r 2.9(1)(c), (d). Appearance includes the right to be represented by counsel or a solicitor.

6 See para **8.7**.

7 Insolvency Rules 1986, r 2.9(1)(g).

8 Such as, in certain circumstances, a landlord with merely a separate estate claim. See para **2.13.5**.

9 Insolvency Rules 1986, r 2.9(2).

10 For instance, the Vice-Chancellor has suggested that in suitable cases the court might require the administrator to hold a meeting of creditors before reporting back to the court within a relatively short period: see *Practice Statement (Administration Orders: Reports)* [1994] 1 WLR 160. This might be appropriate where it is not clear whether the support of creditors would be forthcoming.

11 Section 9(4) of the Insolvency Act 1986, as modified by Sch 2 to the Order.

12 Cf *Re Consumer & Industrial Press Ltd* [1988] BCLC 177; *Re Imperial Motors (UK) Ltd* [1990] BCLC 29.

13 *Cornhill Insurance plc v Cornhill Financial Services Ltd* [1992] BCC 818.

14 *Re Arrows Ltd (No 3)* [1992] BCLC 555; *Re Land & Property Trust Co plc (No 2)* [1991] BCLC 849.

15 Such as, in certain circumstances, the landlord: see footnote 8 above.

16 Cf *Re Rowbotham Baxter Ltd* [1990] BCLC 397.

17 Cf *Re Business Properties Ltd* (1988) 4 BCC 684.

8.14 INTERIM ORDER

In an appropriate case, the court can hold the fort by making an interim order, for example over an adjournment for further information to be gathered. An interim order may restrict the exercise of any powers of the officers of the partnership by reference to requiring the consent of the court, or of an insolvency practitioner, or in some other way[1]. There is no power to appoint an interim administrator, but the court can appoint a person to take control of the property of a partnership and manage it pending the hearing of the application[2].

---

1 Section 9(5) of the Insolvency Act 1986, as modified by Sch 2 to the Order.
2 Cf *Re a Company No 00175 of 1987* (1987) 3 BCC 124.

8.15   ADMINISTRATION ORDER

An administration order must specify the administrator or administrators who are to act[1] and the statutory purposes for which the order is made[2]. The court may appoint more than one administrator; if so, the order must state whether any act required or authorised under any enactment to be done by an administrator is to be done by all or any one or more of the persons for the time being holding the office[3]. The court must give notice to the administrator(s) forthwith (ie immediately)[4], and must send a sealed copy of the order to him[5].

Upon the making of an administration order, any petition for either:

(a)   the winding up of the partnership; or
(b)   the joint bankruptcy of the partners under art 11 of the Order;

must be dismissed by the court[6].

---

1 See s 13(1) of the Insolvency Act 1986, as modified by Sch 2 to the Order.
2 Ibid, s 8(3) (as modified by Sch 2).
3 Section 231(2) in Part VI of the Act; see (b) at para **8.2** above.
4 Insolvency Rules 1986, r 2.10(1).
5 Ibid, r 2.10(4): the reference in the Rule to a second copy being sent by the administrator to the Registrar of Companies is to be ignored (by art 3(2) of the Order).
6 Section 11(1) of the Insolvency Act 1986, as modified by Sch 2 to the Order.

8.16   APPOINTMENT OF AN ADMINISTRATOR

An administrator of a partnership is initially appointed by the making of the administration order[1]. If a vacancy subsequently arises through death[2], resignation[3] or otherwise, the court can fill the vacancy by a further order[4].

Where there is a dispute between different parties over who should be appointed as administrator, the court may have regard to which would be able to carry out the administration more effectively and cheaply, for example, if they have prior knowledge from having investigated the affairs of the partnership for a creditor, and this may outweigh arguments as to potential conflict[5]. Alternatively, in an appropriate case, the court may appoint joint administrators[6].

Upon appointment, an administrator of a partnership:

(a)   may do all such things as may be necessary for the management of the affairs and business of the partnership and of the partnership property[7];
(b)   has the powers which are specified in modified Sch 1 to the Act (as set out in Sch 2 to the Order);
(c)   becomes deemed to act as the agent of the members of the partnership in their capacity as such[8];

(d) has the power to prevent any person from taking part in the management of the partnership business[9];

(e) has the power to appoint any person to be a manager of the partnership business[10];

(f) has the power to call a meeting of the members of the partnership[11];

(g) has the power to call a meeting of the creditors of the partnership[12];

(h) has the power to apply to the court for directions[13].

Upon appointment, the administrator of a partnership must take into his custody or under his control all the property to which the partnership is or appears to be entitled[14]. He must then manage the affairs, business and property of the partnership[15] in accordance with any directions of the court until proposals have been approved by a meeting of the partnership's creditors[16], and in accordance with such proposals once they have been approved[17].

In exercising his duties the administrator is to be judged by the standards of a professional insolvency practitioner of ordinary skill[18].

1 Section 13(1) of the Insolvency Act 1986, as modified by Sch 2 to the Order.

2 If the administrator dies, either his personal representatives, or a partner in his firm who is an insolvency practitioner, or any person producing a copy of the relevant death certificate, may give notice to the court; it is the duty of the personal representatives to see that this is done: see r 2.54.

3 The administrator may resign for ill health, or if he ceases to practise as an insolvency practitioner, or if there is some conflict of interest or change in his personal circumstances which precludes or makes impracticable the further discharge of his duties as administrator (r 2.53(1)). He may resign on other grounds with the leave of the court (r 2.53(2)). Unless he has the leave of the court, he must give at least seven days' notice of his intention to resign to a continuing administrator or, in the absence of such, to the creditors' committee, or in the absence of such, to the partnership and its creditors (r 2.53(3)).

4 Section 13(1), (2) of the Insolvency Act 1986, as modified by Sch 2 to the Order. An application for an order to appoint a replacement administrator may be made by a continuing administrator or, in the absence of such, by the creditors' committee, or in the absence of such, by the members of the partnership or by any creditor or creditors of the partnership: s 13(3) (as modified). It would appear that the same considerations would apply to an application by the members here as apply to the original presentation of a petition by the members (see above).

5 Cf *Re Maxwell Communication Corporation plc* [1992] BCLC 465.

6 Cf *Re Polly Peck International plc* (unreported) (25 October 1990).

7 Section 14(1) of the Insolvency Act 1986, as modified by Sch 2 to the Order.

8 Ibid, s 14(5) (as modified).

9 Ibid, s 14(2)(a) (as modified).

10 Ibid.

11 Ibid, s 14(2)(b) (see below).

12 Ibid.

13 Ibid, s 14(3) (as modified).

14 Section 17(1) of the Insolvency Act 1986, as applied by art 6(1) of the Order.

15 Ibid, s 17(2), as applied by art 6(1) of the Order.

16 Ibid, s 17(2)(a).

17 Ibid, s 17(2)(b).

18 *Re Charnley Davies Ltd* [1990] BCC 605, although it might be argued that the insolvency practitioner should have regard to the nature of the appointment; for example, that he should consider whether he is capable of managing the practice of a firm of solicitors or accountants.

8.17 AGRICULTURAL AND OTHER RECEIVERS

Once an administration order has been made, a receiver of the partnership property or an agricultural receiver of the partnership can only remain in place if the administrator permits. If the administrator requires such a receiver to vacate his office, he must do so[1]. If such a receiver vacates office, his remuneration and expenses, and any indemnity to which he is entitled, must be charged on and paid out of any partnership property which was in his custody or under his control in priority to any security held by the person by or on whose behalf he was appointed[2].

An administrator can dispose of property which is subject to an agricultural floating charge without leave of the court unless an agricultural receiver has been appointed under that security, in which case an application to court is required[3].

1 Section 11(2) of the Insolvency Act 1986, as modified by Sch 2 to the Order.
2 Ibid, s 11(4) (as modified).
4 Ibid, s 15(3) (as modified).

8.18 ADVERTISEMENT AND NOTIFICATION

Once an administration order has been made, the administrator must advertise it forthwith in the *London Gazette*, and also in such newspaper as he thinks most appropriate for ensuring that it will come to the notice of the partnership's creditors[1]. The administrator must give notice to any provisional liquidator who has been appointed in respect of the partnership[2], and if a winding up petition was pending at the time of the order, to the petitioner[3]. Notice must also be given to any person who has appointed or is or may be entitled to appoint an administrative receiver, but this is unlikely to arise.

Every invoice, order for goods or business letter bearing the name (or trading name) of the firm which is issued by or on behalf of the partnership or the administrator when an administration order is in force must also contain:

(a) the name of the administrator;
(b) a statement that the affairs and business of the partnership and the partnership property are being managed by the administrator[4].

In the event of default, the administrator, and any officer of the partnership[5] who without reasonable excuse authorises or permits the default is liable to a fine.

Administration is thus very much a public procedure, and it is thought unlikely that professional partnerships whose reputation involves any element of commercial reliability (such as accountancy firms and city solicitors) would retain the goodwill of their clients through an administration.

1 Insolvency Rules 1986, r 2.10(2).
2 Ibid, r 2.10(3)(c).
3 Ibid.

4 Section 12(1) of the Insolvency Act 1986, as modified by Sch 2 to the Order.
5 Ie any partner, any member by estoppel, and any person who has management or control of the partnership business: art 2(1) of the Order.

8.19 THE STATUTORY MORATORIUM

8.19.1 *The scope of the statutory moratorium*

While an administration order is in force:

(a) no order may be made for the winding up of the partnership[1];
(b) no joint bankruptcy order may be made upon the petition of the partners under art 11 of the Order[2];
(c) no order for the dissolution of the partnership may be made under s 35 of the Partnership Act in respect of the partnership[3].

In addition, the following things may not be done except with the leave of the administrator[4] or the consent of the court (which may be subject to conditions):

(a) no agricultural receiver of the partnership may be appointed[5];
(b) no steps may be taken to enforce any security over the partnership property[6];
(c) no steps may be taken to repossess goods in the possession of one or more of the officers of the partnership in their capacity as such under any 'hire-purchase agreement'[7] (which is defined for these purposes as including conditional sale agreements, chattel leasing agreements and retention of title agreements[8]);
(d) no other proceedings and no execution or other legal process may be commenced or continued, and no distress may be levied, against the partnership or the partnership property[9].

The statutory moratorium which applies once an administration order is in force[10] is fundamental to the whole scheme of the administration procedures which are designed to give an insolvent partnership a breathing space to explore with creditors and financiers whether it is possible to rescue part or all of the undertaking, or at least to produce some better outcome for creditors than would be the case if the partnership were wound up. The courts will therefore take a purposive approach in order to give effect to the statutory provisions, although they will not distort the meaning of the words Parliament has chosen to achieve that result[11].

1 Section 11(3)(a) of the Insolvency Act 1986, as modified by Sch 2 to the Order.
2 Ibid, s 11(3)(b) (as modified).
3 Ibid, s 11(3)(c) (as modified).
4 Once an order has been granted.
5 Ie under the Agricultural Credits Act 1928.
6 Section 11(3)(e) of the Insolvency Act 1986, as modified by Sch 2 to the Order: note that nothing prevents the enforcement of security over the separate property of a partner, as for example where a partner has granted an 'all monies' charge over his home to secure a loan from the bank also used by the partnership.
7 Ibid, s 11(3)(e) (as modified).
8 See s 10(4) of the Insolvency Act 1986, as modified by Sch 2 to the Order.
9 Ibid, s 11(3)(f) (as modified).

10 Like that which is imposed under s 10 of the Act (as modified by Sch 2) once a petition for an administration order is presented, to which the same principles apply.

11 *Bristol Airport plc v Powdrill* [1990] Ch 744; and see *Re a Company (No 001992 of 1988)* (1988) 4 BCC 451.

8.19.2 Enforce security

'Security' in this context includes any mortgage, charge, lien or other similar security[1]. A creditor who has begun to execute a judgment and sent in bailiffs who have entered into a walking possession agreement is a secured creditor for these purposes[2].

1 As defined in s 248(b)(i) of the Insolvency Act 1986. See in this regard the decisions of the Court of Appeal in *Re Paramount Airways Ltd* [1990] Ch 744 and in *Re Atlantic Computer Systems plc* [1992] Ch 505, discussed at para **8.19.9** below.

2 *Re Charles Clarke* [1898] 1 Ch 336; *Peck v Craighead* [1995] 1 BCLC 337.

8.19.3 Goods

It is thought that 'goods' in this context refers to all personal chattels except things in action and money (save where money is a commodity, as in the case of a dealer in old coins)[1].

1 Cf the definition in s 61(1) of the Sale of Goods Act 1979, which is incorporated in the Consumer Credit Act 1974.

8.19.4 Commencement or continuation of proceedings

'Proceedings' is to be given a narrow meaning limited to legal or quasi-legal proceedings. This would include arbitrations and court actions, and proceedings before industrial tribunals[1]. A bankruptcy petition has been said to be a legal (in the sense of judicial) proceeding[2], but service of a statutory demand is not an insolvency proceeding[3], and so apparently not a proceeding at all.

1 *Bristol Airport plc v Powdrill* [1990] Ch 744; cf *Re Hartlebury Printers Ltd* [1992] ICR 559. An application to an industrial tribunal is a 'proceeding', see *Carr v British Helicopters Ltd* [1993] BCC 855.

2 *Re a Debtor No 13A10 of 1994* [1996] BCC 57.

3 *Re a Debtor (No 190 of 1987)* (1988) *The Times*, 21 May. The point has yet to be decided in this context.

8.19.5 'Against the partnership'

The meaning of the phrase 'against the partnership' in this context is probably the single most important issue which will decide how effective the new partnership administration procedure can be. The first signs have not been particularly encouraging[1] but there has yet to be any definitive authority on the point.

It should be remembered that an action against a partnership in the name of the firm is merely an administrative convenience; it is an action against the partners using the firm's name as short-hand. If such an action is stayed, it would be very strange if the plaintiff could still bring an action against one of the partners for the same cause of action.

The expression 'the partnership' in ss 10 and 11 of the Act (as modified) must be a reference to the partnership which is in administration; that is to say, to those who are present partners[2].

Litigation may have been commenced against the entity which bore the same firm-name at a previous time, when the membership was different. On a strict construction of the section, such litigation would not be stayed at all. Insofar as a judgment in such litigation might be enforced against partnership property, it would be desirable for the consent of the administrator or the court to be required.

As a matter of principle, the fact that a stay is imposed against one joint defendant does not mean that the action cannot continue against a co-defendant[3], and so there seems to be no reason why an administration order must bar proceedings against a former partner, or against a person who was formerly employed by the partnership and has become liable 'as a partner' under s 14 of the Partnership Act by being held out to a person who has extended credit in reliance upon that holding out.

Is a bankruptcy petition against an individual partner a proceeding against the partnership? From a certain perspective, at least, it is (or may be). The bankruptcy of an individual partner may well bring about a dissolution of the partnership[4]. The bankruptcy of all the partners would almost certainly frustrate the purposes of an administration. Just as an action against an individual partner for a partnership debt is a species of action against a partnership, so the presentation of a bankruptcy petition against an individual partner for a partnership debt is an attack which is derived from his liability *qua* partner (whereas no such objection can be taken against a statutory demand presented against a partner by a separate estate creditor).

However, it is argued that there is no *express* prohibition on the presentation of a bankruptcy petition by a creditor against a partner in ss 10 or 11 (as modified), whereas there is a prohibition in modified s 10(1)(a) and modified s 11(1)(a) against the making of an order under art 11 of the Order after joint presentation of bankruptcy petitions by individual members for bankruptcy of those members and the winding up of the partnership. That would not provide a definitive answer, if a bankruptcy petition against a partner fell within 'other proceedings ... against the partnership'.

As a matter of policy, it would be preferable if the presentation of a petition against a partner required consent of the administrator or the leave of the court where an administration petition had been presented or an order was in force, so that consideration could be given to the likely effect on the statutory purposes. However, until the position is clarified, it may well be necessary for individual partners who face bankruptcy petitions to propose IVAs even though there is an administration order in force.

The claims of a separate estate creditor (such as, in certain circumstances, a landlord of a partnership with claims only against the four partners named on the lease[5]) are not claims 'against the partnership' directly; it appears that an administration order would not stay proceedings in respect of those claims against the individual partners, although any attempt to levy distress against partnership property would apparently be stayed[6] unless the administrator or the court gave consent.

1 For example, in *Re Sean McBride, Re Patrick McBride* (unreported) 30 January 1996, a deputy bankruptcy registrar was persuaded to make bankruptcy orders against two partners when there was an administration order in force in respect of the partnership. However, the survival of the partnership's undertaking was not one of the purposes of the administration, the partners were not legally represented, and the decision was made without full argument.
2 The definition of 'member' in art 2(1) of the Order distinguishes between the 'member of the partnership' (ie partner) and the 'person who is liable as a partner within the meaning of section 14 of the Partnership Act 1890' (ie the partner by estoppel). 'The partnership' is not defined, but must, it is thought, be taken to mean 'the (present) partners' and not the wider class of those who are members under the Order.
3 See s 3 of the Civil Liability (Contribution) Act 1978 and para **2.16**.
4 Under s 33(1) of the Partnership Act 1890 where there is no provision in the partnership deed to the contrary: see (l) at para **2.9.1**.
5 See para **2.13.5**.
6 Under modified ss 10(1)(c), 11(1)(c) in Sch 2 to the Order.

8.19.6   *Execution*

'Execution' is probably to be given the wide meaning of any process for enforcing or giving effect to a court judgment or order. An application for a charging order has been held to be 'execution' for legal aid purposes[1]. It appears that a judgment against a partnership may still be enforced against the separate property of a partner[2], notwithstanding the existence of an administration order[3].

1 *Parr v Smith* (1994) *The Independent,* 7 March, CA.
2 Cf *Investors and Pensions Advisory Service Ltd v Gray* [1990] BCLC 38.
3 Assuming that the conditions under Rules of the Supreme Court 1965, Ord 81, r 5 have been satisfied: see para **2.16.1**.

8.19.7   *'Other legal process'*

The expression 'other legal process' has been the subject of conflicting authority in the company context[1]. The better view is that the ordinary meaning of 'proceedings' and 'legal process' embraces all steps in legal proceedings from the initiation of proceedings to enforcement of judgment, but not 'non-judicial steps' which do not require the assistance of the court.

1 Compare *Exchange Travel Agency Ltd v Triton Property Trust plc* [1991] BCLC 396 with *Re Olympia & York Canary Wharf Ltd* [1993] BCC 154. In *Re a Debtor No 13A10 of 1994* [1996] BCC 57, Rattee J, considering peaceable re-entry by a landlord in the context of an interim order for an individual voluntary arrangement, preferred Millett J's view in *Re Olympia & York Canary Wharf Ltd.* So did Mr Roger Kaye QC in *McMullen & Sons Ltd v Cerrone* [1994] BCC 25.

8.19.8   *Distress*

'Distress' is an ancient remedy, involving the right to seize goods for unpaid rent or other bills. The Court of Appeal has resisted an attempt to broaden its meaning in a modern context[1].

'Levying distress' is a continuing process[2]; even if bailiffs have taken walking possession before an administration petition has been presented, no further step may be taken without leave.

1 *Bristol Airport v Powdrill* [1990] Ch 744.
2 See *In re Memco Engineering Ltd* [1986] Ch 86; cf *McMullen & Sons Ltd v Cerrone* [1994] 1 BCLC 152 in the context of an interim order for an individual voluntary arrangement.

8.19.9 The grant of consent or leave

In considering whether to give leave for the enforcement of security or the commencement or continuation s of proceedings, etc under modified s 10 or modified s 11 of the Act, the court may impose conditions[1]. An administrator may similarly impose terms when giving his consent[2].

In the *Atlantic Computers* case[3], the Court of Appeal set out detailed guidance on the principles which are applicable where consent or leave is sought; they may be summarised as follows:

(a) the onus is on the person seeking leave to make out his case;
(b) if the grant of leave is unlikely to impede the achievement of the purposes for which the administration has been ordered, leave should normally be given;
(c) in other cases, the court has to carry out a balancing exercise, weighing the legitimate interests of the applicant against the other creditors;
(d) an administration for the benefit of unsecured creditors should not be carried out at the expense of those who have proprietary rights;
(e) where the applicant would otherwise suffer significant loss, leave will normally be granted unless substantially greater loss would then be caused to others;
(f) the conduct of the parties may be a material consideration.

These factors may also be relevant to the question of whether to impose terms if leave is granted, or if it is refused. Proceedings commenced without leave are apparently not a nullity in this context[4].

An administrator is supposed to make his decision on whether to give consent quickly, having regard to the *Atlantic Computer* principles which would be applied by the court. He is not supposed to use consent as a bargaining counter in negotiations where he has regard only to the interests of the unsecured creditors. If he withholds consent unreasonably, he may be penalised in costs[5], and may even be ordered to pay compensation[6].

1 Insolvency Act 1986, ss 10(1)(b), 11(3)(e), (f), as modified by Sch 2 to the Order.
2 *Re Atlantic Computer Systems plc* [1992] Ch 505; cf *Bristol Airport plc v Powdrill* [1990] Ch 744.
3 [1992] Ch 505 at pp 542–544.
4 *Carr v British International Helicopters Ltd* [1993] BCC 855, EAT, at least as far as applications by individuals to an industrial tribunal are concerned; but compare Rattee J's decision in *Re National Employers Mutual General Insurance Association Ltd (in liquidation)* [1995] 1 BCLC 232, in which he held that proceedings commenced against a company in compulsory liquidation without first having obtained the leave of the court *were* a nullity.
5 *Bristol Airport plc v Powdrill* (above).
6 *Barclays Mercantile Business Finance Ltd v Sibec Developments Ltd* [1992] 1 WLR 1253.

8.20 THE STATEMENT OF AFFAIRS

Where an administration order has been made, the administrator must forthwith require the provision of a statement of affairs of the partnership in the prescribed form[1] by some or all of the following:

(a) the present or past officers of the partnership[2];

(b) anyone who took part in the formation of the partnership within one year before the date of the administration order[3];

(c) those who are, or have been within the past year, employed by the partnership if they are capable of giving the information required in the opinion of the administrator[4];

(d) those who are or have been within one year before the date of the administration order officers or employees of a company which has been an officer of the partnership[5] (in other words, directors or employees of a corporate partner).

The administrator must send a notice to each person whom he requires to submit a statement of affairs[6], and must provide the necessary forms on request[7]. The statement of affairs must then be provided within 21 days of notice being given by the administrator[8] unless either the administrator or the court releases the person from the obligation to do so or extends time[9]. Otherwise, failure to comply is an offence punishable by a fine and a daily default fine[10]. Reasonable expenses of a statement of affairs and affidavit will be paid by an administrator out of his receipts.

Each person required to submit a statement of affairs must verify it by affidavit on the same form[11]. In addition, the administrator may require any of the persons listed above to submit an affidavit of concurrence, stating that he concurs with the statement of affairs[12]. Where the maker of an affidavit of concurrence does not agree with the deponent who has made the statement of affairs, or considers the statement to be erroneous or misleading, or where he is without the necessary direct knowledge, the affidavit of concurrence may be qualified[13].

The verified copy of the statement of affairs and any affidavit of concurrence must be filed in court by the administrator[14]. The administrator may apply to the court for an order of limited disclosure in respect of the whole or any part of the statement, if he thinks that it would prejudice the conduct of the administration for the whole statement or the relevant part to be disclosed[15]. The court may then order that the statement or the specified part is not to be filed in court, or that it is to be filed separately and not open to inspection without the leave of the court[16].

---

1 Form 2.9, as specified by the Insolvency Rules 1986, r 2.12(1).

2 Section 22(3)(a) of the Insolvency Act 1986, as applied by art 6(1) of the Order and modified by art 3(4) of the Order; by art 2(1) 'officers' includes partners, persons liable under s 14 of the Partnership Act through holding out, and persons who have management or control of a partnership business.

3 Section 22(3)(b) of the Insolvency Act 1986, as applied by art 6(1) of the Order and modified by art 3(4) of the Order. It is difficult to see how this would apply to a partnership, although conceivably solicitors who drafted a partnership deed or accountants who were involved in the formation of a particular partnership might come within this provision.

4 Section 22(3)(c) of the Insolvency Act 1986, as applied by art 6(1) of the Order and modified by art 3(4) of the Order.
5 Section 22(3)(d) of the Insolvency Act 1986, as applied by art 6(1) of the Order and modified by art 3(4) of the Order.
6 Insolvency Rules 1986, r 2.11(1).
7 Ibid, r 2.11(4).
8 Section 22(4) of the Insolvency Act 1986, as applied by art 6(1) of the Order.
9 Section 22(5) of the Insolvency Act 1986, as applied by art 6(1) of the Order. If a deponent is refused a release or an extension of time by the administrator, he may apply to the court, which must give the deponent an opportunity to attend an ex parte hearing on at least seven days' notice before it decides to dismiss the application. If the court decides not to dismiss the application ex parte at that stage, it gives directions for a hearing at which the administrator may appear and may file a report of any matters which he considers ought to be drawn to the court's attention. The applicant must give the administrator notice of the hearing and serve any evidence at least 14 days before the hearing. The applicant's costs must be borne by him, and although it appears that the court may in exceptional circumstances make an allowance for them out of the partnership's assets, it seems unlikely in practice to do so. See r 2.14.
10 Section 22(6) of the Insolvency Act 1986, as applied by art 6(1) of the Order.
11 Insolvency Rules 1986, r 2.12(1).
12 Ibid, r 2.12.
13 Ibid, r 2.12(3).
14 Ibid, r 2.12(6).
15 Ibid, r 2.13(1).
16 Ibid, r 2.13(2).

8.21 THE ADMINISTRATOR'S PROPOSALS

Within three months of the making of an administration order in respect of a partnership (or such longer period as the court may allow), the administrator must:

(a) send to all those creditors of the partnership of whose addresses he is aware a statement of his proposals for achieving the purpose or purposes specified in the administration order[1];

(b) send a copy of his statement to all the members of the partnership so far as he is aware of their addresses[2], or publish a notice in the *London Gazette* and in the newspaper in which the administration order was advertised[3] stating an address to which members should write for copies of the administrator's statement to be sent to them free of charge[4];

(c) summon a meeting of creditors of the partnership for the purpose of considering his proposals on not less than 14 days' notice[5].

If the administrator fails to comply with these requirements without reasonable excuse, he is liable to a fine[6].

There must be annexed to the administrator's proposals when they are laid before the meeting of the partnership's creditors a statement by the administrator showing:

(a) details relating to his appointment as administrator, the purposes for which the administration order was applied for and made, and any subsequent variation of those purposes[7];

(b) the names of the partners[8];

(c) an account of the circumstances giving rise to the application for an administration order;

(d) if a statement of affairs has been submitted, a copy or summary of it, with the administrator's comments, if any[9];

(e) if no statement of affairs has been submitted, details of the financial position of the partnership, at the latest practicable date (which must, unless the court otherwise orders, be a date not earlier than that of the administration order)[10];

(f) the manner in which the affairs and business of the partnership:

    (i) have, since the date of the administrator's appointment, been managed and financed; and

    (ii) will, if the administrator's proposals are approved, continue to be managed and financed[11];

(g) such other information (if any) as the administrator thinks necessary to enable creditors to vote for the adoption of the proposals[12].

---

1 Section 23(1)(a) of the Insolvency Act 1986, as applied by art 6(1) of the Order and modified by art 3(2) of the Order; the reference to the Registrar of Companies in the section is to be omitted in the partnership context.
2 Section 23(2)(a) of the Insolvency Act 1986, as applied by art 6(1) of the Order and modified by art 3 of the Order.
3 Insolvency Rules 1986, r 2.17.
4 Section 23(2)(b) of the Insolvency Act 1986, as applied by art 6(1) of the Order.
5 Section 23(1)(b) of the Insolvency Act 1986, as applied by art 6(1) of the Order. Note that '14 days' notice' means 14 clear days, leaving out of account the day notice is sent and the day of the meeting itself: *Mytre Investments v Reynolds (No 2)* [1996] BPIR 464; leave to appeal refused by the Court of Appeal, 26 February 1996.
6 Section 23(3) of the Insolvency Act 1986, as applied by art 6(1) of the Order.
7 Insolvency Rules 1986, r 2.16(1)(a).
8 Ibid, r 2.16(1)(b), as modified by art 18(1).
9 Ibid, r 2.16(1)(d).
10 Ibid, r 2.16(1)(e), as modified by art 18(1).
11 Ibid, r 2.16(1)(f), as modified by art 18(1).
12 Ibid, r 2.16(1)(g).

8.22 THE MEETING OF CREDITORS

The meeting of creditors called under s 23 of the Act will be the first opportunity for the partnership's creditors to consider formally the future of the partnership.

8.22.1 Notice of the meeting

The administrator must give notice of the meeting to all the creditors of the partnership who are identified in the statement of affairs or are known to the administrator and had claims against the partnership at the date of the administration order[1]. The meeting must also be advertised by a notice in the same newspaper in which the administration order was advertised, unless the court directs otherwise[2]. In addition, the administrator must send out notices to attend the meeting to any partner or other officer of the partnership (including former partners or other officers) whose presence he considers to be required at the meeting[3].

Contingent and unascertained creditors are to be included within the creditors of a partnership who must be notified of the s 23 meeting. However, it should be noted that there may be significant creditors who would only have claims against the separate estates of individual partners. An example would be a landlord of property used by the partnership who only has claims against four lessee partners and any other separate covenantors[4]. A person who is not a partnership creditor is not entitled to attend and vote at a meeting of creditors within the Rules.

Former partners may have a contingent right of indemnity against the present partnership if they pay off a creditor to whom they are liable from the time when they were full partners. It therefore appears that they should receive notice of the creditors' meeting. The same would apply to other guarantors of partnership liabilities who are not partners.

1 Insolvency Rules 1986, r 2.18, as modified by art 18(1) of the Order.
2 Ibid, r 2.18(2).
3 Ibid, r 2.18(3), as modified by art 18(1) of the Order; the notice is sent out in Form 2.10.
4 See para **2.13.5**.

8.22.2 *Venue and timing*
In fixing a venue for the meeting, the administrator must have regard to the convenience of creditors[1]. The meeting must be summoned for commencement between 10.00 am and 4.00 pm on a business day unless the court directs otherwise[2].

1 Insolvency Rules 1986, r 2.19(2).
2 Ibid, r 2.19(3).

8.22.3 *Chairman*
The chairman of the meeting is either to be the administrator or a person nominated by the administrator in writing, who must either be a person qualified to act as an insolvency practitioner in relation to the partnership, or an employee of the administrator's firm who is experienced in insolvency matters[1].

1 Insolvency Rules 1986, r 2.20.

8.22.4 *If no chairman is present*
If, within 30 minutes from the time fixed for the commencement of the meeting there is no person present to act as chairman[1], the meeting stands adjourned to the same time and place in the following week or, if that is not a business day, to the business day immediately following[2].

1 Ie in compliance with r 2.20, see para **8.22.3** above.
2 Insolvency Rules 1986, r 2.19(6).

8.22.5 *Adjournment*
A meeting may be adjourned from time to time, but not for more than 14 days from the date on which it was fixed to commence[1].

1 Insolvency Rules 1986, r 2.19(7).

8.22.6 Entitlement to vote

A person is only entitled to vote at a meeting if:

(a) he has given to the administrator by 12 noon on the business day before the meeting details in writing of the debt which he claims to be due to him from the company[1] which must include any calculation of the deduction to be made under any of the forms of security the creditor may hold[2];

(b) the creditor's claim has been admitted for voting purposes[3];

(c) if the creditor intends to vote by proxy, a proxy has been lodged with the administrator[4]. The administrator must send out proxy forms with the notice summoning the meeting, in Form 8.2[5].

However, if the chairman is satisfied that the reason why a creditor was unable to comply with the above requirements was circumstances beyond the creditor's control, the chairman may allow him to vote.

1 Insolvency Rules 1986, r 2.22(1)(a).
2 Ibid, r 2.22(1): see paras **8.22.12** to **8.22.15** for the deductions required under rr 2.24–2.27 for purposes of entitlement to vote.
3 Ibid, r 2.22(1)(a).
4 Ibid, r 2.22(1)(b).
5 Ibid, r 2.19(5).

8.22.7 Proxies

A proxy is an authority given by one person ('the principal') to another person ('the proxy-holder') to attend a meeting and speak and vote as his representative[1]. A proxy-holder must be an individual, and must be aged 18 or over[2]. Only one proxy may be given by a person in respect of a meeting, but one or more other individuals may be specified in the alternative, in the order in which they are named in the proxy[3].

A proxy requires the holder to give the principal's vote on matters arising for determination at the meeting, or to abstain, or to propose, in the principal's name, a resolution to be voted on by the meeting, either as directed or in accordance with the holder's own discretion[4]. Where a proxy gives specific directions, this does not, unless the proxy states otherwise, preclude the proxy-holder from voting at his discretion on resolutions put to the meeting which are not dealt with in the proxy[5].

A proxy-holder must not vote in favour of any resolution which would directly or indirectly place him, or any associate of his, in a position to receive any remuneration out of the insolvent estate, unless the proxy specifically directs him to vote in that way[6].

A proxy may be given to whoever is to be the chairman of a meeting[7], in which case the chairman cannot decline to be the proxy-holder[8].

Until recently, there was some doubt as to whether a proxy which was sent by fax was valid. The DTI had stipulated in a standing instruction to Official Receivers that faxed proxies should not be accepted for meetings convened by them, and the Society of Practitioners of Insolvency took a similar view[9]. However, a recent case has indicated that the courts will regard such proxies (and, by extension, documents delivered by other forms of electronic transmission) as effective[10].

Proxies used for voting at any meeting must be retained by the chairman[11] except that, where the chairman was not the administrator, the chairman must deliver the proxies to the administrator forthwith after the meeting[12].

---

1 Insolvency Rules 1986, r 8.1.
2 Ibid, r 8.1(3).
3 Ibid, r 8.1(3).
4 Ibid, r 8.1(6).
5 Ibid, r 8.3(6).
6 Ibid, r 8.6(1).
7 Ibid, r 8.1(4).
8 Ibid, r 8.1(5).
9 Statement of Insolvency Practice 8, para 24.
10 *IR Commissioners v Conbeer* [1996] BCC 189.
11 Insolvency Rules 1986, r 8.4(1).
12 Ibid, r 8.4(2).

8.22.8 *Rights to inspect proxies*
Any person attending a meeting of creditors in respect of an administration of a partnership is entitled, immediately before or in the course of the meeting, to inspect proxies and associated documents (including proofs) sent or given, in accordance with directions contained in any notice convening the meeting, to the chairman for the purpose of the meeting[1].

After the meeting, the administrator must, so long as the proxies lodged with him are in his hands, allow them to be inspected at all reasonable times on any business day, by:

(a) a creditor who has submitted in writing a claim to be a creditor of the partnership[2], unless the person's proof or claim has been wholly rejected for purposes of voting or otherwise[3];
(b) a partner[4].

---

1 Insolvency Rules 1986, r 8.5(4).
2 Ibid, r 8.5(1)(a).
3 Ibid, r 8.5(2).
4 Ibid, r 8.5(3)(a), as modified by art 18(1) of the Order.

8.22.9 *Admission and rejection of claims*
Votes are to be calculated according to the amount of a creditor's debt at the date of the administration order, deducting any amounts paid in respect of the debt after that date[1].

The chairman of the meeting has power to admit or reject a creditor's claim for the purpose of entitlement to vote[2]. That power may be exercised in respect of the whole or any part of the claim.

The administrator (or another person acting as chairman) may call for any document or other evidence to be produced to him where he thinks it necessary for the purpose of substantiating the whole or any part of a claim[3].

1 Insolvency Rules 1986, r 2.22(4).
2 Ibid, r 2.23(1).
3 Ibid, r 2.22(3).

8.22.10   *Valuation of unliquidated or unascertained claims*

Where the amount of a creditor's claim is not settled at the date of the meeting, because it is *unliquidated* (as in a claim for damages) or because it is *unascertained* (as in a claim for future rent or for some other contingent liability), the creditor must not vote unless the chairman agrees to put an estimated minimum value upon the vote for the purpose of voting and admits it for that purpose[1].

No actual agreement with the creditor is required; the chairman only needs to express his willingness to put, and to put, an estimated minimum value on the debt[2]. However, the chairman must make a bona fide attempt to value the creditor's claim[3]. For a contingent claim, this will often involve multiplying the amount claimed by the probability of the contingency occurring which would lead to a claim being made. If the nominee is of the view (on the facts before him) that the contingency is virtually certain to occur, the multiplier should be '1'; in other words, the claim will be valued at its full amount. Where the contingency is very unlikely to occur, it may still in some cases be appropriate to value the claim at a nominal level (eg £1).

1 Insolvency Rules 1986, r 2.22(5).
2 *Doorbar v Alltime Securities* [1995] BCC 1149, CA. That case was a decision on r 5.17, which is in almost identical terms.
3 *In re Cranley Mansions* [1994] 1 WLR 1610; *Doorbar v Alltime Securities* [1994] BCC 994.

8.22.11   *Disputed votes*

The creditors' meeting is not the place to go into lengthy debates about the status of a debt[1]. Where objections are raised as to the nature or amount of a creditor's claim which the chairman is not able to resolve upon a brief inquiry, he must mark the vote as objected to and allow the creditor to vote, subject to the vote being subsequently declared invalid if the objection is sustained[2].

In practice, the administrator will try to negotiate the value of a creditor's claim. If the chairman's decision on the amount of a claim is reversed or varied on an application to the court, the court can order that a fresh meeting is to be summoned or make such other order as it thinks just[3].

1 Cf *Re a Debtor (No 222 of 1990) ex parte Bank of Ireland* [1992] BCLC 137. The case concerned individual voluntary arrangements, but the wording of the respective rules is identical, and there is no reason why the principle should not apply.
2 Insolvency Rules 1986, r 2.23(3).
3 Ibid, r 2.23(4). The court will not order another meeting where it would be pointless to do so, as where it seems clear that the result of the meeting would not be affected by the amount placed by the court on the creditor's claim: cf *Re a Debtor (No 83 of 1988)* [1990] 1 WLR 708; *Re Cove (A Debtor)* [1990] 1 WLR 708; [1990] 1 All ER 949.

8.22.12 *Secured creditors*

A secured creditor is only entitled to vote in respect of the balance (if any) of his debt after deducting the value of his security as estimated by him[1]. Note that there is no provision for any objective quantification of the value of security, and it does not appear that the chairman is entitled to question the secured creditor's estimate. However, where the chairman forms the view that a secured creditor has not valued his security properly or in good faith, it appears that a chairman could reject the whole or part of that creditor's claim[2] or, if he is in doubt, mark it as objected to but allow the creditor to vote[3].

1 Insolvency Rules 1986, r 2.24.
2 Under r 2.23(1).
3 Under r 2.23(3).

8.22.13 *Holders of negotiable instruments*

A creditor must not vote in respect of a claim on, or secured by, a current bill of exchange or promissory note, unless the creditor is prepared to treat the liability to him of every person liable antecedently to the partnership on the bill or note and against whom a bankruptcy order has not been made (or, in the case of a company (or, presumably, a partnership), which has not gone into liquidation), as security, and to deduct the value of such security from the value of the claim for voting purposes[1].

1 Insolvency Rules 1986, r 2.25.

8.22.14 *Retention of title creditors*

A seller of goods to the partnership under a retention of title agreement must deduct from his claim the value, as estimated by him, of any rights arising under that agreement in respect of goods in the possession of the partnership[1]. As with secured creditors generally[2], it does not appear that the chairman is entitled to question the retention of title creditor's estimate. However, where the chairman forms the view that a secured creditor has not valued his security properly or in good faith, it appears that a chairman could reject the whole or part of that creditor's claim[3] or, if he is in doubt, mark it as objected to but allow the creditor to vote[4].

1 Insolvency Rules 1986, r 2.26.
2 See para **8.22.12** above.
3 Under r 2.23(1).
4 Under r 2.23(3).

8.22.15 *Creditors with hire-purchase, conditional sale and chattel leasing agreements*

The owner of goods which the partnership has under a hire-purchase or chattel leasing agreement, or a seller of goods under a conditional sale agreement, is entitled to vote in respect of the amount of the debt due and payable to him by the partnership as at the date of the administration order[1]. Where rights (eg to repossess goods or for a full amount to become payable) become exercisable under the relevant agreement *solely* by virtue of the presentation of the administration petition, or any matter arising in consequence of that, or of the making of the administration order, no account is to be taken of such rights in calculating the amount of the debt for voting purposes[2].

1 Insolvency Rules 1986, r 2.27(1).
2 Ibid, r 2.27(2).

8.22.16 *Majorities*

At a creditors' meeting in administration proceedings, a resolution is passed when a majority (in value) of those present and voting, in person or by proxy, have voted in favour of it[1].

However, this is subject to r 2.28(1A), which provides that any resolution is invalid if those voting against it include more than one half (in value) of the creditors to whom notice of the meeting was sent and who are not, to the best of the chairman's knowledge, persons connected with the partnership[2].

1 Insolvency Rules 1986, r 2.28(1).
2 Ibid, r 2.28(1A), as modified by art 18(1) of the Order. A person is 'connected with' a
  partnership if he is an associate of any partner; see s 249 of the Act and (f) at para **7.2**.

8.22.17 *Minutes*

Partnerships, unlike companies, will not necessarily have a 'minute book'. However, it is clearly desirable that the administrator should keep a formal minute of any meeting held in the course of a partnership administration, and it is suggested that, where the partnership does not already have such a book, a minute book is started for this purpose[1]. The minutes of each meeting must include a list of the creditors who attended, in person or by proxy[2]. If a creditors' committee has been established, the minutes must also include the names and addresses of those elected to be members of the committee[3].

1 Cf Insolvency Rules 1986, r 2.28(2).
2 Insolvency Rules 1986, r 2.28(3).
3 Ibid, r 2.28(3).

8.23 OTHER MEETINGS

8.23.1 *Calling meetings*

Apart from the meeting of creditors under s 23 of the Act, meetings of creditors may be called:

(i)   by the administrator under his general powers[1];
(ii) if the administrator is requested to call a meeting by one-tenth (in value) of the partnership's creditors[2];
(iii) if the administrator is directed to call a meeting by the court[3];
(iv) to consider substantial revisions to the administrator's proposals[4].

In any such case, the Rules as to voting and conduct of meetings set out in para **8.26** also apply, with the variations set out in the following three paragraphs.

1 Under s 14(2)(b) of the Insolvency Act 1986, as modified by Sch 2 to the Order.
2 Under s 17(3)(a) of the Insolvency Act 1986, as applied by art 6(1) of the Order.
3 Section 17(3)(b) of the Insolvency Act 1986, as applied by art 6(1) of the Order.
4 Under s 25(2)(b) of the Insolvency Act 1986, as applied by art 6(1) of the Order.

8.23.2 *Meetings requisitioned by creditors*

Unless the requisitioning creditor is owed more than one-tenth (in value) of the debts of the partnership, the request to the administrator must be accompanied by:

(a) a list of the creditors concurring with the request, showing the amounts of their respective claims[1];
(b) written confirmation of concurrence from each concurring creditor[2];
(c) a statement of the purpose of the proposed meeting[3].

If the administrator considers that the request has properly been made by at least one-tenth (in value) of the partnership's creditors, he must fix a venue for the meeting to be held not more than 35 days from his receipt of the request, and he must give at least 21 days' notice of the meeting to creditors.

A creditor who requests a meeting must pay the costs[4], and must make a deposit on account of those costs before the administrator must call the meeting[5]. However, the meeting may resolve that the costs of the meeting shall instead be paid as an expense of the administration out of the assets of the partnership[6].

1 Insolvency Rules 1986, r 2.21(1)(a).
2 Ibid, r 2.21(1)(b).
3 Ibid.
4 Ibid, r 2.21(3).
5 Ibid, rr 2.21(3), (4).
6 Ibid, r 2.21(5).

8.23.3 *Meetings under s 25(2)*

Where proposals have been approved by the creditors at a meeting called under s 23 of the Act, but an administrator wishes to make substantial revisions to those proposals, he must:

(a) send to all the creditors of the partnership of whose addresses he is aware a statement of his proposed revisions[1]; and
(b) send a copy of his statement to all the members of the partnership so far as he is aware of their addresses[2], or publish a notice in the *London Gazette* and in the newspaper in which the administration order was advertised[3] stating an address to which members should write for copies of the administrator's statement to be sent to them free of charge[4];
(c) summon a meeting of creditors of the partnership for the purpose of considering his proposals on not less than 14 days' notice[5].

The meeting of creditors can approve the proposed revisions with modifications, but only if the administrator consents to each modification[6].

1 Section 25(2)(a) of the Insolvency Act 1986, as applied by art 6(1) of the Order.
2 Section 25(3)(a) of the Insolvency Act 1986, as applied by art 6(1) of the Order and modified by art 3 of the Order.
3 Insolvency Rules 1986, r 2.17(b).
4 Section 25(3)(b) of the Insolvency Act 1986, as applied by art 6(1) of the Order.
5 Section 25(2)(b) of the Insolvency Act 1986, as applied by art 6(1) of the Order. Note that '14 days' notice' means 14 clear days, leaving out of account the day notice is sent and the day of the meeting itself: *Mytre Investments v Reynolds (No 2)* [1996] BPIR 464; leave to appeal refused by the Court of Appeal, 26 February 1996.
6 Section 25(4) of the Insolvency Act 1986, as applied by r 6(1) of the Order.

8.23.4   *Other meetings*

Apart from meetings called under s 23(1) or s 25(2) of the Act, at least 21 clear days' notice of the meeting must be given[1].

Notice must be sent to all creditors who had claims against the partnership at the date of the administration order[2]. The notice must:

(a) specify the purpose for which the meeting is being called;
(b) contain a statement of the effect of r 2.22(1), which provides the conditions which must be satisfied for a creditor to be entitled to vote at the meeting[3].

1 Insolvency Rules 1986, r 2.19(4A).
2 Ibid, r 2.19(4).
3 Ibid: the notices must be in Form 2.11. For r 2.22, see paras **8.22.9** and **8.22.10**.

8.24   REPORT OF MEETING

After the conclusion of a meeting of creditors to consider the administrator's proposals under s 23 of the Act, the administrator must report the result of the meeting to the court[1]. Notice of the result must also be sent within 14 days to every creditor who received notice of the meeting under the Rules, and every other creditor of whom the administrator has since become aware[2].

In the case of a meeting of creditors to consider revised proposals under s 25 of the Act, there is no report to the court, but notice of the result must be sent to creditors, as above[3]. In either case, the notice must, where appropriate, include details of the proposals as approved[4], and details of the proposals which were considered by the meeting and of the revisions and modifications considered must be annexed to the notice[5].

1 Section 24(4) of the Insolvency Act 1986.
2 Section 24(4) of the Insolvency Act 1986 and Insolvency Rules 1986, r 2.30(1).
3 Section 25(6) of the Insolvency Act 1986, as modified by art 3(2) of the Order, and Insolvency Rules 1986, r 2.30.
4 Insolvency Rules 1986, r 2.30(1).
5 Ibid, r 2.29.

8.25   REJECTION OF PROPOSALS

If a meeting called to consider the administrator's proposals under s 23 of the Act declines to approve them (with or without modifications), the court can discharge the administration order and make such consequential provision as it thinks fit, or adjourn the hearing conditionally or unconditionally, or make an interim order or any other order that it thinks fit[1]. When Maxwell Communications Corporation plc collapsed, Hoffmann J suggested that the court could make an order directing that the administrator's proposals could be put into effect even if the creditors had not approved them, or could vary the purposes for which the administration had been granted, or could appoint new administrators[2].

1 Section 24(5) of the Insolvency Act 1986. In the case of a company, if the administration
  order is discharged the administrator must, by s 24(6) of the Act, send an office copy of the
  discharge order to the Registrar of Companies within 14 days; that obligation does not apply
  to the discharge of a partnership administration (by operation of art 3(2) of the Order).
2 *Re Maxwell Communications Corporation plc* [1992] BCLC 465.

8.26   THE CREDITORS' COMMITTEE

8.26.1   Establishment of a creditors' committee
If a meeting of creditors summoned under s 23 of the Act has approved the administrator's proposals (with or without modifications), it may establish a creditors' committee[1]. The Rules provide only in very general terms that the creditors' committee is to assist the administrator in discharging his functions, and act in relation to him in such manner as may be agreed from time to time[2].

1 Insolvency Act 1986, s 26(1).
3 Insolvency Rules 1986, r 2.34(1).

8.26.2   Constitution
The committee must consist of at least three and not more than five creditors of the partnership elected at the meeting[1]. A creditor whose claim has been rejected for purposes of entitlement to vote is ineligible for election, but otherwise any creditor of the partnership may be elected[2]. A body corporate may be a member of the committee[3], but can only act through a duly authorised representative[4]. No person may act as a member of the committee unless and until he has agreed to do so; agreement may be given by a proxy-holder at the meeting establishing the committee, unless the relevant proxy or authorisation[5] contains a statement to the contrary[6]. Nobody can represent more than one committee member, or act both as a member of the committee and as representative of another committee member[7].

1 Insolvency Rules 1986, r 2.32(1). The rule envisages that election is by a single ballot, with
  the five creditors who attract the greatest number of votes (by value) being chosen to form
  the committee: *Re Polly Peck International plc* [1991] BCC 503.
2 Ibid, r 2.32(2).
3 Ibid, r 2.32(3).
4 See r 2.37; a person claiming to represent a member of the committee whose authority
  appears to the chairman of a meeting of the creditors' committee to be deficient may be
  excluded from the meeting: r 2.37(3).
5 Under s 375 of the Companies Act 1985, in the case of the representative of a corporation.
6 Insolvency Rules 1986, r 2.33(2).
7 Ibid, r 2.37(5).

8.26.3 *Certificate of constitution*

The creditors' committee does not come into being and so cannot act until the administrator has issued a certificate of its due constitution. The administrator must not issue this certificate until at least three members have agreed to act[1]. As and when any other members of the committee agree to act, the administrator must issue an amended certificate[2]. The original certificate, and any amended certificate, must be filed in court[3], as must any change in the membership of the committee[4].

1 Insolvency Rules 1986, r 2.32(2A).
2 Ibid, r 2.33(3).
3 Ibid, r 2.33(4).
4 Ibid, r 2.33(5).

8.26.4 *Formal defects*

The acts of the creditors' committee appointed for a partnership administration are valid notwithstanding any defect in the appointment, election or qualifications of any member of the committee or any committee-member's representative or in the formalities of its establishment[1].

1 Insolvency Rules 1986, r 2.46A.

8.26.5 *Meetings*

The administrator must call a first meeting of the creditors' committee not later than three months after its first establishment[1].

Subsequent meetings are to be called:

(a) within 21 days from a request for a meeting to be held being received by the administrator from a member of the committee (or his representative)[2];

(b) for a specified date, if the committee has previously resolved that a meeting be held on that date[3].

Otherwise, it is for the administrator to determine when and where meetings of the creditors' committee are to be held[4]. The administrator must give seven days' written notice of the venue of any meeting to every member of the committee (or to his representative designated for that purpose) unless the requirement of notice has been waived by or on behalf of any member[5].

1 Insolvency Rules 1986, r 2.34(3).
2 Ibid, r 2.34(3)(a).
3 Ibid, r 2.34(3)(b).
4 Ibid, r 2.34(2).
5 Ibid, r 2.34(4).

8.26.6 *Summoning the administrator*

A creditors' committee has a statutory power to require the administrator to attend before it at any reasonable time, on not less than seven days' notice, to furnish it with such information relating to the carrying out of its functions as it may reasonably require[1]. The notice to the administrator must be in writing and signed by a majority of the members of the committee[2]. The committee fixes the day of the meeting, which must be a business day; it is then for the administrator to set the time and place[3].

1 Section 26(2) of the Insolvency Act 1986.
2 Insolvency Rules 1986, r 2.44(1).
3 Ibid, r 2.44(2).

8.26.7   *Chairman of meetings*

The chairman of a meeting of the creditors' committee must be either the administrator or a person nominated by the administrator in writing. If the chairman is nominated by the administrator, he must either be a person qualified to act as an insolvency practitioner in relation to the partnership, or an employee of the administrator's firm who is experienced in insolvency matters[1].

Where a meeting is called because the creditors' committee requires information from the administrator (see above), the members of the creditors' committee may elect one of their number to be chairman of the meeting, in place of the administrator or his nominee[2].

1 Insolvency Rules 1986, r 2.35.
2 Ibid, r 2.44(3).

8.26.8   *Quorum*

A meeting of the committee is duly constituted if due notice of it has been given to all the members, and at least two members are present or represented[1].

1 Insolvency Rules 1986, r 2.36.

8.26.9   *Procedure at meetings*

Each member of the creditors' committee has one vote; a resolution is passed by a simple majority of those present or represented[1].

Every resolution passed must be recorded in writing, either separately or as part of the minutes of the meeting[2]. Where the partnership has a minute book, a record of each resolution must be signed by the chairman of a creditors' committee meeting and placed in the minute book[3].

1 Insolvency Rules 1986, r 2.42.
2 Ibid, r 2.42(2).
3 Ibid, r 2.42(3). As suggested in para **8.22.17**, partnerships, unlike companies, will not necessarily have a 'minute book' but, as it is clearly desirable that the administrator should keep a formal minute of any meeting held in the course of a partnership administration, it is suggested that, where the partnership does not already have such a book, a minute book is started for this purpose.

8.26.10   *Postal resolutions*

The Rules provide a postal procedure to avoid the expense of holding a meeting[1]. The administrator may send a copy of a proposed resolution to every member or his representative. A member of the committee may, within seven days of the administrator sending out a resolution, require him to call a meeting to discuss it[2]. If none of the members insists on a meeting, the members can indicate whether they agree or dissent from each resolution in the manner specified on the copy of the resolution which has been sent out[3]. The resolution is deemed to have been passed by the committee if and when the administrator is notified in writing by a majority of the members of the committee that they concur with it[4].

The Rules require that a copy of every resolution passed under this Rule, and a note that the committee's concurrence was obtained, shall be placed in the partnership's minute book[5].

---

1 Insolvency Rules 1986, r 2.43.
2 Ibid, r 2.43(3).
3 See r 2.43(2).
4 Ibid, r 2.43(4).
5 Ibid, r 2.43(5): see footnote 3 at para **8.26.9**.

8.26.11 *Resignation*

A member of the committee may resign by notice in writing delivered to the administrator[1].

---

1 Insolvency Rules 1986, r 2.38.

8.26.12 *Removal and termination of membership*

A member of the committee may be removed by resolution at a meeting of creditors. At least 14 days' notice must be given of the intention to move such a resolution[1].

Membership of the creditors' committee is automatically terminated if the member:

(a) becomes bankrupt[2], or compounds or arranges with his creditors[3];
(b) at three consecutive meetings of the committee is neither present nor represented (unless at the third of those meetings it is resolved that this rule is not to apply)[4];
(c) ceases to be, or is found never to have been, a creditor[5].

---

1 Insolvency Rules 1986, r 2.40.
2 In which case, his trustee in bankruptcy replaces him as a member of the creditors' committee.
3 Insolvency Rules 1986, r 2.39(1)(a).
4 Ibid, r 2.39(1)(b).
5 Ibid, r 2.39(1)(c).

8.26.13 *Vacancies*

If there is a vacancy on the creditors' committee, it need not be filled, provided that the total number of members does not fall below three[1]. Alternatively, the administrator may appoint any creditor who is qualified under the Rules to be a member of the committee, provided:

(a) a majority of the other members of the committee agree to the appointment; and

(b) the creditor concerned consents to act[2].

1 Insolvency Rules 1986, r 2.41(2).
2 Ibid, r 2.41(3).

8.26.14 *Expenses*

The reasonable travelling expenses directly incurred by members of the creditors' committee or their representatives in relation to attendance at the committee's meetings or otherwise on the committee's business are to be defrayed by the administrator out of the assets of the partnership[1]. This does not apply to a meeting held within three months of the previous meeting, unless the meeting in question has been called by the administrator[2].

1 Insolvency Rules 1986, r 2.45(1).
2 Ibid, r 2.45(2).

8.26.15 *Members' dealings with the partnership*

A member of the committee may still deal with the partnership while the administration order is in force, provided that any transactions are in good faith and for value[1]. On the application of any person interested, the court may set aside any transaction which appears to contravene this rule[2]. If it does so, it may make any consequential directions it thinks fit for compensating the partnership for any loss which it may have incurred in consequence of the transaction.

A member of the committee is in a fiduciary capacity[3], and it is up to him to ensure that he does not put himself in a position where his other interests are in conflict with his duties as a member of the committee. He may have to withdraw from particular discussions, and it may be inappropriate for information to be provided to him where a conflict of interests arises. In an extreme case, the administrator may have to ask the court for directions[4].

1 Insolvency Rules 1986, r 2.46.
2 Ibid, r 2.46(2).
3 Cf *Re F T Hawkins & Co Ltd* [1952] Ch 881.
4 Under s 14(3) of the Insolvency Act 1986, as modified by Sch 2 to the Order.

8.27 MEETINGS OF THE PARTNERSHIP

When a partnership is in administration, meetings of the partners can still be called according to the provisions of the partnership deed (where there is one) or whatever other internal regulatory mechanisms exist. However, where a meeting is summoned by the administrator:

(a) he must have regard to the convenience of the members in fixing the venue[1];

(b) the administrator or a person nominated by him in writing must chair the meeting[2]. Any person nominated must either be qualified to act as an insolvency practitioner in respect of the partnership, or must be an employee of the administrator or his firm who is experienced in insolvency matters[3].

If, within 30 minutes from the time fixed for the commencement of the meeting there is no person present to act as chairman[4], the meeting stands adjourned to the same time and place in the following week or, if that is not a business day, to the business day immediately following[5].

Otherwise, the meeting is to be summoned and conducted as if it were a general meeting of the partnership called under the applicable partnership agreement[6].

One of the reasons why partnerships get into financial difficulties is that they have inadequate or ineffective internal mechanisms for decision-making. It should also be remembered that under the Partnership Act, there is a requirement for unanimity about any change in the nature of the partnership business unless the partners have expressly or impliedly agreed otherwise[7], which can paralyse a partnership. A prospective administrator should always investigate the internal decision-making requirements at an early stage, and would be well-advised to ensure that satisfactory mechanisms are in place[8] before he accepts an appointment, at least where it is contemplated that the partnership is to continue to trade.

---

1 Insolvency Rules 1986, r 2.31(1), as modified by art 18(1) to the Order.
2 Ibid, r 2.31(2).
3 Ibid, r 2.31(3).
4 Ie under r 2.31(2).
5 Ibid, r 2.31(4).
6 Ibid, r 2.31(5).
7 Partnership Act 1890, s 24(8).
8 For example, there should be a written partnership agreement.

8.28 REPORTS BY THE ADMINISTRATOR

The administrator must send out a report on the progress of the administration to all creditors of the partnership within 14 days of the end of every period of six months beginning with the date of approval of proposals or revised proposals (ie by a meeting of creditors under either s 23 or s 25 of the Act, see above)[1].

Within two months[2] after the end of six months from the date of his appointment, and of every subsequent period of six months, the administrator must send to:

(a) the court; and
(b) each member of the creditors' committee;

accounts of the receipts and payments of the partnership[3] in the form of an abstract[4], showing receipts and payments during the relevant six-month period[5].

The administrator must similarly send an abstract of receipts and payments to the court, and to each member of the creditors' committee within 2 months after he ceases to act as administrator[6]. In this case, the abstract must either cover the period from the end of the last 6-month period to the time when he ceased to act as administrator, or alternatively, if there has been no previous abstract, receipts and payments in the period since his appointment as administrator[7].

If the administrator defaults in his obligations to submit abstracts of receipts and payments, he is liable to a fine and, for continued contravention, to a daily default fine[8].

1 Insolvency Rules 1986, r 2.30(2).
2 Unless the court extends time under r 2.52(2).
3 Ibid, r 2.52(1)(a).
4 In Form 2.15.
5 Ibid, r 2.52(3)(a).
6 Ibid, r 2.52(1)(b); again, the court may extend time under r 2.52(2).
7 Ibid, r 2.52(3)(b).
8 Ibid, r 2.52(4).

8.29 FINANCING THE ADMINISTRATION

In almost every case, it will be envisaged that the partnership will continue to trade or conduct business in administration, at least until there has been an opportunity for the creditors to consider the administrator's proposals.

The administrator of a partnership is deemed to act as the agent of the members of the partnership[1]. Third parties who deal with the administrator in good faith and for value are not concerned whether the administrator is acting within his powers[2]; they can assume that he is acting within his authority as agent.

At first sight, this may not appear to be much different from the position which usually pertains in a partnership, where each partner is the agent of the others. The essence of partnership (outside administration) is that the individual partners are personally liable for their mutual debts and for the professional obligations they incur. However, that position ends with the making of an administration order; an officer of the partnership (which includes each of the partners[3]) will not be personally liable either for debts or for obligations of the partnership incurred during the period when the administration order is in force, unless he gives his consent[4]. If the partners have not consented to be personally liable, there is no principal who will technically be liable for the acts of the administrator[5].

Under the administration procedure, it is envisaged that any sums payable in respect of debts or liabilities incurred under a contract entered into by the administrator during the administration will either be paid in the course of the administration[6] or will be charged on and paid out of any property of the partnership in the administrator's possession when he ceases to be administrator[7].

From the point of view of the administrator, it will be necessary to ensure before accepting an appointment that the finance is in place to enable the partnership business to be conducted as envisaged during the administration. Suppliers who contract with a partnership in administration will have all the same concerns that they would have where a company was in administration[8]. In addition, it appears that liability in respect of contracts entered into by a partner, as opposed to by the administrator, would not be charged on assets[9] (while liability in tort would not be protected at all) so clients of a professional partnership in administration would be well-advised to clarify their position before engaging the services of the firm.

1 Section 14(5) of the Insolvency Act 1986, as modified by Sch 2 to the Order.
2 Ibid, s 14(7) (as modified).
3 Insolvent Partnerships Order 1994, art 2(1).
4 Section 14(6) of the Insolvency Act 1986, as modified by Sch 2 to the Order.
5 This might have implications for clients of professional firms who could in theory find that work has been undertaken without liability, and may at least complicate the possibility of claims under professional indemnity insurance policies.
6 Under the administrator's powers in para 12 of Sch 1 to the Insolvency Act 1986, as modified by Sch 2, para 10 to the Order.
7 Section 19(5) of the Insolvency Act 1986, as applied by art 6(1) of the Order.
8 They will try to contract with the administrator personally, and he will usually try to resist that. Unless the contract expressly provides otherwise, contracts entered into by the administrator on behalf of the partnership will not be binding upon the administrator personally. Cf *Re Atlantic Computer Systems plc* [1992] Ch 505.
9 Even where there are any; professional partnerships in particular tend to have relatively few assets.

8.30   THE EFFECT OF ADMINISTRATION ON PARTNERSHIP CONTRACTS

The making of an administration order does not, of itself, terminate contracts the partnership may have made. There may be clauses in some contracts to that effect, but these are more usually found in leases and contracts for the supply of commodities than in contracts for the provision of professional services. A court is unlikely to permit an administrator to ignore contractual obligations to third parties[1] and may grant an injunction in an appropriate case. Particular difficulties may arise where an insolvent firm of solicitors is acting in substantial litigation, or where an insolvent accountancy firm is midway through a major audit at the time when an administration order is made.

It should be borne in mind that the making of an administration order does not affect substantive rights: it merely has procedural consequences on the enforcement of those rights[2]. On the other hand, the likelihood of a partnership being paid for work done to date on a project for a client may well be dependent upon the satisfactory completion of the project; if the client has to instruct another firm, he will almost certainly have a claim for damages which he will be able to set-off against any liability in respect of the work to date.

1 Cf *Astor Chemicals Ltd v Synthetic Technology Ltd* [1990] BCLC 1.
2 *Barclays Mercantile Business Finance Ltd v Sibec Developments Ltd* [1992] 1 WLR 1253.

8.31 DEALING WITH CHARGED PROPERTY

Where partnership property is subject to a charge[1], the court can authorise the administrator to dispose of the property as if it were not subject to a charge if it is satisfied that the disposal would be likely to promote one or more of the purposes for which the administration order has been granted[2]. It must be a condition of any authorisation order that the net proceeds of disposal and any amount required to make that amount up to the open market price for which the asset would have been sold are to be applied towards discharging the sums secured by the relevant security[3].

Where the administrator applies to the court for authority to dispose of charged property[4], the court fixes a venue for the hearing and the administrator must forthwith give notice to the holder of the security[5].

If an order is made under s 15(2) of the Act, authorising disposal, the administrator must give notice of it to the holder of the security[6]. The court must send two sealed copies of its order to the administrator, who must send one of them to that person[7].

1 Other than a floating charge, except where an agricultural receiver has been appointed pursuant to a floating charge: s 15(3) of the Insolvency Act 1986, as modified by Sch 2 to the Order and see para **8.17** above.
2 Section 15(2) of the Insolvency Act 1986, as modified by Sch 2 to the Order.
3 Ibid, s 15(5) (as modified). See *Re ARV Aviation Ltd* [1989] BCLC 664. The court can make an order permitting disposal and direct an inquiry into the open market value.
4 Pursuant to s 15(2) of the Insolvency Act 1986, as modified by Sch 2 to the Order: or goods subject to a hire-purchase agreement (see para **8.32** below).
5 Insolvency Rules 1986, r 2.51(2): or to the owner under the relevant agreement.
6 Ibid, r 2.51(3): or to the owner under the relevant agreement.
7 Ibid, r 2.51(4).

8.32 DEALING WITH PROPERTY HELD UNDER HIRE-PURCHASE AGREEMENTS, ETC

Where partnership property is in the possession of one or more officers of a partnership under a hire-purchase agreement[1] (which for these purposes is defined to include conditional sale agreements, chattel leasing agreements and retention of title agreements[2]), the court can authorise the administrator to dispose of the property as if it were not subject to such an agreement if it is satisfied that the disposal would be likely to promote one or more of the purposes for which the administration order has been granted[3]. As before, it must be a condition of any authorisation order that the net proceeds of disposal and any amount required to make that amount up to the open market price for which the asset would have been sold are to be applied towards discharging the sums payable under the relevant agreement[4].

1 Section 15(2)(b) of the Insolvency Act 1986, as modified by Sch 2 to the Order.
2 Ibid, s 15(7) (as modified).
3 Ibid, s 15(2) (as modified).
4 Ibid, s 15(5) (as modified).

8.33 STATUTORY POWERS OF AN ADMINISTRATOR

Apart from the powers of an administrator of a partnership under Sch 1 to the Act, such an administrator is also given a number of statutory rights and remedies.

8.33.1 Getting in the partnership's property

The administrator can apply to the court for an order that any person who has in his possession or control any property, books, papers or records to which the partnership appears entitled must deliver them up forthwith or within a specified period of time to the administrator[1]. The existence of a dispute between the partnership and the person in possession of such property does not of itself render it inappropriate for the administrator to make such an application[2]. An application may be made even where proceedings by the partnership would be liable to be stayed because of an agreement to submit any dispute relating to the subject matter to the exclusive jurisdiction of a foreign court[3].

---

1 Section 234(2) of the Insolvency Act 1986, as modified by art 3(2) of the Order.
2 *Re London Iron and Steel Co Ltd* [1990] BCLC 372.
3 *Re Leyland Daf Ltd* [1993] BCC 626; affirmed by the Court of Appeal [1994] BCC 166. It is thought the principle applies a fortiori to an arbitration agreement.

8.33.2 Duties to co-operate

There is a positive obligation on the following persons to co-operate with the administrator of a partnership:

(a) those who are or have at any time been officers[1] of the partnership[2];
(b) those who have taken part in the formation of the partnership at any time within one year before the date on which the administration order was made[3];
(c) present employees of the partnership, and those who have been employees within one year before the date on which the administration order was made[4], who are in the administrator's opinion capable of giving information which he requires[5];
(d) present officers, and those who have within one year before the date on which the administration order was made been officers, of a company which was an officer of the partnership[6].

Those persons must give to the administrator such information concerning the partnership and its promotion, formation, business, dealings, affairs or property as the administrator after the date on which the administration order was made may reasonably require[7], and they must attend a meeting with him at such times as he requires[8] so long as the requirement is reasonable[9].

Failure to comply is an offence punishable by a fine; continued contravention is punishable by a daily default fine[10]. In practice, it is more likely to lead to an application to the court under s 236 of the Act (see below).

Information and documents obtained under these powers may properly be disclosed by the administrator of a partnership to the Secretary of State in connection with prospective disqualification proceedings under the Company Directors Disqualification Act 1986, even if the administrator has given an assurance that they would only be used for the purposes of the administration; such disclosure is within such purposes[11].

1 Ie any partner, any member through holding out, and any person who has management or control of the partnership business: art 2(1) of the Order.
2 Insolvency Act 1986, s 235(3)(a).
3 Ibid, s 235(3)(b), (4).
4 Including employment under a contract for services.
5 Ibid, s 235(3)(c).
6 Ibid, s 235(3)(d).
7 Ibid, s 235(2)(a), as modified by art 3(2) of the Order.
8 Eg for informal examination: cf *Re Arrows Ltd (No 4)* [1993] Ch 452.
9 Section 235(2)(b) of the Insolvency Act 1986, as modified by art 3(2) of the Order.
10 Section 235(5) of the Insolvency Act 1986, as modified by art 3(2) of the Order: penalties are imposed under s 430 and Sch 10, applied to an insolvent partnership by art 6(3)(f) of the Order.
11 *Re Polly Peck International plc, ex parte the joint administrators* [1994] BCC 15.

8.33.3   Private examinations
The administrator of a partnership can apply for the court to summon to appear before it:

(a) any officer[1] of the partnership[2];
(b) any person known or suspected to have in his possession any property of the partnership or supposed to be indebted to the partnership[3];
(c) any person whom the court thinks capable of giving information concerning the promotion, formation, business, dealings, affairs or property of the partnership[4].

The court also has the power to require any of the above persons to submit an affidavit containing an account of his dealings with the partnership, or to produce any books, papers or other records in his possession or under his control relating to the partnership or its promotion, formation, business, dealings, affairs or property[5].

If a person does not appear, without reasonable excuse, when summoned to do so[6], or if there are reasonable grounds for believing that a person has absconded[7] or is about to abscond with a view to avoiding his appearance before the court for examination[8], the court may issue a warrant for his arrest[9] and for the seizure of any books, papers, records, money or goods in that person's possession[10].

The court will only order an examination if it is satisfied that it is necessary. It will usually expect an administrator to have obtained what information he can by informal means before making an application for the court to use its draconian powers for private examination. In the first instance, this means first inviting co-operation and attendance at a meeting[11]. It is often useful to send a formal questionnaire at the initial stage, and it may be possible to arrange for the party to attend a formal interview (for example, at the office of the administrator or his solicitor, at which the administrator (or perhaps counsel on his behalf) can question the person and the proceedings can be recorded by a shorthand writer)[12].

In addition, the court must be satisfied that the proposed examination is not oppressive or unfair to the respondent[13]. It is unlikely that a court would grant an order where the administrator has made a firm decision to commence proceedings against the respondent[14], but the fact that criminal charges have already been brought against a respondent is not an absolute bar to an order being made[15]. An officer or former officer of a partnership (and potentially a third party) would not be able to resist an order on grounds of self-incrimination[16].

Until recently, it was frequently the practice to make applications for private examination ex parte as a matter of course. Although there may be cases where such a course is necessary because of particular urgency or for other reasons[17], it will be necessary to demonstrate to the court that an ex parte application is justified[18]. Time and costs may be saved if the respondent is given notice, because it may be possible to clarify the scope of the order.

An application for private examination must be made in writing, sufficiently identifying the respondent[19] and stating the purpose for which it is made[20]. It must be accompanied by a brief statement of the grounds on which it is made[21]. That statement is not normally served on the respondent and he has no automatic right to see it[22]. However, the court has a discretion to permit inspection[23], and the Court of Appeal has said that prima facie, inspection should be allowed where there has been an application to have an order for private examination set aside if the court is of the opinion that it might otherwise be unable to dispose of that application fairly and properly[24]; in such a case, the onus is on the administrator to satisfy the court that confidentiality of all or part of the statement should none the less be maintained. Where the report contains confidential material which the administrator would not want disclosed to the respondent, the report filed should be in two parts; the main part will contain the non-confidential material, and an explanation of why the material in the confidential annexure should not be revealed.

It is not entirely clear whether the court will grant an order for a private examination against a person who is outside the jurisdiction, at least where such an order is unlikely to be effective because it would not be enforced by local courts[25]. However, the court does have jurisdiction to order that a person is to be examined outside the United Kingdom[26].

When a private examination is held, a written record must be made[27] which is usually in the form of a full transcript. It must be signed by the respondent[28] and may subsequently be used as evidence against him in any proceedings[29]. Unless the court directs otherwise (which is unusual) the written record is not filed in court[30], and neither the written record, nor any answers or affidavits are open to inspection by anyone other than the administrator without an order of the court[31]. The Director of the Serious Fraud Office is entitled to the automatic grant of leave to inspect such documents within his statutory powers[32]; it is thought that the court would only grant leave for other third parties to inspect documents if they can satisfy the court that such inspection would be for the benefit of the administration[33].

The administrator must tender to a person who is summoned to attend for private examination a reasonable sum in respect of travelling expenses incurred in connection with his attendance[34]. The court has a discretion to pay an attendee's other costs, but will only do so in exceptional circumstances[35]. Where an examination has been made necessary by the unjustifiable refusal of information, the court can (and usually does) order that the costs are to be paid by the respondent[36]. Otherwise, the administrator's costs are to be paid out of the assets of the partnership, unless the court orders otherwise[37].

1 Ie any partner, any member through holding out, and any person who has management or control of the partnership business: art 2(1) of the Order.
2 Section 236(2)(a) of the Insolvency Act 1986, as modified by art 3(2) of the Order.
3 Ibid, s 236(2)(b) (as modified).
4 Ibid, s 236(2)(c) (as modified).
5 Ibid, s 236(3) (as modified).
6 Ibid, s 236(4)(a).
7 Ie hidden himself or removed himself to avoid legal process.
8 Ibid, s 236(4).
9 Ibid, s 236(5).
10 Ibid, s 236(5)(b).
11 Ie under s 235 of the Insolvency Act 1986 where applicable: see para **8.33.2**.
12 Such a procedure is often more convenient and cheaper than court proceedings.
13 *Re Embassy Art Products Ltd* (1987) 3 BCC 292; *Re Adlards Motor Group Holding Ltd* [1990] BCLC 68; *British & Commonwealth Holdings v Spicer and Oppenheim* [1993] AC 426, HL.
14 *Re Castle New Homes Ltd* [1979] 1 WLR 1075; *Re Cloverbay Ltd (No 2)* [1991] Ch 90.
15 *Re Arrows Ltd (No 2)* [1992] BCC 446.
16 Cf *Re Jeffrey S Levitt Ltd* [1992] Ch 457; *Re A E Farr Ltd* [1992] BCC 151; *Bishopsgate Investment Management Ltd (in provisional liquidation) v Maxwell* [1993] Ch 1. An Australian case suggests the plea *may* be available in the case of a non-officer: *O'Toole v Mitcham* (1978) CLC #40–429.
17 Ex parte application is permitted by the Insolvency Rules 1986, r 9.2(4).
18 *Re Maxwell Communications Corporation plc (No 3)* [1994] BCC 741, [1995] BCLC 521; *Re PFTZM* [1995] BCC 280.
19 Insolvency Rules 1986, r 9.2(2).
20 Ibid, r 9.2(3): the purposes are: (a) to appear before the court; (b) to answer interrogatories; (c) to submit affidavits; (d) to produce books, papers or other records.
21 Ibid, r 9.2(1).
22 Ibid, r 9.5(3).
23 Ibid, r 9.5(2), (3).
24 *Re British & Commonwealth Holdings plc (No 1)* [1992] Ch 342.
25 Dicta in *Re Seagull Manufacturing Co Ltd* [1992] Ch 128 (Mummery J) and [1993] Ch 345 (Court of Appeal) suggest not, as does the decision in *Re Tucker* [1990] Ch 148 under the similar wording of s 25 of the Bankruptcy Act 1914. In the Scottish case *Re McIsaac & Anor, Petitioners; Joint Liquidators of First Tokyo Index Trust Ltd* [1994] BCC 410, it was said that the test was whether an order was effective. The court mistakenly thought that the United States was a relevant territory for the purposes of s 426 of the Act, so an order would be effective.
26 See s 237(3) of the Insolvency Act 1986.
27 Insolvency Rules 1986, r 9.4(6).
28 Ibid, r 9.4(6).
29 Ibid, r 9.4(7).
30 Ibid, r 9.5(1).
31 Ibid, r 9.5(2).
32 See s 2 of the Criminal Justice Act 1987; *Re Arrows Ltd (No 4)* [1993] Ch 452.

33 Cf *Re Esal (Commodities) Ltd* [1989] BCLC 59; *Re Barlow Clowes Gilt Managers Ltd* [1992] Ch 208; *Re Polly Peck International plc* [1994] BCC 15.
34 Insolvency Rules 1986, r 9.6(4); the amount is often tendered at the time the order is served, although the wording of the rule suggests that the travelling costs should have been incurred first.
35 *Re Aveling Barford Ltd* [1989] 1 WLR 36; *Re Cloverbay Ltd* (1989) 5 BCC 732.
36 Insolvency Rules 1986, r 9.6(1); it is therefore necessary to be able to show the court that requests for information were made and refused without justification.
37 Insolvency Rules 1986, r 9.6(3).

8.33.4   Transactions at an undervalue and preferences

The administrator of a partnership has powers to apply to the court in respect of transactions at an undervalue[1] and preferences[2]. However, it is probably unlikely that expenditure in respect of such matters would fall within the ambit of the statutory purposes, and such powers are more likely to be exercised by the liquidator of a partnership.

1 Section 238 of the Insolvency Act 1986, as applied by art 6(2)(b) of the Order.
2 Ibid, s 239, as applied by art 6(2)(b) of the Order.

8.33.5   Extortionate credit transactions

Similarly, the administrator of a partnership has powers to apply to the court in respect of transactions entered into within three years ending with the day the administration order was made, where grossly exorbitant payments were to be made in respect of the provision of credit, or where the ordinary principles of fair dealing were grossly contravened[1].

1 Section 244 of the Insolvency Act 1986, as applied by art 6(2)(b) of the Order.

8.33.6   Transactions defrauding creditors

The administrator may also apply for an order to overturn a transaction which has been entered into at an undervalue for the purpose of putting assets beyond the reach of a person who is making, or may at some time make, a claim against him, or otherwise prejudicing the interests of such a person in relation to the claim which he is making or may make [1].

1 Under s 423 of the Insolvency Act 1986 (which is within Part XVI) as applied by art 6(2)(f) of the Order; the administrator is a permitted applicant under s 424(1)(a) of the Act as modified by art 3(2) of the Order; and by s 424(2) his application is treated as made on behalf of every victim of the transaction.

8.33.7   Unenforceability of liens

A lien or other right to retain possession of any of the books, papers or other records of the partnership is unenforceable against an administrator of the partnership to the extent that its enforcement would deny possession to the administrator[1].

1 Section 246 of the Insolvency Act 1986, as applied by art 6(2)(b) of the Order.

8.33.8 Limits on the exercise of powers

However, it must be borne in mind that the administrator of a partnership is required by s 17(2) of the Act to carry out his functions in accordance with any directions of the court until proposals have been approved, and once proposals have been approved, in accordance with such proposals. The exercise of his powers must thus be directed towards the achievement of the statutory purposes for which the administration order was granted; the administrator may not stray beyond his remit. It may therefore be that some of the powers cannot properly be exercised in an administration, whereas they would appropriately be exercised by a liquidator were the partnership to be wound up.

8.34 THE ADMINISTRATOR'S REMUNERATION

The administrator of a partnership is entitled to be paid for his services[1]. His remuneration is payable out of the assets of the partnership and, upon his ceasing to act, is charged on and payable out of the assets in his custody or under his control at that time[2]. The amount of the administrator's remuneration is to be fixed either:

(a) as a percentage of the value of the property with which he has to deal[3]; or
(b) as a time cost[4].

---

1 Insolvency Rules 1986, r 2.47.
2 Section 19(3), (4) of the Insolvency Act 1986.
3 Insolvency Rules 1986, r 2.47(2)(a).
4 Ibid, r 2.47(2)(b).

8.34.1 Determination by creditors' commitee

If there is a creditors' committee, it is for that committee to determine whether remuneration is to be fixed under (a) or (b); if (a), it is also for the creditors' committee to fix the relevant percentage[1]. In making that determination, the committee must have regard to:

(a) the complexity (or otherwise) of the case[2];
(b) any respects in which, in connection with the partnership's affairs, there falls on the administrator any responsibility of an exceptional kind or degree[3];
(c) the effectiveness with which the administrator appears to be carrying out, or to have carried out, his duties as such[4]; and
(d) the value and nature of the property with which he has to deal[5].

---

1 Insolvency Rules 1986, r 2.47(3).
2 Ibid, r 2.47(4)(a).
3 Ibid, r 2.47(4)(b).
4 Ibid, r 2.47(4)(c).
5 Ibid, r 2.47(4)(d).

8.34.2 Determination by creditors or the court

If there is no creditors' committee, or the committee does not make the requisite determination, the administrator's remuneration may be fixed by a meeting of the partnership's creditors, applying the same principles[1]. Failing that, the administrator can apply to the court[2].

If the administrator considers the rate or amount of remuneration fixed by a creditors' committee to be insufficient, he may request that it be increased by resolution of the creditors[3]. If he is dissatisfied with the remuneration fixed by either a creditors' committee or creditors, he may apply to the court[4].

---

1 Insolvency Rules 1986, r 2.47(5).
2 Ibid, r 2.47(6); cf *Re Charnley Davies Business Services Ltd* (1987) 3 BCC 408; *Re Brooke Marine Ltd* [1988] BCLC 546; *Re Sheridan Securities Ltd* (1988) 4 BCC 200.
3 Insolvency Rules 1986, r 2.48.
4 Ibid, r 2.49.

8.34.3 *Applications to court*

In the event of an application to the court for an increase in the administrator's remuneration, he must give at least 14 days' notice to the members of the creditors' committee, and the committee may nominate one of its members to be heard on the application[1]. Where there is no creditors' committee, notice of the administrator's application must be sent to such one or more of the partnership's creditors as the court may direct, and those creditors may nominate one of their number to be heard on the application[2]. The court may order the costs of such an application, including the costs of any member of the creditors' committee or creditor appearing or being represented, as costs in the administration[3].

If at least 25 per cent (in value) of the creditors concur in the suggestion that the administrator's remuneration is too high, any creditor may apply to the court for an order that it is to be reduced on the grounds that it is, in all the circumstances, excessive[4]. The applicant must have an opportunity to attend the court for an ex parte hearing on at least seven days' notice[5]. If the court thinks no sufficient cause is shown for a reduction, it has a discretion to dismiss the application[6]. Otherwise, it will fix a venue for a hearing, in which case the applicant must send the administrator a notice at least 14 days before the hearing stating the venue and accompanied by a copy of the application and any evidence which the applicant intends to adduce[7]. If the court considers the application to be well-founded, it must make an order fixing the remuneration at a reduced amount or rate[8]. It is unlikely that the court would interfere with the amount set by a creditors' committee or creditors unless it was blatantly excessive[9]. Unless the court orders otherwise, the costs of any such application must be paid by the applicant, and are not payable as an expense of the administration[10].

---

1 Insolvency Rules 1986, r 2.49(2).
2 Ibid, r 2.49(3).
3 Ibid, r 2.49(4).
4 Ibid, r 2.50(1).
5 Ibid, r 2.50(2).
6 Ibid.
7 Ibid, r 2.50(3).
8 Ibid, r 2.50(4).
9 Cf *Re Potters Oils Ltd (No 2)* [1986] 1 WLR 201.
10 Insolvency Rules 1986, r 2.50(5).

8.34.4 Profit costs

If the administrator is a solicitor and employs his own firm, or any partner in it, to act on behalf of the partnership, profit costs must not be paid unless this is authorised by the creditors' committee, the creditors or the court[1].

1 Insolvency Rules 1986, r 2.47(8).

8.34.5 Joint administrators

Joint administrators are supposed to resolve the apportionment of remuneration between themselves[1]; any dispute may be referred to the court[2] or to the creditors' committee or creditors[3].

1 Insolvency Rules 1986, r 2.47(7).
2 Ibid, r 2.47(7)(a).
3 Ibid, r 2.47(7)(b).

8.35 VAT AND BAD DEBT RELIEF

Where an administration order is made, Customs and Excise may from the date of the order to the date of its discharge treat as taxable the person carrying on the business[1]. Normally, this should continue to be the partnership: the administrator merely acts as the partnership's agent[2]. The appointment of the administrator must be notified to Customs and Excise within 21 days[3].

It was formerly the case that an administrator had to issue a certificate to enable creditors to obtain VAT relief on bad debts[4]. Those provisions are now largely redundant[5].

1 Value Added Tax (General) Regulations 1985, SI 1985/886, reg 11(1).
2 Section 14(5) of the Insolvency Act 1986, as modified by Sch 2 of the Order.
3 Value Added Tax (General) Regulations 1985, SI 1985/886, reg 11(2), (3).
4 See rr 2.56–2.58.
5 The provisions continued to apply to supplies made prior to 26 July 1990, by s 11(9) of the Finance Act 1990; it seems unlikely they will have any relevance to the administration of a partnership. The position is today governed by s 36 of the Value Added Tax Act 1994, supplemented by the Value Added Tax (Bad Debt Relief) Regulations 1986, SI 1986/335, and the Value Added Tax (Refunds for Bad Debts) Regulations 1991, SI 1991/371.

8.36 THE ROLE OF THE COURT

The administrator of a partnership is an officer of the court[1]. He is therefore subject to the rule in *Ex parte James* which requires him to behave equitably[2] and he must exercise his powers (such as the power to grant leave to enforce security under s 11(3)(e) (as modified) or the power to make payments) speedily and responsibly, having regard to any orders the court might be expected to make on an application for directions[3].

1 *Re Atlantic Computer Systems plc* [1992] Ch 505.
2 *Re Condon, ex p James* (1874) 9 Ch App 609; note that the rule was somewhat restricted by the decision of Walton J in *Re Clark (A bankrupt)* [1975] 1 WLR 559 and is nowadays regarded as being limited to unfair enrichment of the insolvent estate.
3 *Re Atlantic Computer Systems plc* [1992] Ch 505.

8.36.1 Directions

The court has the power to give directions to an administrator, either on his application or on the application of a creditor, either for leave to take one of the steps specified in s 11(3)(e) and (f) (as modified) against the partnership[1] or generally under s 14(3) of the Act (as modified)[2]. In particular, the court may direct an administrator to make payments as expenses of the administration where liabilities have been incurred for the benefit of the administration; in an appropriate case, this power extends to directing payment in respect of obligations incurred under pre-administration contracts[3].

However, an administrator will be expected to be able to resolve most questions which may arise in the course of an appointment, without incurring the costs of troubling the court.

1 See para **8.19**.
2 On the wording of the section, only the administrator can apply. However in *Re Mirror Group (Holdings) Ltd* [1992] BCC 972, [1993] BCLC 538, Sir Donald Nicholls V-C held that the court has a general power to give directions to its officers on the way in which particular aspects of an administration should be conducted, irrespective of whether the applicant is the administrator. However, it is unlikely that the court would exercise this (apparently inherent) power except in an exceptional case. In normal circumstances, a creditor or member of the partnership will have to persuade the administrator to apply, unless he can bring his case within s 27 of the Act: see below.
3 Cf *Re Atlantic Computer Systems plc* [1992] Ch 505.

8.36.2 Sanction for breach of duty

An administrator of a partnership also owes fiduciary duties to the members of the partnership by virtue of his court appointment as agent of the partnership. These may be summarised as duties to act in good faith, to exercise his powers for proper purposes, not to make any secret profit from his position as administrator, and not to place himself in a position where his duties as administrator conflict with his self-interest or his duties to third parties[1]. He also owes the partnership a duty to exercise reasonable care and skill in the conduct of the administration[2]. Where the administrator of a partnership has been guilty of any misfeasance or breach of duty, he is liable to summary proceedings under s 212 of the Act[3].

1 Cf the position of a liquidator: *Silkstone and Haigh Moor Coal Co v Edey* [1900] 1 Ch 167; *Re Gertzenstein Ltd* [1937] Ch 115; *Re Corbenstoke Ltd (No 2)* [1990] BCLC 60.
2 Cf *Re Charnley Davies Ltd (No 2)* [1990] BCLC 760.
3 Applied by art 6(3)(a) of the Order.

8.36.3 Unfair prejudice

At any time when an administration order is in force in respect of a partnership, any creditor of the partnership, or any member of the partnership[1], may petition the court for relief on the grounds that:

(a) the affairs, business and property of the partnership are being or have been managed by the administrator in a manner which is unfairly prejudicial to the interests of its creditors or members generally, or of some part of its creditors or members (including at least himself)[2]; or

(b) that any actual or proposed act or omission of the administrator is or would be so prejudicial[3].

The court's jurisdiction in this regard is closely analogous to its jurisdiction under s 459 of the Companies Act 1985[4].

Except in cases of urgency, an application in respect of unfair prejudice in the conduct of an administration is made by petition returnable before the registrar or district judge in chambers in the first instance[5], who will give directions and will usually then adjourn the petition to be heard by a judge.

The court has the power to make such order as it thinks fit for giving relief in respect of the matters complained of, and it can also adjourn the hearing conditionally or unconditionally, make an interim order, or make any other order that it thinks fit[6]. In particular, the court's order may:

(a) regulate the future management by the administrator of the partnership's affairs, business and property[7];
(b) require the administrator to refrain from doing or continuing an act complained of by the petitioner, or to do an act which the petitioner has complained that he has omitted to do[8];
(c) require the summoning of a meeting of creditors or members of the partnership for the purpose of considering such matters as the court may direct[9];
(d) discharge the administration order and make such consequential provisions as the court thinks fit[10].

An order in respect of an unfair prejudice petition may not prejudice or prevent the implementation of a partnership voluntary arrangement under s 4 of the Act (as modified)[11]; however, where the complaint is that the PVA itself is prejudicial, a challenge may be brought under s 6 of the Act (as modified)[12].

An order in respect of an unfair prejudice petition also may not prejudice or prevent the implementation of proposals approved under s 24 of the Act or revised proposals approved under s 25 of the Act unless the application was made within 28 days after the proposals were approved[13].

---

1 Ie any partner and anyone who would be liable as a partner through holding out: art 2(1) of the Order.
2 Section 27(1)(a) of the Insolvency Act 1986, as applied by art 6(1) of the Order.
3 Ibid, s 27(1)(b), as applied by art 6(1) of the Order.
4 Cf *Re a Company (No 008699) of 1985)* [1986] BCLC 382; *Re a Company (No 005287 of 1985)* [1986] BCLC 68; *Re Sam Weller & Sons Ltd* [1990] Ch 682. The scope of the court's jurisdiction under s 27 of the Act is discussed in detail in *Re Charnley Davies Ltd* [1990] BCC 605.
5 Insolvency Rules 1986, r 7.6(2), *Practice Direction: Companies Court: Insolvency (No 3 of 1986)* [1987] 1 WLR 53.
6 Section 27(2) of the Insolvency Act 1986, as applied by art 6(1) of the Order.
7 Ibid, s 27(4)(a), as applied by art 6(1) of the Order and modified by art 3(2) of the Order.
8 Ibid, s 27(4)(b), as applied by art 6(1) of the Order.
9 Ibid, s 27(4)(c), as applied by art 6(1) of the Order and modified by art 3(2) of the Order.
10 Ibid, s 27(4)(d), as applied by art 6(1) of the Order.
11 Ibid, s 27(3)(a), as applied by art 6(1) of the Order.
12 See para **7.21**; cf *Re Primlaks (UK) Ltd (No 2)* [1990] BCLC 234.
13 Section 27(3)(b) of the Insolvency Act 1986, as applied by art 6(1) of the Order.

8.37   VACATION OF OFFICE BY THE ADMINISTRATOR

The administrator may at any time be removed from office by order of the court[1]. Grounds for taking this drastic step might be where the administrator was guilty of misconduct, where he was in a position of conflict of interest and duty[2], or where he failed to carry out his duties with sufficient vigour[3]. An order might also be made where the administrator was unreasonably acting contrary to the wishes of creditors.

An administrator must vacate office himself if:

(a)   he ceases to be qualified as an insolvency practitioner in relation to the partnership[4]; or

(b)   the administration order is discharged[5].

---

1   Section 19(1) of the Insolvency Act 1986, as applied by art 6(1) of the Order.
2   Cf *Re Corbenstoke Ltd (No 2)* [1990] BCLC 60.
3   Cf *Re Keypak Homecare Ltd* [1987] BCLC 409.
4   Section 19(2)(a) of the Insolvency Act 1986, as applied by art 6(1) of the Order and modified by art 3(2) of the Order. In these circumstances he vacates office automatically without any further act on his part: cf *Re A J Adams (Builders) Ltd* [1991] BCLC 359.
5   Section 19(2)(b) of the Insolvency Act 1986, as applied by art 6(1) of the Order: see para **8.42.3** below.

8.38   RESIGNATION OF THE ADMINISTRATOR

An administrator of a partnership may give notice of his resignation in the following prescribed circumstances[1]:

(a)   on grounds of ill health[2]; or

(b)   if he intends ceasing to be in practice as an insolvency practitioner[3]; or

(c)   if there is some conflict of interest, or change of personal circumstances, which precludes or makes impracticable the further discharge by him of the duties of an administrator[4]; or

(d)   on other grounds with the leave of the court[5].

The administrator must give seven days' notice of his intention to resign, or of his intention to apply for the leave of the court to resign:

(a)   to any continuing administrator of the partnership[6]; or

(b)   if there is no such administrator, to the creditors' committee[7]; or

(c)   if there is no such administrator and no creditors' committee, to the partnership and its creditors[8].

It is thought that the resignation of an administrator is effective as soon as notice has been given to the court, and that once given, it cannot be withdrawn[9].

If a vacancy has occurred because an administrator has resigned, the court may appoint a replacement[10] upon the application of:

(a) any continuing administrator of the partnership[11]; or

(b) if there is no such administrator, to the creditors' committee[12]; or

(c) if there is no such administrator and no creditors' committee, by the members of the partnership or by any creditor or creditors of the partnership[13].

An order appointing a new administrator must be advertised and notified in the same manner as an administration order[14].

---

1 Section 19(1) of the Insolvency Act 1986 as applied by art 6(1) of the Order.

2 Insolvency Rules 1986, r 2.53(1).

3 Ibid, r 2.53(1)(a).

4 Ibid, r 2.53(1)(b).

5 Ibid, r 2.53(2).

6 Ibid, r 2.53(3)(a).

7 Ibid, r 2.53(3)(b).

8 Ibid, r 2.53(3), as modified by art 18(1) of the Order.

9 Cf *Glossop v Glossop* [1907] 2 Ch 370.

10 Section 13(2) of the Insolvency Act 1986, as modified by Sch 2 to the Order.

11 Ibid, s 13(3)(a) (as modified).

12 Ibid, s 13(3)(b) (as modified).

13 Ibid, s 13(3)(c) (as modified). In such circumstances, it is thought that the same considerations would apply as when the members petition for an administration (see para **8.5.2**) save that it is to be hoped that an administrator as one of the conditions of accepting an appointment will have ensured that there is a workable system for internal decision-taking.

14 Insolvency Rules 1986, r 2.55.

8.39   DEATH OF THE ADMINISTRATOR

If an administrator has died, it is the duty of his personal representatives to give notice of that fact to the court, specifying the date of death[1] unless notice has already been given by:

(a) a partner in the administrator's firm who is also qualified to act as an insolvency practitioner or is a member of any body recognised by the Secretary of State for the authorisation of insolvency practitioners[2]; or

(b) any person producing to the court the relevant death certificate or a copy of it[3].

A person who has ceased to be the administrator of a partnership has his release from the time that notice is given to the court[4].

If a vacancy has occurred because an administrator has died, the court may again appoint a replacement[5] upon the application of:

(a) any continuing administrator of the partnership[6]; or

(b) if there is no such administrator, to the creditors' committee[7]; or

(c) if there is no such administrator and no creditors' committee, by the members of the partnership or by any creditor or creditors of the partnership[8].

An order appointing a new administrator must be advertised and notified in the same manner as an administration order[9].

1 Insolvency Rules 1986, r 2.54(1).
2 Ibid, r 2.54(2).
3 Ibid, r 2.54(3).
4 Section 20(1)(a) of the Insolvency Act 1986, as applied by art 6(1) of the Order and modified by art 3(2) of the Order.
5 Section 13(2) of the Insolvency Act 1986, as modified by Sch 2 to the Order.
6 Ibid, s 13(3)(a) (as modified).
7 Ibid, s 13(3)(b) (as modified).
8 Ibid, s 13(3)(c) (as modified). In such circumstances, it is thought that the same considerations would apply as when the members petition for an administration (see para **8.5.1** above) save that it is to be hoped that an administrator as one of the conditions of accepting an appointment will have ensured that there is a workable system for internal decision-taking.
9 Insolvency Rules 1986, r 2.55.

8.40   CONSEQUENTIAL PROVISIONS ON VACATION OF OFFICE

When a person ceases to be an administrator of a partnership, the following provisions apply.

8.40.1   *Remuneration*

The administrator's remuneration and any expenses properly incurred by him are to be charged upon and paid out of any property of the partnership which is in his custody or under his control at the time he vacates office, in priority to any security over that property[1].

1 Section 19(4) of the Insolvency Act 1986, as applied by art 6(1) of the Order.

8.40.2   *Debts or liabilities*

Any sums payable in respect of debts or liabilities incurred, while the person was administrator, under contracts entered into by him or a predecessor of his in the carrying out of his or the predecessor's functions shall be charged upon and paid out of any property of the partnership which is in his custody or under his control at the time he vacates office, in priority to any charge in respect of the administrator's remuneration and expenses[1].

1 Section 19(5) of the Insolvency Act 1986, as applied by art 6(1) of the Order.

8.40.3   *Contracts of employment*

Any sums payable in respect of liabilities incurred, while the person was administrator, under contracts of employment adopted by him or a predecessor of his in the carrying out of his or the predecessor's functions are, to the extent that the liabilities are 'qualifying liabilities', to be charged upon and paid out of any property of the partnership which is in his custody or under his control at the time he vacates office, in the same priority as any sums payable in respect of contracts (ie ahead of the administrator's remuneration and expenses)[1].

Qualifying liabilities are liabilities under a contract of employment to pay wages, salary or contribution to an occupational pension scheme, if the liability is in respect of services rendered wholly or partly after the adoption of the contract[2]. A contract is 'adopted' if the employee is continued in employment for more than 14 days after the administrator is appointed; it is not possible for an administrator to avoid this result or alter its consequences unilaterally by informing the employees that he is not adopting their contracts[3]. The administrator has 14 days from his appointment to consider contracts of employment; he is not to be taken to have adopted a contract of employment by reason of anything done or omitted to be done within that time[4]. Payment in respect of services rendered before the adoption of the contract is to be disregarded[5]. However, wages or salary payable in respect of a period of holiday or absence from work through sickness or other good cause are deemed to be wages or (as the case may be) salary in respect of services rendered wholly or partly after the adoption of the contract[6]. This includes sums which would have been treated for social security purposes as earnings in respect of that period[7]. A sum payable in lieu of holiday is deemed to be wages or (as the case may be) salary in respect of services rendered in the period by reference to which the holiday entitlement arose[8].

1 Section 19(6) of the Insolvency Act 1986 as applied by art 6(1) of the Order; this section (and subsections (7)–(10)) was added by the Insolvency Act 1994 as a result of the Court of Appeal decision in the *Paramount* case (*Powdrill v Watson* [1995] 2 AC 394).
2 Section 19(7) of the Insolvency Act 1986, as applied by art 6(1) of the Order.
3 *Powdrill v Watson* [1995] 2 AC 394.
4 Section 19(6) of the Insolvency Act 1986, as applied by art 6(1) of the Order.
5 Ibid, s 19(8), as applied by art 6(1) of the Order.
6 Ibid, s 19(9)(a), as applied by art 6(1) of the Order.
7 Ibid, s 19(10), as applied by art 6(1) of the Order.
8 Ibid, s 19(9)(b), as applied by art 6(1) of the Order.

8.41 RELEASE OF THE ADMINISTRATOR

An administrator[1] is released from such time as the court may determine[2]. The court has power to grant the administrator his release immediately upon discharge of the administration order[3], but the usual practice is to delay release for a period, at least until the administrator has delivered his final receipts and payments account[4]. This may permit an application to be made for release to be postponed in order for the administrator's conduct to be investigated[5]. Where there is a claim outstanding against the administrator, the court will not grant a release prior to the claim being determined[6].

Once an administrator has his release, he is discharged from all liability both in respect of acts or omissions of his in the administration and otherwise in relation to his conduct as administrator[7]. However, release does not prevent the exercise of the court's powers under s 212 of the Act for misfeasance or breach of duty[8].

1 Other than an administrator who has died, for which see para **8.39**.
2 Section 20 of the Insolvency Act 1986, as applied by art 6(1) of the Order.
3 *Re Brooke Marine Ltd* [1988] BCLC 546; *Re Olympia & York Canary Wharf Holdings* [1993] BCC 866.
4 Which must be delivered within two months after he ceases to act as administrator, by r 2.52.
5 *Re Sheridan Securities Ltd* (1988) 4 BCC 200; *Re Exchange Travel (Holdings) Ltd* [1992] BCC 954.

6 *Barclays Mercantile Business Finance Ltd v Sibec Developments Ltd* [1992] 1 WLR 1253.
7 Section 20(2) of the Insolvency Act 1986, as applied by art 6(1) of the Order.
8 Ibid, s 20(3), as applied by art 6(1) of the Order; see para **8.36.2** above.

8.42   TERMINATION OR DISCHARGE OF THE ADMINISTRATION

Administration proceedings may be brought to an end by:

(a)   a successful appeal against the making of an administration order[1];
(b)   the rescission of the administration order by the court[2];
(c)   the discharge of the administration order.

1 Under Insolvency Rules 1986, r 7.47(2).
2 Under r 7.47(1); see *Cornhill Insurance plc v Cornhill Financial Services Ltd* [1992] BCC 818.

8.42.1   Appeal

An appeal may be made on usual principles if there has been an error of law, or a wrongful exercise of discretion.

8.42.2   Rescission

The court has power under the Rules to review its own order[1]. This power may be invoked where the court has not been told all the facts[2], or where it can be shown that the court proceeded on the basis of a mistake, or perhaps that the administration order is likely to operate unfairly or oppressively against the interest of a particular creditor or group of creditors, or member or group of members, of the partnership.

1 Insolvency Rules 1986, r 7.47(1).
2 Cf *Re Sharps of Truro Ltd* [1990] BCC 94.

8.42.3   Discharge

A partnership administration order may be discharged:

(a)   upon the application of the administrator[1]; or
(b)   where one of the purposes of the administration order was a PVA, and that has been achieved[2]; or
(c)   if a report is given to the court[3] that a meeting of creditors summoned under s 23 of the Act has declined to approve the administrator's proposals[4]; or
(d)   on an unfair prejudice application by a creditor or member of the partnership[5].

It should be noted that a discharge of the administration of a partnership, unlike that of a company, does not need to be reported officially[6].

1 Section 18(1) of the Insolvency Act 1986, as applied by art 6(1) of the Order; cf *Re Olympia &
   York Canary Wharf Holdings* [1993] BCC 866.
2 Section 5(3)(a)(ii) of the Insolvency Act 1986, as modified by Sch 1 to the Order.
3 Under s 24(4) of the Insolvency Act 1986.
4 Section 24(5) of the Insolvency Act 1986, as applied by art 6(1) of the Order.
5 Ibid, s 27(4)(d), as applied by art 6(1) of the Order: see para **8.36.3**.

6 Sections 18(4), 24(6) and 27(6) of the Act may be disregarded because references to the Registrar of Companies are omitted in applying the Act to an insolvent partnership, by art 3(2) of the Order.

8.42.4 *Application of the administrator*

The administrator may apply to the court at any time for a partnership administration order to be discharged or for it to be varied to specify an additional purpose[1]. He *must* apply for discharge if:

(a) it appears to him that the purpose or each of the purposes specified in the order has either:
   (i)   been achieved; or
   (ii) is incapable of achievement[2]; or
(b) he is required to do so by a meeting of the partnership's creditors summoned for the purpose in accordance with the Rules[3].

On the hearing of such an application for discharge by the administrator, the court has a discretion whether to order discharge, or whether to vary the administration order and make such consequential provision as it thinks fit, or adjourn the hearing conditionally or unconditionally, or make an interim order or such other order as it thinks fit[4].

1 Section 18(1) of the Act, as applied by art 6(1) of the Order; cf *Re Olympia & York Canary Wharf Holdings* [1993] BCC 866.
2 Section 18(2)(a) of the Insolvency Act 1986, as applied by art 6(1) of the Order.
3 Ibid, s 18(2)(b), as applied by art 6(1) of the Order and modified by art 3(2) of the Order.
4 Ibid, s 18(3), as applied by art 6(1) of the Order.

8.42.5 *Application for discharge before proposals are sent to creditors*

If the administrator intends to apply for the administration order to be discharged before he has sent proposals to creditors[1], he must send to all the creditors of the partnership (so far as he is aware of their addresses) at least 10 days before he makes such an application a report containing the following information[2]:

(a) details relating to his appointment as administrator, the purposes for which the administration order was applied for and made, and any subsequent variation of those purposes[3];
(b) the names of the partners[4];
(c) an account of the circumstances giving rise to the application for an administration order;
(d) if a statement of affairs has been submitted, a copy or summary of it, with the administrator's comments, if any[5];
(e) if no statement of affairs has been submitted, details of the financial position of the partnership, at the latest practicable date (which must, unless the court otherwise orders, be a date not earlier than that of the administration order)[6];
(f) the manner in which the affairs and business of the partnership have, since the date of the administrator's appointment, been managed and financed[7].

1 Under s 23(1) of the Insolvency Act 1986.
2 Insolvency Rules 1986, r 2.16(2).
3 Ibid, r 2.16(1)(a).
4 Ibid, r 2.16(1)(b), as modified by art 18(1) of the Order.
5 Ibid, r 2.16(1)(d).
6 Ibid, r 2.16(1)(e), as modified by art 18(1) of the Order.
7 Ibid, r 2.16(1)(f), as modified by art 18(1) of the Order.

8.42.6 *Discharge where a PVA has been approved*

When it has been reported to the court[1] that meetings of a partnership's creditors and members have approved a proposal for a voluntary arrangement in respect of a partnership in administration, the court may[2]:

(a) make an order discharging the administration order[3]; or
(b) give such directions as it thinks appropriate for facilitating the implementation of the approved voluntary arrangement with respect to the conduct of the administration[4].

However, the court may not discharge the administration order until 28 days have elapsed from the time when reports of both meetings have been lodged in court[5], or at any time when an application to challenge the conduct or result of the meetings for material irregularity or unfair prejudice[6] is pending, or an appeal is pending in respect of such an application, or when such an appeal may be brought. In other words, until challenges have been dealt with and the possibility of any appeal has been exhausted, the administration order must remain in force.

It is likely that the administrator would become the supervisor of the PVA, as usually happens with respect to a CVA following the administration of a company. Where someone other than the administrator becomes supervisor, the administrator must forthwith do all that is required for putting the supervisor into possession of the assets included in the arrangement[7], even before the administration has been discharged. If the court subsequently revokes the decision of the meetings, the assets must be handed back.

On taking possession of the assets, the supervisor must discharge any balance due to the administrator by way of remuneration[8] or on account of:

(a) fees, costs, charges and expenses properly incurred and payable under the Act or the Rules[9]; and
(b) any advances made in respect of the partnership, together with interest on such advances at the rate specified in s 17 of the Judgments Act 1838 at the date on which the partnership became subject to the administration order[10].

Alternatively, the supervisor must, before taking possession, give the administrator a written undertaking to discharge the balance of his fees, expenses, advances etc out of the first realisation of any assets[11]. The administrator is protected in that he has a charge on the assets included in the voluntary arrangement in respect of any sums due to him for his fees, expenses, advances etc until they have been discharged, subject only to the deduction from realisations by the supervisor of the proper costs and expenses of such realisations[12]. The supervisor must out of the realisation of assets discharge any guarantees properly given by the administrator for the benefit of the partnership, and must pay his expenses[13].

---

1 Under s 4(6) of the Insolvency Act 1986, as modified by Sch 1 to the Order.
2 By s 5(3) of the Insolvency Act 1986, as modified by Sch 1 to the Order.
3 Ibid, s 5(3)(a)(ii) (as modified).
4 Ibid, s 5(3)(b)(i) (as modified).
5 Ibid, s 5(4)(a) (as modified).
6 See para **7.21** above.
7 Insolvency Rules 1986, r 1.23(1)(b).
8 Ibid, r 1.23(2).
9 Ibid, r 1.23(2)(a).
10 Ibid, r 1.23(2)(b).
11 Ibid, r 1.23(3).
12 Ibid, r 1.23(4).
13 Ibid, r 1.23(5).

8.42.7 *Discharge where the partnership remains insolvent*

Where the partnership remains insolvent (ie where the statutory purposes have not been achievable, or where parts of the business have been sold off or merged with another firm, and an insolvent rump is left), the court will not discharge an administration order unless it is satisfied that proper arrangements will be in place to achieve the realisation of any remaining assets and the distribution of the proceeds to creditors[1].

This will usually be achieved by the administrator exercising his powers[2] to present a petition for the partnership to be wound up and for the administration order to be discharged so that immediately following the grant of the application for discharge, a winding-up order can be made[3]. An administrator may only present a petition to wind up an insolvent partnership under art 7 of the Order[4] and he has no express power in modified Sch 1 to the Act[5] to present a bankruptcy petition against a member of the partnership[6].

A petition by an administrator must contain an application under s 18 of the Act requesting that the administration order be discharged and that the court make any such order consequential upon that discharge as it thinks fit[7]. The procedure applicable to a petition by an administrator is the procedure for a petition by contributories[8]. This is a simplified procedure, with no need for advertisement of the petition[9]. In practice, there is usually no need for any directions, and so the petition is listed in open court from the outset[10].

Where the administrator presents a petition to wind up the insolvent partnership of which he has been administrator, he may be appointed as a provisional liquidator[11], and he may be appointed liquidator of the partnership[12] in which case the Official Receiver does not become liquidator and is relieved of the duties he would otherwise have had to call meetings of creditors or contributories.

In the context of company administrations, the court is sometimes hesitant to appoint an administrator as liquidator where there is some indication that his conduct may give ground for legitimate complaint[13]. There is therefore a provision in the Rules for notification of a company's creditors of the intention to seek an appointment[14]. However, this rule only applies where an appointment is sought in accordance with s 140 of the Act, and is therefore thought not to apply to an appointment as liquidator of an insolvent partnership[15].

An application for discharge will generally be ex parte, and so the usual obligation to make *full and frank* disclosure to the court will apply. The supporting affidavit will therefore need to deal in detail with the conduct of the administration, and with any outstanding claims or complaints against the administrator.

There is no mechanism to wind up an insolvent partnership voluntarily[16]. Whereas in the case of a company it is sometimes possible to arrange for a voluntary winding up to follow immediately upon discharge of an administration, with the result that the value of the assets is not reduced by the ad valorem charge levied on money in the insolvency services account[17], such a tactic is not possible in respect of an insolvent partnership.

It should be noted that because the partnership is wound up under art 7 of the Order, the modifications permitting joint estate claims to rank in priority alongside separate estate claims under Sch 4 to the Order[18] will not initially apply; claims will simply be made for any shortfall on the joint estate against the individual partners as contributories. If it subsequently becomes necessary to present bankruptcy or winding-up petitions against partners, it may be appropriate to ask the court to exercise its supplemental powers under modified s 168 and modified s 303 of the Act[19] to enable the revised priority scheme under Sch 4 to the Order to apply.

Where an insolvent partnership is wound up by the court immediately upon the discharge of an administration order:

(a)   the 'relevant date' for determining the existence and amount of a preferential debt[20] is the date on which the administration order was made[21];

(b)   the 'onset of insolvency' in respect of transactions at an undervalue[22] or preferences[23] is the date of the presentation of the petition on which the partnership administration order was made[24].

---

1   *Re Barrow Borough Transport Ltd* [1990] Ch 227.
2   Under modified s 14(1)(b) and para 19 in modified Sch 1 to the Insolvency Act 1986, as modified by Sch 2, para 10 to the Order.
3   Cf, in the company context, *Re Charnley Davies Business Services Ltd* (1987) 3 BCC 408 and *Re Sheridan Securities Ltd* (1988) 4 BCC 200.
4   By virtue of s 221A(1)(a) of the Insolvency Act 1986, as modified by Sch 3 to the Order; see para **3.2.3** above.
5   As set out in para 10 of Sch 2 to the Order.
6   Unless this could be something 'incidental to the exercise of the foregoing powers' under modified Sch 1, para 20 to the Insolvency Act 1986.
7   Insolvency Rules 1986, r 4.7(7), as applied by art 18(1) of the Order. By s 221A(1) of the Insolvency Act 1986, as modified by Sch 3 to the Order, the petition must be in Form 3 in Sch 9 to the Order. The basic form does not contain the petition for discharge required under the Rules.
8   Ie under Chapter 4 of Part 4 of the Rules: see r 4.7(9).
9   Unless the court orders otherwise under r 4.23(1)(c).

10 Cf r 4.22(2).

11 Section 221A(4) of the Insolvency Act 1986, as modified by Sch 3 to the Order.

12 Ibid, s 221A(5) (as modified).

13 Cf *Re Charnley Davies Business Services Ltd* (1987) 3 BCC 408.

14 Insolvency Rules 1986, r 4.7(10).

15 Which is made under s 221A(5) of the Insolvency Act 1986 in Sch 3.

16 Cf modified s 221(4) of the Insolvency Act 1986 in Sch 3, Sch 4, Sch 5, Sch 6 to the Order.

17 Under regs 5(1) and 18 of the Insolvency Regulations 1994 applying Fee No 10 in Sch, Pt I, of the Insolvency Fees Order 1986.

18 See para **3.3.22**(c).

19 As inserted by art 14 of the Order.

20 Under Sch 6 to the Insolvency Act 1986.

21 Section 387(3)(a) of the Insolvency Act 1986 which is applied by modified s 221(5) of the Act in Sch 3 to the Order.

22 Under s 238 of the Insolvency Act 1986.

23 Under s 239 of the Insolvency Act 1986.

24 By s 240(3)(a) of the Insolvency Act 1986.

Chapter 9

DISQUALIFICATION PROCEEDINGS AGAINST PARTNERS

9.1 INTRODUCTION

Partners and persons who have management or control of the partnership business face, by virtue of the Order, the same sanctions as directors of limited companies for specified misconduct and may be disqualified from office and/or in certain circumstances subjected to personal liability for the debts of partnerships in whose management they have been involved. The Order applies certain provisions (in some cases modified) of the Company Directors Disqualification Act 1986 (the 'CDDA'). The number of cases brought under the CDDA has been steadily increasing due to a policy decision of the Department of Trade and Industry to bring more cases before the courts.

The CDDA allows the court to make a disqualification order under which a person is not allowed, without leave of the court, to be a director of a company, or liquidator or administrator of a company, or a receiver or manager of a company's property or, in any way, whether directly or indirectly, be concerned or take part in the promotion, formation or management of a company, for a specified period beginning with the date of the order of the court[1].

The CDDA only applies to partnerships by virtue of the Order. Under art 16, however, it is only specified sections of the CDDA which apply and there are a number of curious consequences resulting from that. Article 16 provides that where an insolvent partnership is wound up as an unregistered company under Part V of the Act (ie under the provisions of arts 7 to 10 of the Order), the provisions of ss 6 to 10, 15, 19(c) and 20 of, and Sch 1 to, the CDDA shall apply, as modified by Sch 8 to the Order[2].

It follows that since ss 1 to 5 of the CDDA do not apply, there is no discretionary power to disqualify for conviction on an indictable offence, breaches of companies legislation, fraud or summary conviction.

Strangely, because s 1 of the CDDA does not apply, there appears to be no definition of 'a disqualification order' but this must be a legislative error and it is suggested that a disqualification order for the purposes of art 16 must have the same meaning as contained in s 1 of the CDDA.

The next peculiar omission is that since s 22 of the CDDA (the interpretation section) is also not applied by the Order, there appears to be no definition of what is 'a company' for the purposes of the CDDA as applied by the Order. Once again, it is suggested the definition must be the same as that provided in s 22(2)(b) namely, 'any company which may be wound up under Part V of the Insolvency Act [1986]'. Part V of the Act applies to the winding up of an 'unregistered company'. That expression is defined in s 220(1) as:

> 'Any trustee savings bank certified under the enactments relating to such banks, any association and any company, with the following exceptions–

(a)' [repealed]
(b) a company registered in any part of the United Kingdom under the Joint
Stock Companies Acts or under the legislation (past or present) relating to
companies in Great Britain.'

Interestingly, the statutory precursors of s 220, from s 3 of the Joint Stock
Companies Winding-up Act 1848 to s 655 of the Companies Act 1985 defined
'company' as 'any partnership ... any association ... any company'[3].

It is arguable from the fact that the definition included the words 'any
partnership' as part of the list that without such words the section would not
have applied to a partnership. In 1985, the section was moved into the
Insolvency Act 1985 (subsequently the Insolvency Act 1986) and the wording
which applied the section to partnerships was omitted. The effect is that a
partnership is *not* a 'company which may be wound up under Part V' but it *is*
capable of being wound up under Part V as applied or amended by the Order.

If it is correct that a 'disqualification order' bears the meaning in s 1 of the
CDDA:

(a) 'partnership' would not fall within 'company' in s 1(1)(a) or (d); and
(b) there is apparently no scope to apply art 3(2) of the Order, because that
only requires a reference to a company to be construed as a reference to an
'insolvent' partnership, and here disqualification would prospectively
apply to solvent partnerships.

It is worth noting that the same sections of the CDDA were applied by art 6 of
the 1986 Order, which included the words:

'as if any member of a partnership were a director of a company and the
partnership were a company as defined by Section 22(2)(b) of [the CDDA].'

It is not clear why the wording in the 1986 Order has been left out of art 16 of
the Order. Perhaps it was intended to clarify that disqualification does not
operate qua partner but only qua director.

---

1 See s 1 of the CDDA.
2 Sections 2 to 5 of the CDDA provide for disqualification for general misconduct in
connection with companies. Sections 6 to 9 provide for disqualification on the ground of
unfitness. Sections 10 to 12 are headed 'other cases of disqualification' and deal with
participation in wrongful trading, undischarged bankrupts and failure to pay under a county
court administration order. Sections 13 to 15 describe the consequences of contravention
and ss 16 to 19 contain supplementary provisions dealing with the procedure and the setting
up of a register of disqualification orders. Sections 20 to 26 contain miscellaneous and
general provisions. There follow four Schedules the first of which contains a list of matters for
determining the unfitness of directors.
3 See *Re International Tin Council* [1989] Ch 309 per Nourse LJ at 328E–H.

9.2   THE EFFECTS OF DISQUALIFICATION

It is understood that the Department of Trade and Industry ('DTI') takes the
view that a disqualification order made under the CDDA as applied by the
Order has the effect of preventing the individual from acting as a director of a
limited company but not from acting as a partner. Although there has been

some academic debate on this point and although it is anomalous that a person who has perhaps caused unsecured creditors of a partnership to suffer is merely to be deprived from enjoying the benefits of limited liability, it is the authors' view that the DTI is probably correct. As the DTI is the prosecuting authority it seems unlikely that this point will be tested.

The policy of disqualification is said to be that in certain circumstances misconduct should deprive the individual of limited liability. If he has not been enjoying limited liability and unsecured creditors or his partners have suffered in insolvency it seems odd that the court should not have the ability to prevent him from being a partner in another partnership. The view of the DTI is presumably that such a person can always be bankrupted, whereas a director of a limited liability company will prima facie be able to escape personal liability unless held liable, for example, for wrongful trading. From the deterrent point of view, this does not seem to be an adequate explanation.

9.3 PROCEDURE

Under the Insolvent Companies (Reports on Conduct of Directors) No 2 Rules 1986, SI 1986/2134, as applied by the Order[1], the liquidator or an administrator of a partnership must make a report on the conduct of the partners and any other person who had management or control of the partnership business[2].

In respect of disqualification proceedings brought under the Order, only the Secretary of State, or the Official Receiver acting under the direction of the Secretary of State, has locus standi to apply[3]. Except with the leave of the court, application must be made within two years of the day the partnership becomes insolvent. The applicant for the disqualification order must give not less than 10 days' notice of his intention to the person against whom the order is sought[4].

An application for a disqualification order may be heard and determined summarily, without further or other notice to the respondent and, if it is so heard and determined, the court may impose disqualification for a period of up to five years[5]. If at the hearing of the application the court, on the evidence set before it, is minded to impose, in the respondent's case, disqualification for any period longer than five years, it will not make a disqualification order on that occasion but will adjourn the application to be heard (with further evidence, if any) at a later date to be notified[6]. The registrar is empowered to adjourn the case for further consideration on the date fixed for hearing if he forms the provisional opinion that a disqualification order ought to be made, and that a period of disqualification longer than five years is appropriate and, if so, he shall direct whether the case is to be heard by a registrar or, if he thinks it appropriate, by the judge for determination by him. Where a case is adjourned other than to the judge, it may be heard by the registrar who originally dealt with the case or by another registrar[7].

The Official Receiver's report or affidavit evidence must specify the matters relied upon[8] and although the court may in its discretion allow new matters to be raised it will not normally do so unless no injustice is caused to the accused. If necessary, the court will allow him to put in evidence in reply and be given a fair opportunity to answer the new allegations[9].

It has been held by the Court of Appeal that s 8 of the CDDA creates an implied exception to the hearsay rule and that therefore evidence obtained under s 447 of the Companies Act 1985 is admissible in evidence against the respondent[10].

Detailed provisions in relation to the procedure have recently been made in a Practice Direction[11]. The Practice Direction endorses the so-called '*Carecraft* procedure' after the decision of Ferris J, to the effect that the court has jurisdiction to determine a case summarily where there is an agreed schedule of facts and the director has accepted that he should be disqualified for two years[12]. The procedure in such a case is for the applicant to submit a written statement containing any material facts which have been agreed or which are not opposed (for the purposes of the application) and a proposed period for the disqualification can be put forward. This procedure in effect is a kind of plea bargaining between the Secretary of State and the respondent whereby the parties invite the court to make what is in effect a consent order, but of course the court has the power to refuse to do so. If the judge hearing the initial application is not content to impose a disqualification of the suggested length then the matter is adjourned to a different judge and no reference will be made to the agreed statement of facts on the hearing before the second judge.

The Act provides for a potential 15-year disqualification period[13]. The Court of Appeal has held that this period is to be divided into three brackets[14]. The top bracket for periods over 10 years should be reserved for particularly serious cases. These may include cases where a director who has already had one period of disqualification imposed on him falls to be disqualified yet again. The minimum bracket of 2–5 years should be applied where, although disqualification is mandatory, the case is relatively not very serious. A middle bracket of 6–10 years should apply for serious cases which do not merit the top bracket. It has been held that the fact that a respondent was the subject of a bankruptcy order which would prevent him from acting as a director was not a factor which should weigh one way or the other in fixing a period of disqualification under s 6 of the CDDA[15]. In considering whether to make a disqualification order, the court is concerned solely with whether the conduct relied upon, viewed cumulatively and taking into account any extenuating circumstances, fell below the appropriate standards of probity and competence; if so, disqualification is mandatory. The likelihood of the conduct being repeated is not the criterion[16].

1   See Sch 10 to the Order.
2   See definition of 'officer' in art 2 of the Order.
3   See s 7(1) of the CDDA.
4   See s 16(1) of the CDDA.
5   See r 4(c) of the Insolvent Companies (Disqualification of Unfit Directors) Proceedings Rules 1987, SI 1987/2023.
6   See ibid, r 4(d).
7   See ibid, r 7(4), (5) and (6).
8   See *In Re Sevenoaks Stationers (Retail) Limited* [1991] Ch 164.
9   See *Re Jazzgold Limited* [1992] BCC 587.
10 See *Rex Williams Leisure* [1994] Ch 1.

11 See *Practice Direction No 2 of 1995 Directors Disqualification* [1996] BCC 11.
12 See *Re Carecraft Construction Co Limited* [1994] 1 WLR 172.
13 See s 6(4) of the CDDA.
14 See *In Re Sevenoaks Stationers (Retail) Limited* [1991] Ch 164.
15 See *Re Tansoft Limited* [1991] BCLC 339.
16 See *Re Grayan Building Services Limited* [1995] BCC 554.

9.4 DUTY OF COURT TO DISQUALIFY UNFIT OFFICERS OF INSOLVENT PARTNERSHIPS[1]

The court must make a disqualification order against a person in any case where, on an application under s 6 of the CDDA (as modified), it is satisfied:

(a) that he is or has been an officer of a partnership which has at any time become insolvent (whether while he was an officer or subsequently); and

(b) that his conduct as an officer of that partnership (either taken alone or taken together with his conduct as an officer of any other partnership or partnerships, or as a director of any company or companies) makes him unfit to be concerned in the management of a company[2].

For purposes of the modified ss 6 and 7, a partnership becomes insolvent if the court makes an order for it to be wound up as an unregistered company at a time when its assets are insufficient for the payment of its debts and other liabilities and expenses of the winding up, or an administration order is made in relation to the partnership[3] and for the same purposes a company becomes insolvent:

(a) if it goes into liquidation at a time when its assets are insufficient for the payment of its debts and other liabilities and expenses of the winding up; or

(b) an administration order is made in relation to the company; or

(c) an administrative receiver of the company is appointed[4].

References to 'a person's conduct as an officer of any partnership or partnerships or as a director of any company or companies' include, where the partnership or company concerned or any of the partnerships or companies concerned has become insolvent, that person's conduct in relation to any matter connected with or arising out of the insolvency of that partnership or company[5].

'The court' for the purposes of proceedings under the CDDA against a partner means:

(a) in the case of a person who is or has been an officer of a partnership which is being wound up as an unregistered company by the court, the court by which the partnership is being wound up;

(b) in the case of a person who is or has been an officer of a partnership in relation to which an administration order is in force, the court by which that order was made; and

(c) in any other case, the High Court[6].

Under s 6 the minimum period of disqualification is two years and the maximum period is 15 years[7].

1 Section 6 of the CDDA, as modified by Sch 8 to the Order.
2 Ibid, s 6(1) (as modified).
3 Ibid, s 6(2)(a) (as modified).
4 Ibid, s 6(2)(b) (as modified).
5 Ibid, s 6(3) (as modified).
6 In both sections 'director' includes a shadow director: see s 6(4) of the CDDA (as modified).
7 Ibid, s 6(5) (as modified).

9.5 APPLICATIONS TO THE COURT UNDER SECTION 6: REPORTING PROVISIONS[1]

Under s 7 of the CDDA (as modified) 'officer of a partnership' is substituted for 'director of a company' and 'partnership' for 'company' so that:

(a) application may be made by the Secretary of State or, if he so directs in the case of a person who is or has been an officer of a partnership which has been wound up by the court as an unregistered company, by the Official Receiver[2];

(b) the two-year time-limit within which disqualification proceedings have to be commenced is applied beginning with the day on which the partnership of which the person concerned is or has been an officer became insolvent[3];

(c) the office holder responsible for reporting on conduct in the case of a partnership which is being wound up by the court as an unregistered company is the Official Receiver, and in the case of a partnership in relation to which an administration order is in force, the administrator[3];

(d) the Secretary of State or the Official Receiver may require the liquidator, or administrator, or former liquidator or administrator of the partnership to furnish such information with respect to any person's conduct as an officer of a partnership or as a director of a company to produce and permit inspection of such books, papers and other records as are relevant to that person's conduct as such officer or director[5].

1 Section 7 of the CDDA, as modified by Sch 8 to the Order.
2 Ibid, s 7(1) (as modified).
3 Ibid, s 7(2) (as modified).
4 Ibid, s 7(3) (as modified)
5 Ibid, s 7(4) and (5) (as modified).

9.6 DISQUALIFICATION AFTER INVESTIGATION[1]

An officer or former officer of an insolvent partnership[2] may be disqualified even in circumstances where the partnership has not been wound up, provided he was, or had been, an officer of a partnership in relation to which an administration order is in force where it appears to the Secretary of State from a report made by inspectors under s 437 of the Companies Act 1985 or s 94 or s 177 of the Financial Services Act 1986 or from information or documents obtained under:

(a) s 447 or s 448 of the Companies Act 1985;

(b) s 105 of the Financial Services Act 1986;

(c) s 2 of the Criminal Justice Act 1987;

(d) s 52 of the Criminal Justice (Scotland) Act 1987; or

(e) s 83 of the Companies Act 1989,

that it is expedient in the public interest that a disqualification order should be made against such person; in which event, the Secretary of State may apply to the court for a disqualification order to be made against that person[3].

Under s 8 (as modified) only the High Court can make a disqualification order against a person and only where it is satisfied that his conduct in relation to the partnership makes him unfit to be concerned in the management of a company[4].

The maximum period of disqualification under this section is 15 years[5].

---

1 Section 8 of the CDDA, as modified by Sch 8 to the Order.

2 Ibid, s 6(2)(a) (as modified). It appears that if the partnership is no longer in administration despite whatever criticisms have been made of the partner's conduct there is no longer any jurisdiction.

3 Ibid, s 8(1) (as modified).

4 Ibid, s 8(2) and (3) (as modified).

5 Ibid, s 8(4) (as modified).

9.7 MATTERS FOR DETERMINING UNFITNESS OF OFFICERS OF PARTNERSHIPS[1]

Where disqualification proceedings are taken against an officer of a partnership the court must, as respects that person's conduct either taken alone or taken together with his conduct as an officer of any other partnership or partnerships or as a director or shadow director of a company or any company or companies, have regard in particular:

(a) to the matters mentioned in Part I of Sch 1 to the CDDA; and

(b) where the partnership or company, as the case may be, has become insolvent, to the matters mentioned in Part II of Sch 1 to the CDDA[2].

Subsections (2) and (3) of s 6 of the CDDA apply to s 9 and Sch 1 as they apply for the purposes of ss 6 and 7[3]. The references in Sch 1 to an enactment contained in the Companies Act 1985 and the Insolvency Act 1986 include in relation to any time before the coming into force of that enactment, the corresponding enactment in force at that time[4].

The Secretary of State is allowed by order to modify any of the provisions of Sch 1 and to make any transitional provisions he considers necessary or expedient[5].

The power to make orders under s 9 (as modified) is exercisable by statutory instrument subject to annulment in pursuance to resolution of either House of Parliament[6].

---

1 Section 9 of the CDDA, as modified by Sch 8 to the Order.

2 Ibid, s 9(1) and (2) (as modified). 'Misfeasance' being a matter referred to in para 1 of Part I of Sch 1 as being a matter for determining the unfitness of a person to be a director is

generally given a very wide meaning, and is taken to include every misconduct by an officer of a company (or here, a partnership) for which he might have been sued (per Vaughan Williams J in *Re Kingston Cotton Mills Co (No 2)* [1896] 1 Ch 331) or which has resulted in a loss to the company. It does not denote a specific wrongful act (see *Re B Johnson (Builders)* [1955] Ch 634). Insofar as partners are under a fiduciary duty to their co-partners, any breach of duty to co-partners (eg misappropriation of assets or money, or making secret profits) would constitute 'misfeasance'.

3 Section 9(3) of the CDDA (as modified).
4 Ibid, s 9(4) (as modified).
5 Ibid, s 9(5) (as modified).
6 Ibid, s 9(6) (as modified).

9.8 MODIFICATIONS TO SCHEDULE 1 TO THE CDDA[1]

Schedule 1 is headed 'Matters for determining unfitness of officers of partnerships' and is divided into two parts. Part I is headed 'Matters applicable in all cases' and Part II is headed 'Matters applicable where partnership or company has become insolvent'.

Paragraph 1 of Part I provides that there should be taken into account 'any misfeasance or breach of any fiduciary or other duty by the officer in relation to the partnership or, as the case may be, by the director in relation to the company'. The expression 'misfeasance' is not in fact defined either in the Act or the CDDA. It is an expression which is well-known to the common law, but it is curious to see it applied to partnerships[2].

Under para 2 there must taken into account any misapplication or retention by the officer or the director, or any conduct by the officer or the director, giving rise to an obligation to account for any money or other property of the partnership or, as the case may be, of the company.

Under para 3 there must be taken into account the extent of the officer's or the director's responsibility for the partnership or, as the case may be the company, entering into any transaction liable to be set aside under Part XVI of the Act (provisions against debt avoidance). Part XVI comprises three sections (ss 423 to 425) and the substantive section, s 423, is headed 'transactions defrauding creditors'. This section applies to all insolvent partnerships affected by the Order, being expressly applied by art 4 (voluntary arrangements)[3], art 6 (administration orders)[4] and (to all kinds of winding up) by arts 7 to 11[5].

Paragraphs 4 and 5 of the modified Sch 1 are in fact in precisely the same terms as Sch 1 to the CDDA and relate to defaults by an individual as a director of a company under the Companies Act 1985.

Paragraph 6 of the modified Sch 1 provides that there should be taken into account any failure by the officer to comply with any obligation imposed on him by or under ss 8, 9 and 10 of the Limited Partnerships Act 1907[6].

Paragraph 7 of Part II of Sch 1, as modified, provides that there should be taken into account the extent of the officer's or director's responsibility for the causes of the partnership or, as the case may be, the company, becoming insolvent.

Under para 8, as modified, the extent of the officer's or the director's responsibility for any failure by the partnership or, as the case may be, the company to supply any goods or services which have been paid for in whole or in part shall be taken into account.

Under para 9, as modified, there must be taken into account the extent of the officer's or the director's responsibility for the partnership or, as the case may be, the company, entering into any transaction or giving any preference, being a transaction or preference:

(a) liable to be set aside under s 127[7] or ss 238 to 240[8] of the Insolvency Act 1986; or

(b) challengeable under s 242 or s 243 of that Act or under any rule of law in Scotland.

Paragraphs 10 and 11 relate only to a director's responsibilities and are in identical terms to the equivalent paragraphs in the modified Sch 1.

Paragraph 12 makes it a relevant matter to consider any failure by the officer or the director to comply with any obligation imposed on him by, or under, certain provisions of the Insolvency Act 1986 (both as they apply in relation to companies and as they apply in relation to insolvent partnerships under the Order)[9].

---

1 Schedule 1 to the CDDA as modified by Sch 8 to the Order.

2 See footnote 2 to para **9.7**.

3 See art 4(3)(f) of the Order.

4 See art 6(3)(f) of the Order.

5 See art 8(5) and (7), art 10(3) and (5) and art 11(2) of the Order.

6 Under ss 8 and 9 certain matters require to be registered, and under s 10 an advertisement must be placed where a general partner becomes a limited partner and where there has been an assignment of the share of a limited partner.

7 Section 127 deals with the avoidance of property dispositions made after the commencement of the winding up, so that for example a partner who caused property of the partnership to be transferred to a third party (even a creditor) after presentation of the winding-up petition might find that a relevant matter if disqualification proceedings were brought against him.

8 Sections 238 to 240 relate to transactions at an undervalue and preferences, so, once again, a partner who causes the partnership to enter into a transaction at an undervalue or a transaction which constitutes a preference puts himself in danger of disqualification.

9 The provisions are:

(a) s 22 (statement of affairs and administration);

(b) s 131 (statement of affairs and winding up by the court);

(c) s 234 (duty of anyone with property to deliver it up);

(d) s 235 (duty to co-operate with liquidator etc).

Chapter 10

TACTICAL CONSIDERATIONS

10.1 INTRODUCTION

Insolvency of a partnership can be brought about in many various ways. For example, a key partner may die or resign. It may transpire that the partnership has made an unwise property investment or taken on a burdensome lease or has over-extended itself in its borrowings. The partnership may be performing poorly, possibly because of inefficiency, but possibly simply because of local market conditions or a more general economic recession. Once the problem is identified, what can be done? It is critical that partners should identify potential insolvency as soon as possible. The later the problem is identified or admitted the less likely it is that a satisfactory solution will be found so far as the partners are concerned. It is vital to take the best advice early on. Quite apart from the desirability of attempting to salvage the partnership or, failing that, at least the personal assets, to trade while insolvent can expose the partners to all kinds of liabilities including criminal liabilities[1] and, in the case of a professional partnership, may involve a breach of the rules of the relevant supervising authority.

As has been explained in para **1.10**, a creditor is free to bring a bankruptcy petition (or a winding-up petition against a corporate partner) for a debt in excess of £750 against one or more partners without seeking to wind up the partnership. Alternatively, he can petition to wind up the partnership as an unregistered company either with or without concurrent petitions against one or more members.

A partner can petition for the partnership to be wound up without also bringing a petition against another member or he may concurrently petition against all the other members[2]. In a really cataclysmic situation the partners may jointly present bankruptcy petitions, in which case the firm itself will be wound up.

To avoid insolvency proceedings, it may be possible for partners to reach some kind of informal agreement with partnership creditors which falls short of a partnership voluntary arrangement and, in certain situations, it may be possible for the partners to apply for a judicial receiver to be appointed, but probably this will be an interim measure pending one of the other options available under the Order being adopted.

Where individual members of the partnership do not have any appreciable personal assets then it is virtually certain that a creditor would wish to have the partnership wound up. Similarly, where the individual partners, at least collectively, have appreciable assets then it is likely that a creditor would wish to wind up the partnership and bankrupt (or at least threaten to bankrupt) the partner or partners with substantial assets. Although insolvency remedies are described as a class remedy, in practice (at least initially), a creditor tends to regard his debtor as a target for that creditor's own concerns and/or have regard to the costs implications of pursuing his remedies against the debtor.

It can generally be assumed that partners in a firm which has run into financial difficulties will have as their main priority the preservation of their homes and financial assets as far as possible. Secondly, where professional partners are concerned, they will wish to avoid as far as possible the loss of their professional status and future earnings paid. Of course, partners will prefer to see the survival of the whole or rescuable parts of the partnership's business. If that appears impossible, they will fall back on any deal which will allow them as individuals to carry on trading and, in the last resort, the maximisation of the partnership and individual assets.

Consequently, partners in an insolvent partnership will no doubt initiallfy explore the possibility of a PVA or an administration and/or IVAs.

There is the further possible scenario that the partnership has already entered into a PVA, possibly accompanied by one or more IVAs of the individual partners. A creditor not bound by the PVA and/or by the IVAs (for example, someone who was not given notice of the relevant meetings and who therefore is not bound by the arrangements of a post-arrangement creditor) will need to give careful consideration when considering whether to institute winding-up proceedings or bankruptcy proceedings as to what would happen to the assets comprised in the voluntary arrangements[3].

---

1 For example s 357 of the Insolvency Act 1996 makes it an offence for the bankrupt to have made or caused to be made in the period of five years ending with the commencement of the bankruptcy any gift or transfer of, or any charge on, his property. It is a defence to such a charge under s 352 if the defendant proves that, at the time of the conduct constituting the offence, he had no intent to defraud or to conceal the state of his affairs.

2 Note the wide definition of 'member': para **2.11.2**.

3 See para **6.18**.

10.2   THE CREDITORS' POINT OF VIEW

It has been said, over and over again, that winding up and bankruptcy are not to be employed as debt-collecting procedures. The fact remains that, certainly in the case of an undisputed debt, the normal course any creditor pursues is to serve a statutory demand and then if the costs justify it the creditor will present a winding-up or bankruptcy petition in the hope that this will lead to a settlement of the debt or at any rate a satisfactory compounding.

As has already been explained in para **2.16**, it is normally open to a creditor to whom a partnership is indebted in contract to sue either the partnership as a firm or all the partners or any one or more individual partners, but once judgment has been obtained against the partnership then a creditor may be able to enforce that judgment against one or more individual partners with the leave of the court.

Assuming that a creditor has obtained a judgment against the partnership, should he:

(a) simply proceed to wind up the partnership; or
(b) try to bankrupt one or more members of the partnership as well; or
(c) simply proceed to bankrupt one or more partners[1] and leave it to the trustees of those partners to take appropriate proceedings against the partnership for indemnity?

Obviously, if the partnership is eventually wound up, its liquidator will attempt to recover any deficiency from the estates of the individual partners, but that may take time and it is possible that in the intervening period the asset value of the separate estates will for one reason or another have diminished. Furthermore, as is explained in para **5.3.1** there exists at present a doubt (which will only be resolved by the courts) as to whether, where bankruptcies of the partners are not concurrent with the winding up of the partnership, the liquidator of the partnership will in fact rank pari passu with the creditors of the separate estate. The same doubt exists as to the position where a partnership has a petition presented against it concurrently with bankruptcy petitions against, say, two out of six partners and then, following the winding up of the partnership and the bankruptcy orders against the two partners, petitions are presented against the remaining four. If the liquidator does not rank pari passu in the separate estates or all of the separate estates then there is clearly a strong argument for pursuing concurrent bankruptcy proceedings against all individual partners or at least those with any appreciable assets.

The main argument against pursuing a winding-up petition concurrently with one or more bankruptcy petitions is the cost. Article 13 provides that where there are concurrent petitions only one deposit need be paid, but there is still the question of the court fees and the very considerable potential solicitors' costs involved in pursuing concurrent petitions. In the High Court, the winding-up petition will proceed in the Companies Court, whereas the bankruptcy petitions will be dealt with by the court having bankruptcy jurisdiction and, consequently, there will certainly be the necessity for at least two sets of hearings. If there are adjournments the costs could be very high indeed.

It is sometimes the case that a particular partner is known to have substantial assets (perhaps the senior partner). In such circumstances, that partner may be a natural target for a single bankruptcy petition. If this does not itself lead to a settlement, the bankruptcy order may of itself cause a dissolution of the partnership. The wealthy partner's trustee in bankruptcy will, all being well, have the initial funds to pursue the partner's indemnity rights against the partnership. This will lead probably to an eventual liquidation of the partnership.

Special considerations will apply for a creditor who owns a property occupied by a partnership. As has been explained in para **2.13.5**, a landlord may, dependent on the facts of the particular situation, be in doubt as to whether it has a direct claim against the entire partnership or whether it only has a claim against those parties who have contracted as tenants in the lease. Such landlords may not wish to face the potential costs of litigating the question of whether the partnership is itself contractually liable to them and would probably prefer simply to issue bankruptcy proceedings against one or more of the tenant partners. The question may then arise in any future liquidation of the partnership as to whether the landlord has, by its conduct, conceded that it has no direct contractual claim against the partnership and, while any trustee or trustees in bankruptcy of the tenant partners will no doubt have some kind of claim against the partnership, that will be likely to be a deferred claim as has been explained in para **2.13.5**. Solicitors advising landlords granting leases to partnerships should bear this point in mind.

Particular considerations may also apply to banks which have dealings with partnerships. Even where the bank is apparently unsecured vis-à-vis the firm, it may have taken security from individual partners. That security may extend to the liabilities of the partner qua partner if the partnership is indebted to the bank (eg under the usual 'all monies charge' under a domestic mortgage). If that is the position, then the bank will clearly want to consider whether it is in its interests to force a concurrent liquidation and a bankruptcy of the partner or partners concerned.

Although it is possible for an administration petition to be presented by a creditor against a partnership, the experience of the last 10 years is that it is rare for any creditor to attempt to do so, usually because of the lack of all the requisite information. One can conceive however of a bank, which may have more knowledge than most creditors of the affairs of a partnership, considering that it would be in its interests if the insolvent partnership were to go into administration. Take the example of a partnership which is having considerable problems in servicing even the interest on its debt to the bank, but which is representing that in a liquidation the bank would suffer a very considerable shortfall and, at the same time, asking the bank to allow most of the trading income to be used to allow the partnership to survive. The situation may be one where the bank considers that if the partnership were to go into administration the recovery of book debts and/or the sale of work-in-progress would result in a substantial percentage of the debt being recovered and that this would be preferable to continuing support of the partnership business. In such a situation the bank might insist on the partnership considering going into administration and if it refused to do so, the bank might be in a position to present an administration petition itself. Any creditor faced with a partnership that is itself seeking administration or which has called a creditors' meeting to consider a PVA must examine the proposals in either case carefully and, preferably, with professional advice so as to see whether they are in its own interests.

---

1 In the case of *Schooler v Customs and Excise Commissioners* [1995] 2 BCLC 610, the appellant debtor was a married woman who had been carrying on a business in partnership with her husband. The Commissioners of Customs and Excise had presented a bankruptcy petition against her in respect of the partnership debt. She appealed to the Court of Appeal against the dismissal of her appeal to the district judge against a bankruptcy order on the ground that the court did not have jurisdiction to make an order against one member of a partnership in respect of a parnership debt unless the bankruptcy petition was coupled with a petition to wind up the partnership under the provisions of the Insolvent Partnerships Order 1986 or had been preceded by a judgment against the partnership. The appeal was grounded

on the submission that the liability of partners for the debts of a partnership is joint and not joint and several. The Court of Appeal considered that the matter was put beyond doubt by the wording of art 15(3) of the 1986 Order which, so far as material, provided:

'Nothing in this Order is to be taken ... as preventing any creditor or creditors owed one or more debts by an insolvent partnership from presenting a petition under the Act against one or more members of the partnership without including the others and without presenting a petition for the winding-up of the partnership as an unregistered company, and in such a case the debt or debts shall be treated as a debt or debts of the member in question'

Nourse LJ pointed out in the course of his judgment that the equivalent provision contained in art 19(5) of the Order does not contain the words '...and in such a case the debt or debts shall be treated as a debt or debts of the member in question'. However, Nourse LJ also expressed the view that it was impossible to see why the joint debt of a partner should not be 'a debt owed by' that partner for the purposes of s 267(1) of the Act which provides that 'a creditor's petition must be in respect of one or more debts owed by the debtor ...', even though others are jointly indebted with him. Consequently, it would appear that on that basis there is no reason whatsoever why a creditor should not be able to present a bankruptcy petition and for a bankruptcy order to be made on such a petition against one partner in respect of a partnership debt. Why art 19(5) of the Order is in different terms to art 15(3) of the 1986 Order is not at all clear.

10.3   OPTIONS OPEN TO THE INSOLVENT PARTNERSHIP AND ITS PARTNERS

It will be apparent from the discussion of the position of such persons as salaried partners and retired partners that any course of action open to an insolvent partnership may well involve acute conflicts of interest between different categories of partners or persons who may or may not be considered to be partners, and one of the most urgent tasks facing any adviser of an insolvent partnership is to analyse whether such conflicts exist and, if so, whether any of the individual camps need to be separately advised, if not initially, then certainly at the stage when a final decision has to be taken as to a particular course of action.

In the early stages of negotiations, it may suit the true partners to argue with banks and other major creditors that certain individuals are not 'members'[1]. The effect of this would be to reduce the creditors' perception of the pool of assets that would be available in a formal insolvency and to emphasise the likelihood of disputes and litigation. The more complicated the creditors think life will be, the more likely it is that a commercial compromise can be achieved. However, it may be that the assets of salaried 'partners' and those who are alleged to have been held out as partners would make the difference between solvency and insolvency. In those circumstances, the true partners may later want to argue that those same individuals *are* members so as to share the load of liability and reduce the claim against their own private assets.

The partners will want to protect their personal assets and professional status if at all possible. Clearly, if there is time the partners will explore everything short of any formal insolvency regime such as the raising of new capital or new bank facilities. They will have to bear in mind that if they wish to try to suggest a PVA then they will only be able to do so if they can get the requisite level of support internally and the necessary majority of more than three-quarters (in value) of the partnership creditors.

If it is thought possible to avoid bankruptcy of the individual partners then clearly the aim will be to persuade creditors to agree to a PVA, possibly preceded by an administration. If it is considered necessary to ringfence the assets of the partnership pending the creditors' meeting, consideration will have to be given to the partners entering into IVAs. As has already been discussed in para **2.11**, it may be vital to any particular course of action that either the partners be unanimous or that a particular majority be in favour of the intended course of action and, if this particular condition cannot be fulfilled, then this may close the door to particular options.

If bankruptcy is considered to be unavoidable then the main choice will be between the options open under art 10 and art 11 of the Order. Article 10 deals with the winding up of an insolvent partnership on a member's petition where concurrent petitions are presented against all members. Article 11 deals with the situation where individual members present a joint bankruptcy petition but there are no insolvency proceedings involving the winding up of the insolvent partnership itself, the partnership assets and liabilities being dealt with in the individual bankruptcies. A decision as to which of these two alternatives be adopted would probably revolve largely around the question of how complicated the 'winding up' of the insolvent partnership is likely to be; the more complicated it is likely to be, the more likely it is that art 10 should be made use of.

---

1 See para **2.11.2**.

10.4   OPTIONS OPEN TO THE REGULATORS OF A PARTNERSHIP

A partnership may be wound up by a regulator such as the Bank of England under s 92(1) of the Banking Act 1987 and by the Securities Investment Board under s 72(1) of the Financial Services Act 1986. The grounds of such a petition may be that the partnership is insolvent, but it may also be simply on the ground that it is just and equitable that the partnership be wound up (eg because there has been a fraud or, in the case of an unauthorised bank, that it is acting without due authority). If the winding-up order is made only on the just and equitable ground then the Order, subject to the correct interpretation of art 14 (see para **5.3**) does not apply at all, although the partnership will be treated as an unregistered company for the purposes of the winding up. This may have particular importance in relation to the rights of creditors against individual estates of the partners where the old law will continue to apply, so that in relation to any deficiency in the partnership estate, the creditors of the partnership will in most cases be deferred to claims of creditors in the separate estates.

10.5   CONCLUSION

Ultimately, the Order provides only a framework. It is a question for the partners and the creditors as to whether a reconstruction can be agreed or whether there is to be an orderly insolvency administration or simply a liquidation. The problem is not made any easier by the complexities and ambiguities of the Order and, until there is a body of case-law, it will remain difficult for professional advisers to insolvent partnerships to be dogmatic as to whether their solution will necessarily achieve the desired objective.

APPENDICES

Appendix 1

CHECKLISTS AND CASE STUDIES

Checklist of Matters to be Considered when Drafting a PVA

1 INTRODUCTION

The question of who can present a proposal to creditors for a PVA has been discussed in para **7.4** above. Attention is drawn to the necessity for the insolvency practitioner to make sure that he has been duly authorised to act (see para **7.5** above).

The statutory requirements regarding what the proposal must contain are described in para **7.7** above. It is absolutely crucial that the proposal should comply with all the relevant statutory requirements. Otherwise, it is likely to be rejected by the court, or, if the defect is not identified by the court, then it may lead to a successful challenge to the PVA itself.

The first purpose of any PVA proposal must be to convince the creditors that they should vote in favour of it. Consequently, the proposal must explain why a PVA is preferable to any other kind of insolvency regime or other solution to the problem facing the partnership and its creditors. It is equally important that the PVA should bind all the partnership creditors and that it should not contain any provision which could be challenged as being unfairly prejudicial to a particular creditor.

It is important that the PVA should try and envisage every eventuality. It is by no means certain whether it is possible, whatever provision may be inserted to that effect in the PVA, to vary a PVA once it has been approved. One argument is that a variation is simply impossible, the PVA being a statutory contract and there being no provision in the Act permitting variation. An alternative argument is that the court retains a wide-ranging residual discretion under s 7 of the Act and that it may be possible to obtain a variation of the arrangement by a court order. Yet another possibility is that since a PVA is in effect an arrangement between the partnership and its creditors there is no reason why a PVA cannot by express provision in the PVA permit a variation by providing for a particular mechanism whereby that can be achieved. The creditors can approve a PVA which provides, for example, that variations may be permitted, if necessary by convening a meeting of all creditors bound by the PVA and a stipulated majority is obtained (probably such majority should be the same as required for the PVA itself) and subject to potential challenge under s 6 of the Act that may be an effective mechanism. Certainly, such a provision should bind any creditor who voted in favour of the PVA. The residual doubt concerns any creditor who voted against the PVA, but is nevertheless bound by it because the requisite majority was obtained. Can such a creditor be equally bound by a variation by use of this mechanism?

In view of the varied forms that a PVA may take, ranging from continuation of the partnership business to an effective liquidation of the partnership assets (with or without contributions from partners from their individual assets), it would be quite impossible to draft a 'standard' PVA. The best that can be done is to set out a comprehensive checklist of matters that partners and their advisers ought to take into account.

Most proposals ought to include as a preamble to the formal scheme:

(a)	a definition of the firm identifying the partners. In addition, there should be listed other relevant persons intended to be bound by the PVA, such as retired partners and those who are or may fall within the definition of 'member' in the Order;

(b)	a brief description of the partnership business and some account of the trading history of the partnership;

(c)	a description of the events precipitating the insolvency;

(d)	a summary of what the PVA is proposing;

(e)	what a PVA under the Act achieves;

(f)	why the PVA is, in the particular instance, the best solution for the creditors;

(g)	the likely dividend and time or times of payment.

Apart from the proposal itself, there will have to be sent to creditors the statement of affairs (see para **7.9** above) and a list of creditors.

2   CHECKLIST

Definitions

It is useful to set out a list of the expressions used in the PVA and to define them. There are bound to be many references to provisions of the Act and the Rules and possibly the Order, so those enactments should be defined. In many instances, provisions of the Rules will be deemed to be incorporated, but care should be taken as to whether any particular provision needs to be modified and, if so, the modification should be set out in the definition for the purposes of the proposal. Expressions such as 'assets', 'liabilities', 'secured debts' and matters of this kind ought to be comprehensively identified.

Conditions precedent

It will need to be made clear that the proposal is subject to the appropriate vote in favour at the creditors' meeting. It may also be deemed desirable to provide that the PVA is subject to no successful challenge being made to the PVA under s 6 of the Act. If an administration order is being discharged then the PVA may have to be made conditional on the discharge of the administration order. The relationship with any relevant IVA's may need to be spelled out.

Assets and liabilities for the purposes of the PVA

It will be important to define the assets to be included in the PVA and to identify any that are secured to creditors. Assets should usually be listed in a schedule, and valued. Creditors may be unhappy if the valuations are not supported by professional reports. Consideration will need to be given as to whether it is desirable, first from the supervisor's point of view, and, secondly, from the creditors' point of view, to make provision for all assets or certain assets to vest in the supervisor on trust for the creditors.

From the creditors' point of view, it may be highly desirable to try and obviate an argument that, in the event of the PVA failing, the assets fall into the estate of a subsequently appointed liquidator. From the supervisor's point of view, he may not wish to have some or all assets vested in him. For example, a provision that freehold land is to vest in the supervisor may involve him in a potential liability for environmental hazards (under the Environmental Protection Act 1990 as amended by the Environmental Protection Act 1995). A provision that a lease shall vest in the supervisor (assuming that is effective against the landlord) may not be desirable from the supervisor's point of view because of liabilities under the tenant's covenants he will incur. If it is thought desirable in a particular case to provide that some or all of the assets are to vest in the supervisor, consideration will need to be given as to the timing. While at first sight it might seem clear that vesting should take place immediately upon the PVA being approved by the requisite majority, if the PVA is conditional on no successful challenge being made to the PVA under s 6, then it may be that the vesting date ought to be postponed to a date beyond which no appeal can be made under s 6 or any appeal that has been made under s 6 has been disposed of. If the PVA includes a provision for contribution by individual partners from their separate estates then that must be made clear. Equally, it is crucial to identify the liabilities and if, as may well be the case, there is a suggestion that partnership creditors should waive their rights against the separate estates of the individual partners (or at any rate will do so subject to the specified contribution being made from those separate estates), then that must be very clearly stated.

Supervisor(s)

The suggested supervisor(s) must be identified and his or their qualification(s) stated.

Duration

As to the duration of the PVA, it is impossible to be dogmatic as to what it should be. For example, where it is suggested that the partnership will, under the PVA, trade out of its predicament, then presumably the PVA will have to specify a fairly lengthy period with the ability to terminate earlier once all creditors have been paid. If, on the other hand, the PVA in effect suggests a liquidation of all assets then the duration of the PVA may have to be fixed by reference to the time estimated to be needed to realise those assets and to identify and determine the claims, but a fixed period will have to be given. It is a requirement under the Rules to state what the proposed duration is to be.

Treatment of monies

The Rules require that the manner in which funds held for the purposes of the arrangements are to be invested or otherwise dealt with, pending distribution to creditors, must be described in the proposal. The supervisor may want to monitor all payments (or at least payments over a certain amount) or even countersign cheques.

Conduct of the business of the partnership

If it is intended that the partnership should, even for a time, continue to carry on business, then the proposal must make it clear how such business is going to be conducted. Creditors may require business plans, cash-flow forecasts, budgets and regular reporting. The supervisor will wish to try and protect himself against personal liability while, at the same time, the creditors will want to make certain that the partnership is being properly monitored. It may be useful to have a provision deeming the supervisor to be an agent of the partnership, although this will only be effective vis-à-vis creditors bound by the PVA.

Consideration must be given to whether the relationship of the partners inter se should continue to be governed by the existing partnership deed (assuming there is one) or whether as part of the PVA a new deed should be entered into. Quite apart from the desirability of making certain that the arrangements between the partners are properly regulated, the creditors will be concerned in particular about the possibility of changes in the membership of the partnership while the PVA is in force. In the case of a large partnership, it is highly likely that in the lifetime of a PVA there will be changes by reason of death, resignation or admission of new partners. It may be that the creditors will wish to insist that no partner should voluntarily resign without the consent of the supervisor or, possibly, if there is one, of the creditors' committee, or even of the creditors in general meeting. If the creditors are being asked to approve a PVA on the basis that the partnership will over a period of time pay most of the debts, the creditors may be very concerned to make sure that particular partners do not simply leave the partnership. What is to happen if for some reason a partner loses his professional status, such as where The Law Society refuses to renew a solicitor's practising certificate? What if a partner becomes bankrupt?

Financing arrangements

If, as may well be the case, the PVA proposes that special arrangements be made with the partnership's bankers (whose co-operation will probably be fundamental to any survival of the partnership) then those arrangements must be fully described. The Rules require that the details of any further credit facilities which it is intended to arrange for the partnership and how the debts arising are to be paid shall be described in the proposal.

Assets for distribution

Assets may of course include not just the assets at the date of the proposal, but some agreement to contribute a percentage of net profits in future. If there is to be a contribution from future trading, there will have to be detailed provisions as to how that contribution is to be arrived at, particularly if it is expressed as being a percentage of net profits. It should be made clear what the supervisor is to deduct from realisations before making any distribution. Presumably, it will be necessary to discharge preferential creditors first, since unless they otherwise consent, the Act provides that they must not be prejudiced by a PVA compared to their rights in a liquidation. The supervisor will clearly wish to make sure that he gets his remuneration and expenses. He will also wish to consider what monies he may need to retain to deal with problems that may arise in the course of the PVA. If there is a fixed charge on book debts then it must be made clear what precisely is being proposed in relation to book debt recoveries. If there are any assets that are being excluded then such assets must be very clearly identified. If any kind of security is going to be given for the due performance of any obligations to be undertaken in the context of the PVA, either by the partners or third parties and/or any guarantees are being offered by partners or third parties, then full details must be given.

Creditors bound by the PVA

It is probably wise to make it clear in the proposal that preferential creditors will be paid first. There should then follow a definition of 'participating creditors' other than preferential creditors and how such creditors are to be dealt with.

There should be specific provision for what is to happen if an admitted creditor cannot be located. It may be sensible for there to be a provision to the effect that any dividend due to such creditor shall, after a reasonable period and after an effort has been made to locate him, be available for distribution to all other creditors pari passu. Detailed provisions should be made for creating a time bar, failure to comply with which will entitle the supervisor to reject any further claims. Without such a provision the supervisor may have problems in ever completing the administration of the PVA. It may be possible to provide that a creditor not bound by the PVA (eg one who was not given notice of the meeting) can nevertheless be permitted by the supervisor to be admitted, although if the claim is sizeable this may disadvantage other creditors. It will be advisable to provide in such an event that, as in liquidations, no new creditor shall be entitled to disturb the distribution of a dividend but shall be entitled to be paid out of any money for the time being available for the payment of any further dividend to any dividend or dividend which he failed to receive.

Determination of the claims

Detailed provisions will have to be made as to how disputed claims are to be dealt with. These provisions will need to deal not merely with any dispute about liability as such or quantum, but also with arguments about the value of security. There may have to be provisions as to the quantification and timing of claims made in foreign currencies. Although the supervisor may wish to establish a regime under which his determination of the quantum or admission of the claims at all should be final, there is little doubt that an aggrieved creditor could apply to the court under s 7 of the Act and probably the best course would be to provide that any such creditor may make such application, but impose a time-limit within which such application can be made such as 28 days from the receipt of the supervisor's decision. There will have to be provisions for allowing variation or withdrawal of claims, what is to happen where two or more creditors have claims against the partnership in respect of the same debt or liability, and probably that each creditor should bear his own expenses of proving his claim. It may be that the creditors would prefer a mechanism whereby disputes in relation to claims would be referred to arbitration or possibly that use be made of some kind of informal, but nevertheless binding, alternative dispute resolution. This may be particularly true of claims relating to a business of a specialised nature, for example a partnership carrying on the business of a building contractor, where to refer disputes to a surveyor may be better than having them determined by a judge.

Claims of connected persons

Disclosure is required under the Rules of how persons connected with the partnership (see paras **7.7** and **7.18.4** above) who are creditors are proposed to be treated under the PVA. It is suggested that partners and retired partners should be treated as a subordinated class for dividend purposes, receiving no dividend until all other creditors have been paid out in full.

Method of payment

The PVA should specify the manner in which dividends are going to be paid. It may be preferable to provide that dividends may be paid by cheque and sent by post to the creditor's last known address and that encashment of the cheque should be a good discharge of the obligation to pay the dividend.

Landlords

Details must be given of how leases are to be dealt with, as regards accrued and future liabilities. A great deal will of course depend as to whether a particular lease is truly a partnership asset and whether all partners are really debtors of the landlord (see para **2.13.5** above).

The supervisor's remuneration

Full details must be provided as to what remuneration the supervisor will be entitled to and when such remuneration is to be paid, and provision must also be made for the supervisor's expenses and disbursements.

The supervisor's powers and duties

The duties and powers of the supervisor should be set out in full in the interests of clarity and for the supervisor's own protection. The supervisor has no statutory powers, only the person specified in the proposal.

If the supervisor is anxious to limit his liabilities then he must make sure that that is made very clear. The supervisor may ask that he should be exempted from liability for anything he does or does not do while carrying out his functions save as to matters involving bad faith or wilful misconduct. However, it is arguable that by reason of his statutory duties a supervisor cannot, and ought not, ask for a provision whereby he is to be excused from any breach of his duties such as occasioned by his negligence and it is understood that certainly some of the registrars in the High Court have objected to wide-ranging provisions whereby supervisors are to be excused from liability to creditors. If there are joint supervisors then there should be a specific provision as to whether they may act only jointly, or jointly and severally.

Creditors' committee

There is no provision in either the Act or the Rules for any requirement that there should be a creditors' committee; but it is frequently thought desirable, if only for the purposes of getting a voluntary arrangement approved, to make provision for such a committee, in which case provision should also be made as to how such committee is to be constituted and its activities regulated, following the precedent for creditors' committees in the Rules. If there is to be a committee then a decision has to be taken in the PVA as to precisely what its powers are to be. It is not unusual to find provisions in voluntary arrangements whereby the supervisor if he considers that there has been a default should, if the creditors' committee so directs, be permitted to petition for the winding up of the company or to petition for bankruptcy in the case of an individual. Some supervisors do not like the creditors' committee to be given any kind of a power of veto or a power to direct what should or should not be done. It is essential therefore that the PVA should make it quite clear what the functions of the committee are, and what, if any, powers it is suggested the committee should have. This particular point is one where the creditors will sometimes put forward and insist on an appropriate modification being made to the terms of the voluntary arrangement.

Default

Many IVAs are sadly deficient as to what is to happen if there is a default by the individual. It is most important that the PVA should make it clear as to what is to constitute a default and what the consequences of such default are to be (eg should the supervisor be under an obligation to petition for winding up). If creditors have agreed to accept, say, 50p in the £1 and when the default occurs have only received 25p in the £1, is the original liability to be revived or are they limited in any subsequent liquidation to the balance of the promised dividend? Even more important is to make it clear what is to happen to the assets comprised in the PVA at the time of the supervening insolvency. Are they to be regarded as being held on trust for the creditors participating in the PVA, or do they fall into the estate of the liquidator and therefore become available, not only to the creditors in the PVA, but creditors subsequently incurred? Purely from the point of view of the creditors being asked to approve a PVA, the former is clearly the desirable course.

Variation of the PVA

There is no mechanism in either the Act or the Rules for any variation of the PVA once it has been adopted.

It may well be thought desirable to provide for a mechanism within the PVA for flexibility and variation. Such a provision has often been included in CVA's and PVA's. Frequently, it will provide that modifications should require the same majority as is required for the PVA itself, namely more than 75% (in value) of the creditors bound by the PVA. The legal effect of such clauses is the subject of some debate and has not been settled by the courts.

Case Studies: Calculation of Assets and Liabilities of Partners on Liquidation

EXAMPLE 1

BACKGROUND   There is a deficiency of £300 in the joint estate but a surplus in each of the separate estates of A and B (£200 and £300 respectively).

A B Partnership

		£
Partnership assets		1,500
	Liabilities	1,800
	Deficiency	(300)
Personal estate of A		
	Assets	700
	Liabilities	500
	Surplus	200
Personal estate of B		
	Assets	1,000
	Liabilities	700
	Surplus	300

OUTCOME   Partnership creditors will rank equally in the separate estates of A and B for £150 each.

The result is the same as under the pre-1994 Order.

EXAMPLE 2

BACKGROUND   There is a surplus of £700 in the joint estate and a surplus of £300 in the separate estate of B but a deficiency of £200 in A's separate estate.

A B Partnership

		£
Partnership assets		1,700
	Liabilities	1,000
	Surplus	700
Personal estate of A		
	Assets	500
	Liabilities	700
	Deficiency	(200)
Personal estate of B		
	Assets	1,000
	Liabilities	700
	Surplus	300

OUTCOME   Assuming A and B share equally in partnership assets, the separate
                 estates of A and B increase by £350 each. After satisfying the
                 deficiency in A's separate estate, A's estate will have a surplus of £150.

                 The result is the same as under the pre-1994 Order.

EXAMPLE 3

BACKGROUND   The expenses of winding up of the joint estate exceed the assets of
             the joint estate by £200. The separate estates of A and B are sufficient
             to meet the winding-up expenses of those estates, leaving A with a net
             surplus of £200 and B with a net surplus of £100 (before meeting any
             liabilities of the separate estates). The unpaid expenses of the
             winding up of the joint estate are apportioned equally among the
             separate estates.

A B Partnership

	£
Partnership assets	200
Expenses of winding up	400
Deficiency	(200)
Personal estate of A	
Assets	400
Less expenses of winding up personal estate	200
Less A's share of deficiency in the expenses of the winding up of the joint estate	100
Balance available for creditors	100
Personal estate of B	
Assets	300
Less expenses of winding up personal estate	200
Less B's share of deficiency in the expenses of the winding up of the joint estate	100
Amount available for the creditors in B's estate	0

OUTCOME   £100 of the unpaid winding-up expenses of the joint estate are
                 allocated to each of A's and B's separate estates. The amount
                 available for the creditors of A's separate estate after paying these
                 expenses is reduced to £100. B's separate estate is reduced to £0 as
                 a result of the allocation and his creditors receive nothing.

NB: If B's assets were £250, such that B's separate estate could only bear £50 of the
     winding-up expenses of the joint estate, the remaining £50 would be paid out of
     A's separate estate and A's separate estate would bear £150 in total of the
     winding-up expenses of the joint estate.

EXAMPLE 4

BACKGROUND   There are deficiencies in the joint estate and in all the separate
estates.

Pre-1994 Order situation

A B C Partnership

	£	
Partnership assets	250,000	
Liabilities	500,000	
Deficiency	(250,000)	(dividend 50%)

Personal estate of A		
Assets	425,000	
Liabilities	675,000	
Deficiency	(250,000)	(dividend 63%)

Personal estate of B		
Assets	90,000	
Liabilities	100,000	
Deficiency	(10,000)	(dividend 90%)

Personal estate of C		
Assets	185,000	
Liabilities	420,000	
Deficiency	(235,000)	(dividend 44%)

OUTCOME   Partnership creditors cannot rank for a dividend in the separate
estates because the separate creditors have not been paid in full (and
vice versa).

This is the situation before the 1994 Order came into force.

EXAMPLE 5

BACKGROUND   There are deficiencies in the joint estate and in all the separate
estates. However, the liquidator of the joint estate is able to claim in
respect of the deficiency in the joint estate from each of separate
estates.

Post-1994 Order situation

1. Assume scenario in Example 4.
2. Under 1994 Order, partnership ranks for deficiency pari passu with separate estate
creditors. Hence, separate estates have to admit claims for additional £250,000:

Personal estate of A	£	
Assets	425,000	
Liabilities	925,000	
Deficiency	(500,000)	(dividend 45.9%)

Personal estate of B	£	
Assets	90,000	
Liabilities	350,000	
Deficiency	(260,000)	(dividend 25.7%)

Personal estate of C	£	
Assets	185,000	
Liabilities	670,000	
Deficiency	(485,000)	(dividend 27.6%)

	£	
Partnership assets	250,000	
Dividends from A, B and C	248,000	
Liabilities	500,000	
Deficiency	(2,000)	(dividend 99.6%)

OUTCOME   The liabilities of each of the separate estates increase by the amount of the deficiency in the joint estate. The liquidator of the joint estate therefore ranks in respect of the deficiency of the joint estate (£250,000) equally with the separate creditors in the separate estates.

Therefore, the dividend received by the liquidator of the joint estate is calculated as follows:

(i) **A's estate:**   £
     Assets: 425,000
     Liabilities   (675,000)
                       + (250,000)
                          (925,000)

Dividend = 45.9%

The liquidator of the joint estate receives a dividend of £114,864.86 (45.9% of £250,000).

(ii) **B's estate:**   £
      Assets: 90,000
      Liabilities   (100,000)
                       + (250,000)
                          (350,000)

Dividend = 25.7%

The liquidator of the joint estate receives a dividend of £64,285.71 (25.7% of £250,000).

(iii) **C's estate:** £
Assets: 185,000
Liabilities (420,000)
+ (250,000)
(670,000)

Dividend = 27.62%

The liquidator of the joint estate receives a dividend of
£69,029.85 (27.6% of £250,000).

Final outcome:

Joint estate is: £
Partnership assets 250,000.00
Dividend from A's estate 114,864.86
Dividend from B's estate 64,285.71
Dividend from C's estate 69,029.85
498,180.42

Partnership liabilities (500,000)

Dividend = 99.6%

EXAMPLE 6

BACKGROUND There is a surplus in the joint estate of £300,000 (after paying off
partnership creditors). There are deficiencies in each of the separate
estates of X, Y and Z. Under the partnership agreement, profits and
losses are shared by the partners in the ratios 5:3:2. X, Y and Z are
each owed £180,000, £150,000 and £70,000 respectively on capital
account.

XYZ Partnership

	Partnership	X	Y	Z
	£	£	£	£
Assets	800,000	350,000	200,000	100,000
Liabilities	*500,000*	550,000	500,000	120,000
Surplus	300,000			
Profit ratios		5	3	2
Amount owing on capital account	400,000	180,000	150,000	70,000
Deficiency suffered	*100,000*	*50,000*	*30,000*	*20,000*
Transfers to separate estates	300,000	130,000	120,000	50,000

XYZ Partnership

	Partnership	X	Y	Z
	£	£	£	£
Assets	800,000	350,000	200,000	100,000
Payments in (or out)	*(300,000)*	*130,000*	*120,000*	*50,000*
Available	500,000	480,000	320,000	150,000
Liabilities	500,000	550,000	500,000	120,000
Dividend	100%	87%	64%	100%

OUTCOME   The amount owed to the partners on capital account exceeds the surplus in the joint estate by £100,000. The deficiency is apportioned amongst the partners in accordance with the partnership agreement. The amount each partner receives is calculated by deducting the deficiency to be incurred by each partner from the amount owed to him. The resultant amount is then added to the assets of the separate estate of each partner for distribution to that partner's separate creditors. After taking into account the surplus distributed from the joint estate, the separate creditors of X, Y and Z receive a dividend of 87%, 64% and 100% respectively.

EXAMPLE 7

BACKGROUND   The assets of the partnership are £300,000 with total liabilities of £500,000. There is therefore a deficiency in the joint estate of £200,000. There is also a deficiency in the separate estates of X and Y but a surplus in the separate estate of Z.

XYZ Partnership

	Partnership	X	Y	Z
	£	£	£	£
Assets	300,000	350,000	200,000	150,000
Payments in from separate estates	*250,476*			
Total funds	550,476			
Liabilities	500,000	550,000	500,000	100,000
Deficiency from joint estate	*200,000*	*200,000*	*200,000*	*200,000*
Total claims	*500,000*	*750,000*	*700,000*	*300,000*
Dividend	100%	47%	29%	50%

OUTCOME   The liabilities of each of the separate estates increase by the amount of the deficiency in the joint estate. The liquidator of the joint estate ranks equally in respect of the deficiency in the joint estate with the separate creditors of the partners. Therefore, the claims in the separate estates each increase by £200,000. This results in a dividend for all creditors including the liquidator of the partnership in the estates of X, Y and Z of 47%, 29% and 50% respectively. The liquidator of the partnership will therefore receive the following dividends from the separate estates:

dividend from X's estate: £93,333 (47% of £200,000)
dividend from Y's estate: £57,143 (29% of £200,000)
dividend from Z's estate: £100,000 (50% of £200,000)

Total: £250,476

When the dividends received from the separate estates are added to the partnership assets, there are sufficient assets to pay partnership creditors in full leaving a surplus of £50,476 in the joint estate.

EXAMPLE 8

BACKGROUND   The surplus of £50,476 in the joint estate is distributed to the separate estates in the same way as shown above.

XYZ Partnership (Partners share losses in ratio 5:3:2)

	Partnership	**X**	**Y**	**Z**
	£	£	£	£
Assets	550,476	350,000	200,000	150,000
Payments in (or out)	*(50,476)*	*5,236*	*45,143*	*95*
Total funds available	500,000	355,236	245,143	150,095
Liabilities	500,000	550,000	500,000	100,000
Dividend	100%	64%	49%	100%

OUTCOME   The partners X, Y and Z are owed £180,000, £150,000 and £70,000 respectively on capital account. The deficiency suffered by the partners is therefore £349,524 (ie £400,000 representing the total amount owing to all the partners on the capital account, less the surplus in the joint estate of £50,476). The deficiency is allocated to the partners in the ratios 5:3:2. This results in the allocation of the deficiency to X, Y and Z in the sums of £174,762, £104,857 and £69,905 respectively. Deducting these amounts from the amount owed to each partner on the capital account results in a payment to the separate estates of X, Y and Z of £5,236, £45,143 and £95 respectively.

As a result, the separate creditors receive a final dividend in the estates of X, Y and Z of 64%, 49% and 100% respectively.

Effect of Administration Orders or PVAs on Various Professions

	Mandatory exclusion	Discretionary exclusion	Grounds for discretionary exclusion (appeals)
The Institute of Chartered Accountants in England and Wales Tel: 01908 248100		✓	Disciplinary Committee – Lack of integrity or competence.
Chartered Association of Certified Accountants Tel: 0171 242 6855		✓	Misconduct. Material breach of the voluntary arrangement.
The Institute of Financial Accountants Tel: 01732 458080		✓	Bringing the Institute into disrepute.
The Law Society (Solicitors Complaints Bureau) Tel: 01926 820082 OR Ethics and Guidance Helpline Tel: 0171 242 1222		✓	Each case considered on its own merits.
The Institute of Legal Executives Tel: 01234 841000		✓	Each case considered on its own merits by the Disciplinary Tribunal.
The Royal Institution of Chartered Surveyors Tel: 0171 222 7000		✓	Financial imprudence; scale of loss to creditors; misapplication of clients' monies; failure to maintain professional indemnity insurance cover.
National Association of Estate Agents Tel: 01926 496800	✓		Re-instatement is at the discretion of the membership sub-committee and includes whether creditors fully paid.
Architects Registration Council of the United Kingdom Tel: 0171 580 5861		✓	None except in connection with other forms of misconduct.
British Medical Association Tel: 0171 387 4499		✓	None stated – Exclusion very unlikely for PVA or administration order.
Royal Pharmaceutical Society of Great Britain Tel: 0171 735 9141		✓	Very unlikely. Dishonesty in the conduct of business.

SUMMARY COMMENTS

Accountants

The main ground for exclusion amongst accountants is misconduct/lack of integrity. The ICAEW and ACCA currently monitor all IVAs entered into by members. Whilst not certain, it is likely that there will be monitoring of any PVA or administration order. Accountancy bodies do already seek information from one another on mixed partnerships where partners are made bankrupt or enter into an IVA. The Institute of Financial Accountants also takes a very serious view on the insolvency of any member, and will refer the matter to their Disciplinary Committee to consider.

Solicitors

The position of solicitors in partnership seeking an administration order or PVA will be considered on the merits of the individual case. The Law Society exercises control over insolvent solicitors principally through the practising certificate. It can either (a) grant or refuse an application for a practising certificate, or (b) issue a certificate subject to certain conditions.

Practising certificates are renewed on a yearly basis and can only be refused at the renewal stage. It is unlikely that The Law Society will refuse a renewal where the solicitor's moratorium with his creditors is the only factor involved.

The Law Society does not have to wait until a renewal application is made to impose conditions on the practising certificate. The most common condition will be the requirement to file the accountant's report half yearly or quarterly rather than on the usual yearly basis.

As from 1 September 1996, The Law Society refers these matters to a new body known as the Office for Solicitors' Professional Regulation.

Legal Executives

Generally, a legal executive would be an employee in a solicitor's office but, with licensed conveyancers and such like, it is not beyond the realms of possibility that legal executives might form a partnership with other professionals. The Institute of Legal Executives would refer any instance of a PVA or administration order involving legal executives to its disciplinary tribunal, which has the power to exclude persons from membership or, alternatively, to impose lesser sanctions.

Chartered Surveyors

The Royal Institution of Chartered Surveyors considers the insolvency of any member to be a disciplinary matter. Each case is considered on its own merits and one issue is how the member has dealt with the insolvency. Whilst it is no panacea, if members entering into a PVA or an administration order show some responsibility to their creditors, this may be a positive factor in considering disciplinary proceedings. It is regarded as very important that effective professional indemnity insurance cover is maintained.

Estate Agents

The professional body with one of the strictest codes of practice in respect of PVAs and administration orders is the National Association of Estate Agents. Their articles provide for the mandatory exclusion of any member who is the subject of a bankruptcy order, or who makes any arrangement or composition with his/her creditors. Re-instatement is at the discretion of the membership sub-committee which will consider the circumstances of the insolvency and whether creditors have been paid in full, per art 8(a) of the Association's articles.

Architects

Insolvency is not of itself an area of misconduct for an architect, and only complaints of misconduct in other areas of practice associated with insolvency could result in a case of 'disgraceful conduct' being proven which might lead to an architect's name being removed from the Register of Architects (Registration) Council of the United Kingdom. Many architectural practices are in fact limited companies.

Doctors

The British Medical Association is not a disciplinary or regulatory body. There is no exclusion of members as a consequence of their bankruptcy or an IVA and it is unlikely that doctors in partnership within a surgery would be subject to exclusion if seeking a PVA or administration order.

Pharmacists

Most retail pharmacy businesses are owned by limited companies. Nevertheless, some retail pharmacies are partnerships. In England and Wales such a partnership must consist only of pharmacists although, in Scotland, only one partner needs to be a pharmacist. Under s 69 of the Medicines Act 1968, such a retail business must be registered with the Royal Pharmaceutical Society of Great Britain. Under s 72 of the same Act, a personal representative could continue such a business although only a pharmacist could actually dispense prescription drugs.

Appendix 2

STATUTORY MATERIALS

Insolvent Partnerships Order 1994, SI 1994/2421

ARRANGEMENT OF ARTICLES

PART I
GENERAL

PART II
VOLUNTARY ARRANGEMENTS

PART III
ADMINISTRATION ORDERS

PART IV
CREDITORS' ETC. WINDING-UP PETITIONS

PART V
MEMBERS' PETITIONS

PART VI
PROVISIONS APPLYING TO INSOLVENCY PROCEEDINGS IN RELATION TO INSOLVENT PARTNERSHIPS

PART I

GENERAL

1 Citation, commencement and extent

(1) This Order may be cited as the Insolvent Partnerships Order 1994 and shall come into force on 1st December 1994.

(2) This Order—

(a) in the case of insolvency proceedings in relation to companies and partnerships, relates to companies and partnerships which the courts in England and Wales have jurisdiction to wind up; and

(b) in the case of insolvency proceedings in relation to individuals, extends to England and Wales only.

(3) In paragraph (2) the term "insolvency proceedings" has the meaning ascribed to it by article 2 below.

2 Interpretation: definitions

(1) In this Order, except in so far as the context otherwise requires—

"the Act" means the Insolvency Act 1986;
"agricultural charge" has the same meaning as in the Agricultural Credits Act 1928;
"agricultural receiver" means a receiver appointed under an agricultural charge;
"corporate member" means an insolvent member which is a company;
"the court", in relation to an insolvent partnership, means the court which has jurisdiction to wind up the partnership;
"individual member" means an insolvent member who is an individual;
"insolvency order" means—

(a) in the case of an insolvent partnership or a corporate member, a winding-up order; and

(b) in the case of an individual member, a bankruptcy order;

"insolvency petition" means, in the case of a petition presented to the court—

(a) against a corporate member, a petition for its winding up by the court;

(b) against an individual member, a petition for a bankruptcy order to be made against that individual,

where the petition is presented in conjunction with a petition for the winding up of the partnership by the court as an unregistered company under the Act;
"insolvency proceedings" means any proceedings under the Act, this Order or the Insolvency Rules 1986;
"insolvent member" means a member of an insolvent partnership, against whom an insolvency petition is being or has been presented;
"joint bankruptcy petition" means a petition by virtue of article 11 of this Order;
"joint debt" means a debt of an insolvent partnership in respect of which an order is made by virtue of Part IV or V of this Order;
"joint estate" means the partnership property of an insolvent partnership in respect of which an order is made by virtue of Part IV or V of this Order;
"joint expenses" means expenses incurred in the winding up of an insolvent partnership or in the winding up of the business of an insolvent partnership and the administration of its property;
"limited partner" has the same meaning as in the Limited Partnerships Act 1907;
"member" means a member of a partnership and any person who is liable as a partner within the meaning of section 14 of the Partnership Act 1890;
"officer", in relation to an insolvent partnership, means—

(a) a member; or

(b) a person who has management or control of the partnership business;

"partnership property" has the same meaning as in the Partnership Act 1890;

"postponed debt" means a debt the payment of which is postponed by or under any provision of the Act or of any other enactment;

"responsible insolvency practitioner" means—

(a) in winding up, the liquidator of an insolvent partnership or corporate member; and

(b) in bankruptcy, the trustee of the estate of an individual member,

and in either case includes the official receiver when so acting;

"separate debt" means a debt for which a member of a partnership is liable, other than a joint debt;

"separate estate" means the property of an insolvent member against whom an insolvency order has been made;

"separate expenses" means expenses incurred in the winding up of a corporate member, or in the bankruptcy of an individual member; and

"trustee of the partnership" means a person authorised by order made by virtue of article 11 of this Order to wind up the business of an insolvent partnership and to administer its property.

(2) The definitions in paragraph (1), other than the first definition, shall be added to those in section 436 of the Act.

(3) References in provisions of the Act applied by this Order to any provision of the Act so applied shall, unless the context otherwise requires, be construed as references to the provision as so applied.

(4) Where, in any Schedule to this Order, all or any of the provisions of two or more sections of the Act are expressed to be modified by a single paragraph of the Schedule, the modification includes the combination of the provisions of those sections into the one or more sections set out in that paragraph.

3 Interpretation: expressions appropriate to companies

(1) This article applies for the interpretation in relation to insolvent partnerships of expressions appropriate to companies in provisions of the Act and of the Company Directors Disqualification Act 1986 applied by this Order, unless the contrary intention appears.

(2) References to companies shall be construed as references to insolvent partnerships and all references to the registrar of companies shall be omitted.

(3) References to shares of a company shall be construed—

(a) in relation to an insolvent partnership with capital, as references to rights to share in that capital; and

(b) in relation to an insolvent partnership without capital, as references to interests—

(i) conferring any right to share in the profits or liability to contribute to the losses of the partnership, or

(ii) giving rise to an obligation to contribute to the debts or expenses of the partnership in the event of a winding up.

(4) Other expressions appropriate to companies shall be construed, in relation to an insolvent partnership, as references to the corresponding persons, officers, documents or organs (as the case may be) appropriate to a partnership.

PART II

VOLUNTARY ARRANGEMENTS

4 Voluntary arrangement of insolvent partnership

(1) The provisions of Part I of the Act shall apply in relation to an insolvent partnership, those provisions being modified in such manner that, after modification, they are as set out in Schedule 1 to this Order.

(2) For the purposes of the provisions of the Act applied by paragraph (1), the provisions of the Act specified in paragraph (3) below, insofar as they relate to company voluntary arrangements, shall also apply in relation to insolvent partnerships.

(3) The provisions referred to in paragraph (2) are—

    (a) section 233 in Part VI,
    (b) Part VII, with the exception of section 250,
    (c) Part XII,
    (d) Part XIII,
    (e) sections 411, 413, 414 and 419 in Part XV, and
    (f) Parts XVI to XIX.

5 Voluntary arrangements of members of insolvent partnership

(1) Where insolvency orders are made against an insolvent partnership and an insolvent member of that partnership in his capacity as such, Part I of the Act shall apply to corporate members and Part VIII to individual members of that partnership, with the modification that any reference to the creditors of the company or of the debtor, as the case may be, includes a reference to the creditors of the partnership.

(2) Paragraph (1) is not to be construed as preventing the application of Part I or (as the case may be) Part VIII of the Act to any person who is a member of an insolvent partnership (whether or not a winding-up order has been made against that partnership) and against whom an insolvent order has not been made under this Order or under the Act.

PART III

ADMINISTRATION ORDERS

6 Administration order in relation to insolvent partnership

(1) The provisions of Part II of the Act shall apply in relation to an insolvent partnership, certain of those provisions being modified in such manner that, after modification, they are as set out in Schedule 2 to this Order.

(2) For the purposes of the provisions of the Act applied by paragraph (1), the provisions of the Act specified in paragraph (3) below, insofar as they relate to administration orders, shall also apply in relation to insolvent partnerships.

(3) The provisions referred to in paragraph (2) are—

    (a) section 212 in Part IV,
    (b) Part VI,

(c) Part VII, with the exception of section 250,
(d) Part XIII,
(e) sections 411, 413, 414 and 419 in Part XV, and
(f) Parts XVI to XIX.

PART IV

CREDITORS' ETC. WINDING-UP PETITIONS

7 Winding up of insolvent partnership as unregistered company on petition of creditor etc. where no concurrent petition presented against member

(1) Subject to paragraph (2) below, the provisions of Part V of the Act shall apply in relation to the winding up of an insolvent partnership as an unregistered company on the petition of a creditor, of a responsible insolvency practitioner[, of the Secretary of State or of any other person other than a member,] where no insolvency petition is presented by the petitioner against a member or former member of that partnership in his capacity as such.

(2) Certain of the provisions referred to in paragraph (1) are modified in their application in relation to insolvent partnerships which are being wound up by virtue of that paragraph in such manner that, after modification, they are as set out in Part I of Schedule 3 to this Order.

(3) The provisions of the Act specified in Part II of Schedule 3 to this Order shall apply as set out in that Part for the purposes of section 221(5) of the Act, as modified by Part I of that Schedule.

Amendments—words in square brackets substituted by the Insolvent Partnerships (Amendment) Order 1996, SI 1996/1308.

8 Winding up of insolvent partnership as unregistered company on creditor's petition where concurrent petitions presented against one or more members

(1) Subject to paragraph (2) below, the provisions of Part V of the Act (other than sections 223 and 224), shall apply in relation to the winding up of an insolvent partnership as an unregistered company on a creditor's petition where insolvency petitions are presented by the petitioner against the partnership and against one or more members or former members of the partnership in their capacity as such.

(2) Certain of the provisions referred to in paragraph (1) are modified in their application in relation to insolvent partnerships which are being wound up by virtue of that paragraph in such manner that, after modification, they are as set out in Part I of Schedule 4 to this Order.

(3) The provisions of the Act specified in Part II of Schedule 4 to this Order shall apply as set out in that Part for the purposes of section 221(5) of the Act, as modified by Part I of that Schedule.

(4) The provisions of the Act specified in paragraph (5) below, insofar as they relate to winding up of companies by the court in England and Wales on a creditor's petition, shall apply in relation to the winding up of a corporate member or former corporate member (in its capacity as such) of an insolvent partnership which is being wound up by virtue of paragraph (1).

(5) The provisions referred to in paragraph (4) are—

(a) Part IV,
(b) Part VI,
(c) Part VII, and
(d) Parts XII to XIX.

(6) The provisions of the Act specified in paragraph (7) below, insofar as they relate to the bankruptcy of individuals in England and Wales on a petition presented by a creditor, shall apply in relation to the bankruptcy of an individual member or former individual member (in his capacity as such) of an insolvent partnership which is being wound up by virtue of paragraph (1).

(7) The provisions referred to in paragraph (6) are—

(a) Part IX (other than sections 269, 270, 287 and 297), and
(b) Parts X to XIX.

(8) Certain of the provisions referred to in paragraphs (4) and (6) are modified in their application in relation to the corporate or individual members or former corporate or individual members of insolvent partnerships in such manner that, after modification, they are as set out in Part II of Schedule 4 to this Order.

(9) The provisions of the Act applied by this Article shall further be modified so that references to a corporate or individual member include any former such member against whom an insolvency petition is being or has been presented by virtue of this Article.

PART V

MEMBERS' PETITIONS

9 Winding up of insolvent partnership as unregistered company on member's petition where no concurrent petition presented against member

The following provisions of the Act shall apply in relation to the winding up of an insolvent partnership as an unregistered company on the petition of a member where no insolvent petition is presented by the petitioner against a member of that partnership in his capacity as such—

(a) sections 117 and 221, modified in such manner that, after modification, they are as set out in Schedule 5 to this Order; and
(b) the other provisions of Part V of the Act, certain of those provisions being modified in such manner that, after modification, they are as set out in Part I of Schedule 3 to this Order.

10 Winding up of insolvent partnership as unregistered company on member's petition where concurrent petitions presented against all members

(1) The following provisions of the Act shall apply in relation to the winding up of an insolvent partnership as an unregistered company on a member's petition where insolvency petitions are presented by the petitioner against the partnership and against all its members in their capacity as such—

(a) sections 117, 124, 125, 221, 264, 265, 271 and 272 of the Act, modified in such manner that, after modification, they are as set out in Schedule 6 to this Order; and

(b) sections 220, 225 and 227 to 229 in Part V of the Act, section 220 being modified
in such manner that, after modification, it is as set out in Part I of Schedule 4 to
this Order.

(2) The provisions of the Act specified in paragraph (3) below, insofar as they relate to
winding up of companies by the court in England and Wales on a member's petition,
shall apply in relation to the winding up of a corporate member (in its capacity as such)
of an insolvent partnership which is wound up by virtue of paragraph (1).

(3) The provisions referred to in paragraph (2) are—

(a) Part IV,
(b) Part VI,
(c) Part VII, and
(d) Parts XII to XIX.

(4) The provisions of the Act specified in paragraph (5) below, insofar as they relate to
the bankruptcy of individuals in England and Wales where a bankruptcy petition is
presented by a debtor, shall apply in relation to the bankruptcy of an individual member
(in his capacity as such) of an insolvent partnership which is being wound up by virtue of
paragraph (1).

(5) The provisions referred to in paragraph (4) are—

(a) Part IX (other than sections 273, 274, 287 and 297), and
(b) Parts X to XIX.

(6) Certain of the provisions referred to in paragraphs (2) and (4) are modified in their
application in relation to the corporate or individual members of insolvent partnerships
in such manner that, after modification, they are as set out in Part II of Schedule 4 to this
Order, save that the provisions on summary administration of a debtor's estate shall
apply in relation to the individual members of insolvent partnerships in such manner
that, after modification, those provisions are as set out in Schedule 7 to this Order.

11 Insolvency proceedings not involving winding up of insolvent partnership as unregistered company where individual members present joint bankruptcy petition

(1) The provisions of the Act specified in paragraph (2) below shall apply in relation to
the bankruptcy of the individual members of an insolvent partnership where those
members jointly present a petition to the court for orders to be made for the bankruptcy
of each of them in his capacity as a member of the partnership, and the winding up of
the partnership business and administration of its property, without the partnership
being wound up as an unregistered company under Part V of the Act.

(2) The provisions referred to in paragraph (1) are—

(a) Part IX (other than sections 273, 274 and 287), and
(b) Parts X to XIX,

insofar as they relate to the insolvency of individuals in England and Wales where a
bankruptcy petition is presented by a debtor.

(3) Certain of the provisions referred to in paragraph (1) are modified in their
application in relation to the individual members of insolvent partnerships in such
manner that, after modification, they are as set out in Schedule 7 to this Order.

PART VI

PROVISIONS APPLYING IN INSOLVENCY PROCEEDINGS IN RELATION TO INSOLVENT PARTNERSHIPS

12 Winding up of unregistered company which is a member of insolvent partnership being wound up by virtue of this Order

Where an insolvent partnership or other body which may be wound up under Part V of the Act as an unregistered company is itself a member of an insolvent partnership being so wound up, articles 8 and 10 above shall apply in relation to the latter insolvent partnership as though the former body were a corporate member of that partnership.

13 Deposit on petitions

(1) Where an order under section 414(4) or 415(3) of the Act (security for fees) provides for any sum to be deposited on presentation of a winding-up or bankruptcy petition, that sum shall, in the case of petitions presented by virtue of articles 8 and 10 above, only be required to be deposited in respect of the petition for winding up the partnership, but shall be treated as a deposit in respect of all those petitions.

(2) Production of evidence as to the sum deposited on presentation of the petition for winding up the partnership shall suffice for the filing in court of an insolvency petition against an insolvent member.

14 Supplemental powers of court

(1) At the end of section 168 of the Act there shall be inserted the following subsections—

"(5A) Where at any time after a winding-up petition has been presented to the court against any person (including an insolvent partnership or other body which may be wound up under Part V of the Act as an unregistered company), whether by virtue of the provisions of the Insolvent Partnerships Order 1994 or not, the attention of the court is drawn to the fact that the person in question is a member of an insolvent partnership, the court may make an order as to the future conduct of the insolvency proceedings and any such order may apply any provisions of that Order with any necessary modifications.

(5B) Any order or directions under subsection (5A) may be made or given on the application of the official receiver, any responsible insolvency practitoner, the trustee of the partnership or any other interested person and may include provisions as to the administration of the joint estate of the partnership, and in particular how it and the separate estate of any member are to be administered.

(5C) Where the court makes an order under section 72(1)(a) of the Financial Services Act 1986 or section 92(1)(a) of the Banking Act 1987 for the winding up of an insolvent partnership, the court may make an order as to the future conduct of the winding-up proceedings, and any such order may apply any provisions of the Insolvent Partnerships Order 1994 with any necessary modifications.".

(2) At the end of section 303 of the Act there shall be inserted the following subsections—

"(2A) Where at any time a bankruptcy petition has been presented to the court against any person, whether under the provisions of the Insolvent Partnership Order 1994 or not, the attention of the court is drawn to the fact that the person in question is a member of an insolvent partnership, the court may make an order as to the future conduct of the insolvency proceedings and any such order may apply any provisions of that Order with any necessary modifications.

(2B) Where a bankruptcy petition has been presented against more than one individual in the circumstances mentioned in subsection (2A) above, the court may give such directions for consolidating the proceedings, or any of them, as it thinks just.

(2C) Any order or directions under subsection (2A) or (2B) may be made or given on the application of the official receiver, any responsible insolvency practitioner, the trustee of the partnership or any other interested person and may include provisions as to the administration of the joint estate of the partnership, and in particular how it and the separate estate of any member are to be administered.".

15 Meaning of "act as insolvency practitioner"

(1) After section 388(2) of the Act there shall be inserted the following—

"(2A) A person acts as an insolvency practitioner in relation to an insolvent partnership by acting—

  (a) as its liquidator, provisional liquidator or administrator, or
  (b) as trustee of the partnership under article 11 of the Insolvent Partnerships Order 1994, or
  (c) as supervisor of a voluntary arrangement approved in relation to it under Part I of this Act.".

(2) In section 388(3) the words "to a partnership and" shall be omitted.

PART VII

DISQUALIFICATION

16 Application of Company Directors Disqualification Act 1986

Where an insolvent partnership is wound up as an unregistered company under Part V of the Act, the provisions of sections 6 and 10, 15, 19(c) and 20 of, and Schedule 1 to, the Company Directors Disqualification Act 1986 shall apply, certain of those provisions being modified in such manner that, after modification, they are as set out in Schedule 8 to this Order.

PART VIII

MISCELLANEOUS

17 Forms

(1) The forms contained in Schedule 9 to this Order shall be used in and in connection with proceedings by virtue of this Order, whether in the High Court or a county court.

(2) The forms shall be used with such variations, if any, as the circumstances may require.

18 Application of subordinate legislation

(1) The subordinate legislation specified in Schedule 10 to this Order shall apply as from time to time in force and with such modifications as the context requires for the purpose of giving effect to the provisions of the Act and of the Company Directors Disqualification Act 1986 which are applied by this Order.

(2) In the case of any conflict between any provision of the subordinate legislation applied by paragraph (1) and any provision of this Order, the latter provision shall prevail.

19 Supplemental and transitional provisions

(1) This Order does not apply in relation to any case in which a winding-up or a bankruptcy order was made under the Insolvent Partnerships Order 1986 in relation to a partnership or an insolvent member of a partnership, and where this Order does not apply the law in force immediately before this Order came into force continues to have effect.

(2) Where winding-up or bankruptcy proceedings commenced under the provisions of the Insolvent Partnerships Order 1986 were pending in relation to a partnership or an insolvent member of a partnership immediately before this Order came into force, either—

- (a) those proceedings shall be continued, after the coming into force of this Order, in accordance with the provisions of this Order, or
- (b) if the court so directs, they shall be continued under the provisions of the 1986 Order, in which case the law in force immediately before this Order came into force continues to have effect.

(3) For the purpose of paragraph (2) above, winding-up or bankruptcy proceedings are pending if a statutory or written demand has been served on a winding-up or bankruptcy petition has been presented.

(4) Nothing in this Order is to be taken as preventing a petition being presented against an insolvent partnership under—

- (a) section 53 or 54 of the Insurance Companies Act 1982 (winding up: insurance companies),
- (b) section 72(2)(d) of the Financial Services Act 1986 (winding up: investment business),
- (c) section 92 of the Banking Act 1987 (winding up: authorised institutions), or
- (d) any other enactment.

(5) Nothing in this Order is to be taken as preventing any creditor or creditors owed one or more debts by an insolvent partnership from presenting a petition under the Act against one or more members of the partnership liable for that debt or those debts (as the case may be) without including the others and without presenting a petition for the winding up of the partnership as an unregistered company.

(6) Bankruptcy proceedings may be consolidated by virtue of article 14(2) above irrespective of whether they were commenced under the Bankruptcy Act 1914 or the Insolvency Act 1986 or by virtue of the Insolvent Partnerships Order 1986 or this Order, and the court shall, in the case of proceedings commenced under or by virtue of different enactments, make provision for the manner in which the consolidated proceedings are to be conducted.

20 Revocation

The Insolvent Partnerships Order 1986 is hereby revoked.

SCHEDULE 1

MODIFIED PROVISIONS OF PART I OF THE ACT (COMPANY VOLUNTARY ARRANGEMENTS) AS APPLIED BY ARTICLE 4

For Part I of the Act there shall be substituted—

"PART I
PARTNERSHIP VOLUNTARY ARRANGEMENTS

The proposal

1 Those who may propose an arrangement

(1) The members of an insolvent partnership (other than one for which an administration order is in force, or which is being wound up as an unregistered company, or in respect of which an order has been made by virtue of article 11 of the Insolvent Partnerships Order 1994) may make a proposal under this Part to the partnership's creditors for a composition in satisfaction of the debts of the partnership or a scheme of arrangement of its affairs (from here on referred to, in either case, as a 'voluntary arrangement').

(2) A proposal under this Part is one which provides for some person ('the nominee') to act in relation to the voluntary arrangement either as trustee or otherwise for the purpose of supervising its implementation; and the nominee must be a person who is qualified to act as an insolvent practitioner in relation to the insolvent partnership.

(3) Such a proposal may also be made—

(a) where an administration order is in force in relation to the partnership, by the administrator,
(b) where the partnership is being wound up as an unregistered company, by the liquidator, and
(c) where an order has been made by virtue of article 11 of the Insolvent Partnerships Order 1994, by the trustee of the partnership.

2 Procedure where nominee is not the liquidator, administrator or trustee

(1) This section applies where the nominee under section 1 is not the liquidator, administrator or trustee of the insolvent partnership.

(2) The nominee shall, within 28 days (or such longer period as the court may allow) after he is given notice of the proposal for a voluntary arrangement, submit a report to the court stating—

(a) whether, in his opinion, meetings of the members of the partnership and of the partnership's creditors should be summoned to consider the proposal, and
(b) if in his opinion such meetings should be summoned, the date on which, and time and place at which, he proposes the meetings should be held.

(3) The nominee shall also state in his report whether there are in existence any insolvency proceedings in respect of the insolvent partnership or any of its members.

(4) For the purposes of enabling the nominee to prepare his report, the person intending to make the proposal shall submit to the nominee—

- (a) a document setting out the terms of the proposed voluntary arrangement, and
- (b) a statement of the partnership's affairs containing—
    - (i) such particulars of the partnership's creditors and of the partnership's debts and other liabilities and of the partnership property as may be prescribed, and
    - (ii) such other information as may be prescribed.

(5) The court may, on an application made by the person intending to make the proposal, in a case where the nominee has failed to submit the report required by this section, direct that the nominee be replaced as such by another person qualified to act as an insolvency practitioner in relation to the insolvent partnership.

3 Summoning of meetings

(1) Where the nominee under section 1 is not the liquidator, administrator or trustee of the insolvent partnership, and it has been reported to the court that such meetings as are mentioned in section 2(2) should be summoned, the person making the report shall (unless the court otherwise directs) summon those meetings for the time, date and place proposed in the report.

(2) Where the nominee is the liquidator, administrator or trustee of the insolvent partnership, he shall summon meetings of the members of the partnership and of the partnership's creditors to consider the proposal for such a time, date and place as he thinks fit.

(3) The persons to be summoned to a creditors' meeting under this section are every creditor of the partnership of whose claim and address the person summoning the meeting is aware.

Consideration and implementation of proposal

4 Decisions of meetings

(1) The meetings summoned under section 3 shall decide whether to approve the proposed voluntary arrangement (with or without modifications).

(2) The modifications may include one conferring the functions proposed to be conferred on the nominee on another person qualified to act as an insolvency practitioner in relation to the insolvent partnership.

But they shall not include any modification by virtue of which the proposal ceases to be a proposal such as is mentioned in section 1.

(3) A meeting so summoned shall not approve any proposal or modification which affects the right of a secured creditor of the partnership to enforce his security, except with the concurrence of the creditor concerned.

(4) Subject as follows, a meeting so summoned shall not approve any proposal or modification under which—

- (a) any preferential debt of the partnership is to be paid otherwise than in priority to such of its debts as are not preferential debts, or
- (b) a preferential creditor of the partnership is to be paid an amount in respect of a preferential debt that bears to that debt a smaller proportion than is borne to another preferential debt by the amount that is to be paid in respect of that other debt.

However, the meeting may approve such a proposal or modification with the concurrence of the preferential creditor concerned.

(5) Subject as above, each of the meetings shall be conducted in accordance with the rules.

(6) After the conclusion of either meeting in accordance with the rules, the chairman of the meeting shall report the result of the meeting to the court, and, immediately after reporting to the court, shall give notice of the result of the meeting to all those who were sent notice of the meeting in accordance with the rules.

(7) References in this section to preferential debts and preferential creditors are to be read in accordance with section 386 in Part XII of this Act.

5 Effect of approval

(1) This section has effect where each of the meetings summoned under section 3 approves the proposed voluntary arrangement either with the same modifications or without modifications.

(2) The approved voluntary arrangement—

   (a) takes effect as if made by the members of the partnership at the creditors' meeting, and
   (b) binds every person who in accordance with the rules had notice of, and was entitled to vote at, that meeting (whether or not he was present or represented at the meeting) as if he were a party to the voluntary arrangement.

(3) Subject as follows, if the partnership is being wound up as an unregistered company, or an administration order or an order by virtue of article 11 of the Insolvent Partnerships Order 1994 is in force, the court may do one or both of the following, namely—

   (a) by order—
      (i) stay all proceedings in the winding up or in the proceedings under the order made by virtue of the said article 11 (as the case may be), including any related insolvency proceedings of a member of the partnership in his capacity as such, or
      (ii) discharge the administration order;
   (b) give such directions as it thinks appropriate for facilitating the implementation of the approved voluntary arrangement with respect to—
      (i) the conduct of the winding up, of the proceedings by virtue of the said article 11 or of the administration (as the case may be), and
      (ii) the conduct of any related insolvency proceedings as referred to in paragraph (a)(i) above.

(4) The court shall not make an order under subsection (3)(a)—

   (a) at any time before the end of the period of 28 days beginning with the first day on which each of the reports required by section 4(6) has been made to the court, or
   (b) at any time when an application under the next section or an appeal in respect of such an application is pending, or at any time in the period within which such an appeal may be brought.

6 Challenge of decisions

(1) Subject to this section, an application to the court may be made, by any of the persons specified below, on one or both of the following grounds, namely—

(a) that a voluntary arrangement approved at the meetings summoned under section 3 unfairly prejudices the interests of a creditor, member or contributory of the partnership;

(b) that there has been some material irregularity at or in relation to either of the meetings.

(2) The persons who may apply under this section are—

(a) a person entitled, in accordance with the rules, to vote at either of the meetings;

(b) the nominee or any person who has replaced him under section 2(5) or 4(2); and

(c) if the partnership is being wound up as an unregistered company or an administration order or order by virtue of article 11 of the Insolvent Partnerships Order 1994 is in force, the liquidator, administrator or trustee of the partnership.

(3) An application under this section shall not be made after the end of the period of 28 days beginning with the first day on which each of the reports required by section 4(6) has been made to the court.

(4) Where on such an application the court is satisfied as to either of the grounds mentioned in subsection (1), it may do one or both of the following, namely—

(a) revoke or suspend the approvals given by the meetings or, in a case falling within subsection (1)(b), any approval given by the meeting in question;

(b) give a direction to any person for the summoning of further meetings to consider any revised proposal the person who made the original proposal may make or, in a case falling within subsection (1)(b), a further meeting of the members of the partnership or (as the case may be) of the partnership's creditors to reconsider the original proposal.

(5) Where at any time after giving a direction under subsection (4)(b) for the summoning of meetings to consider a revised proposal the court is satisfied that the person who made the original proposal does not intend to submit a revised proposal, the court shall revoke the direction and revoke or suspend any approval given at the previous meetings.

(6) In a case where the court, on an application under this section with respect to any meeting—

(a) gives a direction under subsection (4)(b), or

(b) revokes or suspends an approval under subsection (4)(a) or (5),

the court may give such supplemental directions as it thinks fit, and, in particular, directions with respect to things done since the meeting under any voluntary arrangement approved by the meeting.

(7) Except in pursuance of the preceding provisions of this section, an approval given at a meeting summoned under section 3 is not invalidated by any irregularity at or in relation to the meeting.

7 Implementation of proposal

(1) This section applies where a voluntary arrangement approved by the meetings summoned under section 3 has taken effect.

(2) The person who is for the time being carrying out in relation to the voluntary arrangement the functions conferred—

(a) by virtue of the approval on the nominee, or

(b) by virtue of section 2(5) or 4(2) on a person other than the nominee,

shall be known as the supervisor of the voluntary arrangement.

(3) If any of the partnership's creditors or any other person is dissatisfied by any act, omission or decision of the supervisor, he may apply to the court; and on the application the court may—

(a) confirm, reverse or modify any act or decision of the supervisor,

(b) give him directions, or

(c) make such other order as it thinks fit.

(4) The supervisor—

(a) may apply to the court for directions in relation to any particular matter arising under the voluntary arrangement, and

(b) is included among the persons who may apply to the court for the winding up of the partnership as an unregistered company or for an administration order to be made in relation to it.

(5) The court may, whenever—

(a) it is expedient to appoint a person to carry out the functions of the supervisor, and

(b) it is inexpedient, difficult or impracticable for an appointment to be made without the assistance of the court,

make an order appointing a person who is qualified to act as an insolvency practitioner in relation to the partnership, either in substitution for the existing supervisor or to fill a vacancy.

(6) The power conferred by subsection (5) is exercisable so as to increase the number of persons exercising the functions of supervisor or, where there is more than one person exercising those functions, so as to replace one or more of those persons.".

SCHEDULE 2

MODIFIED PROVISIONS OF PART II OF THE ACT (ADMINISTRATION ORDERS) AS APPLIED BY ARTICLE 6

1 Sections 8 to 15 of, and Schedule 1 to, the Act are set out as modified in this Schedule.

2 Section 8: Power of court to make order

Section 8 is modified so as to read as follows:—

"**8.**—(1) Subject to this section, if the court—

(a) is satisfied that a partnership is unable to pay its debts (within the meaning given to that expression by section 222, 223 or 224 of this Act), and

(b) considers that the making of an order under this section would be likely to achieve one or more of the purposes mentioned below,

the court may make an administration order in relation to the partnership.

(2) An administration order is an order directing that, during the period for which the order is in force, the affairs and business of the partnership and the partnership property shall be managed by a person ('the administrator') appointed for the purpose by the court.

(3) The purposes for whose achievement an administration order may be made are—

    (a) the survival of the whole or any part of the undertaking of the partnership as a going concern;

    (b) the approval of a voluntary arrangement under Part I; and

    (c) a more advantageous realisation of the partnership property than would be effected on a winding up;

and the order shall specify the purpose or purposes for which it is made.

(4) An administration order shall not be made in relation to a partnership after an order has been made for it to be wound up by the court as an unregistered company, nor after an order has been made in relation to it by virtue of article 11 of the Insolvent Partnerships Order 1994, nor where it is—

    (a) an insurance company within the meaning of the Insurance Companies Act 1982, or

    (b) an authorised institution or former authorised institution within the meaning of the Banking Act 1987.".

3 Section 9: Application for order

Section 9 is modified so as to read as follows—

"**9.**—(1) An application to the court for an administration order shall be by petition in Form 1 in Schedule 9 to the Insolvent Partnerships Order 1994 presented either by the members of an insolvent partnership in their capacity as such, or by a creditor or creditors (including any contingent or prospective creditor or creditors), or by all or any of those parties, together or separately.

(2) Where a petition is presented to the court—

    (a) notice of the petition shall be given forthwith to any person who has appointed, or is or may be entitled to appoint, an agricultural receiver of the partnership, and to such other persons as may be prescribed, and

    (b) the petition shall not be withdrawn except with the leave of the court.

(3) Where the court is satisfied that there is an agricultural receiver of the partnership, the court shall dismiss the petition unless it is also satisfied either—

    (a) that the person by whom or on whose behalf the receiver was appointed has consented to the making of the order, or

    (b) that, if an administration order were made, any security by virtue of which the receiver was appointed would—

        (i) be liable to be released or discharged under sections 238 to 240 in Part VI (transactions at an undervalue and preferences),

        (ii) be avoided under section 245 in that Part (avoidance of floating charges), or

        (iii) be challengeable under section 242 (gratuitous alienations) or 243 (unfair preferences) in that Part, or under any rule of law in Scotland.

(4) Subject to subsection (3), on hearing a petition the court may dismiss it, or adjourn the hearing conditionally or unconditionally, or make an interim order or any other order that it thinks fit.

(5) Without prejudice to the generality of subsection (4), an interim order under that subsection may restrict the exercise of any powers of the officers of the partnership (whether by reference to the consent of the court or of a person qualified to act as an insolvency practitioner in relation to the partnership, or otherwise).".

4 Section 10: Effect of application

Section 10 is modified so as to read as follows—

"**10.**—(1) During the period beginning with the presentation of a petition for an administration order and ending with the making of such an order or the dismissal of the petition—

    (a) no order may be made for the winding up of the insolvent partnership, nor may any order be made by virtue of article 11 of the Insolvent Partnerships Order 1994 or under section 35 of the Partnership Act 1890 in respect of the partnership;

    (b) no steps may be taken to enforce any security over the partnership property, or to repossess goods in the possession, under any hire-purchase agreement, of one or more of the officers of the partnership in their capacity as such, except with the leave of the court and subject to such terms as the court may impose; and

    (c) no other proceedings and no execution or other legal process may be commenced or continued, and no distress may be levied, against the partnership or the partnership property except with the leave of the court and subject to such terms as aforesaid.

(2) Nothing in subsection (1) requires the leave of the court—

    (a) for the presentation of a petition for the winding up of the partnership,

    (b) for the presentation of a petition by virtue of article 11 of the Insolvent Partnerships Order 1994 in respect of the partnership,

    (c) for the appointment of an agricultural receiver of the partnership, or

    (d) for the carrying out by such a receiver (whenever appointed) of any of his functions.

(3) Where—

    (a) a petition for an administration order is presented at a time when there is an agricultural receiver of the partnership, and

    (b) the person by or on whose behalf the receiver was appointed has not consented to the making of the order,

the period mentioned in subsection (1) is deemed not to begin unless and until that person so consents.

(4) References in this section and the next to hire-purchase agreements include conditional sale agreements, chattel leasing agreements and retention of title agreements.

(5) In the application of this section and the next to Scotland, references to execution being commenced or continued include references to diligence being carried out or continued, and references to distress being levied shall be omitted.".

5 Section 11: Effect of order

Section 11 is modified so as to read as follows—

"**11.**—(1) On the making of an administration order, any petition for the winding up of the insolvent partnership and any petition for an order to be made by virtue of article 11 of the Insolvent Partnerships Order 1994 shall be dismissed.

(2) Where an administration order has been made, any agricultural receiver of the partnership and any receiver of the partnership property shall vacate office on being required to do so by the administrator.

(3) During the period for which an administration order is in force—

(a) no order may be made for the winding up of the partnership;

(b) no order may be made by virtue of article 11 of the Insolvent Partnerships Order 1994 in respect of the partnership;

(c) no order may be made under section 35 of the Partnership Act 1890 in respect of the partnership;

(d) no agricultural receiver of the partnership may be appointed except with the consent of the administrator or the leave of the court and subject (where the court gives leave) to such terms as the court may impose;

(e) no other steps may be taken to enforce any security over the partnership property, or to repossess goods in the possession, under any hire-purchase agreement, of one or more of the officers of the partnership in their capacity as such, except with the consent of the administrator or the leave of the court and subject (where the court gives leave) to such terms as the court may impose; and

(f) no other proceedings and no execution or other legal process may be commenced or continued, and no distress may be levied, against the partnership or the partnership property except with the consent of the administrator or the leave of the court and subject (where the court gives leave) to such terms as aforesaid.

(4) Where at any time an agricultural receiver or a receiver of part of the partnership property has vacated office under subsection (2)—

(a) his remuneration and any expenses properly incurred by him, and

(b) any indemnity to which he is entitled out of the partnership property,

shall be charged on and (subject to subsection (3) above) paid out of any partnership property which was in his custody or under his control at that time in priority to any security held by the person by or on whose behalf he was appointed.".

6 Section 12: Notification of order

Section 12 is modified so as to read as follows—

"**12.**—(1) Every invoice, order for goods or business letter which, at a time when an administration order is in force in relation to an insolvent partnership, is issued by or on behalf of the partnership or the administrator, being a document on or in which the name under which the partnership carries on business appears, shall also contain the administrator's name and a statement that the affairs and business of the partnership and the partnership property are being managed by the administrator.

(2) If default is made in complying with this section, any of the following persons who without reasonable excuse authorises or permits the default, namely, the administrator and any officer of the partnership, is liable to a fine.".

7 Section 13: Appointment of administrator

Section 13 is modified so as to read as follows—

"**13.**—(1) The administrator of a partnership shall be appointed either by the administration order or by an order under the next subsection.

(2) If a vacancy occurs by death, resignation or otherwise in the office of the administrator, the court may by order fill the vacancy.

(3) An application for an order under subsection (2) may be made—

(a) by any continuing administrator of the partnership; or

(b) where there is no such administrator, by a creditors' committee established under section 26 below; or

(c) where there is no such administrator and no such committee, by the members of the partnership or by any creditor or creditors of the partnership.".

8 Section 14: General powers

Section 14 is modified so as to read as follows—

"**14.**—(1) The administrator of an insolvent partnership—

(a) may do all such things as may be necessary for the management of the affairs and business of the partnership and of the partnership property, and

(b) without prejudice to the generality of paragraph (a), has the powers specified in Schedule 1 to this Act;

and in the application of that Schedule to the administrator of a partnership the words "he" and "him" refer to the administrator.

(2) The administrator also has power—

(a) to prevent any person from taking part in the management of the partnership business and to appoint any person to be a manager of that business, and

(b) to call any meeting of the members or creditors of the partnership.

(3) The administrator may apply to the court for directions in relation to any particular matter arising in connection with the carrying out of his functions.

(4) Any power exercisable by the officers of the partnership, whether under the Partnership Act 1890, the partnership agreement or otherwise, which could be exercised in such a way as to interfere with the exercise by the administrator of his powers is not exercisable except with the consent of the administrator, which may be given either generally or in relation to particular cases.

(5) Subject to subsection (6) below, in exercising his powers the administrator is deemed to act as the agent of the members of the partnership in their capacity as such.

(6) An officer of the partnership shall not, unless he otherwise consents, be personally liable for the debts and obligations of the partnership incurred during the period when the administration order is in force.

(7) A person dealing with the administrator in good faith and for value is not concerned to inquire whether the administrator is acting within his powers.".

9 Section 15: Power to deal with charged property, etc.

Section 15 is modified so as to read as follows—

"**15.**—(1) The administrator of a partnership may dispose of or otherwise exercise his powers in relation to any partnership property which is subject to a security to which this subsection applies as if the property were not subject to the security.

(2) Where, on an application by the administrator, the court is satisfied that the disposal (with or without other assets) of—

(a) any partnership property subject to a security to which this subsection applies, or

(b) any goods in the possession of one or more officers of the partnership in their capacity as such under a hire-purchase agreement,

would be likely to promote the purpose or one or more of the purposes specified in the administration order, the court may by order authorise the administrator to dispose of the property as if it were not subject to the security or to dispose of the goods as if all rights of the owner under the hire-purchase agreement were vested in the members of the partnership.

(3) Subsection (1) applies to any security which, as created, was a floating charge unless an agricultural receiver has been appointed under that security; and subsection (2) applies to any other security.

(4) Where property is disposed of under subsection (1), the holder of the security has the same priority in respect of any partnership property directly or indirectly representing the property disposed of as he would have had in respect of the property subject to the security.

(5) It shall be a condition of an order under subsection (2) that—

    (a) the net proceeds of the disposal, and
    (b) where those proceeds are less than such amount as may be determined by the court to be the net amount which would be realised on a sale of the property or goods in the open market by a willing vendor, such sums as may be required to make good the deficiency,

shall be applied towards discharging the sums secured by the security or payable under the hire-purchase agreement.

(6) Where a condition imposed in pursuance of subsection (5) relates to two or more securities, that condition requires the net proceeds of the disposal and, where paragraph (b) of that subsection applies, the sums mentioned in that paragraph to be applied towards discharging the sums secured by those securities in the order of their priorities.

(7) References in this section to hire-purchase agreements include conditional sale agreements, chattel leasing agreements and retention of title agreements.".

10 Schedule 1 is modified so as to read as follows—

"SCHEDULE 1   Section 14
POWERS OF ADMINISTRATOR

1 Powers to take possession of, collect and get in the partnership property and, for that purpose, to take such proceedings as may seem to him expedient.

2 Power to sell or otherwise dispose of the partnership property by public auction or private auction or private contract or, in Scotland, to sell, feu, hire out or otherwise dispose of the partnership property by public roup or private bargain.

3 Power to raise or borrow money and grant security therefor over the partnership property.

4 Power to appoint a solicitor or accountant or other professionally qualified person to assist him in the performance of his functions.

5 Power to bring or defend any action or other legal proceedings in the name and on behalf of any member of the partnership in his capacity as such or of the partnership.

6 Power to refer to arbitration any question affecting the partnership.

7 Power to effect and maintain insurances in respect of the partnership business and property.

8 Power to do all acts and execute, in the name and on behalf of the partnership or of any member of the partnership in his capacity as such, any deed, receipt or other document.

9 Power to draw, accept, make and endorse any bill of exchange or promissory note in the name and on behalf of any member of the partnership in his capacity as such or of the partnership.

10 Power to appoint any agent to do any business which he is unable to do himself or which can more conveniently be done by an agent and power to employ and dismiss employees.

11 Power to do all such things (including the carrying out of works) as may be necessary for the realisation of the partnership property.

12 Power to make any payment which is necessary or incidental to the performance of his functions.

13 Power to carry on the business of the partnership.

14 Power to establish subsidiary undertakings of the partnership.

15 Power to transfer to subsidiary undertakings of the partnership the whole or any part of the business of the partnership or of the partnership property.

16 Power to grant or accept a surrender of a lease or tenancy of any of the partnership property, and to take a lease or tenancy of any property required or convenient for the business of the partnership.

17 Power to make any arrangement or compromise on behalf of the partnership or of its members in their capacity as such.

18 Power to rank and claim in the bankruptcy, insolvency, sequestration or liquidation of any person indebted to the partnership and to receive dividends, and to accede to trust deeds for the creditors of any such person.

19 Power to present or defend a petition for the winding up of the partnership under the Insolvent Partnerships Order 1994.

20 Power to do all other things incidental to the exercise of the foregoing powers.".

SCHEDULE 3

PROVISIONS OF THE ACT WHICH APPLY WITH MODIFICATIONS FOR THE PURPOSES OF ARTICLE 7 TO WINDING UP OF INSOLVENT PARTNERSHIP ON PETITION OF CREDITOR ETC. WHERE NO CONCURRENT PETITION PRESENTED AGAINST MEMBER

PART I
MODIFIED PROVISIONS OF PART V OF THE ACT

1. Sections 220 to 223 of the Act are set out as modified in Part I of this Schedule, and sections 117, 131, 133, 234 and Schedule 4 are set out as modified in Part II.

2 Section 220: Meaning of "unregistered company"

Section 220 is modified so as to read as follows—

"**220.** For the purposes of this Part, the expression 'unregistered company' includes any insolvent partnership.".

3 Section 221: Winding up of unregistered companies

Section 221 is modified so as to read as follows—

"**221.**—(1) Subject to subsections (2) and (3) below and to the provisions of this Part, any insolvent partnership may be wound up under this Act if it has, or at any time had, in England and Wales either—

  (a) a principal place of business, or
  (b) a place of business at which business is or has been carried on in the course of which the debt (or part of the debt) arose which forms the basis of the petition for winding up the partnership.

(2) Subject to subsection (3) below, an insolvent partnership shall not be wound up under this Act if the business of the partnership has not been carried on in England and Wales at any time in the period of 3 years ending with the day on which the winding-up petition is presented.

(3) If an insolvent partnership had a principal place of business situated in Scotland or in Northern Ireland, the court shall not have jurisdiction to wind up the partnership unless it had a principal place of business in England and Wales—

  (a) in the case of a partnership with a principal place of business in Scotland, at any time in the period of 1 year, or
  (b) in the case of a partnership with a principal place of business in Northern Ireland, at any time in the period of 3 years,

ending with the day on which the winding-up petition is presented.

(4) No insolvent partnership shall be wound up under this Act voluntarily.

(5) To the extent that they are applicable to the winding up of a company by the court in England and Wales on the petition of a creditor or of the Secretary of State, all the provisions of this Act and the Companies Act about winding up apply to the winding up of an insolvent partnership as an unregistered company—

  (a) with the exceptions and additions mentioned in the following subsections of this section and in section 221A, and
  (b) with the modifications specified in Part II of Schedule 3 to the Insolvent Partnerships Order 1994.

(6) Sections 73(1), 74(2)(a) to (d) and (3), 75 to 78, 83, 122, 123, 202, 203, 205 and 250 shall not apply.

(7) The circumstances in which an insolvent partnership may be wound up as an unregistered company are as follows—

  (a) if the partnership is dissolved, or has ceased to carry on business, or is carrying on business only for the purpose of winding up its affairs;
  (b) if the partnership is unable to pay its debts;
  (c) if the court is of the opinion that it is just and equitable that the partnership should be wound up.

(8) Every petition for the winding up of an insolvent partnership under Part V of this Act shall be verified by affidavit in Form 2 in Schedule 9 to the Insolvent Partnerships Order 1994.

Petition by liquidator, administrator, trustee or supervisor to wind up insolvent partnership as unregistered company

221A.—(1) A petition in Form 3 in Schedule 9 to the Insolvent Partnerships Order 1994 for winding up an insolvent partnership may be presented by—

    (a) the liquidator or administrator of a corporate member or of a former corporate member, or

    (b) the administrator of the partnership, or

    (c) the trustee of an individual member's, or of a former individual member's, estate, or

    (d) the supervisor of a voluntary arrangement approved under Part I of this Act in relation to a corporate member or the partnership, or under Part VIII of this Act in relation to an individual member,

if the ground of the petition is one of the circumstances set out in section 221(7).

(2) In this section "petitioning insolvency practitioner" means a person who has presented a petition under subsection (1).

(3) If the ground of the petition presented under subsection (1) is that the partnership is unable to pay its debts and the petitioning insolvency practitioner is able to satisfy the court that an insolvency order has been made against the member whose liquidator or trustee he is because of that member's inability to pay a joint debt, that order shall, unless it is proved otherwise to the satisfaction of the court, be proof for the purposes of section 221(7) that the partnership is unable to pay its debts.

(4) Where a winding-up petition is presented under subsection (1), the court may appoint the petitioning insolvency practitioner liquidator of the partnership under section 135 (appointment and powers of provisional liquidator).

(5) Where a winding-up order is made against an insolvent partnership after the presentation of a petition under subsection (1), the court may appoint the petitioning insolvency practitioner as liquidator of the partnership; and where the court makes an appointment under this subsection, section 140(3) (official receiver not to become liquidator) applies as if an appointment had been made under that section.

(6) Where a winding-up petition is presented under subsection (1), in the event of the partnership property being insufficient to satisfy the costs of the petitioning insolvency practitioner the costs may be paid out of the assets of the corporate or individual member, as the case may be, as part of the expenses of the liquidation, administration, bankruptcy or voluntary arrangement of that member, in the same order of priority as expenses properly chargeable or incurred by the practitioner in getting in any of the assets of the member.".

4 Section 222: Inability to pay debts: unpaid creditor for £750 or more

Section 222 is modified so as to read as follows—

"**222.**—(1) An insolvent partnership is deemed (for the purposes of section 221) unable to pay its debts if there is a creditor, by assignment or otherwise, to whom the partnership is indebted in a sum exceeding £750 then due and—

    (a) the creditor has served on the partnership, in the manner specified in subsection (2) below, a written demand in the prescribed form requiring the partnership to pay the sum so due, and

    (b) the partnership has for 3 weeks after the service of the demand neglected to pay the sum or to secure or compound for it to the creditor's satisfaction.

(2) Service of the demand referred to in subsection (1)(a) shall be effected—

    (a) by leaving it at a principal place of business of the partnership in England and Wales, or

(b) by leaving it at a place of business of the partnership in England and Wales at which business is carried on in the course of which the debt (or part of the debt) referred to in subsection (1) arose, or

(c) by delivering it to an officer of the partnership, or

(d) by otherwise serving it in such manner as the court may approve or direct.

(3) The money sum for the time being specified in subsection (1) is subject to increase or reduction by regulations under section 417 in Part XV; but no increase in the sum so specified affects any case in which the winding-up petition was presented before the coming into force of the increase.".

5 Section 223: Inability to pay debts: debt remaining unsatisfied after action brought

Section 223 is modified so as to read as follows—

"**223.**—(1) An insolvent partnership is deemed (for the purposes of section 221) unable to pay its debts if an action or other proceeding has been instituted against any member for any debt or demand due, or claimed to be due, from the partnership, or form him in his character of member, and—

(a) notice in writing of the institution of the action or proceeding has been served on the partnership in the manner specified in subsection (2) below, and

(b) the partnership has not within 3 weeks after service of the notice paid, secured or compounded for the debt or demand, or procured the action or proceeding to be stayed or sisted, or indemnified the defendant or defender to his reasonable satisfaction against the action or proceeding, and against all costs, damages and expenses to be incurred by him because of it.

(2) Service of the notice referred to in subsection (1)(a) shall be effected—

(a) by leaving it at a principal place of business of the partnership in England and Wales, or

(b) by leaving it at a place of business of the partnership in England and Wales at which business is carried on in the course of which the debt or demand (or part of the debt or demand) referred to in subsection (1) arose, or

(c) by delivering it to an officer of the partnership, or

(d) by otherwise serving it in such manner as the court may approve or direct."

PART II

OTHER MODIFIED PROVISIONS OF THE ACT ABOUT WINDING UP BY THE COURT

6 Section 117: High Court and county court jurisdiction

Section 117 is modified so as to read as follows—

"**117.**—(1) Subject to subsections (3) and (4) below, the High Court has jurisdiction to wind up any insolvent partnership as an unregistered company by virtue of article 7 of the Insolvent Partnerships Order 1994 if the partnership has, or at any time had, in England and Wales either—

(a) a principal place of business, or

(b) a place of business at which business is or has been carried on in the course of which the debt (or part of the debt) arose which forms the basis of the petition for winding up the partnership.

(2) Subject to subsections (3) and (4) below, a petition for the winding up of an insolvent partnership by virtue of the said article 7 may be presented to a county court

in England and Wales if the partnership has, or at any time had, within the insolvency district of that court either—

(a) a principal place of business, or
(b) a place of business at which business is or has been carried on in the course of which the debt (or part of the debt) arose which forms the basis of the winding-up petition.

(3) Subject to subsection (4) below, the court only has jurisdiction to wind up an insolvent partnership if the business of the partnership has been carried on in England and Wales at any time in the period of 3 years ending with the day on which the petition for winding it up is presented.

(4) If an insolvent partnership has a principal place of business situated in Scotland or in Northern Ireland, the court shall not have jurisdiction to wind up the partnership unless it had a principal place of business in England and Wales—

(a) in the case of a partnership with a principal place of business in Scotland, at any time in the period of 1 year, or
(b) in the case of a partnership with a principal place of business in Northern Ireland, at any time in the period of 3 years,

ending with the day on which the petition for winding up is presented.

(5) The Lord Chancellor may by order in a statutory instrument exclude a county court from having winding-up jurisdiction, and for the purposes of that jurisdiction may attach its district, or any part thereof, to any other county court, and may by statutory instrument revoke or vary any such order.

In exercising the powers of this section, the Lord Chancellor shall provide that a county court is not to have winding-up jurisdiction unless it has for the time being jurisdiction for the purposes of Parts VIII to XI of this Act (individual insolvency).

(6) Every court in England and Wales having winding-up jurisdiction has for the purposes of that jurisdiction all the powers of the High Court; and every prescribed officer of the court shall perform any duties which an officer of the High Court may discharge by order of a judge of that court or otherwise in relation to winding up.".

7 Section 131: Statement of affairs of insolvent partnership

Section 131 is modified so as to read as follows—

"**131.**—(1) Where the court has, by virtue of article 7 of the Insolvent Partnerships Order 1994, made a winding-up order or appointed a provisional liquidator in respect of an insolvent partnership, the official receiver may require some or all of the persons mentioned in subsection (3) below to make out and submit to him a statement in the prescribed form as to the affairs of the partnership.

(2) The statement shall be verified by affidavit by the persons required to submit it and shall show—

(a) particulars of the debts and liabilities of the partnership and of the partnership property;
(b) the names and addresses of the partnership's creditors;
(c) the securities held by them respectively;
(d) the dates when the securities were respectively given; and
(e) such further or other information as may be prescribed or as the official receiver may require.

(3) The persons referred to in subsection (1) are—

    (a) those who are or have been officers of the partnership;

    (b) those who have taken part in the formation of the partnership at any time within one year before the relevant date;

    (c) those who are in the employment of the partnership, or have been in its employment within that year, and are in the official receiver's opinion capable of giving the information required;

    (d) those who are or have been within that year officers of, or in the employment of, a company which is, or within that year was, an officer of the partnership.

(4) Where any persons are required under this section to submit a statement of affairs to the official receiver, they shall do so (subject to the next subsection) before the end of the period of 21 days beginning with the day after that on which the prescribed notice of the requirement is given to them by the official receiver.

(5) The official receiver, if he thinks fit, may—

    (a) at any time release a person from an obligation imposed on him under subsection (1) or (2) above; or

    (b) either when giving the notice mentioned in subsection (4) or subsequently, extend the period so mentioned;

and where the official receiver has refused to exercise a power conferred by this subsection, the court, if it thinks fit, may exercise it.

(6) In this section—

"employment" includes employment under a contract for services; and
"the relevant date" means—

    (a) in a case where a provisional liquidator is appointed, the date of his appointment; and

    (b) in a case where no such appointment is made, the date of the winding-up order.

(7) If a person without reasonable excuse fails to comply with any obligation imposed under this section, he is liable to a fine and, for continued contravention, to a daily default fine."

8 Section 133: Public examination of officers of insolvent partnerships

Section 133 is modified so as to read as follows—

"**133.**—(1) Where an insolvent partnership is being wound up by virtue of article 7 of the Insolvent Partnerships Order 1994, the official receiver may at any time before the winding up is complete apply to the court for the public examination of any person who—

    (a) is or has been an officer of the partnership; or

    (b) has acted as liquidator or administrator of the partnership or as receiver or manager or, in Scotland, receiver of its property; or

    (c) not being a person falling within paragraph (a) or (b), is or has been concerned, or has taken part, in the formation of the partnership.

(2) Unless the court otherwise orders, the official receiver shall make an application under subsection (1) if he is requested in accordance with the rules to do so by one-half, in value, of the creditors of the partnership.

(3) On an application under subsection (1), the court shall direct that a public examination of the person to whom the application relates shall be held on a day appointed by the court; and that person shall attend on that day and be publicly

examined as to the formation or management of the partnership or as to the conduct of its business and affairs, or his conduct or dealings in relation to the partnership.

(4) The following may take part in the public examination of a person under this section any may question that person concerning the matters mentioned in subsection (3), namely—

    (a) the official receiver;
    (b) the liquidator of the partnership;
    (c) any person who has been appointed as special manager of the partnership's property or business;
    (d) any creditor of the partnership who has tendered a proof in the winding up.".

9 Section 234: Getting in the partnership property

Section 234 is modified so as to read as follows—

"**234.**—(1) This section applies where, by virtue of article 7 of the Insolvent Partnerships Order 1994—

    (a) an insolvent partnership is being wound up, or
    (b) a provisional liquidator of an insolvent partnership is appointed;
and "the office-holder" means the liquidator or the provisional liquidator, as the case may be.

(2) Any person who is or has been an officer of the partnership, or who is an executor or administrator of the estate of a deceased officer of the partnership, shall deliver up to the office-holder, for the purposes of the exercise of the office-holder's functions under this Act and (where applicable) the Company Directors Disqualification Act 1986, possession of any partnership property which he holds for purposes of the partnership.

(3) Where any person has in his possession or control any property, books, papers or records to which the partnership appears to be entitled, the court may require that person forthwith (or within such period as the court may direct) to pay, deliver, convey, surrender or transfer the property, books, papers or records to the office-holder or as the court may direct.

(4) Where the office-holder—

    (a) seizes or disposes of any property which is not partnership property, and
    (b) at the time of seizure or disposal believes, and has reasonable grounds for believing, that he is entitled (whether in pursuance of an order of the court or otherwise) to seize or dispose of that property,
the next subsection has effect.

(5) In that case the office-holder—

    (a) is not liable to any person in respect of any loss or damage resulting from the seizure or disposal except in so far as that loss or damage is caused by the office-holder's own negligence, and
    (b) has a lien on the property, or the proceeds of its sale, for such expenses as were incurred in connection with the seizure or disposal."

10 Schedule 4 is modified so as to read as follows—

"SCHEDULE 4
POWERS OF LIQUIDATOR IN A WINDING UP

PART I
POWERS EXERCISABLE WITH SANCTION

1 Power to pay any class of creditors in full.

2 Power to make any compromise or arrangement with creditors or persons claiming to be creditors, or having or alleging themselves to have any claim (present or future, certain or contingent, ascertained or sounding only in damages) against the partnership, or whereby the partnership may be rendered liable.

3 Power to compromise, on such terms as may be agreed—

   (a) all debts and liabilities capable of resulting in debts, and all claims (present or future, certain or contingent, ascertained or sounding only in damages) subsisting or supposed to subsist between the partnership and a contributory or alleged contributory or other debtor or person apprehending liability to the partnership, and

   (b) all questions in any way relating to or affecting the partnership property or the winding up of the partnership,

and take any security for the discharge of any such debt, liability or claim and give a complete discharge in respect of it.

4 Power to bring or defend any action or other legal proceeding in the name and on behalf of any member of the partnership in his capacity as such or of the partnership.

5 Power to carry on the business of the partnership so far as may be necessary for its beneficial winding up.

PART II
POWERS EXERCISABLE WITHOUT SANCTION

6 Power to sell any of the partnership property by public auction or private contract, with power to transfer the whole of it to any person or to sell the same in parcels.

7 Power to do all acts and execute, in the name and on behalf of the partnership or of any member of the partnership in his capacity as such, all deeds, receipts and other documents.

8 Power to prove, rank and claim in the bankruptcy, insolvency or sequestration of any contributory for any balance against his estate, and to receive dividends in the bankruptcy, insolvency or sequestration in respect of that balance, as a separate debt due from the bankrupt or insolvent, and rateably with the other separate creditors.

9 Power to draw, accept, make and endorse any bill of exchange or promissory note in the name and on behalf of any member of the partnership in his capacity as such or of the partnership, with the same effect with respect to the liability of the partnership or of any member of the partnership in his capacity as such as if the bill or note had been drawn, accepted, made or endorsed in the course of the partnership's business.

10 Power to raise on the security of the partnership property any money requisite.

11 Power to take out in his official name letters of administration to any deceased contributory, and to do in his official name any other act necessary for obtaining payment of any money due from a contributory or his estate which cannot conveniently be done in the name of the partnership.

In all such cases the money due is deemed, for the purpose of enabling the liquidator to take out the letters of administration or recover the money, to be due to the liquidator himself.

12 Power to appoint an agent to do any business which the liquidator is unable to do himself.

13 Power to do all such other things as may be necessary for winding up the partnership's affairs and distributing its property."

SCHEDULE 4

PROVISIONS OF THE ACT WHICH APPLY WITH MODIFICATIONS FOR THE PURPOSES OF ARTICLE 8 TO WINDING UP OF INSOLVENT PARTNERSHIP ON CREDITOR'S PETITION WHERE CONCURRENT PETITIONS ARE PRESENTED AGAINST ONE OR MORE MEMBERS

PART I
MODIFIED PROVISION OF PART V OF THE ACT

1 (1) Sections 220 to 222 of the Act are set out as modified in Part I of this Schedule, and the provisions of the Act specified in sub-paragraph (2) below are set out as modified in Part II.

(2) The provisions referred to in sub-paragraph (1) are sections 117, 122 to 125, 131, 133, 136, 137, 139 to 141, 143, 146, 147, 168, 172, 174, 175, 189, 211, 230, 231, 234, 264, 265, 267, 268, 271, 283, 284, 288, 292 to 296, 298 to 303, 305, 314, 328, 331 and 356, and Schedule 4.

2 Section 220: Meaning of "unregistered company"

Section 220 is modified so as to read as follows—

"**220.** For the purposes of this Part, the expression "unregistered company" includes any insolvent partnership.".

3 Section 221: Winding up of unregistered companies

Section 221 is modified so as to read as follows—

"**221.**—(1) Subject to subsection (2) and (3) below and to the provisions of this Part, any insolvent partnership may be wound up under this Act if it has, or at any time had, in England and Wales either—

  (a) a principal place of business, or
  (b) a place of business at which business is or has been carried on in the course of which the debt (or part of the debt) arose which forms the basis of the petition for winding up the partnership.

(2) Subject to subsection (3) below, an insolvent partnership shall not be wound up under this Act if the business of the partnership has not been carried on in England and Wales at any time in the period of 3 years ending with the day on which the winding-up petition is presented.

(3) If an insolvent partnership has a principal place of business situated in Scotland or in Northern Ireland, the court shall not have jurisdiction to wind up the partnership unless it had a principal place of business in England and Wales—

(a) in the case of a partnership with a principal place of business in Scotland, at any time in the period of 1 year, or

(b) in the case of a partnership with a principal place of business in Northern Ireland, at any time in the period of 3 years,

ending with the day on which the winding-up petition is presented.

(4) No insolvent partnership shall be wound up under this Act voluntarily.

(5) To the extent that they are applicable to the winding up of a company by the court in England and Wales on a creditor's petition, all the provisions of this Act and the Companies Act about winding up apply to the winding up of an insolvent partnership as an unregistered company—

(a) with the exceptions and additions mentioned in the following subsections of this section, and

(b) with the modifications specified in Part II of Schedule 4 to the Insolvent Partnerships Order 1994.

(6) Sections 73(1), 74(2)(a) to (d) and (3), 75 to 78, 83, 154, 202, 203, 205 and 250 shall not apply.

(7) Unless the contrary intention appears, a member of a partnership against whom an insolvency order has been made by virtue of article 8 of the Insolvent Partnerships Order 1994 shall not be treated as a contributory for the purposes of this Act.

(8) The circumstance in which an insolvent partnership may be wound up as an unregistered company is that the partnership is unable to pay its debts.

(9) Every petition for the winding up of an insolvent partnership under Part V of this Act shall be verified by affidavit in Form 2 in Schedule 9 to the Insolvent Partnerships Order 1994.".

4 Section 222: Inability to pay debts: unpaid creditor for £750 or more

Section 222 is modified so as to read as follows—

"**222.**—(1) An insolvent partnership is deemed (for the purposes of section 221) unable to pay its debts if there is a creditor, by assignment or otherwise, to whom the partnership is indebted in a sum exceeding £750 then due and—

(a) the creditor has served on the partnership, in the manner specified in subsection (2) below, a written demand in Form 4 in Schedule 9 to the Insolvent Partnerships Order 1994 requiring the partnership to pay the sum so due,

(b) the creditor has also served on any one or more members or former members of the partnership liable to pay the sum due (in the case of a corporate member by leaving it at its registered office and in the case of an individual member by serving it in accordance with the rules) a demand in Form 4 in Schedule 9 to that Order, requiring that member or those members to pay the sum so due, and

(c) the partnership and its members have for 3 weeks after the service of the demands, or the service of the last of them if served at different times, neglected to pay the sum or to secure or compound for it to the creditor's satisfaction.

(2) Service of the demand referred to in subsection (1)(a) shall be effected—

(a) by leaving it at a principal place of business of the partnership in England and Wales, or

(b) by leaving it at a place of business of the partnership in England and Wales at which business is carried on in the course of which the debt (or part of the debt) referred to in subsection (1) arose, or

(c) by delivering it to an officer of the partnership, or

(d) by otherwise serving it in such manner as the court may approve or direct.

(3) The money sum for the time being specified in subsection (1) is subject to increase or reduction by regulations under section 417 in Part XV; but no increase in the sum so specified affects any case in which the winding-up petition was presented before the coming into force of the increase.".

PART II
OTHER MODIFIED PROVISIONS OF THE ACT ABOUT WINDING UP BY THE COURT AND BANKRUPTCY OF INDIVIDUALS

5 Sections 117 and 265: High Court and county court jurisdiction

Sections 117 and 265 are modified so as to read as follows—

"**117.**—(1) Subject to the provisions of this section, the High Court has jurisdiction to wind up any insolvent partnership as an unregistered company by virtue of article 8 of the Insolvent Partnerships Order 1994 if the partnership has, or at any time had, in England and Wales either—

(a) a principal place of business, or

(b) a place of business at which business is or has been carried on in the course of which the debt (or part of the debt) arose which forms the basis of the petition for winding up the partnership.

(2) Subject to subsections (3) and (4) below, a petition for the winding up of an insolvent partnership by virtue of the said article 8 may be presented to a county court in England and Wales if the partnership has, or at any time had, within the insolvency district of that court either—

(a) a principal place of business, or

(b) a place of business at which business is or has been carried on in the course of which the debt (or part of the debt) arose which forms the basis of the winding-up petition.

(3) Subject to subsection (4) below, the court only has jurisdiction to wind up an insolvent partnership if the business of the partnership has been carried on in England and Wales at any time in the period of 3 years ending with the day on which the petition for winding it up is presented.

(4) If an insolvent partnership has a principal place of business situated in Scotland or in Northern Ireland, the court shall not have jurisdiction to wind up the partnership unless it had a principal place of business in England and Wales—

(a) in the case of a partnership with a principal place of business in Scotland, at any time in the period of 1 year, or

(b) in the case of a partnership with a principal place of business in Northern Ireland, at any time in the period of 3 years,

ending with the day on which the petition for winding it up is presented.

(5) Subject to subsection (6) below, the court has jurisdiction to wind up a corporate member or former corporate member, or make a bankruptcy order against an individual member or former individual member, of a partnership against which a petition has been presented by virtue of article 8 of the Insolvent Partnerships Order 1994 if it has jurisdiction in respect of the partnership.

(6) Petitions by virtue of the said article 8 for the winding up of an insolvent partnership and the bankruptcy of one or more members or former members of that partnership may not be presented to a district registry of the High Court.

(7) The Lord Chancellor may by order in a statutory instrument exclude a county court from having winding-up jurisdiction, and for the purposes of that jurisdiction may attach its district, or any part thereof, to any other county court, and may by statutory instrument revoke or vary any such order.

In exercising the powers of this section, the Lord Chancellor shall provide that a county court is not to have winding-up jurisdiction unless it has for the time being jurisdiction for the purposes of Parts VIII to XI of this Act (individual insolvency).

(8) Every court in England and Wales having winding-up jurisdiction has for the purposes of that jurisdiction all the powers of the High Court; and every prescribed officer of the court shall perform any duties which an officer of the High Court may discharge by order of a judge of that court or otherwise in relation to winding up.".

6 Circumstances in which members of insolvent partnerships may be wound up or made bankrupt by the court: Section 122—corporate member Section 267—individual member

(a) Section 122 is modified so as to read as follows—

"**122.** A corporate member or former corporate member may be wound up by the court if it is unable to pay its debts.".

(b) Section 267 is modified so as to read as follows—

"**267.**—(1) Where a petition for the winding up of an insolvent partnership has been presented to the court by virtue of article 8 of the Insolvent Partnerships Order 1994, a creditor's petition against any individual member or former individual member of that partnership by virtue of that article must be in respect of one or more joint debts owed by the insolvent partnership, and the petitioning creditor or each of the petitioning creditors must be a person to whom the debt or (the case may be) at least one of the debts is owed.

(2) Subject to section 268, a creditor's petition may be presented to the court in respect of a joint debt or debts only if, at the time the petition is presented—

- (a) the amount of the debt, or the aggregate amount of the debts, is equal to or exceeds the bankruptcy level,
- (b) the debt, or each of the debts, is for a liquidated sum payable to the petitioning creditor, or one or more of the petitioning creditors, immediately, and is unsecured,
- (c) the debt, or each of the debts, is a debt for which the individual member or former member is liable and which he appears to be unable to pay, and
- (d) there is no outstanding application to set aside a statutory demand served (under section 268 below) in respect of the debt or any of the debts.

(3) "The bankruptcy level" is £750; but the Secretary of State may by order in a statutory instrument substitute any amount specified in the order for that amount or (as the case may be) for the amount which by virtue of such an order is for the time being the amount of the bankruptcy level.

(4) An order shall not be made under subsection (3) unless a draft of it has been laid before, and approved by a resolution of, each House of Parliament.".

7 Definition of inability to pay debts: Section 123—corporate member Section 268—individual member

(a) Section 123 is modified so as to read as follows—

"**123.**—(1) A corporate member or former member is deemed unable to pay its debts if there is a creditor, by assignment or otherwise, to whom the partnership is indebted in a sum exceeding £750 then due for which the member or former member is liable and—

(a) the creditor has served on that member or former member and the partnership, in the manner specified in subsection (2) below, a written demand in Form 4 in Schedule 9 to the Insolvent Partnerships Order 1994 requiring that member or former member and the partnership to pay the sum so due, and

(b) the corporate member or former member and the partnership have for 3 weeks after the service of the demands, or the service of the last of them if served at different times, neglected to pay the sum or to secure or compound for it to the creditor's satisfaction.

(2) Service of the demand referred to in subsection (1)(a) shall be effected, in the case of the corporate member or former corporate member, by leaving it at its registered office, and, in the case of the partnership—

(a) by leaving it at a principal place of business of the partnership in England and Wales, or

(b) by leaving it at a place of business of the partnership in England and Wales at which business is carried on in the course of which the debt (or part of the debt) referred to in subsection (1) arose, or

(c) by delivering it to an officer of the partnership, or

(d) by otherwise serving it in such manner as the court may approve or direct.

(3) The money sum for the time being specified in subsection (1) is subject to increase or reduction by order under section 416 in Part XV.".

(b) Section 268 is modified so as to read as follows—

"**268.**—(1) For the purposes of section 267(2)(c), an individual member or former individual member appears to be unable to pay a joint debt for which he is liable if the debt is payable immediately and the petitioning creditor to whom the insolvent partnership owes the joint debt has served—

(a) on the individual member or former individual member in accordance with the rules a demand (known as "the statutory demand"), in Form 4 in Schedule 9 to the Insolvent Partnerships Order 1994, and

(b) on the partnership in the manner specified in subsection (2) below a demand (known as "the written demand") in the same form,

requiring the member or former member and the partnership to pay the debt or to secure or compound for it to the creditor's satisfaction, and at least 3 weeks have elapsed since the service of the demands, or the service of the last of them if served at different times, and neither demand has been complied with nor the demand against the member set aside in accordance with the rules.

(2) Service of the demand referred to in subsection (1)(b) shall be effected—

(a) by leaving it as a principal place of business of the partnership in England and Wales, or

(b) by leaving it at a place of business of the partnership in England and Wales at which business is carried on in the course of which the debt (or part of the debt) referred to in subsection (1) arose, or

(c) by delivering it to an officer of the partnership, or

(d) by otherwise serving it in such manner as the court may approve or direct.".

8 Sections 124 and 264: Applications to wind up insolvent partnership and to wind up or bankrupt insolvent member

Sections 124 and 264 are modified so as to read as follows—

"**124.**—(1) An application to the court by virtue of article 8 of the Insolvent Partnerships Order 1994 for the winding up of an insolvent partnership as an unregistered company and the winding up or bankruptcy (as the case may be) of at least one of its members or former members shall—

(a) in the case of the partnership, be by petition in Form 5 in Schedule 9 to that Order,

(b) in the case of a corporate member or former corporate member, be by petition in Form 6 in that Schedule, and

(c) in the case of an individual member or former individual member, be by petition in Form 7 in that Schedule.

(2) Each of the pertitions mentioned in subsection (1) may be presented by any creditor or creditors to whom the partnership and the member or former member in question is indebted in respect of a liquidated sum payable immediately.

(3) The petitions mentioned in subsection (1)—

(a) shall all be presented to the same court and, except as the court otherwise permits or directs, on the same day, and

(b) except in the case of the petition mentioned in subsection (1)(c), shall be advertised in Form 8 in the said Schedule 9.

(4) At any time after presentation of a petition under this section the petitioner may, with the leave of the court obtained on application and on such terms as it thinks just, add other members or former members of the partnership as parties to the proceedings in relation to the insolvent partnership.

(5) Each petition presented under this section shall contain particulars of other petitions being presented in relation to the partnership, identifying the partnership and members concerned.

(6) The hearing of the petition against the partnership fixed by the court shall be in advance of the hearing of any petition against an insolvent member.

(7) On the day appointed for the hearing of the petition against the partnership, the petitioner shall, before the commencement of the hearing, hand to the court Form 9 in Schedule 9 to the Insolvent Partnerships Order 1994, duly completed.

(8) Any member of the partnership or any person against whom a winding-up or bankruptcy petition has been presented in relation to the insolvent partnership is entitled to appear and to be heard on any petition of the winding up of the partnership.

(9) A petitioner under this section may at the hearing withdraw a petition if—

(a) subject to subsection (10) below, he withdraws at the same time every other petition which he has presented under this section; and

    (b) he gives notice to the court at least 3 days before the date appointed for the hearing of the relevant petition of his intention to withdraw the petition.

(10) A petitioner need not comply with the provisions of subsection (9)(a) in the case of a petition against an insolvent member if the court is satisfied on application made to it by the petitioner that, because of difficulties in serving the petition or for any other reason, the continuance of that petition would be likely to prejudice or delay the proceedings on the petition which he has presented against the partnership or on any petition which he has presented against any other insolvent member.

(11) Where notice is given under subsection (9)(b), the court may, on such terms as it thinks just, substitute as petitioner, both in respect of the partnership and in respect of each insolvent member against whom a petition has been presented, any creditor of the partnership who in its opinion would have a right to present the petitions, and if the court makes such a substitution the petitions in question will not be withdrawn.

(12) Reference in subsection (11) to substitution of a petitioner includes reference to change of carriage of the petition in accordance with the rules.".

9 Sections 125 and 271: Powers of court on hearing of petitions against insolvent partnership and members

Sections 125 and 271 are modified so as to read as follows—

"**125.**—(1) Subject to the provisions of section 125A, on hearing a petition under section 124 against an insolvent partnership or any of its insolvent members, the court may dismiss it, or adjourn the hearing conditionally or unconditionally or make any other order that it thinks fit; but the court shall not refuse to make a winding-up order against the partnership or a corporate member on the ground only that the partnership property or (as the case may be) the member's assets have been mortgaged to an amount equal to or in excess of that property or those assets, or that the partnership has no property or the member no assets.

(2) An order under subsection (1) in respect of an insolvent partnership may contain directions as to the future conduct of any insolvency proceedings in existence against any insolvent member in respect of whom an insolvency order has been made.

Hearing of petitions against members

125A.—(1) On the hearing of a petition against an insolvent member the petitioner shall draw the court's attention to the result of the hearing of the winding-up petition against the partnership and the following subsections of this section shall apply.

(2) If the court has neither made a winding-up order, nor dismissed the winding-up petition, against the partnership the court may adjourn the hearing of the petition against the member until either event has occurred.

(3) Subject to subsection (4) below, if a winding-up order has been made against the partnership, the court may make a winding-up order against the corporate member in respect of which, or (as the case may be) a bankruptcy order against the individual member in respect of whom, the insolvency petition was presented.

(4) If no insolvency order is made under subsection (3) against any member within 28 days of the making of the winding-up order against the partnership, the proceedings against the partnership shall be conducted as if the winding-up petition against the partnership had been presented by virtue of article 7 of the Insolvent Partnerships Order 1994 and the proceedings against any member shall be conducted under this

Act without the modifications made by that Order (other than the modifications made to sections 168 and 303 by article 14).

(5) If the court has dismissed the winding-up petition against the partnership, the court may dismiss the winding-up petition against the corporate member or (as the case may be) the bankruptcy petition against the individual member. However, if an insolvency order is made against a member, the proceedings against that member shall be conducted under this Act without the modifications made by the Insolvent Partnerships Order 1994 (other than the modifications made to sections 168 and 303 of this Act by article 14 of that Order).

(6) The court may dismiss a petition against an insolvent member if it considers it just to do so because of a change in circumstances since the making of the winding-up order against the partnership.

(7) The court may dismiss a petition against an insolvent member who is a limited partner, if—

(a) the member lodges in court for the benefit of the creditors of the partnership sufficient money or security to the court's satisfaction to meet his liability for the debts and obligations of the partnership; or

(b) the member satisfies the court that he is no longer under any liability in respect of the debts and obligations of the partnership.

(8) Nothing in sections 125 and 125A or in sections 267 and 268 prejudices the power of the court, in accordance with the rules, to authorise a creditor's petition to be amended by the omission of any creditor or debt and to be proceeded with as if things done for the purposes of those sections had been done only by or in relation to the remaining creditors or debts.".

10 Sections 131 and 288: Statements of affairs—Insolvent partnerships; corporate members; individual members

Sections 131 and 288 are modified so as to read as follows—

"**131.**—(1) This section applies where the court has, by virtue of article 8 of the Insolvent Partnerships Order 1994—

(a) made a winding-up order or appointed a provisional liquidator in respect of an insolvent partnership, or

(b) made a winding-up order or appointed a provisional liquidator in respect of any corporate member of that partnership, or

(c) made a bankruptcy order in respect of any individual member of that partnership.

(2) The official receiver may require some or all of the persons mentioned in subsection (4) below to make out and submit to him a statement as to the affairs of the partnership or member in the prescribed form.

(3) The statement shall be verified by affidavit by the persons required to submit it and shall show—

(a) particulars of the debts and liabilities of the partnership or of the member (as the case may be), and of the partnership property and member's assets;

(b) the names and addresses of the creditors of the partnership or of the member (as the case may be);

(c) the securities held by them respectively;

(d) the dates when the securities were respectively given; and

(e) such further or other information as may be prescribed or as the official receiver may require.

(4) The persons referred to in subsection (2) are—

(a) those who are or have been officers of the partnership;
(b) those who are or have been officers of the corporate member;
(c) those who have taken part in the formation of the partnership or of the corporate member at any time within one year before the relevant date;
(d) those who are in the employment of the partnership or of the corporate member, or have been in such employment within that year, and are in the official receiver's opinion capable of giving the information required;
(e) those who are or have been within that year officers of, or in the employment of, a company which is, or within that year was, an officer of the partnership or an officer of the corporate member.

(5) Where any persons are required under this section to submit a statement of affairs to the official receiver, they shall do so (subject to the next subsection) before the end of the period of 21 days beginning with the day after that on which the prescribed notice of the requirement is given to them by the official receiver.

(6) The official receiver, if he thinks fit, may—

(a) at any time release a person from an obligation imposed on him under subsection (2) or (3) above; or
(b) either when giving the notice mentioned in subsection (5) or subsequently, extend the period so mentioned;

and where the official receiver has refused to exercise a power conferred by this subsection, the court, if it thinks fit, may exercise it.

(7) In this section—

"employment" includes employment under a contract for services; and
"the relevant date" means—
(a) in a case where a provisional liquidator is appointed, the date of his appointment; and
(b) in a case where no such appointment is made, the date of the winding-up order.

(8) Any person who without reasonable excuse fails to comply with any obligation imposed under this section (other than, in the case of an individual member, an obligation in respect of his own statement of affairs), is liable to a fine and, for continued contravention, to a daily default fine.

(9) An individual member who without reasonable excuse fails to comply with any obligation imposed under this section in respect of his own statement of affairs, is guilty of a contempt of court and liable to be punished accordingly (in addition to any other punishment to which he may be subject).".

11 Section 133: Public examination of officers of insolvent partnerships

Section 133 is modified so far as insolvent partnerships are concerned so as to read as follows—

"**133.**—(1) Where an insolvent partnership is being wound up by virtue of article 8 of the Insolvent Partnerships Order 1994, the official receiver may at any time before the winding up is complete apply to the court for the public examination of any person who—

(a) is or has been an officer of the partnership; or

(b) has acted as liquidator or administrator of the partnership or as receiver or manager or, in Scotland, receiver of its property;

(c) not being a person falling within paragraph (a) or (b), is or has been concerned, or has taken part, in the formation of the partnership.

(2) Unless the court otherwise orders, the official receiver shall make an application under subsection (1) if he is requested in accordance with the rules to do so by one-half, in value, of the creditors of the partnership.

(3) On an application under subsection (1), the court shall direct that a public examination of the person to whom the application relates shall be held on a day appointed by the court; and that person shall attend on that day and be publicly examined as to the formation or management of the partnership or as to the conduct of its business and affairs, or his conduct or dealings in relation to the partnership.

(4) The following may take part in the public examination of a person under this section and may question that person concerning the matters mentioned in subsection (3), namely—

(a) the official receiver;

(b) the liquidator of the partnership;

(c) any person who has been appointed as special manager of the partnership's property or business;

(d) any creditor of the partnership who has tendered a proof in the winding up.

(5) On an application under subsection (1), the court may direct that the public examination of any person under this section in relation to the affairs of an insolvent partnership be combined with the public examination of any person under this Act in relation to the affairs of a corporate member of that partnership against which, or an individual member of the partnership against whom, an insolvency order has been made.".

12 Sections 136, 293 and 294: Functions of official receiver in relation to office of responsible insolvency practitioner

Sections 136, 293 and 294 are modified so as to read as follows—

"**136.**—(1) The following provisions of this section and of section 136A have effect, subject to section 140 below, where insolvency orders are made in respect of an insolvent partnership and one or more of its insolvent members by virtue of article 8 of the Insolvent Partnerships Order 1994.

(2) The official receiver, by virtue of his office, becomes the responsible insolvency practitioner of the partnership and of any insolvent member and continues in office until another person becomes responsible insolvency practitioner under the provisions of this Part.

(3) The official receiver is, by virtue of his office, the responsible insolvency practitioner of the partnership and of any insolvent member during any vacancy.

(4) At any time when he is the responsible insolvency practitioner of the insolvent partnership and of any insolvent member, the official receiver may summon a combined meeting of the creditors of the partnership and the creditors of such member, for the purpose of choosing a person to be responsible insolvency practitioner in place of the official receiver.

Duty of official receiver to summon meetings

136A.—(1) It is the duty of the official receiver—

(a) as soon as practicable in the period of 12 weeks beginning with the day on which the insolvency order was made against the partnership, to decide whether to exercise his power under section 136(4) to summon a meeting, and

(b) if in pursuance of paragraph (a) he decides not to exercise that power, to give notice of his decision, before the end of that period, to the court and to the creditors of the partnership and the creditors of any insolvent member against who an insolvency order has been made, and

(c) (whether or not he has decided to exercise that power) to exercise his power to summon a meeting under section 136(4) if he is at any time requested to do so in accordance with the rules by one-quarter, in value, of either—

    (i) the partnership's creditors, or

    (ii) the creditors of any insolvent member against whom an insolvency order has been made,

and accordingly, where the duty imposed by paragraph (c) arises before the official receiver has performed a duty imposed by paragraph (a) or (b), he is not required to perform the latter duty.

(2) A notice given under subsection (1)(b) to the creditors shall contain an explanation of the creditors' power under subsection (1)(c) to require the official receiver to summon a combined meeting of the creditors of the partnership and of any insolvent member.

(3) If the official receiver, in pursuance of subsection (1)(a), has decided to exercise his power under section 136(4) to summon a meeting, he shall hold that meeting in the period of 4 months beginning with the day on which the insolvency order was made against the partnership.

(4) If (whether or not he has decided to exercise that power) the official receiver is requested, in accordance with the provisions of subsection (1)(c), to exercise his power under section 136(4) to summon a meeting, he shall hold that meeting in accordance with the rules.

(5) Where a meeting of creditors of the partnership and of any insolvent member has been held under section 136(4), and an insolvency order is subsequently made against a further insolvent member by virtue of article 8 of the Insolvent Partnerships Order 1994—

(a) any person chosen at that meeting to be responsible insolvency practitioner in place of the official receiver shall also be the responsible insolvency practitioner of the member against whom the subsequent order is made, and

(b) subsection (1) of this section shall not apply.".

13 Sections 137, 295, 296 and 300: Appointment of responsible insolvency practitioner by Secretary of State

Sections 137, 295, 296 and 300 are modified so as to read as follows—

"**137.**—(1) This section and the next apply where the court has made insolvency orders in respect of an insolvent partnership and one or more of its insolvent members by virtue of article 8 of the Insolvent Partnerships Order 1994.

(2) The official receiver may, at any time when he is the responsible insolvency practitioner of the partnership and of any insolvent member, apply to the Secretary of State for the appointment of a person as responsible insolvency practitioner of both the partnership and of such member in his place.

(3) If a meeting is held in pursuance of a decision under section 136A(1)(a), but no person is chosen to be responsible insolvency practitioner as a result of that meeting, it is the duty of the official receiver to decide whether to refer the need for an appointment to the Secretary of State.

Consequences of section 137 application

137A.—(1) On an application under section 137(2), or a reference made in pursuance of a decision under section 137(3), the Secretary of State shall either make an appointment or decline to make one.

(2) If on an application under section 137(2), or a reference made in pursuance of a decision under section 137(3), no appointment is made, the official receiver shall continue to be responsible insolvency practitioner of the partnership and its insolvent member or members, but without prejudice to his power to make a further application or reference.

(3) Where a responsible insolvency practitioner has been appointed by the Secretary of State under subsection (1) of this section, and an insolvency order is subsequently made against a further insolvent member by virtue of article 8 of the Insolvent Partnerships Order 1994, then the practitioner so appointed shall also be the responsible insolvency practitioner of the member against whom the subsequent order is made.

(4) Where a responsible insolvency practitioner has been appointed by the Secretary of State under subsection (1), or has become responsible insolvency practitioner of a further insolvent member under subsection (3), that practitioner shall give notice of his appointment or further appointment (as the case may be) to the creditors of the insolvent partnership and the creditors of the insolvent member or members against whom insolvency orders have been made or, if the court so allows, shall advertise his appointment in accordance with the direction of the court.

(5) Subject to subsection (6) below, in that notice or advertisement the responsible insolvency practitioner shall—

    (a) state whether he proposes to summon, under section 141 below, a combined meeting of the creditors of the insolvent partnership and of the insolvent member or members against whom insolvency orders have been made, for the purpose of determining whether a creditors' committee should be established under that section, and

    (b) if he does not propose to summon such a meeting, set out the power under that section of the creditors of the partnership and of the insolvent member or members to require him to summon one.

(6) Where in a case where subsection (3) applies a meeting has already been held under section 141 below, the responsible insolvency practitioner shall state in the notice or advertisement whether a creditors' committee was established at that meeting and—

    (a) if such a committee was established, shall state whether he proposes to appoint additional members of the committee under section 141A(3), and

    (b) if such a committee was not established, shall set out the power under section 141 of the creditors of the partnership and of the insolvent member or members to require him to summon a meeting for the purpose of determining whether a creditors' committee should be established under that section.".

14 Section 139: Rules applicable to meetings of creditors

Section 139 is modified so as to read as follows—

"**139.**—(1) This section applies where the court has made insolvency orders against an insolvent partnership and one or more of its insolvent members by virtue of article 8 of the Insolvent Partnerships Order 1994.

(2) Subject to subsection (4) below, the rules relating to the requisitioning, summoning, holding and conducting of meetings on the winding up of a company are to apply (with the necessary modifications) to the requisitioning, summoning, holding and conducting of—

(a) separate meetings of the creditors of the partnership or of any corporate member against which an insolvency order has been made, and

(b) combined meetings of the creditors of the partnership and the creditors of the insolvent member or members.

(3) Subject to subsection (4) below, the rules relating to the requisitioning, summoning, holding and conducting of meetings on the bankruptcy of an individual are to apply (with the necessary modifications) to the requisitioning, summoning, holding and conducting of separate meetings of the creditors of any individual member against whom an insolvency order has been made.

(4) Any combined meeting of creditors shall be conducted as if the creditors of the partnership and of the insolvent member or members were a single set of creditors.".

15 Section 140: Appointment by the court following administration or voluntary arrangement

Section 140 is modified so as to read as follows—

"**140.**—(1) This section applies where insolvency orders are made in respect of an insolvent partnership and one or more of its insolvent members by virtue of article 8 of the Insolvent Partnerships Order 1994.

(2) Where the orders referred to in subsection (1) are made immediately upon the discharge of an administration order in respect of the partnership, the court may appoint as responsible insolvency practitioner the person who has ceased on the discharge of the administration order to be the administrator of the partnership.

(3) Where the orders referred to in subsection (1) are made at a time when there is a supervisor of a voluntary arrangement approved in relation to the partnership under Part I, the court may appoint as responsible insolvency practitioner the person who is the supervisor at the time when the winding-up order against the partnership is made.

(4) Where the court makes an appointment under this section, the official receiver does not become the responsible insolvency practitioner as otherwise provided by section 136(2), and he has no duty under section 136A(1)(a) or (b) in respect of the summoning of creditors' meetings.".

16 Sections 141, 301 and 302: Creditors' Committee: Insolvent partnership and members

Sections 141, 301 and 302 are modified so as to read as follows—

"**141.**—(1) This section applies where—

(a) insolvency orders are made in respect of an insolvent partnership and one or more of its insolvent members by virtue of article 8 of the Insolvent Partnerships Order 1994, and

(b) a combined meeting of creditors has been summoned for the purpose of choosing a person to be responsible insolvency practitioner of the partnership and of any such insolvent member or members.

(2) The meeting of creditors may establish a committee ('the creditors' committee') which shall consist of creditors of the partnership or creditors of any insolvent member against whom an insolvency order has been made, or both.

(3) The responsible insolvency practitioner of the partnership and of its insolvent member or members (not being the official receiver) may at any time, if he thinks fit, summon a combined general meeting of the creditors of the partnership and of such member or members for the purpose of determining whether a creditors' committee should be established and, if it is so determined, of establishing it.

The responsible insolvency practitioner (not being the official receiver) shall summon such a meeting if he is requested, in accordance with the rules, to do so by one-tenth, in value, of either—

(a) the partnership's creditors, or
(b) the creditors of any insolvent member against whom an insolvency order has been made.

Functions and membership of creditors' committee

141A.—(1) The committee established under section 141 shall act as liquidation committee for the partnership and for any corporate member against which an insolvency order has been made, and as creditors' committee for any individual member against whom an insolvency order has been made, and shall as appropriate exercise the functions conferred on liquidation and creditors' committees in a winding up or bankruptcy by or under this Act.

(2) The rules relating to liquidation committees are to apply (with the necessary modifications and with the exclusion of all references to contributories) to a committee established under section 141.

(3) Where the appointment of the responsible insolvency practitioner also takes effect in relation to a further insolvent member under section 136A(5) or 137A(3), the practitioner may appoint any creditor of that member (being qualified under the rules to be a member of the committee) to be an additional member of any creditors' committee already established under section 141, provided that the creditor concerned consents to act.

(4) The court may at any time, on application by a creditor of the partnership or of any insolvent member against whom an insolvency order has been made, appoint additional members of the creditors' committee.

(5) If additional members of the creditors' committee are appointed under subsection (3) or (4), the limit on the maximum number of members of the committee specified in the rules shall be increased by the number of additional members so appointed.

(6) The creditors' committee is not to be able or required to carry out its functions at any time when the official receiver is responsible insolvency practitioner of the partnership and of its insolvent member or members; but at any such time its functions are vested in the Secretary of State except to the extent that the rules otherwise provide.

(7) Where there is for the time being no creditors' committee, and the responsible insolvency practitioner is a person other than the official receiver, the functions of

such a committee are vested in the Secretary of State except to the extent that the rules otherwise provide.".

17 Sections 143, 168(4) and 305: General functions of responsible insolvency practitioner

Sections 143, 168(4) and 305 are modified so as to read as follows—

"**143.**—(1) The functions of the responsible insolvency practitioner of an insolvent partnership and of its insolvent member or members against whom insolvency orders have been made by virtue of article 8 of the Insolvent Partnerships Order 1994, are to secure that the partnership property and the assets of any such corporate member, and the estate of any such individual member, are got in, realised and distributed to their respective creditors and, if there is a surplus of such property or assets or in such estate, to the persons entitled to it.

(2) In the carrying out of those functions, and in the management of the partnership property and of the assets of any corporate member and of the estate of any individual member, the responsible insolvency practitioner is entitled, subject to the provisions of this Act, to use his own discretion.

(3) It is the duty of the responsible insolvency practitioner, if he is not the official receiver—

(a) to furnish the official receiver with such information,
(b) to produce to the official receiver, and permit inspection by the official receiver of, such books, papers and other records, and
(c) to give the official receiver such other assistance,

as the official receiver may reasonably require for the purposes of carrying out his functions in relation to the winding up of the partnership and any corporate member or the bankruptcy of any individual member.

(4) The official name of the responsible insolvency practitioner in his capacity as trustee of an individual member shall be "the trustee of the estate of . . ., a bankrupt" (inserting the name of the individual member); but he may be referred to as "the trustee in bankruptcy" of the particular member.".

18 Sections 146 and 331: Duty to summon final meeting of creditors

Sections 146 and 331 are modified so as to read as follows—

"**146.**—(1) This section applies, subject to subsection (3) of this section and section 332 below, if it appears to the responsible insolvency practitioner of an insolvent partnership which is being wound up by virtue of article 8 of the Insolvent Partnerships Order 1994 and of its insolvent member or members that the winding up of the partnership or of any corporate member, or the administration of any individual member's estate, is for practical purposes complete and the practitioner is not the official receiver.

(2) The responsible insolvency practitioner shall summon a final general meeting of the creditors of the partnership or of the insolvent member or members (as the case may be) or a combined final general meeting of the creditors of the partnership and of the insolvent member or members which—

(a) shall as appropriate receive the practitioner's report of the winding up of the insolvent partnership or of any corporate member or of the administration of the estate of any individual member, and

(b) shall determine whether the practitioner should have his release under section 174 in Chapter VII of this Part in respect of the winding up of the partnership or of the corporate member, or the administration of the individual member's estate (as the case may be).

(3) The responsible insolvency practitioner may, if he thinks fit, give the notice summoning the final general meeting at the same time as giving notice of any final distribution of the partnership property or the property of the insolvent member or members; but, if summoned for an earlier date, that meeting shall be adjourned (and, if necessary, further adjourned) until a date on which the practitioner is able to report to the meeting that the winding up of the partnership or of any corporate member, or the administration of any individual member's estate, is for practical purposes complete.

(4) In the carrying out of his functions in the winding up of the partnership and of any corporate member and the administration of any individual member's estate, it is the duty of the responsible insolvency practitioner to retain sufficient sums from the partnership property and the property of any such insolvent member to cover the expenses of summoning and holding any meeting required by this section.".

19 Section 147: Power of court to stay proceedings

Section 147 is modified, so far as insolvent partnerships are concerned, so as to read as follows—

"**147.**—(1) The court may, at any time after an order has been made by virtue of article 8 of the Insolvent Partnerships Order 1994 for winding up an insolvent partnership, on the application either of the responsible insolvency practitioner or the official receiver or any creditor or contributory, and on proof to the satisfaction of the court that all proceedings in the winding up of the partnership ought to be stayed, make an order staying the proceedings, either altogether or for a limited time, on such terms and conditions as the court thinks fit.

(2) If, in the course of hearing an insolvency petition presented against a member of an insolvent partnership, the court is satisfied that an application has been or will be made under subsection (1) in respect of a winding-up order made against the partnership, the court may adjourn the petition against the insolvent member, either conditionally or unconditionally.

(3) Where the court makes an order under subsection (1) staying all proceedings on the order for winding up an insolvent partnership—

(a) the court may, on hearing any insolvency petition presented against an insolvent member of the partnership, dismiss the petition; and
(b) if any insolvency order has already been made by virtue of article 8 of the Insolvent Partnerships Order 1994 in relation to an insolvent member of the partnership, the court may make an order annulling or rescinding that insolvency order, or may make any other order that it thinks fit.

(4) The court may, before making any order under this section, require the official receiver to furnish to it a report with respect to any facts or matters which are in his opinion relevant to the application.".

20 Sections 168, 303 and 314(7): Supplementary powers of responsible insolvency practitioner

Sections 168(1) to (3) and (5), 303 and 314(7) are modified so as to read as follows—

"**168.**—(1) This section applies where the court has made insolvency orders in respect of an insolvent partnership and one or more of its insolvent members by virtue of article 8 of the Insolvent Partnerships Order 1994.

(2) The responsible insolvency practitioner of the partnership and of such member or members may at any time summon either separate or combined general meetings of—

(a) the creditors or contributories of the partnership, and
(b) the creditors or contributories of the member or members,

for the purpose of ascertaining their wishes.

(3) It is the duty of the responsible insolvency practitioner—

(a) to summon separate meetings at such times as the creditors of the partnership or of the member (as the case may be), or the contributories of any corporate member, by resolution (either at the meeting appointing the responsible insolvency practitioner or otherwise) may direct, or whenever requested in writing to do so by one-tenth in value of such creditors or contributories (as the case may be); and
(b) to summon combined meetings at such times as the creditors of the partnership and of the member or members by resolution (either at the meeting appointing the responsible insolvency practitioner or otherwise) may direct, or whenever requested in writing to do so by one-tenth in value of such creditors.

(4) The responsible insolvency practitioner may apply to the court (in the prescribed manner) for directions in relation to any particular matter arising in the winding up of the insolvent partnership or in the winding up or bankruptcy of an insolvent member.

(5) If any person is aggrieved by an act or decision of the responsible insolvency practitioner, that person may apply to the court; and the court may confirm, reverse or modify the act or decision complained of, and make such order in the case as it thinks just.".

21 Sections 172 and 298: Removal etc. of responsible insolvency practitioner or of provisional liquidator

Sections 172 and 298 are modified so as to read as follows—

"**172.**—(1) This applies with respect to the removal from office and vacation of office of—

(a) the responsible insolvency practitioner of an insolvent partnership which is being wound up by virtue of article 8 of the Insolvent Partnerships Order 1994 and of its insolvent member or members against whom insolvency orders have been made, or
(b) a provisional liquidator of an insolvent partnership, and of any corporate member of that partnership, against which a winding-up petition is presented by virtue of that article,

and, subject to subsections (6) and (7) below, any removal from or vacation of office under this section relates to all offices held in the proceedings relating to the partnership.

(2) Subject as follows, the responsible insolvency practitioner or provisional liquidator may be removed from office only by an order of the court.

(3) If appointed by the Secretary of State, the responsible insolvency practitioner may be removed from office by a direction of the Secretary of State.

(4) A responsible insolvency practitioner or provisional liquidator, not being the official receiver, shall vacate office if he ceases to be a person who is qualified to act as an insolvency practitioner in relation to the insolvent partnership or any insolvent member of it against whom an insolvency order has been made.

(5) The responsible insolvency practitioner may, with the leave of the court (or, if appointed by the Secretary of State, with the leave of the court or the Secretary of State), resign his office by giving notice of his resignation to the court.

(6) Where a final meeting has been held under section 146 (final meeting of creditors of insolvent partnership or of insolvent members), the responsible insolvency practitioner whose report was considered at the meeting shall vacate office as liquidator of the insolvent partnership or of any corporate member or as trustee of the estate of any individual member (as the case may be) as soon as he has given notice to the court (and, in the case of a corporate member, to the registrar of companies) that the meeting has been held and of the decisions (if any) of the meeting.

(7) The responsible insolvency practitioner shall vacate office as trustee of the estate of an individual member if the insolvency order against that member is annulled.".

22 Sections 174 and 299: Release of responsible insolvency practitioner or of provisional liquidator

Sections 174 and 299 are modified so as to read as follows—

"**174.**—(1) This section applies with respect to the release of—

(a) the responsible insolvency practitioner of an insolvent partnership which is being wound up by virtue of article 8 to the Insolvent Partnerships Order 1994 and of its insolvent member or members against whom insolvency orders have been made, or

(b) a provisional liquidator of an insolvent partnership, and of any corporate member of that partnership, against which a winding-up petition is presented by virtue of that article.

(2) Where the official receiver has ceased to be the responsible insolvency practitioner and a person is appointed in his stead, the official receiver has his release with effect from the following time, that is to say—

(a) in a case where that person was nominated by a combined general meeting of creditors of the partnership and of any insolvent member or members, or was appointed by the Secretary of State, the time at which the official receiver gives notice to the court that he has been replaced;

(b) in a case where that person is appointed by the court, such time as the court may determine.

(3) If the official receiver while he is a responsible insolvency practitioner gives notice to the Secretary of State that the winding up of the partnership or of any corporate member or the administration of the estate of any individual member is for practical purposes complete, he has his release as liquidator or trustee (as the case may be) with effect from such time as the Secretary of State may determine.

(4) A person other than the official receiver who has ceased to be a responsible insolvency practitioner has his release with effect from the following time, that is to say—

(a) in the case of a person who has died, the time at which notice is given to the court in accordance with the rules that that person has ceased to hold office;

(b) in the case of a person who has been removed from office by the court or by the Secretary of State, or who has vacated office under section 172(4), such time as the Secretary of State may, on an application by that person, determine;

(c) in the case of a person who has resigned, such time as may be directed by the court (or, if he was appointed by the Secretary of State, such time as may be directed by the court or as the Secretary of State may, on an application by that person, determine);

(d) in the case of a person who has vacated office under section 172(6)—

(i) if the final meeting referred to in that subsection has resolved against that person's release, such time as the Secretary of State may, on an application by that person, determine, and

(ii) if that meeting has not so resolved, the time at which that person vacated office.

(5) A person who has ceased to hold office as a provisional liquidator has his release with effect from such time as the court may, on an application by him, determine.

(6) Where a bankruptcy order in respect of an individual member is annulled, the responsible insolvency practitioner at the time of the annulment has his release with effect from such time as the court may determine.

(7) Where the responsible insolvency practitioner or provisional liquidator (including in both cases the official receiver when so acting) has his release under this section, he is, with effect from the time specified in the preceding provisions of this section, discharged from all liability both in respect of acts or omissions of his in the winding up of the insolvent partnership or any corporate member or the administration of the estate of any individual member (as the case may be) and otherwise in relation to his conduct as responsible insolvency practitioner or provisional liquidator.

But nothing in this section prevents the exercise, in relation to a person who has had his release under this section, of the court's powers under section 212 (summary remedy against delinquent directors, liquidators, etc.) or section 304 (liability of trustee).".

23 Sections 175 and 328: Priority of expenses and debts

Sections 175 and 328(1) to (3) and (6) are modified so as to read as follows—

"Priority of expenses

175.—(1) The provisions of this section shall apply in a case where article 8 of the Insolvent Partnerships Order 1994 applies, as regards priority of expenses incurred by a responsible insolvency practitioner of an insolvent partnership, and of any insolvent member of that partnership against whom an insolvency order has been made.

(2) The joint estate of the partnership shall be applicable in the first instance in payment of the joint expenses and the separate estate of each insolvent member shall be applicable in the first instance in payment of the separate expenses relating to that member.

(3) Where the joint estate is insufficient for the payment in full of the joint expenses, the unpaid balance shall be apportioned equally between the separate estates of the insolvent members against whom insolvency orders have been made and shall form part of the expenses to be paid out of those estates.

(4) Where any separate estate of an insolvent member is insufficient for the payment in full of the separate expenses to be paid out of that estate, the unpaid balance shall form part of the expenses to be paid out of the joint estate.

(5) Where after the transfer of any unpaid balance in accordance with subsection (3) or (4) any estate is insufficient for the payment in full of the expenses to be paid out of that estate, the balance then remaining unpaid shall be apportioned equally between the other estates.

(6) Where after an apportionment under subsection (5) one or more estates are insufficient for the payment in full of the expenses to be paid out of those estates, the total of the unpaid balances of the expenses to be paid out of those estates shall continue to be apportioned equally between the other estates until provision is made for the payment in full of the expenses or there is no estate available for the payment of the balance finally remaining unpaid, in which case it abates in equal proportions between all the estates.

(7) Without prejudice to subsections (3) to (6) above, the responsible insolvency practitioner may, with the sanction of any creditors' committee established under section 141 or with the leave of the court obtained on application—

- (a) pay out of the joint estate as part of the expenses to be paid out of that estate any expenses incurred for any separate estate of an insolvent member; or
- (b) pay out of any separate estate of an insolvent member any part of the expenses incurred for the joint estate which affects that separate estate.

Priority of debts in joint estate

175A.—(1) The provisions of this section and the next (which are subject to the provisions of section 9 of the Partnership Act 1890 as respects the liability of the estate of a deceased member) shall apply as regards priority of debts in a case where article 8 of the Insolvent Partnerships Order 1994 applies.

(2) After payment of expenses in accordance with section 175 and subject to section 175C(2), the joint debts of the partnership shall be paid out of its joint estate in the following order of priority—

- (a) the preferential debts;
- (b) the debts which are neither preferential debts nor postponed debts;
- (c) interest under section 189 on the joint debts (other than postponed debts);
- (d) the postponed debts;
- (e) interest under section 189 on the postponed debts.

(3) The responsible insolvency practitioner shall adjust the rights among themselves of the members of the partnership as contributories and shall distribute any surplus to the members or, where applicable, to the separate estates of the members, according to their respective rights and interests in it.

(4) The debts referred to in each of paragraphs (a) and (b) of subsection (2) rank equally between themselves, and in each case if the joint estate is insufficient for meeting them, they abate in equal proportions between themselves.

(5) Where the joint estate is not sufficient for the payment of the joint debts in accordance with paragraphs (a) and (b) of subsection (2), the responsible insolvency practitioner shall aggregate the value of those debts to the extent that they have not been satisfied or are not capable of being satisfied, and that aggregate amount shall be

a claim against the separate estate of each member of the partnership against whom an insolvency order has been made which—

(a) shall be a debt provable by the responsible insolvency practitioner in each such estate, and

(b) shall rank equally with the debts of the member referred to in section 175B(1)(b) below.

(6) Where the joint estate is sufficient for the payment of the joint debts in accordance with paragraphs (a) and (b) of subsection (2) but not for the payment of interest under paragraph (c) of that subsection, the responsible insolvency practitioner shall aggregate the value of that interest to the extent that it has not been satisfied or is not capable of being satisfied, and that aggregate amount shall be a claim against the separate estate of each member of the partnership against whom an insolvency order has been made which—

(a) shall be a debt provable by the responsible insolvency practitioner in each such estate, and

(b) shall rank equally with the interest on the separate debts referred to in section 175B(1)(c) below.

(7) Where the joint estate is not sufficient for the payment of the postponed joint debts in accordance with paragraph (d) of subsection (2), the responsible insolvency practitioner shall aggregate the value of those debts to the extent that they have not been satisfied or are not capable of being satisfied, and that aggregate amount shall be a claim against the separate estate of each member of the partnership against whom an insolvency order has been made which—

(a) shall be a debt provable by the responsible insolvency practitioner in each such estate, and

(b) shall rank equally with the postponed debts of the member referred to in section 175B(1)(d) below.

(8) Where the joint estate is sufficient for the payment of the postponed joint debts in accordance with paragraph (d) of subsection (2) but not for the payment of interest under paragraph (e) of that subsection, the responsible insolvency practitioner shall aggregate the value of that interest to the extent that it has not been satisfied or is not capable of being satisfied, and that aggregate amount shall be a claim against the separate estate of each member of the partnership against whom an insolvency order has been made which—

(a) shall be a debt provable by the responsible insolvency practitioner in each such estate, and

(b) shall rank equally with the interest on the postponed debts referred to in section 175B(1)(e) below.

(9) Where the responsible insolvency practitioner receives any distribution from the separate estate of a member in respect of a debt referred to in paragraph (a) of subsection (5), (6), (7) or (8) above, that distribution shall become part of the joint estate and shall be distributed in accordance with the order of priority set out in subsection (2) above.

Priority of debts in separate estate

175B.—(1) The separate estate of each member of the partnership against whom an insolvency order has been made shall be applicable, after payment of expenses in accordance with section 175 and subject to section 175C(2) below, in payment of the separate debts of that member in the following order of priority—

    (a) the preferential debts;

    (b) the debts which are neither preferential debts nor postponed debts (including any debt referred to in section 175A(5)(a));

    (c) interest under section 189 on the separate debts and under section 175A(6);

    (d) the postponed debts of the member (including any debt referred to in section 175A(7)(a));

    (e) interest under section 189 on the postponed debts of the member and under section 175A(8).

(2) The debts referred to in each of paragraphs (a) and (b) of subsection (1) rank equally between themselves, and in each case if the separate estate is insufficient for meeting them, they abate in equal proportions between themselves.

(3) Where the responsible insolvency practitioner receives any distribution from the joint estate or from the separate estate of another member of the partnership against whom an insolvency order has been made, that distribution shall become part of the separate estate and shall be distributed in accordance with the order of priority set out in subsection (1) of this section.

Provisions generally applicable in distribution of joint and separate estates

175C.—(1) Distinct accounts shall be kept of the joint estate of the partnership and of the separate estate of each member of that partnership against whom an insolvency order is made.

(2) No member of the partnership shall prove for a joint or separate debt in competition with the joint creditors, unless the debt has arisen—

    (a) as a result of fraud, or

    (b) in the ordinary course of a business carried on separately from the partnership business.

(3) For the purpose of establishing the value of any debt referred to in section 175A(5)(a) or (7)(a), that value may be estimated by the responsible insolvency practitioner in accordance with section 322 or (as the case may be) in accordance with the rules.

(4) Interest under section 189 on preferential debts ranks equally with interest on debts which are neither preferential debts nor postponed debts.

(5) Sections 175A and 175B are without prejudice to any provision of this Act or of any other enactment concerning the ranking between themselves of postponed debts and interest thereon, but in the absence of any such provision postponed debts and interest thereon rank equally between themselves.

(6) If any two or more members of an insolvent partnership constitute a separate partnership, the creditors of such separate partnership shall be deemed to be a separate set of creditors and subject to the same statutory provisions as the separate creditors of any member of the insolvent partnership.

(7) Where any surplus remains after the administration of the estate of a separate partnership, the surplus shall be distributed to the members or, where applicable, to the separate estates of the members of that partnership according to their respective rights and interests in it.

(8) Neither the official receiver, the Secretary of State nor a responsible insolvency practitioner shall be entitled to remuneration or fees under the Insolvency Rules 1986, the Insolvency Regulations 1986 or the Insolvency Fees Order 1986 for his services in connection with—

(a) the transfer of a surplus from the joint estate to a separate estate under section 175A(3),
(b) a distribution from a separate estate to the joint estate in respect of a claim referred to in section 175A(5), (6), (7) or (8), or
(c) a distribution from the estate of a separate partnership to the separate estates of the members of that partnership under subsection (7) above.".

24 Sections 189 and 328: Interest on debts

Sections 189 and 328(4) and (5) are modified so as to read as follows—

"**189.**—(1) In the winding up of an insolvent partnership or the winding up or bankruptcy (as the case may be) of any of its insolvent members interest is payable in accordance with this section, in the order of priority laid down by sections 175A and 175B, on any debt proved in the winding up or bankruptcy, including so much of any such debt as represents interest on the remainder.

(2) Interest under this section is payable on the debts in question in respect of the periods during which they have been outstanding since the winding-up order was made against the partnership or any corporate member (as the case may be) or the bankruptcy order was made against any individual member.

(3) The rate of interest payable under this section in respect of any debt ('the official rate' for the purposes of any provision of this Act in which that expression is used) is whichever is the greater of—

(a) the rate specified in section 17 of the Judgments Act 1838 on the day on which the winding-up or bankruptcy order (as the case may be) was made, and
(b) the rate applicable to that debt apart from the winding up or bankruptcy.".

25 Sections 211 and 356: False representations to creditors

Sections 211 and 356(2)(d) are modified so as to read as follows—

"**211.**—(1) This section applies where insolvency orders are made against an insolvent partnership and any insolvent member or members of it by virtue of article 8 of the Insolvent Partnerships Order 1994.

(2) Any person, being a past or present officer of the partnership or a past or present officer (which for these purposes includes a shadow director) of a corporate member against which an insolvency order has been made—

(a) commits an offence if he makes any false representation or commits any other fraud for the purpose of obtaining the consent of the creditors of the partnership (or any of them) or of the creditors of any of its members (or any of such creditors) to an agreement with reference to the affairs of the partnership or of any of its members or to the winding up of the partnership or of a corporate member, or the bankruptcy of an individual member, and
(b) is deemed to have committed that offence if, prior to the winding up or bankruptcy (as the case may be), he has made any false representation, or committed any other fraud, for that purpose.

(3) A person guilty of an offence under this section is liable to imprisonment or a fine, or both.".

26 Sections 230, 231 and 292: Appointment to office of responsible insolvency practitioner or provisional liquidator

Sections 230, 231 and 292 are modified so as to read as follows—

"**230.**—(1) This section applies with respect to the appointment of—

    (a) the responsible insolvency practitioner of an insolvent partnership which is being wound up by virtue of article 8 of the Insolvent Partnerships Order 1994 and of one or more of its insolvent members, or

    (b) a provisional liquidator of an insolvent partnership, or of any of its corporate members, against which a winding-up petition is presented by virtue of that article,

but is without prejudice to any enactment under which the official receiver is to be, or may be, responsible insolvency practitioner or provisional liquidator.

(2) No person may be appointed as responsible insolvency practitioner unless he is, at the time of the appointment, qualified to act as an insolvency practitioner both in relation to the insolvent partnership and to the insolvent member or members.

(3) No person may be appointed as provisional liquidator unless he is, at the time of the appointment, qualified to act as an insolvency practitioner both in relation to the insolvent partnership and to any corporate member in respect of which he is appointed.

(4) If the appointment or nomination of any person to the office of responsible insolvency practitioner or provisional liquidator relates to more than one person, or has the effect that the office is to be held by more than one person, then subsection (5) below applies.

(5) The appointment or nomination shall declare whether any act required or authorised under any enactment to be done by the responsible insolvency practitioner or by the provisional liquidator is to be done by all or any one or more of the persons for the time being holding the office in question.

(6) The appointment of any person as responsible insolvency practitioner takes effect only if that person accepts the appointment in accordance with the rules. Subject to this, the appointment of any person as responsible insolvency practitioner takes effect at the time specified in his certificate of appointment.

Conflicts of interest

230A.—(1) If the responsible insolvency practitioner of an insolvent partnership being wound up by virtue of article 8 of the Insolvent Partnerships Order 1994 and of one or more of its insolvent members is of the opinion at any time that there is a conflict of interest between his functions as liquidator of the partnership and his functions as responsible insolvency practitioner of any insolvent member, or between his functions as responsible insolvency practitioner of two or more insolvent members, he may apply to the court for directions.

(2) On an application under subsection (1), the court may, without prejudice to the generality of its power to give directions, appoint one or more insolvency practitioners either in place of the applicant to act as responsible insolvency practitioner

of both the partnership and its insolvent member or members or to act as joint responsible insolvency practitioner with the applicant.".

27 Section 234: Getting in the partnership property

Section 234 is modified, so far as insolvent partnerships are concerned, so as to read as follows—

"**234.**—(1) This section applies where—

(a) insolvency orders are made by virtue of article 8 of the Insolvent Partnerships Order 1994 in respect of an insolvent partnership and its insolvent member or members, or

(b) a provisional liquidator of an insolvent partnership and any of its corporate members is appointed by virtue of that article;

and 'the office-holder' means the liquidator or the provisional liquidator, as the case may be.

(2) Any person who is or has been an officer of the partnership, or who is an executor or administrator of the estate of a deceased officer of the partnership, shall deliver up to the office-holder, for the purposes of the exercise of the office-holder's functions under this Act and (where applicable) the Company Directors Disqualification Act 1986, possession of any partnership property which he holds for the purposes of the partnership.

(3) Where any person has in his possession or control any property, books, papers or records to which the partnership appears to be entitled, the court may require that person forthwith (or within such period as the court may direct) to pay, deliver, convey, surrender or transfer the property, books, papers or records to the office-holder or as the court may direct.

(4) Where the office-holder—

(a) seizes or disposes of any property which is not partnership property, and

(b) at the time of seizure or disposal believes, and has reasonable grounds for believing, that he is entitled (whether in pursuance of an order of the court or otherwise) to seize or dispose of that property,

the next subsection has effect.

(5) In that case the office-holder—

(a) is not liable to any person in respect of any loss or damage resulting from the seizure or disposal except in so far as that loss or damage is caused by the office-holder's own negligence, and

(b) has a lien on the property, or the proceeds of its sale, for such expenses as were incurred in connection with the seizure or disposal.".

28 Section 283: Definition of individual member's estate

Section 283 is modified so as to read as follows—

"**283.**—(1) Subject as follows, the estate of an individual member for the purposes of this Act comprises—

(a) all property belonging to or vested in the individual member at the commencement of the bankruptcy, and

(b) any property which by virtue of any of the provisions of this Act is comprised in that estate or is treated as falling within the preceding paragraph.

(2) Subsection (1) does not apply to—

(a) such tools, books, vehicles and other items of equipment as are not partnership property and as are necessary to the individual member for use personally by him in his employment, business or vocation;

(b) such clothing, bedding, furniture, household equipment and provisions as are not partnership property and as are necessary for satisfying the basic domestic needs of the individual member and his family.

This subsection is subject to section 308 in Chapter IV (certain excluded property reclaimable by trustee).

(3) Subsection (1) does not apply to—

(a) property held by the individual member on trust for any other person, or

(b) the right of nomination to a vacant ecclesiastical benefice.

(4) References in any provision of this Act to property, in relation to an individual member, include references to any power exercisable by him over or in respect of property except in so far as the power is exercisable over or in respect of property not for the time being comprised in the estate of the individual member and—

(a) is so exercisable at a time after either the official receiver has had his release in respect of that estate under section 174(3) or a meeting summoned by the trustee of that estate under section 146 has been held, or

(b) cannot be so exercised for the benefit of the individual member;

and a power exercisable over or in respect of property is deemed for the purposes of any provision of this Act to vest in the person entitled to exercise it at the time of the transaction or event by virtue of which it is exercisable by that person (whether or not it becomes so exercisable at that time).

(5) For the purposes of any such provision of this Act, property comprised in an individual member's estate is so comprised subject to the rights of any person other than the individual member (whether as a secured creditor of the individual member or otherwise) in relation thereto, but disregarding any rights which have been given up in accordance with the rules.

(6) This section has effect subject to the provisions of any enactment not contained in this Act under which any property is to be excluded from a bankrupt's estate.".

29 Section 284: Individual member: Restrictions on dispositions of property

Section 284 is modified so as to read as follows—

"**284.**—(1) Where an individual member is adjudged bankrupt by virtue of article 8 of the Insolvent Partnerships Order 1994, any disposition of property made by that member in the period to which this section applies is void except to the extent that it is or was made with the consent of the court, or is or was subsequently ratified by the court.

(2) Subsection (1) applies to a payment (whether in cash or otherwise) as it applies to a disposition of property and, accordingly, where any payment is void by virtue of that subsection, the person paid shall hold the sum paid for the individual member as part of his estate.

(3) This section applies to the period beginning with the day of the presentation of the petition for the bankruptcy order and ending with the vesting, under Chapter IV of this Part, of the individual member's estate in a trustee.

(4) The preceding provisions of this section do not give a remedy against any person—

(a) in respect of any property or payment which he received before the commencement of the bankruptcy in good faith, for value and without notice that the petition had been presented, or

(b) in respect of any interest in property which derives from an interest in respect of which there is, by virtue of this subsection, no remedy.

(5) Where after the commencement of his bankrutpcy the individual member has incurred a debt to a banker or other person by reason of the making of a payment which is void under this section, that debt is deemed for the purposes of any provision of this Act to have been incurred before the commencement of the bankruptcy unless—

(a) that banker or person had notice of the bankruptcy before the debt was incurred, or

(b) it is not reasonably practicable for the amount of the payment to be recovered from the person to whom it was made.

(6) A disposition of property is void under this section notwithstanding that the property is not or, as the case may be, would not be comprised in the individual member's estate; but nothing in this section affects any disposition made by a person of property held by him on trust for any other person other than a disposition made by an individual member of property held by him on trust for the partnership.".

30 Schedule 4 is modified so as to read as follows—

"SCHEDULE 4
POWERS OF LIQUIDATOR IN A WINDING UP

PART I
POWERS EXERCISABLE WITH SANCTION

1 Power to pay any class of creditors in full.

2 Power to make any compromise or arrangement with creditors or persons claiming to be creditors, or having or alleging themselves to have any claim (present or future, certain or contingent, ascertained or sounding only in damages) against the partnership, or whereby the partnership may be rendered liable.

3 Power to compromise, on such terms as may be agreed—

(a) all debts and liabilities capable of resulting in debts, and all claims (present or future, certain or contingent, ascertained or sounding only in damages) subsisting or supposed to subsist between the partnership and a contributory or alleged contributory or other debtor or person apprehending liability to the partnership, and

(b) all questions in any way relating to or affecting the partnership property or the winding up of the partnership,

and take any security for the discharge of any such debt, liability or claim and give a complete discharge in respect of it.

4 Power to bring or defend any action or other legal proceeding in the name and on behalf of any member of the partnership in his capacity as such or of the partnership.

5 Power to carry on the business of the partnership so far as may be necessary for its beneficial winding up.

PART II
POWERS EXERCISABLE WITHOUT SANCTION

6 Power to sell any of the partnership property by public auction or private contract, with power to transfer the whole of it to any person or to sell the same in parcels.

7 Power to do all acts and execute, in the name and on behalf of the partnership or of any member of the partnership in his capacity as such, all deeds, receipts and other documents.

8 Power to prove, rank and claim in the bankruptcy, insolvency or sequestration of any contributory for any balance against his estate, and to receive dividends in the bankruptcy, insolvency or sequestration in respect of that balance, as a separate debt due from the bankrupt or insolvent, and rateably with the other separate creditors.

9 Power to draw, accept, make and endorse any bill of exchange of promissory note in the name and on behalf of any member of the partnership in his capacity as such or of the partnership, with the same effect with respect to the liability of the partnership or of any member of the partnership in his capacity as such as if the bill or note had been drawn, accepted, made or endorsed in the course of the partnership's business.

10 Power to raise on the security of the partnership property any money requisite.

11 Power to take out in his official name letters of administration to any deceased contributory, and to do in his official name any other act necessary for obtaining payment of any money due from a contributory or his estate which cannot conveniently be done in the name of the partnership.

In all such cases the money due is deemed, for the purpose of enabling the liquidator to take out the letters of administration or recover the money, to be due to the liquidator himself.

12 Power to appoint an agent to do any business which the liquidator is unable to do himself.

13 Power to do all such other things as may be necessary for winding up the partnership's affairs and distributing its property.".

SCHEDULE 5

PROVISIONS OF THE ACT WHICH APPLY WITH MODIFICATIONS FOR THE PURPOSES OF ARTICLE 9 TO WINDING UP OF INSOLVENT PARTNERSHIP ON MEMBER'S PETITION WHERE NO CONCURRENT PETITION PRESENTED AGAINST MEMBER

1 Section 117: High Court and county court jurisdiction

Section 117 is modified so as to read as follows—

"**117.**—(1) Subject to subsections (3) and (4) below, the High Court has jurisdiction to wind up any insolvent partnership as an unregistered company by virtue of article 9 of the Insolvent Partnerships Order 1994 if the partnership has, or at any time had, a principal place of business in England and Wales.

(2) Subject to subsections (3) and (5) below, a petition for the winding up of an insolvent partnership by virtue of the said article 9 may be presented to a county court in England and Wales if the partnership has, or at any time had, a principal place of business within the insolvency district of that court.

(3) Subject to subsection (4) below, the court only has jurisdiction to wind up an insolvent partnership if the business of the partnership has been carried on in England and Wales at any time in the period of 3 years ending with the day on which the petition for winding it up is presented.

(4) If an insolvent partnership has a principal place of business situated in Scotland or in Northern Ireland, the court shall not have jurisdiction to wind up the partnership unless it had a principal place of business in England and Wales—

    (a) in the case of a partnership with a principal place of business in Scotland, at any time in the period of 1 year, or

    (b) in the case of a partnership with a principal place of business in Northern Ireland, at any time in the period of 3 years,

ending with the day on which the petition for winding it up is presented.

(5) The Lord Chancellor may by order in a statutory instrument exclude a county court from having winding-up jurisdiction, and for the purposes of that jurisdiction may attach its district, or any part thereof, to any other county court, and may by statutory instrument revoke or vary any such order.

In exercising the powers of this section, the Lord Chancellor shall provide that a county court is not to have winding-up jurisdiction unless it has for the time being jurisdiction for the purposes of Parts VIII to XI of this Act (individual insolvency).

(6) Every court in England and Wales having winding-up jurisdiction has for the purposes of that jurisdiction all the powers of the High Court; and every prescribed officer of the court shall perform any duties which an officer of the High Court may discharge by order of a judge of that court or otherwise in relation to winding up.".

2 Section 221: Winding up of unregistered companies

Section 221 is modified so as to read as follows—

"**221.**—(1) Subject to subsections (2) and (3) below and to the provisions of this Part, any insolvent partnership which has, or at any time had, a principal place of business in England and Wales may be wound up under this Act.

(2) Subject to subsection (3) below an insolvent partnership shall not be wound up under this Act if the business of the partnership has not been carried on in England and Wales at any time in the period of 3 years ending with the day on which the winding-up petition is presented.

(3) If an insolvent partnership has a principal place of business situated in Scotland or in Northern Ireland, the court shall not have jurisdiction to wind up the partnership unless it had a principal place of business in England and Wales—

    (a) in the case of a partnership with a principal place of business in Scotland, at any time in the period of 1 year, or

    (b) in the case of a partnership with a principal place of business in Northern Ireland, at any time in the period of 3 years,

ending with the day on which the winding-up petition is presented.

(4) No insolvent partnership shall be wound up under this Act voluntarily.

(5) To the extent that they are applicable to the winding up of a company by the court in England and Wales on a member's petition or on a petition by the company, all the provisions of this Act and the Companies Act about winding up apply to the winding up of an insolvent partnership as an unregistered company—

(a) with the exceptions and additions mentioned in the following subsections of this section and in section 221A, and

(b) with the modifications specified in Part II of Schedule 3 to the Insolvent Partnerships Order 1994.

(6) Sections 73(1), 74(2)(a) to (d) and (3), 75 to 78, 83, 122, 123, 124(2) and (3), 202, 203, 205 and 250 shall not apply.

(7) The circumstances in which an insolvent partnership may be wound up as an unregistered company are as follows—

(a) if the partnership is dissolved, or has ceased to carry on business, or is carrying on business only for the purpose of winding up its affairs;

(b) if the partnership is unable to pay its debts;

(c) if the court is of the opinion that it is just and equitable that the partnership should be wound up.

(8) Every petition for the winding up of an insolvent partnership under Part V of this Act shall be verified by affidavit in Form 2 in Schedule 9 to the Insolvent Partnerships Order 1994.

Who may present petition

221A.—(1) A petition for winding up an insolvent partnership may be presented by any member of the partnership if the partnership consists of not less than 8 members.

(2) A petition for winding up an insolvent partnership may also be presented by any member of it with the leave of the court (obtained on his application) if the court is satisfied that—

(a) the member has served on the partnership, by leaving at a principal place of business of the partnership in England and Wales, or by delivering to an officer of the partnership, or by otherwise serving in such manner as the court may approve or direct, a written demand in Form 10 in Schedule 9 to the Insolvent Partnerships Order 1994 in respect of a joint debt or debts exceeding £750 then due from the partnership but paid by the member, other than out of partnership property;

(b) the partnership has for 3 weeks after the service of the demand neglected to pay the sum or to secure or compound for it to the member's satisfaction; and

(c) the member has obtained a judgment, decree or order of any court against the partnership for reimbursement to him of the amount of the joint debt or debts so paid and all reasonable steps (other than insolvency proceedings) have been taken by the member to enforce that judgment, decree or order.

(3) Subsection (2)(a) above is deemed included in the list of provisions specified in subsection (1) of section 416 of this Act for the purposes of the Secretary of State's order-making power under that section.".

SCHEDULE 6

PROVISIONS OF THE ACT WHICH APPLY WITH MODIFICATIONS FOR
THE PURPOSES OF ARTICLE 10 TO WINDING UP OF INSOLVENT
PARTNERSHIP ON MEMBER'S PETITION WHERE CONCURRENT
PETITIONS ARE PRESENTED AGAINST ALL THE MEMBERS

1 Sections 117 and 265: High Court and county court jurisdiction

Sections 117 and 265 are modified so as to read as follows—

"**117.**—(1) Subject to the provisions of this section, the High Court has jurisdiction to
wind up any insolvent partnership as an unregistered company by virtue of article 10
of the Insolvent Partnerships Order 1994 if the partnership has, or at any time had, a
principal place of business in England and Wales.

(2) Subject to the provisions of this section, a petition for the winding up of an
insolvent partnership by virtue of the said article 10 may be presented to a county
court in England and Wales if the partnership has, or at any time had, a principal
place of business within the insolvency district of that court.

(3) Subject to subsection (4) below, the court only has jurisdiction to wind up an
insolvent partnership if the business of the partnership has been carried on in
England and Wales at any time in the period of 3 years ending with the day on which
the petition for winding it up is presented.

(4) If an insolvent partnership has a principal place of business situated in Scotland or
in Northern Ireland, the court shall not have jurisdiction to wind up the partnership
unless it had a principal place of business in England and Wales—

    (a) in the case of a partnership with a principal place of business in Scotland, at any
        time in the period of 1 year, or
    (b) in the case of a partnership with a principal place of business in Northern
        Ireland, at any time in the period of 3 years.
ending with the day on which the petition for winding it up is presented.

(5) Subject to subsection (6) below, the court has jurisdiction to wind up a corporate
member, or make a bankruptcy order against an individual member, of a partnership
against which a petition has been presented by virtue of article 10 of the Insolvent
Partnerships Order 1994 if it has jurisdiction in respect of the partnership.

(6) Petitions by virtue of the said article 10 for the winding up of an insolvent
partnership and the bankruptcy of one or more members of that partnership may not
be presented to a district registry of the High Court.

(7) The Lord Chancellor may by order in a statutory instrument exclude a county
court from having winding-up jurisdiction, and for the purposes of that jurisdiction
may attach its district, or any part thereof, to any other county court, and may by
statutory instrument revoke or vary any such order.

In exercising the powers of this section, the Lord Chancellor shall provide that a
county court is not to have winding-up jurisdiction unless it has for the time being
jurisdiction for the purposes of Parts VIII to XI of this Act (individual insolvency).

(8) Every court in England and Wales having winding-up jurisdiction has for the
purposes of that jurisdiction all the powers of the High Court; and every prescribed
officer of the court shall perform any duties which an officer of the High Court may
discharge by order of a judge of that court or otherwise in relation to winding up.".

2 Sections 124, 264 and 272: Applications to wind up insolvent partnership and to wind up or bankrupt insolvent members

Sections 124, 264 and 272 are modified so as to read as follows—

"**124.**—(1) An application to the court by a member of an insolvent partnership by virtue of article 10 of the Insolvent Partnerships Order 1994 for the winding up of the partnership as an unregistered company and the winding up or bankrutpcy (as the case may be) of all its members shall—

    (a) in the case of the partnership, be by petition in Form 11 in Schedule 9 to that Order,

    (b) in the case of a corporate member, be by petition in Form 12 in that Schedule, and

    (c) in the case of an individual member, be by petition in Form 13 in that Schedule.

(2) Subject to subsection (3) below, a petition under subsection (1)(a) may only be presented by a member of the partnership on the grounds that the partnership is unable to pay its debts and if—

    (a) petitions are at the same time presented by that member for insolvency orders against every member of the partnership (including himself or itself); and

    (b) each member is willing for an insolvency order to be made against him or it and the petition against him or it contains a statement to this effect.

(3) If the court is satisfied, on application by any member of an insolvent partnership, that presentation of petitions under subsection (1) against the partnership and every member of it would be impracticable, the court may direct that petitions be presented against the partnership and such member or members of it as are specified by the court.

(4) The petitions mentioned in subsection (1)—

    (a) shall all be presented to the same court and, except as the court otherwise permits or directs, on the same day, and

    (b) except in the case of the petition mentioned in subsection (1)(c) shall be advertised in Form 8 in the said Schedule 9.

(5) Each petition presented under this section shall contain particulars of the other petitions being presented in relation to the partnership, identifying the partnership and members concerned.

(6) The hearing of the petition against the partnership fixed by the court shall be in advance of the hearing of the petitions against the insolvent members.

(7) On the day appointed for the hearing of the petition against the partnership, the petitioner shall, before the commencement of the hearing, hand to the court Form 9 in Schedule 9 to the Insolvent Partnerships Order 1994, duly completed.

(8) Any person against whom a winding-up or bankruptcy petition has been presented in relation to the insolvent partnership is entitled to appear and to be heard on any petition for the winding up of the partnership.

(9) A petitioner under this section may at the hearing withdraw the petition if—

    (a) subject to subsection (10) below, he withdraws at the same time every other petition which he has presented under this section; and

(b) he gives notice to the court at least 3 days before the date appointed for the hearing of the relevant petition of his intention to withdraw the petition.

(10) A petitioner need not comply with the provisions of subsection (9)(a) in the case of a petition against a member, if the court is satisfied on application made to it by the petitioner that, because of difficulties in serving the petition or for any other reason, the continuance of that petition would be likely to prejudice or delay the proceedings on the petition which he has presented against the partnership or on any petition which he has presented against any other insolvent member.".

3 Sections 125 and 271: Powers of court on hearing of petitions against insolvent partnership and members

Sections 125 and 271 are modified so as to read as follows—

"**125.**—(1) Subject to the provisions of section 125A, on hearing a petition under section 124 against an insolvent partnership or any of its insolvent members, the court may dismiss it, or adjourn the hearing conditionally or unconditionally or make any other order that it thinks fit; but the court shall not refuse to make a winding-up order against the partnership or a corporate member on the ground only that the partnership property or (as the case may be) the member's assets have been mortgaged to an amount equal to or in excess of that property or those assets, or that the partnership has no property or the member no assets.

(2) An order under subsection (1) in respect of an insolvent partnership may contain directions as to the future conduct of any insolvency proceedings in existence against any insolvent member in respect of whom an insolvency order has been made.

Hearing of petitions against members

125A.—(1) On the hearing of a petition against an insolvent member the petitioner shall draw the court's attention to the result of the hearing of the winding-up petition against the partnership and the following subsections of this section shall apply.

(2) If the court has neither made a winding-up order, nor dismissed the winding-up petition, against the partnership the court may adjourn the hearing of the petition against the member until either event has occurred.

(3) Subject to subsection (4) below, if a winding-up order has been made against the partnership, the court may make a winding-up order against the corporate member in respect of which, or (as the case may be) a bankruptcy order against the individual member in respect of whom, the insolvency petition was presented.

(4) If no insolvency order is made under subsection (3) against any member within 28 days of the making of the winding-up order against the partnership, the proceedings against the partnership shall be conducted as if the winding-up petition against the partnership had been presented by virtue of article 7 of the Insolvent Partnerships Order 1994, and the proceedings against any member shall be conducted under this Act without the modifications made by that Order (other than the modifications made to sections 168 and 303 by article 14).

(5) If the court has dismissed the winding-up petition against the partnership, the court may dismiss the winding-up petition against the corporate member or (as the case may be) the bankruptcy petition against the individual member. However, if an insolvency order is made against a member, the proceedings against that member shall be conducted under this Act without the modifications made by the Insolvent Partnerships Order 1994 (other than the modifications made to sections 168 and 303 of this Act by article 14 of that Order).

(6) The court may dismiss a petition against an insolvent member if it considers it just to do so because of a change in circumstances since the making of the winding-up order against the partnership.

(7) The court may dismiss a petition against an insolvent member who is a limited partner, if—

(a) the member lodges in court for the benefit of the creditors of the partnership sufficient money or security to the court's satisfaction to meet his liability for the debts and obligations of the partnership; or

(b) the member satisfies the court that he is no longer under any liability in respect of the debts and obligations of the partnership.".

4 Section 221: Winding up of unregistered companies

Section 221 is modified so as to read as follows—

"**221.**—(1) Subject to subsections (2) and (3) below and to the provisions of this Part, any insolvent partnership which has, or at any time had, a principal place of business in England and Wales may be wound up under this Act.

(2) Subject to subsection (3) below, an insolvent partnership shall not be wound up under this Act if the business of the partnership has not been carried on in England and Wales at any time in the period of 3 years ending with the day on which the winding-up petition is presented.

(3) If an insolvent partnership has a principal place of business situated in Scotland or in Northern Ireland, the court shall not have jurisdiction to wind up the partnership unless it had a principal place of business in England and Wales—

(a) in the case of a partnership with a principal place of business in Scotland, at any time in the period of 1 year, or

(b) in the case of a partnership with a principal place of business in Northern Ireland, at any time in the period of 3 years,

ending with the day on which the winding-up petition is presented.

(4) No insolvent partnership shall be wound up under this Act voluntarily.

(5) To the extent that they are applicable to the winding up of a company by the court in England and Wales on a member's petition, all the provisions of this Act and the Companies Act about winding up apply to the winding up of an insolvent partnership as an unregistered company—

(a) with the exceptions and additions mentioned in the following subsections of this section, and

(b) with the modifications specified in Part II of Schedule 4 to the Insolvent Partnerships Order 1994.

(6) Sections 73(1), 74(2)(a) to (d) and (3), 75 to 78, 83, 124(2) and (3), 154, 202, 203, 205 and 250 shall not apply.

(7) Unless the contrary intention appears, the members of the partnership against whom insolvency orders are made by virtue of article 10 of the Insolvent Partnerships Order 1994 shall not be treated as contributions for the purposes of this Act.

(8) The circumstances in which an insolvent partnership may be wound up as an unregistered company are that the partnership is unable to pay its debts.

(9) Every petition for the winding up of an insolvent partnership under Part V of this Act shall be verified by affidavit in Form 2 in Schedule 9 to the Insolvent Partnerships Order 1994.".

SCHEDULE 7

PROVISIONS OF THE ACT WHICH APPLY WITH MODIFICATIONS FOR THE PURPOSES OF ARTICLE 11 WHERE JOINT BANKRUPTCY PETITION PRESENTED BY INDIVIDUAL MEMBERS WITHOUT WINDING UP PARTNERSHIP AS UNREGISTERED COMPANY

1   (1) The provisions of the Act specified in sub-paragraph (2) below, are set out as modified in this Schedule.

(2) The provisions referred to in sub-paragraph (1) above are sections 264 to 266, 272, 275, 283, 284, 290, 292 to 301, 305, 312, 328, 331 and 387.

2 Section 264: Presentation of joint bankruptcy petition

Section 264 is modified so as to read as follows—

"**264.**—(1) Subject to section 266(1) below, a joint bankruptcy petition may be presented to the court by virtue of article 11 of the Insolvent Partnerships Order 1994 by all the members of an insolvent partnership in their capacity as such provided that all the members are individuals and none of them is a limited partner.

(2) A petition may not be presented under paragraph (1) by the members of an insolvent partnership which is an authorised institution or former authorised institution within the meaning of the Banking Act 1987.

(3) The petition—

- (a) shall be in Form 14 in Schedule 9 to the Insolvent Partnerships Order 1994; and
- (b) shall contain a request that the trustee shall wind up the partnership business and administer the partnership property without the partnership being wound up as an unregistered company under Part V of this Act.

(4) The petition shall either—

- (a) be accompanied by an affidavit in Form 15 in Schedule 9 to the Insolvent Partnerships Order 1994 made by the member who signs the petition, showing that all the members are individual members (and that none of them is a limited partner) and concur in the presentation of the petition, or
- (b) contain a statement that all the members are individual members and be signed by all the members.

(5) On presentation of a petition under this section, the court may make orders in Form 16 in Schedule 9 to the Insolvent Partnerships Order 1994 for the bankruptcy of the members and the winding up of the partnership business and administration of its property.".

3 Section 265: Conditions to be satisfied in respect of members

Section 265 is modified so as to read as follows—

"**265.**—(1) Subject to the provisions of this section, a joint bankruptcy petition by virtue of article 11 of the Insolvent Partnerships Order 1994 may be presented—

- (a) to the High Court (other than to a district registry of that Court) if the partnership has, or at any time had, a principal place of business in England and Wales, or

(b) to a county court in England and Wales if the partnership has, or at any time had, a principal place of business within the insolvency district of that court.

(2) A joint bankruptcy petition shall not be presented to the court by virtue of article 11 unless the business of the partnership has been carried on in England and Wales at any time in the period of 3 years ending with the day on which the joint bankruptcy petition is presented.".

4 Section 266: Other preliminary conditions

Section 266 is modified so as to read as follows—

"**266.**—(1) If the court is satisfied, on application by any member of an insolvent partnership, that the presentation of the petition under section 264(1) by all the members of the partnership would be impracticable, the court may direct that the petition be presented by such member or members as are specified by the court.

(2) A joint bankruptcy petition shall not be withdrawn without the leave of the court.

(3) The court has a general power, if it appears to it appropriate to do so on the grounds that there has been a contravention of the rules or for any other reason, to dismiss a joint bankruptcy petition or to stay proceedings on such a petition; and, where it stays proceedings on a petition, it may do so on such terms and conditions as it thinks fit.".

5 Section 272: Grounds of joint bankruptcy petition

Section 272 is modified so as to read as follows—

"**272.**—(1) A joint bankruptcy petition may be presented to the court by the members of a partnership only on the grounds that the partnership is unable to pay its debts.

(2) The petition shall be accompanied by—

    (a) a statement of each member's affairs in Form 17 in Schedule 9 to the Insolvent Partnerships Order 1994, and
    (b) a statement of the affairs of the partnership in Form 18 in that Schedule, sworn by one or more members of the partnership.

(3) The statements of affairs required by subsection (2) shall contain—

    (a) particulars of the member's or (as the case may be) partnership's creditors, debts and other liabilities and of their assets, and
    (b) such other information as is required by the relevant form.".

6 Section 275: Summary administration

Section 275 is modified so as to read as follows—

"**275.**—(1) Where orders have been made against the members of an insolvent partnership by virtue of article 11 of the Insolvent Partnerships Order 1994, and the case is as specified in the next subsection, the court shall, if it appears to it appropriate to do so, issue a certificate for the summary administration of any member's estate.

(2) That case is where it appears to the court—

    (a) that the aggregate amount of the unsecured joint debts of the partnership and unsecured separate debts of the member concerned is less than the small bankruptcies level prescribed for the purposes of section 273 (as that section applies apart from the Insolvent Partnerships Order 1994), and

(b) that within the period of 5 years ending with the presentation of the joint bankruptcy petition the member concerned has neither been adjudged bankrupt nor made a composition with his creditors in satisfaction of his debts or a scheme of arrangement of his affairs.

(3) The court may at any time revoke a certificate issued under this section if it appears to it that, on any grounds existing at the time the certificate was issued, the certificate ought not to have been issued.".

7 Section 283: Definition of member's estate

Section 283 is modified so as to read as follows—

"**283.**—(1) Subject as follows, a member's estate for the purposes of this Act comprises—

(a) all property belonging to or vested in the member at the commencement of the bankruptcy, and
(b) any property which by virtue of any of the provisions of this Act is comprised in that estate or is treated as falling within the preceding paragraph.

(2) Subsection (1) does not apply to—

(a) such tools, books, vehicles and other items of equipment as are not partnership property and as are necessary to the member for use personally by him in his employment, business or vocation;
(b) such clothing, bedding, furniture, household equipment and provisions as are not partnership property and as are necessary for satisfying the basic domestic needs of the member and his family.

This subsection is subject to section 308 in Chapter IV (certain excluded property reclaimable by trustee).

(3) Subsection (1) does not apply to—

(a) property held by the member on trust for any other person, or
(b) the right of nomination to a vacant ecclesiastical benefice.

(4) References in any provision of this Act to property, in relation to a member, include references to any power exercisable by him over or in respect of property except insofar as the power is exercisable over or in respect of property not for the time being comprised in the member's estate and—

(a) is so exercisable at a time after either the official receiver has had his release in respect of that estate under section 299(2) in Chapter III or a meeting summoned by the trustee of that estate under section 331 in Chapter IV has been held, or
(b) cannot be so exercised for the benefit of the member;

and a power exercisable over or in respect of property is deemed for the purposes of any provision of this Act to vest in the person entitled to exercise it at the time of the transaction or event by virtue of which it is exercisable by that person (whether or not it becomes so exercisable at that time).

(5) For the purposes of any such provision of this Act, property comprised in a member's estate is so comprised subject to the rights of any person other than the member (whether as a secured creditor of the member or otherwise) in relation thereto, but disregarding any rights which have been given up in accordance with the rules.

(6) This section has effect subject to the provisions of any enactment not contained in this Act under which any property is to be excluded from a bankrupt's estate.".

8 Section 284: Restrictions on dispositions of property

Section 284 is modified so as to read as follows—

"**284.**—(1) Where a member is adjudged bankrupt on a joint bankruptcy petition, any disposition of property made by that member in the period to which this section applies is void except to the extent that it is or was made with the consent of the court, or is or was subsequently ratified by the court.

(2) Subsection (1) applies to a payment (whether in cash or otherwise) as it applies to a disposition of property and, accordingly, where any payment is void by virtue of that subsection, the person paid shall hold the sum paid for the member as part of his estate.

(3) This section applies to the period beginning with the day of the presentation of the joint bankruptcy petition and ending with the vesting, under Chapter IV of this Part, of the member's estate in a trustee.

(4) The preceding provisions of this section do not give a remedy against any person—

    (a) in respect of any property or payment which he received before the commencement of the bankruptcy in good faith, for value, and without notice that the petition had been presented, or

    (b) in respect of any interest in property which derives from an interest in respect of which there is, by virtue of this subsection, no remedy.

(5) Where after the commencement of his bankruptcy the member has incurred a debt to a banker or other person by reason of the making of a payment which is void under this section, that debt is deemed for the purposes of any provision of this Act to have been incurred before the commencement of the bankruptcy unless—

    (a) that banker or person had notice of the bankruptcy before the debt was incurred, or

    (b) it is not reasonably practicable for the amount of the payment to be recovered from the person to whom it was made.

(6) A disposition of property is void under this section notwithstanding that the property is not or, as the case may be, would not be comprised in the member's estate; but nothing in this section affects any disposition made by a person of property held by him on trust for any other person other than a disposition made by a member of property held by him on trust for the partnership.".

9 Section 290: Public examination of member

Section 290 is modified so as to read as follows—

"**290.**—(1) Where orders have been made against the members of an insolvent partnership on a joint bankruptcy petition, the official receiver may at any time before the discharge of any such member apply to the court for the public examination of that member.

(2) Unless the court otherwise orders, the official receiver shall make an application under subsection (1) if notice requiring him to do so is given to him, in accordance with the rules, by one of the creditors of the member concerned with the concurrence

of not less than one-half, in value, of those creditors (including the creditor giving notice).

(3) On an application under subsection (1), the court shall direct that a public examination of the member shall be held on a day appointed by the court; and the member shall attend on that day and be publicly examined as to his affairs, dealings and property and as to those of the partnership.

(4) The following may take part in the public examination of the member and may question him concerning the matters mentioned in subsection (3), namely—

    (a) the official receiver,

    (b) the trustee of the member's estate, if his appointment has taken effect,

    (c) any person who has been appointed as special manager of the member's estate or business or of the partnership property or business,

    (d) any creditor of the member who has tendered a proof in the bankruptcy.

(5) On an application under subsection (1), the court may direct that the public examination of a member under this section be combined with the public examination of any other person.

(6) If a member without reasonable excuse fails at any time to attend his public examination under this section he is guilty of a contempt of court and liable to be punished accordingly (in addition to any other punishment to which he may be subject).".

10 Section 292: Power to appoint trustee

Section 292 is modified so as to read as follows—

"**292.**—(1) The power to appoint a person as both trustee of the estates of the members of an insolvent partnership against whom orders are made on a joint bankruptcy petition and as trustee of the partnership is exercisable—

    (a) by a combined general meeting of the creditors of the members and of the partnership;

    (b) under section 295(2), 296(2) or 300(3) below in this Chapter, by the Secretary of State.

(2) No person may be appointed as trustee of the members' estates and as trustee of the partnership unless he is, at the time of the appointment, qualified to act as an insolvency practitioner both in relation to the insolvent partnership and to each of the members.

(3) Any power to appoint a person as trustee of the members' estates and of the partnership includes power to appoint two or more persons as joint trustees; but such an appointment must make provision as to the circumstances in which the trustees must act together and the circumstances in which one or more of them may act for the others.

(4) The appointment of any person as trustee of the members' estates and of the partnership takes effect only if that person accepts the appointment in accordance with the rules. Subject to this, the appointment of any person as trustee takes effect at the time specified in his certificate of appointment.

(5) This section is without prejudice to the provisions of this Chapter under which the official receiver is, in certain circumstances, to be trustee of the members' estates and of the partnership.

Conflicts of interest

292A.—(1) If the trustee of the members' estates and of the partnership is of the opinion at any time that there is a conflict of interest between his functions as trustee of the members' estates and his functions as trustee of the partnership, or between his functions as trustee of the estates of two or more members, he may apply to the court for directions.

(2) On an application under subsection (1), the court may, without prejudice to the generality of its power to give directions, appoint one or more insolvency practitioners either in place of the applicant to act both as trustee of the members' estates and as trustee of the partnership, or to act as joint trustee with the applicant.".

11 Sections 293 and 294: Summoning of meeting to appoint trustee

Sections 293 and 294 are modified so as to read as follows—

"**293.**—(1) Where orders are made by virtue of article 11 of the Insolvent Partnerships Order 1994, the official receiver, by virtue of his office, becomes the trustee of the estates of the members and the trustee of the partnership and continues in office until another person becomes trustee under the provisions of this Part.

(2) The official receiver is, by virtue of his office, the trustee of the estates of the members and the trustee of the partnership during any vacancy.

(3) At any time when he is trustee, the official receiver may summon a combined meeting of the creditors of the members and the creditors of the partnership, for the purpose of appointing a trustee in place of the official receiver.

(4) It is the duty of the official receiver—

    (a) as soon as practicable in the period of 12 weeks beginning with the day on which the first order was made by virtue of article 11 of the Insolvent Partnerships Order 1994, to decide whether to exercise his power under subsection (3) to summon a meeting, and

    (b) if in pursuance of paragraph (a) he decides not to exercise that power, to give notice of his decision, before the end of that period, to the court and to those creditors of the members and those of the partnership who are known to the official receiver or identified in a statement of affairs submitted under section 272, and

    (c) (whether or not he has decided to exercise that power) to exercise his power to summon a meeting under subsection (3) if he is at any time requested to do so by one-quarter, in value, of either—

        (i) the creditors of any member against whom an insolvency order has been made, or

        (ii) the partnership's creditors,

and accordingly, where the duty imposed by paragraph (c) arises before the official receiver has performed a duty imposed by paragraph (a) or (b), he is not required to perform the latter duty.

(5) A notice given under subsection (4)(b) to the creditors shall contain an explanation of the creditors' power under subsection (4)(c) to require the official receiver to summon a combined meeting of the creditors of the partnership and of the members against whom insolvency orders have been made.

(6) If the official receiver, in pursuance of subsection (4)(a), has decided to exercise his power under subsection (3) to summon a meeting, he shall hold that meeting in the period of 4 months beginning with the day on which the first order was made by virtue of article 11 of the Insolvent Partnerships Order 1994.

(7) If (whether or not he has decided to exercise that power) the official receiver is requested, in accordance with the provisions of subsection (4)(c), to exercise his power under subsection (3) to summon a meeting, he shall hold that meeting in accordance with the rules.

(8) Where a meeting of creditors of the partnership and of the members has been held, and an insolvency order is subsequently made against a further insolvent member by virtue of article 11 of the Insolvent Partnerships Order 1994—

> (a) any person chosen at the meeting to be responsible insolvency practitioner in place of the official receiver shall also be the responsible insolvency practitioner of the member against whom the subsequent order is made, and
> (b) subsection (4) of this section shall not apply.".

12 Section 295: Failure of meeting to appoint trustee

Section 295 is modified so as to read as follows—

"**295.**—(1) If a meeting of creditors summoned under section 293 is held but no appointment of a person as trustee is made, it is the duty of the official receiver to decide whether to refer the need for an appointment to the Secretary of State.

(2) On a reference made in pursuance of that decision, the Secretary of State shall either make an appointment or decline to make one.

(3) If—

> (a) the official receiver decides not to refer the need for an appointment to the Secretary of State, or
> (b) on such a reference the Secretary of State declines to make an appointment,
> the official receiver shall give notice of his decision or, as the case may be, of the Secretary of State's decision to the court.".

13 Section 296: Appointment of trustee by Secretary of State

Section 296 is modified so as to read as follows—

"**296.**—(1) At any time when the official receiver is the trustee of the members' estates and of the partnership by virtue of any provision of this Chapter he may apply to the Secretary of State for the appointment of a person as trustee instead of the official receiver.

(2) On an application under subsection (1) the Secretary of State shall either make an appointment or decline to make one.

(3) Such an application may be made notwithstanding that the Secretary of State has declined to make an appointment either on a previous application under subsection (1) or on a reference under section 295 or under section 300(2) below.

(4) Where a trustee has been appointed by the Secretary of State under subsection (2) of this section, and an insolvency order is subsequently made against a further insolvent member by virtue of article 11 of the Insolvent Partnerships Order 1994, then the trustee so appointed shall also be the trustee of the member against whom the subsequent order is made.

(5) Where the trustee of the members' estates and of the partnership has been appointed by the Secretary of State (whether under this section or otherwise) or has become trustee of a further insolvent member under subsection (4), the trustee shall

give notice of his appointment or further appointment (as the case may be) to the creditors of the members and the creditors of the partnership or, if the court so allows, shall advertise his appointment in accordance with the court's directions.

(6) Subject to subsection (7) below, in that notice or advertisement the trustee shall—

    (a) state whether he proposes to summon a combined general meeting of the creditors of the members and of the creditors of the partnership for the purpose of establishing a creditors' committee under section 301, and

    (b) if he does not propose to summon such a meeting, set out the power of the creditors under this Part to require him to summon one.

(7) Where in a case where subsection (4) applies a meeting referred to in subsection (6)(a) has already been held, the trustee shall state in the notice or advertisement whether a creditors' committee was established at that meeting and—

    (a) if such a committee was established, shall state whether he proposes to appoint additional members of the committee under section 301A(3), and

    (b) if such a committee was not established, shall set out the power of the creditors to require him to summon a meeting for the purpose of determining whether a creditors' committee should be established.".

14 Section 297: Rules applicable to meetings of creditors

Section 297 is modified so as to read as follows—

"**297.**—(1) This section applies where the court has made orders by virtue of article 11 of the Insolvent Partnerships Order 1994.

(2) Subject to subsection (3) below, the rules relating to the requisitioning, summoning, holding and conducting of meetings on the bankruptcy of an individual are to apply (with the necessary modifications) to the requisitioning, summoning, holding and of conducting of separate meetings of the creditors of each member and of combined meetings of the creditors of the partnership and the creditors of the members.

(3) Any combined meeting of creditors shall be conducted as if the creditors of the members and of the partnership were a single set of creditors.".

15 Section 298: Removal of trustee; vacation of office

Section 298 is modified so as to read as follows—

"**298.**—(1) Subject as follows, the trustee of the estates of the members and of the partnership may be removed from office only by an order of the court.

(2) If the trustee was appointed by the Secretary of State, he may be removed by a direction of the Secretary of State.

(3) The trustee (not being the official receiver) shall vacate office if he ceases to be a person who is for the time being qualified to act as an insolvency practitioner in relation to any member or to the partnership.

(4) The trustee may, with the leave of the court (or, if appointed by the Secretary of State, with the leave of the court or the Secretary of State), resign his office by giving notice of his resignation to the court.

(5) Subject to subsections (6) and (7) below, any removal from or vacation of office under this section relates to all offices held in the proceedings by virtue of article 11 of the Insolvent Partnerships Order 1994.

(6) The trustee shall vacate office on giving notice to the court that a final meeting has been held under section 331 in Chapter IV (final meeting of creditors of insolvent partnership or of members) and of the decision (if any) of that meeting.

(7) The trustee shall vacate office as trustee of a member if the order made by virtue of article 11 of the Insolvent Partnerships Order 1994 in relation to that member is annulled.".

16 Section 299: Release of trustee

Section 299 is modified so as to read as follows—

"**299.**—(1) Where the official receiver has ceased to be the trustee of the members' estates and of the partnership and a person is appointed in his stead, the official receiver shall have his release with effect from the following time, that is to say—

    (a) where that person is appointed by a combined general meeting of creditors of the members and of the partnership or by the Secretary of State, the time at which the official receiver gives notice to the court that he has been replaced, and

    (b) where that person is appointed by the court, such time as the court may determine.

(2) If the official receiver while he is the trustee gives notice to the Secretary of State that the administration of the estate of any member, or the winding up of the partnership business and administration of its affairs, is for practical purposes complete, he shall have his release as trustee of any member or as trustee of the partnership (as the case may be) with effect from such time as the Secretary of State may determine.

(3) A person other than the official receiver who has ceased to be the trustee of the estate of any member or of the partnership shall have his release with effect from the following time, that is to say—

    (a) in the case of a person who has died, the time at which notice is given to the court in accordance with the rules that that person has ceased to hold office;

    (b) in the case of a person who has been removed from office by the court or by the Secretary of State, or who has vacated office under section 298(3), such time as the Secretary of State may, on an application by that person, determine;

    (c) in the case of a person who has resigned, such time as may be directed by the court (or, if he was appointed by the Secretary of State, such time as may be directed by the court or as the Secretary of State may, on an application by that person, determine);

    (d) in the case of a person who has vacated office under section 298(6)—

        (i) if the final meeting referred to in that subsection has resolved against that person's release, such time as the Secretary of State may, on an application by that person, determine; and

        (ii) if that meeting has not so resolved, the time at which the person vacated office.

(4) Where an order by virtue of article 11 of the Insolvent Partnerships Order 1994 is annulled in so far as it relates to any member, the trustee at the time of the annulment has his release in respect of that member with effect from such time as the court may determine.

(5) Where the trustee (including the official receiver when so acting) has his release under this section, he shall, with effect from the time specified in the preceding provisions of this section, be discharged from all liability both in respect of acts or

omissions of his in the administration of the estates of the members and in the winding up of the partnership business and administration of its affairs and otherwise in relation to his conduct as trustee.

But nothing in this section prevents the exercise, in relation to a person who has had his release under this section, of the court's powers under section 304 (liability of trustee).".

17 Section 300: Vacancy in office of trustee

Section 300 is modified so as to read as follows—

"**300.**—(1) This section applies where the appointment of any person as trustee of the members' estates and of the partnership fails to take effect or, such an appointment having taken effect, there is otherwise a vacancy in the office of trustee.

(2) The official receiver may refer the need for an appointment to the Secretary of State and shall be trustee until the vacancy is filled.

(3) On a reference to the Secretary of State under subsection (2) the Secretary of State shall either make an appointment or decline to make one.

(4) If on a reference under subsection (2) no appointment is made, the official receiver shall continue to be trustee, but without prejudice to his power to make a further reference.

(5) References in this section to a vacancy include a case where it is necessary, in relation to any property which is or may be comprised in a member's estate, to revive the trusteeship of that estate after the holding of a final meeting summoned under section 331 or the giving by the official receiver of notice under section 299(2).".

18 Section 301: Creditors' committee

Section 301 is modified so as to read as follows—

"**301.**—(1) Subject as follows, a combined general meeting of the creditors of the members and of the partnership (whether summoned under the preceding provisions of this Chapter or otherwise) may establish a committee (known as 'the creditors' committee') to exercise the functions conferred on it by or under this Act.

(2) A combined general meeting of the creditors of the members and of the partnership shall not establish such a committee, or confer any functions on such a committee, at any time when the official receiver is the trustee, except in connection with an appointment made by that meeting of a person to be trustee instead of the official receiver.

Functions and membership of creditors' committee

301A.—(1) The committee established under section 301 shall act as creditors' committee for each member and as liquidation committee for the partnership, and shall as appropriate exercise the functions conferred on creditors' and liquidation committees in a bankruptcy or winding up by or under this Act.

(2) The rules relating to liquidation committees are to apply (with the necessary modifications and with the exclusion of all references to contributories) to a committee established under section 301.

(3) Where the appointment of the trustee also takes effect in relation to a further insolvent member under section 293(8) or 296(4), the trustee may appoint any creditor of that member (being qualified under the rules to be a member of the

committee) to be an additional member of any creditors' committee already established under section 301, provided that the creditor concerned consents to act.

(4) The court may at any time, on application by a creditor of any member or of the partnership, appoint additional members of the creditors' committee.

(5) If additional members of the creditors' committee are appointed under subsection (3) or (4), the limit on the maximum number of members of the committee specified in the rules shall be increased by the number of additional members so appointed.".

19 Section 305: General functions and powers of trustee

Section 305 is modified so as to read as follows—

"**305.**—(1) The function of the trustee of the estates of the members and of the partnership is to get in, realise and distribute the estates of the members and the partnership property in accordance with the following provisions of this Chapter.

(2) The trustee shall have all the functions and powers in relation to the partnership and the partnership property that he has in relation to the members and their estates.

(3) In the carrying out of his functions and in the management of the members' estates and the partnership property the trustee is entitled, subject to the following provisions of this Chapter, to use his own discretion.

(4) It is the duty of the trustee, if he is not the official receiver—

    (a) to furnish the official receiver with such information,
    (b) to produce to the official receiver, and permit inspection by the official receiver of, such books, papers and other records, and
    (c) to give the official receiver such other assistance,

as the official receiver may reasonably require for the purpose of enabling him to carry out his functions in relation to the bankruptcy of the members and the winding up of the partnership business and administration of its property.

(5) The official name of the trustee in his capacity as trustee of a member shall be "the trustee of the estate of ...., a bankrupt" (inserting the name of the member concerned); but he may be referred to as "the trustee in bankruptcy" of the particular member.

(6) The official name of the trustee in his capacity as trustee of the partnership shall be "the trustee of ...., a partnership" (inserting the name of the partnership concerned).".

20 Section 312: Obligation to surrender control to trustee

Section 312 is modified so as to read as follows—

"**312.**—(1) This section applies where orders are made by virtue of article 11 of the Insolvent Partnerships Order 1994 and a trustee is appointed.

(2) Any person who is or has been an officer of the partnership in question, or who is an executor or administrator of the estate of a deceased officer of the partnership, shall deliver up to the trustee of the partnership, for the purposes of the exercise of the trustee's functions under this Act, possession of any partnership property which he holds for the purposes of the partnership.

(3) Each member shall deliver up to the trustee possession of any property, books, papers or other records of which he has possession or control and of which the trustee is required to take possession.

This is without prejudice to the general duties of the members as bankrupts under section 333 in this Chapter.

(4) If any of the following is in possession of any property, books, papers or other records of which the trustee is required to take possession, namely—

(a) the official receiver,

(b) a person who has ceased to be trustee of a member's estate,

(c) a person who has been the administrator of the partnership or supervisor of a voluntary arrangement approved in relation to the partnership under Part I,

(d) a person who has been the supervisor of a voluntary arrangement approved in relation to a member under Part VIII,

the official receiver or, as the case may be, that person shall deliver up possession of the property, books, papers or records to the trustee.

(5) Any banker or agent of a member or of the partnership, or any other person who holds any property to the account of, or for, a member or the partnership shall pay or deliver to the trustee all property in his possession or under his control which forms part of the member's estate or which is partnership property and which he is not by law entitled to retain as against the member, the partnership or the trustee.

(6) If any person without reasonable excuse fails to comply with any obligation imposed by this section, he is guilty of a contempt of court and liable to be punished accordingly (in addition to any other punishment to which he may be subject).".

21 Section 328: Priority of expenses and debts

Section 328 is modified so as to read as follows—

"Priority of expenses

328.—(1) The provisions of this section shall apply in a case where article 11 of the Insolvent Partnerships Order 1994 applies, as regards priority of expenses incurred by a person acting as trustee of the estates of the members of an insolvent partnership and as trustee of that partnership.

(2) The joint estate of the partnership shall be applicable in the first instance in payment of the joint expenses and the separate estate of each insolvent member shall be applicable in the first instance in payment of the separate expenses relating to that member.

(3) Where the joint estate is insufficient for the payment in full of the joint expenses, the unpaid balance shall be apportioned equally between the separate estates of the insolvent members against whom insolvency orders have been made and shall form part of the expenses to be paid out of those estates.

(4) Where any separate estate of an insolvent member is insufficient for the payment in full of the separate expenses to be paid out of that estate, the unpaid balance shall form part of the expenses to be paid out of the joint estate.

(5) Where after the transfer of any unpaid balance in accordance with subsection (3) or (4) any estate is insufficient for the payment in full of the expenses to be paid out of that estate, the balance then remaining unpaid shall be apportioned equally between the other estates.

(6) Where after an apportionment under subsection (5) one or more estates are insufficient for the payment in full of the expenses to be paid out of those estates, the total of the unpaid balances of the expenses to be paid out of those estates shall continue to be apportioned equally between the other estates until provision is made

for the payment in full of the expenses or there is no estate available for the payment of the balance finally remaining unpaid, in which case it abates in equal proportions between all the estates.

(7) Without prejudice to subsections (3) to (6) above, the trustee may, with the sanction of any creditors' committee established under section 301 or with the leave of the court obtained on application—

(a) pay out of the joint estate as part of the expenses to be paid out of that estate any expenses incurred for any separate estate of an insolvent member; or

(b) pay out of any separate estate of an insolvent member any part of the expenses incurred for the joint estate which affects that separate estate.

Priority of debts in joint estate

328A.—(1) The provisions of this section and the next (which are subject to the provisions of section 9 of the Partnership Act 1890 as respects the liability of the estate of a deceased member) shall apply as regards priority of debts in a case where article 11 of the Insolvent Partnerships Order 1994 applies.

(2) After payment of expenses in accordance with section 328 and subject to section 328C(2), the joint debts of the partnership shall be paid out of its joint estate in the following order of priority—

(a) the preferential debts;
(b) the debts which are neither preferential debts nor postponed debts;
(c) interest under section 328D on the joint debts (other than postponed debts);
(d) the postponed debts;
(e) interest under section 328D on the postponed debts.

(3) The responsible insolvency practitioner shall adjust the rights among themselves of the members of the partnership as contributories and shall distribute any surplus to the members or, where applicable, to the separate estates of the members, according to their respective rights and interests in it.

(4) The debts referred to in each of paragraphs (a) and (b) of subsection (2) rank equally between themselves, and in each case if the joint estate is insufficient for meeting them, they abate in equal proportions between themselves.

(5) Where the joint estate is not sufficient for the payment of the joint debts in accordance with paragraphs (a) and (b) of subsection (2), the responsible insolvency practitioner shall aggregate the value of those debts to the extent that they have not been satisfied or are not capable of being satisfied, and that aggregate amount shall be a claim against the separate estate of each member of the partnership against whom an insolvency order has been made which—

(a) shall be a debt provable by the responsible insolvency practitioner in each such estate, and

(b) shall rank equally with the debts of the member referred to in section 328B(1)(b) below.

(6) Where the joint estate is sufficient for the payment of the joint debts in accordance with paragraphs (a) and (b) of subsection (2) but not for the payment of interest under paragraph (c) of that subsection, the responsible insolvency practitioner shall aggregate the value of that interest to the extent that it has not been satisfied or is not capable of being satisfied, and that aggregate amount shall be a claim against the separate estate of each member of the partnership against whom an insolvency order has been made which—

(a) shall be a debt provable by the responsible insolvency practitioner in each such estate, and

(b) shall rank equally with the interest on the separate debts referred to in section 328B(1)(c) below.

(7) Where the joint estate is not sufficient for the payment of the postponed joint debts in accordance with paragraph (d) of subsection (2), the responsible insolvency practitioner shall aggregate the value of those debts to the extent that they have not been satisfied or are not capable of being satisfied, and that aggregate amount shall be a claim against the separate estate of each member of the partnership against whom an insolvency order has been made which—

(a) shall be a debt provable by the responsible insolvency practitioner in each such estate, and

(b) shall rank equally with the postponed debts of the member referred to in section 328B(1)(d) below.

(8) Where the joint estate is sufficient for the payment of the postponed joint debts in accordance with paragraph (d) of subsection (2) but not for the payment of interest under paragraph (e) of that subsection, the responsible insolvency practitioner shall aggregate the value of that interest to the extent that it has not been satisfied or is not capable of being satisfied, and that aggregate amount shall be a claim against the separate estate of each member of the partnership against whom an insolvency order has been made which—

(a) shall be a debt provable by the responsible insolvency practitioner in each such estate, and

(b) shall rank equally with the interest on the postponed debts referred to in section 328B(1)(e) below.

(9) Where the responsible insolvency practitioner receives any distribution from the separate estate of a member in respect of a debt referred to in paragraph (a) of subsection (5), (6), (7) or (8) above, that distribution shall become part of the joint estate and shall be distributed in accordance with the order of priority set out in subsection (2) above.

Priority of debts in separate estate

328B.—(1) The separate estate of each member of the partnership against whom an insolvency order has been made shall be applicable, after payment of expenses in accordance with section 328 and subject to section 328C(2) below, in payment of the separate debts of that member in the following order of priority—

(a) the preferential debts;

(b) the debts which are neither preferential debts nor postponed debts (including any debt referred to in section 328A(5)(a));

(c) interest under section 328D on the separate debts and under section 328A(6);

(d) the postponed debts of the member (including any debt referred to in section 328A(7)(a));

(e) interest under section 328D on the postponed debts of the member and under section 328A(8).

(2) The debts referred to in each of paragraphs (a) and (b) of subsection (1) rank equally between themselves, and in each case if the separate estate is insufficient for meeting them, they abate in equal proportions between themselves.

(3) Where the responsible insolvency practitioner receives any distribution from the joint estate or from the separate estate of another member of the partnership against

whom an insolvency order has been made, that distribution shall become part of the separate estate and shall be distributed in accordance with the order of priority set out in subsection (1) of this section.

Provisions generally applicable in distribution of joint and separate estates

328C.—(1) Distinct accounts shall be kept of the joint estate of the partnership and of the separate estate of each member of that partnership against whom an insolvency order is made.

(2) No member of the partnership shall prove for a joint or separate debt in competition with the joint creditors, unless the debt has arisen—

    (a) as a result of fraud, or
    (b) in the ordinary course of a business carried on separately from the partnership business.

(3) For the purpose of establishing the value of any debt referred to in section 328A(5)(a) or (7)(a), that value may be estimated by the responsible insolvency practitioner in accordance with section 322.

(4) Interest under section 328D on preferential debts ranks equally with interest on debts which are neither preferential debts nor postponed debts.

(5) Sections 328A and 328B are without prejudice to any provision of this Act or of any other enactment concerning the ranking between themselves of postponed debts and interest thereon, but in the absence of any such provision postponed debts and interest thereon rank equally between themselves.

(6) If any two or more members of an insolvent partnership constitute a separate partnership, the creditors of such separate partnership shall be deemed to be a separate set of creditors and subject to the same statutory provisions as the separate creditors of any member of the insolvent partnership.

(7) Where any surplus remains after the administration of the estate of a separate partnership, the surplus shall be distributed to the members or, where applicable, to the separate estates of the members of that partnership according to their respective rights and interests in it.

(8) Neither the official receiver, the Secretary of State nor a responsible insolvency practitioner shall be entitled to remuneration or fees under the Insolvency Rules 1986, the Insolvency Regulations 1986 or the Insolvency Fees Order 1986 for his services in connection with—

    (a) the transfer of a surplus from the joint estate to a separate estate under section 328A(3),
    (b) a distribution from a separate estate to the joint estate in respect of a claim referred to in section 328A(5), (6), (7) or (8), or
    (c) a distribution from the estate of a separate partnership to the separate estates of the members of that partnership under subsection (7) above.".

Interest on debts

328D.—(1) In the bankruptcy of each of the members of an insolvent partnership and in the winding up of that partnership's business and administration of its property, interest is payable in accordance with this section, in the order of priority laid down by sections 328A and 328B, on any debt proved in the bankruptcy including so much of any such debt as represents interest on the remainder.

(2) Interest under this section is payable on the debts in question in respect of the periods during which they have been outstanding since the relevant order was made by virtue of article 11 of the Insolvent Partnerships Order 1994.

(3) The rate of interest payable under this section in respect of any debt ("the official rate" for the purposes of any provision of this Act in which that expression is used) is whichever is the greater of—

    (a) the rate specified in section 17 of the Judgments Act 1838 on the day on which the relevant order was made, and

    (b) the rate applicable to that debt apart from the bankruptcy or winding up.".

22 Section 331: Final meeting

Section 331 is modified so as to read as follows—

"**331.**—(1) Subject as follows in this section and the next, this section applies where—

    (a) it appears to the trustee of the estates of the members and of the partnership that the administration of any member's estate or the winding up of the partnership business and administration of the partnership property is for practical purposes complete, and

    (b) the trustee is not the official receiver.

(2) The trustee shall summon a final general meeting of the creditors of any such member or of the partnership (as the case may be) or a combined final general meeting of the creditors of any such members or (as the case may be) the creditors of any such members and of the partnership which—

    (a) shall as appropriate receive the trustee's report of the administration of the estate of the member or members or of the winding up of the partnership business and administration of the partnership property, and

    (b) shall determine whether the trustee should have his release under section 299 in Chapter III in respect (as the case may be) of the administration of the estate of the member or members, or of the winding up of the partnership business and administration of the partnership property.

(3) The trustee may, if he thinks fit, give the notice summoning the final general meeting at the same time as giving notice under section 330(1); but, if summoned for an earlier date, that meeting shall be adjourned (and, if necessary, further adjourned) until a date on which the trustee is able to report that the administration of the estate of the member or members or the winding up of the partnership business and administration of the partnership property is for practical purposes complete.

(4) In the administration of the members' estates and the winding up of the partnership business and administration of the partnership property it is the trustee's duty to retain sufficient sums from the property of the members and of the partnership to cover the expenses of summoning and holding any meeting required by this section.".

23 Section 387: The "relevant date"

Section 387 is modified so as to read as follows—

"**387.** Where an order has been made in respect of an insolvent partnership by virtue of article 11 of the Insolvent Partnerships Order 1994, references in Schedule 6 to this Act to the relevant date (being the date which determines the existence and amount of a preferential debt) are to the date on which the said order was made.".

SCHEDULE 8

MODIFIED PROVISIONS OF COMPANY DIRECTORS DISQUALIFICATION ACT 1986 FOR THE PURPOSES OF ARTICLE 16

[Sections 6 to 9 of, and Sch 1 to, the Company Directors Disqualification Act 1986 are modified by this Schedule. These sections are reproduced at pp 413 to 418 below.]

SCHEDULE 9

FORMS

Form No	*Description*
1	Petition for administration order.
2	Affidavit verifying petition to wind up partnership.
3	Petition to wind up partnership by liquidator, administrator, trustee or supervisor.
4	Written/statutory demand by creditor.
5	Creditor's petition to wind up partnership (presented in conjunction with petitions against members).
6	Creditor's petition to wind up corporate member (presented in conjunction with petition against partnership).
7	Creditor's bankruptcy petition against individual member (presented in conjunction with petition against partnership).
8	Advertisement of winding-up petition(s) against partnership (and any corporate members).
9	Notice to court of progress on petitions presented.
10	Demand by member.
11	Members' petition to wind up partnership (presented in conjunction with petitions against members).
12	Members' petition to wind up corporate member (presented in conjunction with petition against partnership).
13	Members' bankruptcy petition against individual member (presented in conjunction with petition against partnership).
14	Joint bankruptcy petition against individual members.
15	Affidavit of individual member(s) as to concurrence of all members in presentation of joint bankruptcy petition against individual members.
16	Bankruptcy orders on joint bankruptcy petition presented by individual members.
17	Statement of affairs of member of partnership.
18	Statement of affairs of partnership.

**Schedule 2 para 3
S9(1)**

Petition for Administration Order

(a) Insert name of
partnership

In the matter of (a) _____

_____

**(hereinafter referred to as "the partnership") and
in the matter of the Insolvent Partnerships Order 1994**

(b) Insert title of court
and number of
proceedings (to be
allocated by court)

To (b) _____

_____ No: _____ of _____

(c) Insert full name(s)
and address(es) of
petitioner(s)

The petition of (c) _____

_____

_____

(d) Delete if petition
not presented by the
partnership's
members

presented (d) [by the members] under section 9 of
the Insolvency Act 1986 as modified by the
Insolvent Partnerships Order 1994

(e) Insert address of
principal place
of business

1. The principal place of business of the
partnership is at (e)

_____

_____

_____

(f) Insert nature of
partnership's
business

2. The nature of the partnership's business is (f)

_____

3. The petitioner(s) believe(s) that the partnership
is unable to pay its debts and that an administration
order would be likely to achieve:

(g) Delete such as are
inapplicable

(g) (i) the survival of the whole or any part of the
undertaking of the partnership as a going
concern

(ii) the approval of a voluntary arrangement with
its creditors under Part I of the Insolvency
Act 1986 as modified by the Insolvent
Partnerships Order 1994

(iii) a more advantageous realisation of the
partnership property than would be effected
on a winding up

for the reasons stated in the affidavit of _____

_____

filed in support hereof.

4. The petitioner(s) propose(s) that during the period for which the order is in force the affairs, business and property of the partnership be managed by

(h) Insert full name(s)					(h) _____
and address(es)
of proposed					_____
administrator(s)

_____

who is (are) to the best of the petitioner's(s') knowledge and belief qualified to act as (an) insolvency practitioner(s) in relation to the partnership.

The petitioner(s) therefore pray(s) as follows:–

(1) that the court make an administration order in

(j) Insert full name of					relation to (j) _____
partnership

_____

(k) Insert name(s) of					(2) that (k) _____
proposed
administrator(s)					_____

_____

be appointed to be the administrator(s) of the said partnership

(l) Insert details of any					(3) (l) _____
ancillary orders
sought					_____

or

(4) that such other order may be made in the premises as shall be just.

Note:
It is intended to serve this petition on _____

_____

_____

_____

(m) Insert here name,					This petition was issued by (m) _____
address, telephone
number and reference					_____
(if any) of a
solicitor acting for					_____
the petitioner(s)

_____

_____ (solicitor for)

the petitioner(s) whose address for service is:

_____

_____

_____

(n) Delete as applicable

(o) Insert name and
     address of court

(p) Insert name and
     address of
     District Registry

ENDORSEMENT

This petition against the partnership having been presented to the court on _____ will be heard at (n) [Royal Courts of Justice, Strand, London WC2A 2LL] [(o) _____

_____ County Court

_____

_____]

[(p) _____ District

Registry _____

_____]

on:

Date _____

Time _____

(or as soon thereafter as the petition can be heard)

Schedule 3 para 3
S221(8)
Schedule 4 para 3
S221(9)
Schedule 5 para 2
S221(8)
Schedule 6 para 4
S221(9)

Affidavit Verifying Petition to Wind Up Partnership

(a) Insert name of partnership subject to petition

In the matter of (a) _____

_____

and in the matter of the Insolvent Partnerships Order 1994

(b) Insert name and address of person making oath

I (b) _____

_____

_____

Make oath and say as follows:–

(c) Delete if affidavit not made by petitioner in person

1. (c) I am the petitioner. The statements in the petition now produced and shown to me marked "A" are (d) [true] [true to the best of my knowledge, information and belief].

(d) Delete as applicable

OR

(e) Delete if affidavit is made by petitioner in person

1. (e) I am (f) _____
of the petitioner.

(f) State capacity eg. director, secretary, solicitor, etc

2. (e) I am duly authorised by the petitioner to make this affidavit on (d) [its] [his] behalf.

3. (e) I have been concerned in the matters giving rise to the petition and have the requisite knowledge of the matters referred to in

(g) State means of knowledge of matters sworn to in affidavit

the petition because (g) _____

_____

_____

_____

4. (e) The statements in the petition now produced and shown to me marked "A" are (d) [true] [true to the best of my knowledge, information and belief].

Sworn at _____

Date _____

Signature(s) _____

Before me (signature) _____

(h) Insert name and full address and whether solicitor or commissioner of oaths or duly authorised officer

(h) _____

_____

_____

A solicitor or commissioner of oaths or duly authorised officer

FORM 3

Schedule 3 para 3
S221A(1)

Petition to Wind Up Partnership by Liquidator, Administrator, Trustee or Supervisor

(a) Insert name of partnership subject to petition

In the matter of (a) _____

(hereinafter referred to as "the partnership") and in the matter of the Insolvent Partnerships Order 1994

(b) Insert title of court and number of proceedings (to be allocated by court)

To (b) _____

_____ **No:** _____ **of** _____

(c) Insert full name(s) and address(es) of petitioner(s)

The petition of (c) _____

_____

_____

(d) Delete as necessary

(e) Insert name of insolvent

1.   I am/We are the (d) [joint] liquidator(s)/administrator(s)/trustee(s)/supervisor(s) of (e) _____

who is/was a member of the partnership, the nature of whose business is/was

(f) Insert the nature of the partnership's business

(f) _____

2.   (d) [The principal place of business of the partnership] [A place of business at which business was carried on by the partnership in the course of which the debt (or part of the debt) arose which forms the basis of this petition] is at (g) _____

(g) Insert address of business applicable to show jurisdiction of the court

_____

_____

within the jurisdiction of the court.

(h) Delete as necessary. If the partnership has a principal place of business in both England and Wales and in Scotland the relevant period is 1 year. In any other case it is 3 years

3.   The partnership has carried on its business in England and Wales at some time during the period of (h) [3 years] [1 year] ending with the day on which this petition is presented.

(j) Set out the grounds on which a winding-up order is sought

4.   (j) _____

_____

_____

5. In the circumstances the partnership should be wound up.

The petitioner(s) therefore pray(s) as follows:–
(1) that (a) _____

may be wound up by the court under the provisions of the Insolvency Act 1986 as modified by the Insolvent Partnerships Order 1994
OR
(2) that such other order may be made as the court thinks fit.

Note:

(k)   Add full name and
      address of any other
      person on whom it is
      intended to serve
      this petition

It is intended to serve this petition on the
partnership [and] (k) _____

_____

_____

ENDORSEMENT

This petition against the partnership having been presented to the court on _____ will be heard at (l) [Royal Courts of Justice, Strand, London WC2A 2LL]

(l)   Delete as applicable

(m) Insert name and address of court

[(m) _____

_____ County Court

_____

_____]

(n) Insert name and address of District Registry

[(n) _____ District

Registry _____

_____]

on:

Date _____

Time _____

(or as soon thereafter as the petition can be heard)

The solicitor to the petitioner is:–

Name _____

Address _____

_____

_____

Tel. no. _____

Reference _____

[whose agents are:–

Name _____

Address _____

_____

_____

Tel. no. _____

Reference _____]

Schedule 4 para 4 and para 7
S222(1)(a)
S222(1)(b)
S123(1)(a)
S268(1)(a)

Written/Statutory Demand by Creditor

(a) Insert name   **In the matter of (a)** _____
of partnership   **and in the matter of the Insolvent Partnerships Order 1994**

WARNING TO DEBTOR – READ THE FOLLOWING NOTES CAREFULLY

- This is an important document. Please read the demand and the notes entitled "How to comply with a demand" and "How to have a demand set aside (applicable to individual members only)" on page 5 below.

- If the partnership has received this, the partnership must act upon it **within 21 days** or a winding-up order could be made against the partnership.

- If a corporate member of the partnership has received this, that member must act upon it **within 21 days** or a winding-up order could be made against the company.

- If, having received this as an individual member of the partnership, you wish to have this demand set aside, you must make application to do so **within 18 days** from its service on you. If you do not apply to set aside **within 18 days** or otherwise deal with this demand as set out in the notes **within 21 days** after its service on you, you could be made bankrupt and your property and goods taken away from you.

  If you are in any doubt about your position you should seek advice **immediately** from a solicitor or your nearest Citizens Advice Bureau.

To: _____

Address: _____

_____

_____

This DEMAND is served on you by the creditor:

Name: _____

Address: _____

_____

_____

DEMAND

Notes for Creditor

- If the creditor is entitled to the debt by way of assignment, details of the original creditor and any intermediary assignees should be given in part B on page 4.
- If the amount of the debt includes interest not previously notified to the partnership as included in its liability, details should be given, including the grounds upon which interest is charged. The amount of interest must be shown separately.
- Any other charge accruing due from time to time may be claimed. The amount or rate of the charge must be identified and the grounds on which it is claimed must be stated.
- In either case the amount claimed must be limited to that which has accrued due at the date of the demand.
- If the creditor holds any security, the amount of the debt should be the sum the creditor is prepared to regard as unsecured for the purposes of this demand. Brief details of the total debt should be included and the nature of the security and the value put upon it by the creditor, as at the date of the demand, must be specified.
- If signatory of the demand is a solicitor or other agent of the creditor, the name of his/her firm should be given.

The creditor claims that the partnership owes the sum of £_____, full particulars of which are set out on page 3;

The creditor demands that the partnership or a member or former member of the partnership named in part C of this notice do pay the above debt or secure or compound for it to the creditor's satisfaction.

[The creditor making this demand is a Minister of the Crown or a Government Department and it is intended to present a winding-up and/or bankruptcy petitions in the High Court in London]

[Delete if inappropriate]

Signature of individual _____

Name _____
(BLOCK LETTERS)

Date _____

*Position with or relationship to creditor:

_____

*I am authorised to make this demand on the creditor's behalf.

Address _____

_____

_____

Tel. no. _____   Ref. _____

N.B.   The person making this demand must complete the whole of this page, page 3, page 4 and page 5.

*Delete if signed by the creditor himself.

Particulars of Debt.
These particulars must include (a) when the debt was incurred, (b) the consideration for the debt (or if there is no consideration the way in which it arose), and (c) the amount due as at the date of this demand

Notes for Creditor
Please make sure that you have read the notes on page 2 before completing this page.

Note:
If space is insufficient continue on reverse of page and clearly indicate on this page that you are doing so.

PART A

The individual or individuals to whom any communication regarding this demand may be addressed is/are:–

Name _____ | _____
(BLOCK LETTERS)
Address _____ | _____

_____ | _____

_____ | _____

Telephone number _____ | _____

Reference _____ | _____

PART B

For completion if the creditor is entitled to the debt by way of assignment

	Name	Date(s) of Assignment
Original creditor		
Assignees		

PART C

It is intended that a demand in respect of the debt shown on page 2 will also be served on the following:–

_____

_____

_____

_____

HOW TO COMPLY WITH A DEMAND

If the partnership or a corporate member wishes to avoid a winding-up petition being presented against it, it must pay the debt shown on page 2, particulars of which are set out on page 3 of this notice, within the period of **21 days after** its service. Alternatively, the partnership can attempt to come to a settlement with the creditor. To do this the partnership should:

- inform the individual (or one of the individuals) named in part A above immediately that it is willing and able to offer security for the debt to the creditor's satisfaction; or

- inform the individual (or one of the individuals) named in part A immediately that it is willing and able to compound for the debt to the creditor's satisfaction.

If the partnership disputes the demand in whole or in part it should:

- contact the individual (or one of the individuals) named in part A immediately.

REMEMBER! The partnership has only 21 days after the date of the service on it of this document before the creditor may present a winding-up petition against the partnership and winding-up or bankruptcy petitions against those members listed in part C of this notice.

HOW TO HAVE A DEMAND SET ASIDE (applicable to individual members only)

If you are an individual member of the partnership and you consider that you have grounds to have this demand set aside or if you do not quickly receive a satisfactory written reply from the individual named at part A whom you have contacted you should **apply within 18 days** from the date of service of this demand on you to the (a) [High Court of Justice, Strand, London WC2A 2LL] [(b) _____ County Court whose address is

_____]

to have the demand set aside.

Any application to set aside the demand (Form 6.4 in Schedule 4 to the Insolvency Rules 1986) should be made within 18 days from the date of service upon you and be supported by an affidavit (Form 6.5 in Schedule 4 to those Rules) stating the grounds on which the demand should be set aside. The forms may be obtained from the appropriate court when you attend to make the application.

REMEMBER! From the date of service on you of this document
- **you have only 18 days to apply to the court to have the demand set aside, and**
- **you have only 21 days before the creditor may present a bankruptcy petition against you.**

(a) Delete as applicable

(b) Insert name and address of court

Schedule 4 para 8
S124(1)(a)

Creditor's Petition to Wind Up Partnership (Presented in Conjunction with Petitions against Members)

(a) Insert name of partnership subject to petition

In the matter of (a) _____

_____

(hereinafter referred to as "the partnership") and in the matter of the Insolvent Partnerships Order 1994

(b) Insert title of court and number of proceedings (to be allocated by court)

To (b) _____

_____ **No:** _____ **of** _____

(c) Insert full name(s) and address(es) of petitioner(s)

The petition of (c) _____

_____

_____

(d) Insert the nature of the partnership's business

1.   The nature of the partnership's business is/was (d) _____

_____

(e) Delete as necessary

(f) Insert address of business applicable to show jurisdiction of the court

2.   (e) [The principal place of business of the partnership] [A place of business at which business was carried on by the partnership in the course of which the debt (or part of the debt) arose which forms the basis of this petition] is at (f) _____

_____

_____

within the jurisdiction of the court.

(g) Delete as necessary. If the partnership has a principal place of business in both England and Wales and in Scotland the relevant period is 1 year. In any other case it is 3 years

3.   The partnership has carried on its business in England and Wales at some time during the period of (g) [3 years] [1 year] ending with the day on which this petition is presented.

4.   The partnership is justly and truly indebted to me [us] in the aggregate sum of £ _____. The above-mentioned debt is for a liquidated sum payable immediately.

(h) Insert date of service

(j) State manner of service of demand

On (h) _____ a demand was served upon the partnership by (j) _____

_____

in respect of the above-mentioned debt. To the best of my knowledge and belief the demand has not been complied with.

(k) Insert full name of
    member(s)

On (h) _____ (a) demand(s) was/were
served upon (k) _____
(a) member(s) of the partnership by (j) _____

_____
in respect of the above-mentioned debt. To the best
of my knowledge and belief the demand(s) has/have
not been complied with.

5. The partnership is unable to pay its debts
and in the circumstances the partnership should
be wound up.

The petitioner(s) therefore pray(s) as follows:–

(1) that (a) _____
may be wound up by the court under the provisions of the Insolvency Act 1986 as
modified by the Insolvent Partnerships Order 1994.

OR

(2) that such other order may be made as the court thinks fit.

NOTE 1:

Petitions are also being presented against the following members of the partnership:

NAME	ADDRESS	TYPE OF PETITION (WINDING-UP OR BANKRUPTCY)	DATE DEMAND SERVED

NOTE 2:

It is intended to serve this petition on the partnership.

ENDORSEMENT

This petition having been presented to the court
on _____ will be heard
at (l) [Royal Courts of Justice, Strand, London
WC2A 2LL]

[(m) _____ County Court

_____

_____]

on:

Date _____

Time _____
    (or as soon thereafter as the petition can be
    heard)

The solicitor to the petitioner is:

Name _____

Address _____

_____

_____

Tel. no. _____

Reference _____

[whose agents are:

Name _____

Address _____

_____

_____

Tel. no. _____

Reference _____]

(l) Delete as applicable

(m) Insert name and
address of court

Schedule 4 para 8
S124(1)(b)

Creditor's Petition to Wind Up Corporate Member (Presented in Conjunction with Petition against Partnership)

(a) Insert name of corporate member subject to winding-up petition

In the matter of (a) _____

_____

(hereinafter referred to as "the company") and in the matter of the Insolvent Partnerships Order 1994

(b) Insert title of court and number of proceedings (to be allocated by court)

To (b) _____

_____ No: _____ of _____

(c) Insert full name(s) and address(es) of petitioner(s)

The petition of (c) _____

_____ .

_____

(d) Insert date of incorporation

1. The company was incorporated on (d) _____ under the Companies Act 19

(e) Insert address of registered office

2. The registered office of the company is at (e)

_____

_____

_____

3. The nominal capital of the company is £ _____ divided into _____ shares of £ _____ each. The amount of the capital paid up or credited as paid up is £ _____

4. The principal objects for which the company was established are as follows:–

_____

_____

_____

_____

and other objects stated in the memorandum of association of the company.

(f) Insert full name of
partnership against
which winding-up
petition has been
presented to this
court

(g) Delete as necessary.
If the partnership has
a principal place of
business in both
England and Wales
and in Scotland the
relevant period is
1 year. In any other
case it is 3 years

(h) Insert appropriate
date

(j) State manner of
service of demand

5.   The subject of this petition is a member of (f)

_____

which has carried on business in England and Wales
at some time during the period of (g) [3 years] [1 year]
ending with (h) _____ , the day on which a
winding-up petition was presented to this court
against the partnership.

6.   The partnership is justly and truly indebted
to me[us] in the aggregate sum of £ _____.
The above-mentioned debt is for a liquidated sum
payable immediately. On (h) _____
a demand was served upon the company and the
partnership by (j) _____

_____

in respect of the above-mentioned debt. To the
best of my knowledge and belief the demand has not
been complied with.

7.   The partnership is unable to pay its debts
and in the circumstances the corporate member
should be wound up.

The petitioner(s) therefore pray(s) as follows:–

(1) that (a)_____
may be wound up by the court under
the provisions of the Insolvency Act 1986 as
modified by the Insolvent Partnerships Order 1994.

OR

(2) that such other order may be made as the court
thinks fit.

NOTE 1:

Petitions are also being presented against the following members of the partnership:

NAME	ADDRESS	TYPE OF PETITION (WINDING-UP OR BANKRUPTCY)	DATE DEMAND SERVED

NOTE 2:

It is intended to serve this petition on (a) _____

_____

FORM 6 (*cont'd*)

ENDORSEMENT

(k)   Delete as applicable

(l)   Insert name and
      address of court

This petition having been presented to the court on
_____ will be heard at (k) [Royal
Courts of Justice, Strand, London WC2A 2LL]

[(l) _____ County Court

_____

_____]

on:
Date _____

Time _____
(or as soon thereafter as the petition can be heard)

The solicitor to the petitioner is:

Name _____

Address _____

_____

_____

Tel. no. _____

Reference _____

[whose agents are:

Name _____

Address _____

_____

_____

Tel. no. _____

Reference _____]

Schedule 4 para 8
S124(1)(c)

Creditor's Bankruptcy Petition against Individual Member (Presented in Conjunction with Petition against Partnership)

(a) Insert name of individual member subject to petition

In the matter of (a) _____

_____

and in the matter of the Insolvent Partnerships Order 1994

(b) Insert title of court and number of proceedings (to be allocated by court)

To (b) _____

_____ No: _____ of _____

(c) Insert full name(s) and address(es) of petitioner(s)

I/We (c) _____

_____

_____

_____

(d) Insert full name, place of residence and occupation of individual member

petition the court that a bankruptcy order may be made against (d) _____

_____

_____

_____

(e) Insert in full any other name(s) by which the member is or has been known

[also known as (e) _____

_____]

(f) Insert trading name (adding "with another or others", if this is so), business address and nature of business

[and carrying on business as (f) _____

_____

_____

_____]

(g) Insert any former address(es) at which the member has resided after the time at which the petition debt of the partnership (j) was incurred

[and lately residing at (g) _____

_____

_____

_____]

(h) Give the same details as specified in note (f) above for any other businesses which have been carried on at or after the time at which the petition debt of the partnership (j) was incurred or at which the member may have incurred debts or liabilities still unpaid or unsatisfied

[and lately carrying on business as (h) _____

_____

_____

_____]

On the grounds that:

(j) Insert name of partnership subject to winding-up petition

he is a member of (j) _____
which has carried on business in England and Wales
at some time during the period of (k) [3 years] [1 year]
ending with (l) _____ , the day on which a
winding-up petition was presented to this court
against the partnership.

(k) Delete as necessary. If the partnership has a principal place of business in both England and Wales and in Scotland the relevant period is 1 year. In any other case it is 3 years

The partnership is justly and truly indebted to
me [us] in the aggregate sum of £ _____

(l) Insert appropriate date

The above-mentioned debt is for a liquidated sum
payable immediately.

(m) State date and manner of service of demand

On (m) _____ a demand was served upon the
member and the partnership by (m) _____

_____

_____

in respect of the above-mentioned debt.

To the best of my knowledge and belief the demand
has neither been complied with nor set aside in
accordance with the Rules and no application
made to set it aside is outstanding.

The partnership is unable to pay its debts,
and in the circumstances a bankruptcy order
should be made against (a) _____

_____

Note 1:
Petitions are also being presented against the following members of the partnership:

NAME	ADDRESS	TYPE OF PETITION (WINDING-UP OR BANKRUPTCY)	DATE DEMAND SERVED

Note 2:
It is intended to serve this petition on (a) _____

_____

ENDORSEMENT

This petition having been presented to the court on _____ it is ordered that the petition shall be heard as follows:

Date _____

Time _____

Place _____

_____

(n) Insert name of member

and you, the above-named (n) _____ are to take notice that if you intend to oppose the petition you must not later than 7 days before the date fixed for the hearing:

(i) file in court a notice in Form 6.19 of the Insolvency Rules 1986 specifying the grounds on which you object to the making of a bankruptcy order; and

(ii) send a copy of the notice to the petitioner or his solicitor.

(o) Only to be completed where the petitioning creditor is represented by a solicitor

The solicitor to the petitioner is (o):

Name _____

Address _____

_____

_____

Tel. no. _____

Reference _____

[whose agents are:

Name _____

Address _____

_____

_____

Tel. no. _____

Reference _____]

FORM 8

Schedule 4 para 8 **S124(3)(b)** **Schedule 6 para 2** **S124(4)(b)**	**Advertisement of Winding-Up** **Petition(s) against Partnership** **(and any Corporate Members)**

(a) Insert name of
partnership

In the matter of (a) _____

_____

**(hereinafter referred to as "the partnership") and in
the matter of the Insolvent Partnerships Order 1994**

(b) Insert title of court
and number of
proceedings (to be
allocated by court)

In the (b) _____

_____ No: _____ of _____

(c) Insert full name(s) of
partnership, and any
corporate members, and
partnership's principal
place of business or
place debt incurred
and nature of its
business

Petition(s) to wind up (c) _____

_____

_____

_____

(d) Insert date

presented on (d) _____

(e) Insert name and
address of petitioner

by (e) _____

_____

(f) Delete as applicable

(f) [claiming to be a creditor of the partnership]
will be heard at (f) [The Royal Courts of Justice,
Strand, London WC2A 2LL] [(g) _____

(g) Insert name and
address of court

County Court, _____

_____

_____]

on:

Date _____

Time _____
(or as soon thereafter as the petition can be heard)

Any person intending to appear on the hearing of the
petition(s) (whether in support or opposition) must
give notice of intention to do so to the petitioner
or his/its solicitor in accordance with Rule 4.16 of
the Insolvency Rules 1986 by 1600 hours on

(h) Insert date, which
should be the
business day before
that appointed for
the hearing

(h) _____

The petitioner's solicitor is (j) _____

(j) Where applicable
insert name and address
of solicitor

_____

_____

_____

_____

Dated _____

Note:
Details of individual members of the partnership against whom bankruptcy petitions
are being presented in conjunction with the winding-up petition against the
partnership <u>MUST NOT BE</u> included in this advertisement.

FORM 9

Schedule 4 para 8
Schedule 6 para 2
S124(1)(a)(b)(c)
S124(7)

Notice to Court of Progress on Petitions Presented

In the matter of (a) _____
and in the matter of the Insolvent Partnerships Order 1994

(a) Insert name of partnership

To (b) _____

_____ No: _____ of _____

(b) Insert name of court and number of proceedings (to be allocated by court)

Petitions are being presented in these proceedings as follows:

Name	Address	Type of petition (winding-up or bankruptcy)	Current position (details as to service of petition, whether pending, dismissed or order made, must be stated)
(c)			
_____	_____	_____	_____
_____	_____	_____	_____
_____	_____	_____	_____
_____	_____	_____	_____
_____	_____	_____	_____

(c) Insert name and details of all partners against whom petitions are being presented

Schedule 5 para 2
S221A(2)(a)

Demand by Member

(a) Insert name of
    partnership

In the matter of (a) _____
**(hereinafter referred to as "the partnership") and in the
matter of the Insolvent Partnerships Order 1994**

Warning	
• This is an important document. This demand must be dealt with **within 21 days** of its service upon the partnership or a winding-up order could be made in respect of the partnership.	• **Please read the demand and the notes "How to comply with a demand" carefully**

Demand

To _____

Address _____

_____

This demand is served by the member:

_____

Address _____

_____

The member claims that the partnership owes the following debt which he/she has
paid other than out of partnership property:

When incurred	Description of debt	Amount due as at the date of this demand	Date of order, decree, or judgment of court obtained by member and steps that he/she has taken to enforce it
(1)	(2)	(3)	(4)
_____	_____	_____	_____
_____	_____	_____	_____
_____	_____	_____	_____
_____	_____	_____	_____
_____			_____

Amount of debt
£ [   ]

The member demands that the partnership do pay the above debt or secure or
compound for it to his/her satisfaction.   •

Signature _____

Name of signatory (BLOCK LETTERS) _____

Date _____

Position with or relationship to member _____

_____ duly authorised _____

Address _____

_____

Tel. no. _____

Reference _____

Notes

- If signatory is a solicitor or other agent of the creditor the name of his/her firm should be given.

- The person making the demand must complete the whole of pages 1 and 2 and part A overleaf.

PART A

The person(s) to whom any communication regarding this demand should be addressed is/are

Name(s) _____

Address(es) _____

_____

Tel. no.(s) _____

How to comply with a demand

To avoid insolvency proceedings being taken, the debt set out on page 1 of this notice must be paid **within the period of 21 days of service** of the written demand. Alternatively, a settlement can be reached with the member. To do this the person named in part A above must be informed immediately:–

- of any security offered for the debt to the member's satisfaction, or

- of any terms available for settlement of the debt to the member's satisfaction.

If the debt is disputed in whole or in part contact the person named in part A immediately.

REMEMBER! **There are only 21 days from the date of the service of this document before the member may present the winding-up petition.**

FORM 11

Schedule 6 para 2
S124(1)(a)

Members' Petition to Wind Up Partnership (Presented in Conjunction with Petitions against Members)

In the matter of (a) _____

_____

(hereinafter referred to as "the partnership") and in the matter of the Insolvent Partnerships Order 1994

(a) Insert name of partnership subject to petition

(b) Insert title of court and number of proceedings (to be allocated by court)

To (b) _____

_____ No: _____ of _____

(c) Insert full name(s) and address(es) of petitioner(s)

The petition of (c) _____

_____

_____

1.   The nature of the partnership business is/was (d) _____

(d) Insert the nature of the partnership's business

_____

(e) Insert address of business applicable to show jurisdiction of the court

2.   The principal place of business of the partnership is at (e) _____

_____

_____

within the jurisdiction of the court.

(f) Delete as necessary. If the partnership has a principal place of business in both England and Wales and in Scotland the relevant period is 1 year. In any other case it is 3 years

3.   The partnership has carried on its business in England and Wales at some time during the period of (f) [3 years] [1 year] ending with the day on which this petition is presented.

This petition is presented by the members of the partnership.

Note: the petition should be presented by all members unless the court has otherwise directed under section 124(3) of the Insolvency Act 1986 as modified by the Insolvent Partnerships Order 1994

4.   The partnership is unable to pay its debts and in the circumstances the partnership should be wound up.

The petitioner(s) therefore pray(s) as follows:–

(1) that (a) _____
may be wound up by the court under the provisions of the Insolvency Act 1986 as modified by the Insolvent Partnerships Order 1994.

OR

(2) that such other order may be made as the court thinks fit.

NOTE 1:

Petitions are also being presented against the following members of the partnership:

NAME	ADDRESS	TYPE OF PETITION (WINDING-UP OR BANKRUPTCY)

NOTE 2:

It is intended to serve this petition on the partnership.

(g) Delete as applicable

(h) Insert name and
address of court

ENDORSEMENT

This petition having been presented to the court
on _____ will be heard
at (g) [Royal Courts of Justice, Strand, London
WC2A 2LL]

[(h) _____ County Court

_____

_____]

on:

Date _____

Time _____
(or as soon thereafter as the petition can be
heard)

The solicitor to the petitioner is:

Name _____

Address _____

_____

_____

Tel. no. _____

Reference _____

[whose agents are:

Name _____

Address _____

_____

_____

Tel. no. _____

Reference _____]

Schedule 6 para 2
S124(1)(b)

Members' Petition to Wind Up Corporate Member (Presented in Conjunction with Petition against Partnership)

(a) Insert name of corporate member subject to winding-up petition

In the matter of (a) _____

_____

(hereinafter referred to as "the company") and in the matter of the Insolvent Partnerships Order 1994

(b) Insert title of court and number of proceedings (to be allocated by court)

To (b) _____

_____ No: _____ of _____

(c) Insert full name(s) and address(es) of petitioner(s)

The petition of (c) _____

_____

_____

(d) Insert date of incorporation

1. The company was incorporated on (d)

_____ under
the Companies Act 19

(e) Insert address of registered office

2. The registered office of the company is at (e) ___

_____

_____

_____

3. The nominal capital of the company is £_____
divided into _____ shares of £_____ each. The
amount of capital paid up or credited as paid up
is £ _____

4. The principal objects for which the company was
established are as follows:–

_____

_____

_____

and other objects stated in the memorandum of
association of the company.

(f) Insert full name of partnership against which winding-up petition has been presented to this court

5. The subject of this petition is a member of (f)

_____

which has carried on business in England and Wales at some time during the period of (g) [3 years] [1 year] ending with (h) _____ , the day on which a winding-up petition was presented to this court against the partnership.

(g) Delete as necessary. If the partnership has a principal place of business in both England and Wales and in Scotland the relevant period is 1 year. In any other case it is 3 years

(h) Insert appropriate date

Note: the petition should be presented by all members unless the court has otherwise directed under section 124(3) of the Insolvency Act 1986 as modified by the Insolvent Partnerships Order 1994. If the court has so directed, then each member against whom a petition is being presented should state that he is willing for an insolvency order to be made against him.

6. A petition has been presented against the partnership by its members and this petition is presented in conjunction with that petition.

7. The partnership is unable to pay its debts, each member is willing for an insolvency order to be made against that member and in the circumstances the corporate member should be wound up. The petitioner(s) therefore pray(s) as follows:–

(1) that (a) _____
may be wound up by the court under the provisions of the Insolvency Act 1986 as modified by the Insolvent Partnerships Order 1994.

OR

(2) that such other order may be made as the court thinks fit.

NOTE 1:

Petitions are also being presented against the following members of the partnership:

NAME	ADDRESS	TYPE OF PETITION (WINDING-UP OR BANKRUPTCY)

NOTE 2:

It is intended to serve this petition on (a) _____

(j) Delete as applicable

(k) Insert name and
     address of court

ENDORSEMENT

This petition having been presented to the court
on _____ will be heard at (j)
[Royal Courts of Justice, Strand, London
WC2A 2LL]

[(k)_____ County Court

_____

_____

_____]

on:

Date _____

Time _____

(or as soon thereafter as the petition can be
heard)

The solicitor to the petitioner is:

Name _____

Address _____

_____

_____

Tel. no. _____

Reference _____

[whose agents are:

Name _____

Address _____

_____

_____

Tel. no. _____

Reference _____]

FORM 13

Schedule 6 para 2 **S124(1)(c)**	**Members' Bankruptcy Petition against Individual Member (Presented in Conjunction with Petition against Partnership)**

(a) Insert name of individual member subject to petition

In the matter of (a) _____

_____

and in the matter of the Insolvent Partnerships Order 1994

(b) Insert title of court and number of proceedings (to be allocated by court)

To (b) _____

_____ No: _____ of _____

(c) Insert full name(s) and address(es) of petitioner(s)

I/We   (c) _____

_____

_____

(d) Insert full name, place of residence and occupation of member

petition the court that a bankruptcy order may be made against (d) _____

_____

_____

(e) Insert in full any other name(s) by which the member is or has been known

[also known as (e) _____

_____]

(f) Insert trading name (adding "with another or others", if this is so), business address and nature of business

[and carrying on business as (f) _____

_____

_____

_____]

(g) Insert any former address(es) at which the member has resided after the time at which the petition debt of the partnership (j) was incurred

[and lately residing at (g) _____

_____

_____

_____]

(h) Give the same details as specified in note (f) above for any other businesses which have been carried on at or after the time at which the petition debt of the partnership (j) was incurred or at which the member may have incurred debts or liabilities still unpaid or unsatisfied

[and lately carrying on business as (h) _____

_____

_____

_____]

FORM 13 (*cont'd*)

On the grounds that:

(j) Insert name of partnership subject to winding-up petition

he is a member of (j) _____

_____

(k) Delete as necessary. If the partnership has a principal place of business in both England and Wales and in Scotland the relevant period is 1 year. In any other case it is 3 years

which has carried on business in England and Wales at some time during the period of (k) [3 years] [1 year] ending with (l) _____ , the day on which a winding-up petition was presented to this court against the partnership.

(l) Insert appropriate date

Note: the petition should be presented by all members unless the court has otherwise directed under section 124(3) of the Insolvency Act 1986 as modified by the Insolvent Partnerships Order 1994. If the court has so directed, then each member against whom a petition is being presented should state that he is willing for an insolvency order to be made against him.

A petition has been presented against the partnership by its members and this petition is presented in conjunction with that petition.

The partnership is unable to pay its debts, each member is willing for an insolvency order to be made against that member and in the circumstances a bankruptcy order should be made against (a)

_____

NOTE 1:

Petitions are also being presented against the following members of the partnership:

NAME	ADDRESS	TYPE OF PETITION (WINDING-UP OR BANKRUPTCY)

NOTE 2:

It is intended to serve this petition on (a) _____

_____

Signature _____

Date _____

FORM 13 (*cont'd*)

ENDORSEMENT

This petition having been presented to the court on _____ it is ordered that the petition shall be heard as follows:

Date _____

Time _____

Place _____

_____

_____

_____

(m) Insert name of member

and you, the above-named (m) _____

_____ ,

are to take notice that if you intend to oppose the petition you must not later than 7 days before the day fixed for the hearing:

(i) file in court a notice in Form 6.19 of the Insolvency Rules 1986 specifying the grounds on which you object to the making of a bankruptcy order; and

(ii) send a copy of the notice to the petitioner or his solicitor.

(n) Only to be completed where the petitioner is represented by a solicitor

The solicitor to the petitioner is (n):

Name _____

Address _____

_____

_____

Tel. no. _____

Reference _____

[whose agents are:

Name _____

Address _____

_____

_____

Tel. no. _____

Reference _____]

Schedule 7 para 2
S264(3)(a)

Joint Bankruptcy Petition against Individual Members

(a) Insert name of partnership subject to petition

In the matter of (a) _____

_____

(hereinafter referred to as "the partnership") and in the matter of the Insolvent Partnerships Order 1994

(b) Insert title of court and number of proceedings (to be allocated by court)

To (b) _____

_____ No: _____ of _____

Details of members

(c) Insert separately for each member their full name, any other names by which they are or have been known and their occupation

*(1) I, (c) _____

_____

(d) Insert separately for each member their residential address

(d) _____

_____

_____

[and carrying on/lately carrying on business as

(e) Excluding the partnership, insert separately for each member the trading name, business address and nature of any business carried on at, or after, the time the partnership debts were incurred

(e) _____

_____

_____

_____]

AND

*(2) I, (c) _____

_____

(d) _____

_____

_____

[and carrying on/lately carrying on business as

(e) _____

_____

_____

_____]

*Continue with separate numbered paragraphs for each member

AND

*(3) I, (c) _____

_____

(d) _____

_____

_____

[and carrying on/lately carrying on
business as (e) _____

_____

_____

_____]

(f) Insert trading name,
business address(es)
and nature of
partnership business
the subject of
this petition

being all the members of (f) _____

_____

_____

_____

and all of us being individual members and none of
us being limited partners

and being unable to pay the debts of the partnership

and the members of the partnership having carried
on its business in England and Wales at some time
during the period of 3 years ending with the day
on which this petition is presented

petition the court that bankruptcy orders be made
against us and that the trustee of our estates
wind up the partnership business and administer the
partnership property.

Signature(s) _____
                    (member(s) of partnership)

Date _____

Notes

(1) The petition should be
presented by <u>all</u> members
unless the court
has otherwise directed
under section 266(1) of the
Insolvency Act 1986 as
modified by the
Insolvent Partnerships
Order 1994.

(2) If this petition is not
signed by all the partners
presenting it, it must be
accompanied by an
affidavit in Form 15 made
by the partner or one of
the partners who signs the
petition showing that all
the partners are individual
members and not limited
partners and that all the
partners presenting the
petition concur in its
presentation (s264(4)).

Schedule 7 para 2
S264(4)(a)

Affidavit of Individual Member(s) as to Concurrence of All Members in Presentation of Joint Bankruptcy Petition against Individual Members

Note: Only use this Form if the petition has not been signed by all members presenting it.

(a) Insert name of partnership subject to petition

In the matter of (a) _____

_____

and in the matter of the Insolvent Partnerships Order 1994

(b) Insert full name(s) and occupation(s) of deponent(s)

I/We (b) _____

_____

_____

(c) Insert full address(es) of deponent(s)

of (c) _____

_____

_____

_____

MAKE OATH AND SAY that:–

1. I am/we are member(s) of (a) _____

_____

a partnership against all of whose members a joint bankruptcy petition has today been presented (hereinafter referred to as "the partnership").

2. All members of the partnership are individual members and not limited partners and all partners presenting this petition concur in its presentation.

Sworn at _____

Date _____

Signature(s) _____

Before me (Signature) _____

(d) Insert name and full address of solicitor or commissioner of oaths or duly authorised officer

(d) _____

_____

_____

A solicitor or commissioner of oaths or duly authorised officer.

Before swearing the affidavit, the solicitor or commissioner or duly authorised officer is particularly requested to make sure that the full name, address and description of the deponent(s) are stated, and to initial any crossings-out or other alterations in the printed form. A deficiency in the affidavit in any of the above respects will mean that it is refused by the court, and will need to be re-sworn.

Schedule 7 para 2
S264(5)

Bankruptcy Orders on Joint Bankruptcy Petition Presented by Individual Members

(a)   Insert names of individual members

In the matter of (a) _____

_____

(hereinafter referred to as "the partnership") and in the matter of the Insolvent Partnerships Order 1994

(b)   Insert title of court and number of proceedings (to be allocated by court)

In the (b) _____

_____ No: _____ of _____

(c)   Insert date

Upon the petition of the above named individual members which was presented on (c) _____

And upon hearing _____

_____

And upon reading the petition and statements of affairs

(d)   Insert full description of individual members as set out in the petition

It is ordered that (d) _____

_____

_____

_____

and (d) _____

_____

_____

_____

[and (d) _____

_____

_____

_____]

be adjudged bankrupt.

(e)   Insert name of any bankrupt in respect of whom a certificate of summary administration is issued under section 275 of the Insolvency Act 1986 as modified by the Insolvent Partnerships Order 1994

[And it is certified that the estate(s) of (e) _____

_____

_____

_____

the bankrupt(s) be administered in a summary manner].

FORM 16 *(cont'd)*

And it is also ordered that the trustee of the bankrupts' estates be trustee of the partnership estate and that he wind up the affairs of the partnership and administer the partnership property.

Date _____

Time _____ hours

Important Notice to Bankrupts

(f) Delete as appropriate

(g) Insert address of official receiver's office

(f) [The] [One of the] official receiver(s) attached to the court is by virtue of this order trustee of the bankrupts' estates and trustee of the partnership. You are requested to attend upon the official receiver of the court at (g) _____

_____

_____

_____

immediately after you have received this order.

The official receiver's offices are open Monday to Friday (except on holidays) from 10.00 to 16.00 hours.

(h) Order to be
    endorsed where
    individual members
    are represented
    by a solicitor

ENDORSEMENT (h)

The solicitor(s) to the individual members is (are):–

Name of individual member: _____

_____

Name of solicitor: _____

_____

Address _____

_____

_____

Tel. no. _____

Reference _____

Name of individual member: _____

_____

Name of solicitor: _____

_____

Address _____

_____

_____

Tel. no. _____

Reference _____

Name of individual member: _____

_____

Name of solicitor: _____

_____

Address _____

_____

_____

Tel. no. _____

Reference _____

**Schedule 7 para 5
S272(2)(a)**

Statement of Affairs of Member of Partnership

(a) Insert name of
partnership

In the matter of (a) _____

_____

**(hereinafter referred to as "the partnership") and
in the matter of the Insolvent Partnerships Order 1994**

(b) Insert title of court
and number of
proceedings (to be
allocated by court)

In the (b) _____

_____ **No:** _____ **of** _____

(c) Insert name of
member

Re (c) _____
a member of the partnership.

**Show your current financial position by completing all
the pages of this form which will then be your
statement of affairs**

*Note: the partnership property and creditors will be
shown separately on Form 18 which must be completed and sworn by a member of the partnership*

AFFIDAVIT

**When you have completed the rest of this form,
this affidavit must be sworn before a solicitor or
commissioner of oaths or an officer of the court
duly authorised to administer oaths**

(d) Insert full name and
occupation

I (d) _____

_____

(e) Insert full address

of (e) _____

_____

_____

Make oath and say that the several pages exhibited
hereto and marked _____ are to the
best of my knowledge and belief a full, true and
complete statement of my affairs as at today's date.

Sworn at _____

Date _____

Signature _____

Before me (Signature) _____

(f) Insert name and full
address of solicitor,
commissioner of
oaths or duly
authorised officer

(f) _____

_____

_____

A solicitor or commissioner of oaths or duly authorised
officer.

**Before swearing the affidavit, the solicitor or commis-
sioner or duly authorised officer is particularly requested to make sure that the full name, address and
description of the deponent are stated, and to initial
any crossings-out or other alterations to the printed
form. A deficiency in the affidavit in any of the above
respects will mean that it is refused by the court, and
will need to be re-sworn.**

FORM 17 *(cont'd)*

A

LIST OF SECURED CREDITORS OF MEMBER

Is anyone claiming something of yours to clear or reduce their claim?

Tick Box
Yes ☐
No ☐

If '**YES**' give details below:

Name of creditor	Address (with postcode)	Amount owed to creditor £	What of yours is claimed and what is it worth?
1.			
2.			
3.			

Signature _____

Date _____

B

LIST OF UNSECURED CREDITORS OF MEMBER

1	2	3	4	5
No	Name of creditor or claimant	Address (with postcode)	Amount the creditor says you owe him/her £	Amount you think you owe £

Signature _____ Date _____

C

ASSETS OF MEMBER

Now show anything else of yours which may be of value:

£

(a) Cash at bank or building society _____ _____

(b) Household furniture and belongings _____ _____

(c) Life policies _____ _____

(d) Money owed to you _____ _____

(e) Stock in trade _____ _____

(f) Motor vehicles _____ _____

(g) Other property:–

_____ _____

_____ _____

_____ _____

_____ _____

_____ _____

_____ _____

_____ _____

_____ _____

_____ _____

_____ _____

TOTAL _____

Signature _____ Date _____

Schedule 7 para 5
S272(2)(b)

Statement of Affairs of Partnership

(a) Insert name of
     partnership

In the matter of (a) _____

(hereinafter referred to as "the partnership") and in the matter of the Insolvent Partnerships Order 1994

(b) Insert title of court
     and number of
     proceedings (to be
     allocated by court)

In the (b) _____

_____ No: _____ of _____

STATEMENT OF AFFAIRS OF THE PARTNERSHIP

(c) Insert date of
     presentation of
     bankruptcy petition
     against members

on the (c) _____ , the date of the
presentation of the bankruptcy petition against the
members of the partnership.

Show the partnership's current financial position by completing all the pages of this form which will then be your statement of the partnership's affairs.

Note: individual members' property and creditors will be shown separately on Form 17 which must be completed and sworn by members of the partnership

AFFIDAVIT
When you have completed the rest of this form, this affidavit must be sworn before a solicitor or commissioner of oaths or an officer of the court duly authorised to administer oaths

(d) Insert full name and
     occupation

I (d) _____

_____

(e) Insert full address

of (e) _____

_____

_____

a member of (a) _____

_____

Make oath and say that the several pages exhibited
hereto and marked _____
are to the best of my knowledge and belief a full,
true and complete statement as to the affairs of the
above-named partnership as at (c) _____,
the date of the presentation of the bankruptcy petition
against the members of the partnership, and that the
said partnership carried on business as

_____

Sworn at _____

Date _____

Signature(s) _____

Before me (Signature) _____

(f)   Insert name and full   (f) _____
       address of solicitor
       or commissioner of   _____
       oaths or duly
       authorised officer   _____   .

                                 _____

A solicitor or commissioner of oaths or duly authorised
officer

**Before swearing the affidavit, the solicitor or
commissioner or duly authorised officer is particularly
requested to make sure that the full name, address
and description of the deponent are stated, and to
initial any crossings-out or other alterations in the
printed form. A deficiency in the affidavit in any of the
above respects will mean that it is refused by the
court, and will need to be re-sworn.**

FORM 18 *(cont'd)*

A

LIST OF SECURED CREDITORS OF PARTNERSHIP

Is anyone claiming something of the partnership's to clear or reduce their claim?

Tick Box
Yes   No

If '**YES**' give details below:

Name of creditor	Address (with postcode)	Amount owed to creditor £	What of the partnership's is claimed and what is it worth?
1.			
2.			
3.			

Signature

Date

B

LIST OF UNSECURED CREDITORS OF PARTNERSHIP

1	2	3	4	5
No	Name of creditor or claimant	Address (with postcode)	Amount the creditor says the partner-ship owes him/her £	Amount you think the partnership owes £

Signature _____ Date _____

C

PARTNERSHIP PROPERTY

Show all partnership property not already included on Part A

Description	Book value £	Estimated to realise £
TOTAL	£	£

Signature _____ Date _____

SCHEDULE 10

SUBORDINATE LEGISLATION APPLIED

The Insolvency Practitioners Tribunal (Conduct of Investigations) Rules 1986

The Insolvency Practitioners (Recognised Professional Bodies) Order 1986

The Insolvency Rules 1986

The Insolvency Regulations 1986

The Insolvency Proceedings (Monetary Limits) Order 1986

The Administration of Insolvent Estates of Deceased Persons Order 1986

The Insolvency (Amendment of Subordinate Legislation) Order 1986

The Insolvency Fees Order 1986

The Companies (Disqualification Orders) Regulations 1986

The Co-operation of Insolvency Courts (Designation of Relevant Countries and Territories) Order 1986

The Insolvent Companies (Reports on Conduct of Directors) No. 2 Rules 1986

The Insolvent Companies (Disqualification of Unfit Directors) Proceedings Rules 1987

The Insolvency Practitioners Regulations 1990

Partnership Act 1890

ARRANGEMENT OF SECTIONS

Nature of partnership

Relations of partners to persons dealing with them

Relations of partners to one another

Dissolution of partnership and its consequences

Supplemental

Nature of partnership

1 Definition of partnership

(1) Partnership is the relation which subsists between persons carrying on a business in common with a view of profit.

(2) But the relation between members of any company or association which is—

- (a) Registered as a Company under the Companies Act 1862 or any other Act of Parliament for the time being in force and relating to the registration of joint stock companies; or
- (b) Formed or incorporated by or in pursuance of any other Act of Parliament or letters patent, or Royal Charter; or
- (c) A company engaged in working mines within and subject to the jurisdiction of the Stannaries:

is not a partnership within the meaning of this Act.

2 Rules for determining existence of partnership

In determining whether a partnership does or does not exist, regard shall be had to the following rules:

(1) Joint tenancy, tenancy in common, joint property, common property, or part ownership does not of itself create a partnership as to anything so held or owned, whether the tenants or owners do or do not share any profits made by the use thereof.

(2) The sharing of gross returns does not of itself create a partnership, whether the persons sharing such returns have or have not a joint or common right or interest in any property from which or from the use of which the returns are derived.

(3) The receipt by a person of a share of the profits of a business is *prima facie* evidence that he is a partner in the business, but receipt of such a share, or of a payment

contingent on or varying with the profits of a business, does not of itself make him a partner in the business; and in particular—

(a) The receipt by a person of a debt or other liquidated amount by instalments or otherwise out of the accruing profits of a business does not of itself make him a partner in the business or liable as such:

(b) A contract for the remuneration of a servant or agent of a person engaged in a business by a share of the profits of the business does not of itself make the servant or agent a partner in the business or liable as such:

(c) A person being the widow or child of a deceased partner, and receiving by way of annuity a portion of the profits made in the business in which the deceased person was a partner, is not by reason only of such receipt a partner in the business or liable as such:

(d) The advance of money by way of loan to a person engaged or about to engage in any business on a contract with that person that the lender shall receive a rate of interest varying with the profits, or shall receive a share of the profits arising from carrying on the business, does not of itself make the lender a partner with the person or persons carrying on the business or liable as such. Provided that the contract is in writing, and signed by or on behalf of all the parties thereto:

(e) A person receiving by way of annuity or otherwise a portion of the profits of a business in consideration of the sale by him of the goodwill of the business is not by reason only of such receipt a partner in the business or liable as such.

3 Postponement of rights of person lending or selling in consideration of share of profits in case of insolvency

In the event of any person to whom money has been advanced by way of loan upon such a contract as is mentioned in the last foregoing section, or of any buyer of a goodwill in consideration of a share of the profits of the business, being adjudged a bankrupt, entering into an arrangement to pay his creditors less than [100p] in the pound, or dying in insolvent circumstances, the lender of the loan shall not be entitled to recover anything in respect of his loan, and the seller of the goodwill shall not be entitled to recover anything in respect of the share of profits contracted for, until the claims of the other creditors of the borrower or buyer for valuable consideration in money or money's worth have been satisfied.

4 Meaning of firm

(1) Persons who have entered into partnership with one another are for the purposes of this Act called collectively a firm, and the name under which their business is carried on is called the firm-name.

(2) (*Applies in Scotland only.*)

Relations of partners to persons dealing with them

5 Power of partner to bind the firm

Every partner is an agent of the firm and his other partners for the purpose of the business of the partnership; and the acts of every partner who does any act for carrying on in the usual way business of the kind carried on by the firm of which he is a member bind the firm and his partners, unless the partner so acting has in fact no authority to act for the firm in the particular matter, and the person with whom he is dealing either knows that he has no authority, or does not know or believe him to be a partner.

6 Partners bound by acts on behalf of firm

An act or instrument relating to the business of the firm done or executed in the firm-name, or in any other manner showing an intention to bind the firm, by any person thereto authorised, whether a partner or not, is binding on the firm and all the partners.

Provided that this section shall not affect any general rule of law relating to the execution of deeds or negotiable instruments.

7 Partner using credit of firm for private purposes

Where one partner pledges the credit of the firm for a purpose apparently not connected with the firm's ordinary course of business, the firm is not bound, unless he is in fact specially authorised by the other partners; but this section does not affect any personal liability incurred by an individual partner.

8 Effect of notice that firm will not be bound by acts of partner

If it has been agreed between the partners that any restriction shall be placed on the power of any one or more of them to bind the firm, no act done in contravention of the agreement is binding on the firm with respect to persons having notice of the agreement.

9 Liability of partners

Every partner in a firm is liable jointly with the other partners, and in Scotland severally also, for all debts and obligations of the firm incurred while he is a partner; and after his death his estate is also severally liable in a due course of administration for such debts and obligations, so far as they remain unsatisfied, but subject in England or Ireland to the prior payment of his separate debts.

10 Liability of the firm for wrongs

Where, by any wrongful act or omission of any partner acting in the ordinary course of the business of the firm, or with the authority of his co-partners, loss or injury is caused to any person not being a partner in the firm, or any penalty is incurred, the firm is liable therefor to the same extent as the partner so acting or omitting to act.

11 Misapplication of money or property received for or in custody of the firm

In the following cases; namely—

(a) Where one partner acting with the scope of his apparent authority receives the money or property of a third person and misapplies it; and
(b) Where a firm in the course of its business receives money or property of a third person, and the money or property so received is misapplied by one or more of the partners while it is in the custody of the firm;

the firm is liable to make good the loss.

12 Liability for wrongs joint and several

Every partner is liable jointly with his co-partners and also severally for everything for which the firm while he is a partner therein becomes liable under either of the two last preceding sections.

13 Improper employment of trust-property for partnership purposes

If a partner, being a trustee, improperly employs trust-property in the business or on the account of the partnership, no other partner is liable for the trust property to the persons beneficially interested therein:

Provided as follows:—

(1) This section shall not affect any liability incurred by any partner by reason of his having notice of a breach of trust; and

(2) Nothing in this section shall prevent trust money from being followed and recovered from the firm if still in its possession or under its control.

14 Persons liable by "holding out"

(1) Every one who by words spoken or written or by conduct represents himself, or who knowingly suffers himself to be represented, as a partner in a particular firm, is liable as a partner to any one who has on the faith of any such representation given credit to the firm, whether the representation has or has not been made or communicated to the person so giving credit by or with the knowledge of the apparent partner making the representation or suffering it to be made.

(2) Provided that where after a partner's death the partnership business is continued in the old firm's name, the continued use of that name or of the deceased partner's name as part thereof shall not of itself make his executors or administrators estate or effects liable for any partnership debts contracted after his death.

15 Admissions and representations of partners

An admission or representation made by any partner concerning the partnership affairs, and in the ordinary course of its business, is evidence against the firm.

16 Notice to acting partner to be notice to the firm

Notice to any partner who habitually acts in the partnership business of any matter relating to partnership affairs operates as notice to the firm, except in the case of a fraud on the firm committed by or with the consent of that partner.

17 Liabilities of incoming and outgoing partners

(1) A person who is admitted as a partner into an existing firm does not thereby become liable to the creditors of the firm for anything done before he became a partner.

(2) A partner who retires from a firm does not thereby cease to be liable for partnership debts or obligations incurred before his retirement.

(3) A retiring partner may be discharged from any existing liabilities, by an agreement to that effect between himself and the members of the firm as newly constituted and the creditors, and this agreement may be either expressed or inferred as a fact from the course of dealing between the creditors and the firm as newly constituted.

18 Revocation of continuing guaranty by change in firm

A continuing guaranty or cautionary obligation given either to a firm or to a third person in respect of the transactions of a firm is, in the absence of agreement to the contrary, revoked as to future transactions by any change in the constitution of the firm to which, or of the firm in respect of the transactions of which, the guaranty or obligation was given.

Relations of partners to one another

19 Variation by consent of terms of partnership

The mutual rights and duties of partners, whether ascertained by agreement or defined by this Act, may be varied by the consent of all the partners, and such consent may be either express or inferred from a course of dealing.

20 Partnership property

(1) All property and rights and interests in property originally brought into the partnership stock or acquired, whether by purchase or otherwise, on account of the firm, or for the purposes and in the course of the partnership business, are called in this Act partnership property, and must be held and applied by the partners exclusively for the purposes of the partnership and in accordance with the partnership agreement.

(2) Provided that the legal estate or interest in any land, or in Scotland the title to and interest in any heritable estate, which belongs to the partnership shall devolve according to the nature and tenure thereof, and the general rules of law thereto applicable, but in trust, so far as necessary, for the persons beneficially interested in the land under this section.

(3) Where co-owners of an estate or interest in any land, or in Scotland of any heritable estate, not being itself partnership property, are partners as to profits made by the use of that land or estate, and purchase other land or estate out of the profits to be used in like manner, the land or estate so purchased belongs to them, in the absence of an agreement to the contrary, not as partners, but as co-owners for the same respective estates and interests as are held by them in the land or estate first mentioned at the date of the purchase.

21 Property bought with partnership money

Unless the contrary intention appears, property bought with money belonging to the firm is deemed to have been bought on account of the firm.

22 Conversion into personal estate of land held as partnership property

Where land or any heritable interest therein has become partnership property, it shall, unless the contrary intention appears, be treated as between the partners (including the representatives of a deceased partner), and also as between the heirs of a deceased partner and his executors or administrators, as personal or moveable and not real or heritable estate.

23 Procedure against partnership property for a partner's separate judgment debt

(1) A writ of execution shall not issue against any partnership property except on a judgment against the firm.

(2) The High Court, or a judge thereof, or a county court, may, on the application by summons of any judgment creditor of a partner, make an order charging that partner's interest in the partnership property and profits with payment of the amount of the judgment debt and interest thereon, and may by the same or a subsequent order appoint a receiver of that partner's share of profits (whether already declared or accruing), and of any other money which may be coming to him in respect of the partnership, and direct all accounts and inquiries, and give all other orders and directions which might have been directed or given if the charge had been made in

favour of the judgment creditor by the partner, or which the circumstances of the case may require.

(3) The other partner or partners shall be at liberty at any time to redeem the interest charged, or in case of a sale being directed, to purchase the same.

(4) This section shall apply in the case of a cost-book company as if the company were a partnership within the meaning of this Act.

(5) This section shall not apply to Scotland.

24 Rules as to interests and duties of partners subject to special agreement

The interests of partners in the partnership property and their rights and duties in relation to the partnership shall be determined, subject to any agreement express or implied between the partners, by the following rules:—

(1) All the partners are entitled to share equally in the capital and profits of the business, and must contribute equally towards the losses whether of capital or otherwise sustained by the firm.

(2) The firm must indemnify every partner in respect of payments made and personal liabilities incurred by him—
   (a) In the ordinary and proper conduct of the business of the firm; or,
   (b) In or about anything necessarily done for the preservation of the business or property of the firm.

(3) A partner making, for the purpose of the partnership, any actual payment or advance beyond the amount of capital which he has agreed to subscribe, is entitled to interest at the rate of five per cent. per annum from the date of the payment or advance.

(4) A partner is not entitled, before the ascertainment of profits, to interest on the capital subscribed by him.

(5) Every partner may take part in the management of the partnership business.

(6) No partner shall be entitled to remuneration for acting in the partnership business.

(7) No person may be introduced as a partner without the consent of all existing partners.

(8) Any difference arising as to ordinary matters connected with the partnership business may be decided by a majority of the partners, but no change may be made in the nature of the partnership business without the consent of all existing partners.

(9) The partnership books are to be kept at the place of business of the partnership (or the principal place, if there is more than one), and every partner may, when he thinks fit, have access to and inspect and copy any of them.

25 Expulsion of partner

No majority of the partners can expel any partner unless a power to do so has been conferred by express agreement between the partners.

26 Retirement from partnership at will

(1) Where no fixed term has been agreed upon for the duration of the partnership, any partner may determine the partnership at any time on giving notice of his intention so to do to all the other partners.

(2) Where the partnership has originally been constituted by deed, a notice in writing, signed by the partner giving it, shall be sufficient for this purpose.

27 Where partnership for term is continued over, continuance on old terms presumed

(1) Where a partnership entered into for a fixed term is continued after the term has expired, and without any express new agreement, the rights and duties of the partners remain the same as they were at the expiration of the term, so far as is consistent with the incidents of a partnership at will.

(2) A continuance of the business by the partners or such of them as habitually acted therein during the term, without any settlement or liquidation of the partnership affairs, is presumed to be a continuance of the partnership.

28 Duty of partners to render accounts, etc

Partners are bound to render true accounts and full information of all things affecting the partnership to any partner or his legal representatives.

29 Accountability of partners for private profits

(1) Every partner must account to the firm for any benefit derived by him without the consent of the other partners from any transaction concerning the partnership, or from any use by him of the partnership property name or business connexion.

(2) This section applies also to transactions undertaken after a partnership has been dissolved by the death of a partner, and before the affairs thereof have been completely wound up, either by any surviving partner or by the representatives of the deceased partner.

30 Duty of partner not to compete with firm

If a partner, without the consent of the other partners, carries on any business of the same nature as and competing with that of the firm, he must account for and pay over to the firm all profits made by him in that business.

31 Rights of assignee of share in partnership

(1) An assignment by any partner of his share in the partnership, either absolute or by way of mortgage or redeemable charge, does not, as against the other partners, entitle the assignee, during the continuance of the partnership, to interfere in the management or administration of the partnership business or affairs, or to require any accounts of the partnership transactions, or to inspect the partnership books, but entitles the assignee only to receive the share of profits to which the assigning partner would otherwise be entitled, and the assignee must accept the account of profits agreed to by the partners.

(2) In case of a dissolution of the partnership, whether as respects all the partners or as respects the assigning partner, the assignee is entitled to receive the share of the partnership assets to which the assigning partner is entitled as between himself and the other partners, and, for the purpose of ascertaining that share, to an account as from the date of the dissolution.

Dissolution of partnership and its consequences

32 Dissolution by expiration or notice

Subject to any agreement between the partners, a partnership is dissolved—

    (a) If entered into for a fixed term, by the expiration of that term:

(b) If entered into for a single adventure or undertaking, by the termination of that adventure or undertaking:

(c) If entered into for an undefined time, by any partner giving notice to the other or others of his intention to dissolve the partnership.

In the last-mentioned case the partnership is dissolved as from the date mentioned in the notice as the date of dissolution, or, if no date is so mentioned, as from the date of the communication of the notice.

33 Dissolution by bankruptcy, death or charge

(1) Subject to any agreement between the partners, every partnership is dissolved as regards all the partners by the death or bankruptcy of any partner.

(2) A partnership may, at the option of the other partners, be dissolved if any partner suffers his share of the partnership property to be charged under this Act for his separate debt.

34 Dissolution by illegality of partnership

A partnership is in every case dissolved by the happening of any event which makes it unlawful for the business of the firm to be carried on or for the members of the firm to carry it on in partnership.

35 Dissolution by the Court

On application by a partner the Court may decree a dissolution of the partnership in any of the following cases:

(a) ...

(b) When a partner, other than the partner suing, becomes in any other way permanently incapable of performing his part of the partnership contract:

(c) When a partner, other than the partner suing, has been guilty of such conduct as, in the opinion of the Court, regard being had to the nature of the business, is calculated to prejudicially affect the carrying on of the business:

(d) When a partner, other than the partner suing, wilfully or persistently commits a breach of the partnership agreement, or otherwise so conducts himself in matters relating to the partnership business that it is not reasonably practicable for the other partner or partners to carry on the business in partnership with him:

(e) When the business of the partnership can only be carried on at a loss:

(f) Whenever in any case circumstances have arisen which, in the opinion of the Court, render it just and equitable that the partnership be dissolved.

36 Rights of persons dealing with firm against apparent members of firm

(1) Where a person deals with a firm after a change in its constitution he is entitled to treat all apparent members of the old firm as still being members of the firm until he has notice of the change.

(2) An advertisement in the London Gazette as to a firm whose principal place of business is in England or Wales, in the Edinburgh Gazette as to a firm whose principal place of business is in Scotland, and in the Dublin Gazette as to a firm whose principal place of business is in Ireland, shall be notice as to persons who had not dealings with the firm before the date of the dissolution or change so advertised.

(3) The estate of a partner who dies, or who becomes bankrupt, or of a partner who, not having been known to the person dealing with the firm to be a partner, retires from the

firm, is not liable for partnership debts contracted after the date of the death, bankruptcy, or retirement respectively.

37 Right of partners to notify dissolution

On the dissolution of a partnership or retirement of a partner any partner may publicly notify the same, and may require the other partner or partners to concur for that purpose in all necessary or proper acts, if any, which cannot be done without his or their concurrence.

38 Continuing authority of partners for purposes of winding up

After the dissolution of a partnership the authority of each partner to bind the firm, and the other rights and obligations of the partners, continue notwithstanding the dissolution so far as may be necessary to wind up the affairs of the partnership, and to complete transactions begun but unfinished at the time of the dissolution, but not otherwise.

Provided that the firm is in no case bound by the acts of a partner who has become bankrupt; but this proviso does not affect the liability of any person who has after the bankruptcy represented himself or knowingly suffered himself to be represented as a partner of the bankrupt.

39 Rights of partners as to application of partnership property

On the dissolution of a partnership every partner is entitled, as against the other partners in the firm, and all persons claiming through them in respect of their interests as partners, to have the property of the partnership applied in payment of the debts and liabilities of the firm, and to have the surplus assets after such payment applied in payment of what may be due to the partners respectively after deducting what may be due from them as partners to the firm; and for that purpose any partner or his representatives may on the termination of the partnership apply to the Court to wind up the business and affairs of the firm.

40 Apportionment of premium where partnership prematurely dissolved

Where one partner has paid a premium to another on entering into a partnership for a fixed term, and the partnership is dissolved before the expiration of that term otherwise than by the death of a partner, the Court may order the repayment of the premium, or of such part thereof as it thinks just, having regard to the terms of the partnership contract and to the length of time during which the partnership has continued; unless

(a) the dissolution is, in the judgment of the Court, wholly or chiefly due to the misconduct of the partner who paid the premium; or

(b) the partnership has been dissolved by an agreement containing no provision for a return of any part of the premium.

41 Rights where partnership dissolved for fraud or misrepresentation

Where a partnership contract is rescinded on the ground of the fraud or misrepresentation of one of the parties thereto, the party entitled to rescind is, without prejudice to any other right, entitled—

(a) to a lien on, or right of retention of, the surplus of the partnership assets, after satisfying the partnership liabilities, for any sum of money paid by him for the purchase of a share in the partnership and for any capital contributed by him, and is

(b) to stand in the place of the creditors of the firm for any payments made by him in respect of the partnership liabilities, and

(c) to be indemnified by the person guilty of the fraud or making the representation against all the debts and liabilities of the firm.

42 Right of outgoing partner in certain cases to share profits made after dissolution

(1) Where any member of a firm has died or otherwise ceased to be a partner, and the surviving or continuing partners carry on the business of the firm with its capital or assets without any final settlement of accounts as between the firm and the outgoing partner or his estate, then, in the absence of any agreement to the contrary, the outgoing partner or his estate is entitled at the option of himself or his representatives to such share of the profits made since the dissolution as the Court may find to be attributable to the use of his share of the partnership assets, or to interest at the rate of five per cent. per annum on the amount of his share of the partnership assets.

(2) Provided that where by the partnership contract an option is given to surviving or continuing partners to purchase the interest of a deceased or outgoing partner, and that option is duly exercised, the estate of the deceased partner, or the outgoing partner or his estate, as the case may be, is not entitled to any further or other share of profits; but if any partner assuming to act in exercise of the option does not in all material respects comply with the terms thereof, he is liable to account under the foregoing provisions of this section.

43 Retiring or deceased partner's share to be a debt

Subject to any agreement between the partners, the amount due from surviving or continuing partners to an outgoing partner or the representatives of a deceased partner in respect of the outgoing or deceased partner's share is a debt accruing at the date of the dissolution or death.

44 Rule for distribution of assets on final settlement of accounts

In settling accounts between the partners after a dissolution of partnership, the following rules shall, subject to any agreement, be observed:

(a) Losses, including losses and deficiencies of capital, shall be paid first out of profits, next out of capital, and lastly, if necessary, by the partners individually in the proportion in which they were entitled to share profits:

(b) The assets of the firm including the sums, if any, contributed by the partners to make up losses or deficiencies of capital, shall be applied in the following manner and order:

1. In paying the debts and liabilities of the firm to persons who are not partners therein:
2. In paying to each partner rateably what is due from the firm to him for advances as distinguished from capital:
3. In paying to each partner rateably what is due from the firm to him in respect of capital:
4. The ultimate residue, if any, shall be divided among the partners in the proportion in which profits are divisible.

Supplemental

45 Definitions of "court" and "business"

In this Act, unless the contrary intention appears,—

The expression "court" includes every court and judge having jurisdiction in the case:

The expression "business" includes every trade, occupation, or profession.

46 Saving for rules of equity and common law

The rules of equity and of common law applicable to partnership shall continue in force except so far as they are inconsistent with the express provisions of this Act.

47 *(Applies in Scotland only.)*

48, 49 *(Repealed)*

50 Short title

This Act may be cited as the Partnership Act 1890.

Limited Partnerships Act 1907

ARRANGEMENT OF SECTIONS

1 Short title

This Act may be cited for all purposes as the Limited Partnerships Act 1907.

2 (*Repealed*)

3 Interpretation of terms

In the construction of this Act the following words and expressions shall have the meanings respectively assigned to them in this section, unless there be something in the subject or context repugnant to such construction—

"Firm," "firm name," and "business" have the same meanings as in the Partnership Act 1890:

"General partner" shall mean any partner who is not a limited partner as defined by this Act.

4 Definition and constitution of limited partnership

(1) ... Limited partnerships may be formed in the manner and subject to the conditions by this Act provided.

(2) A limited partnership shall not consist ... of more than twenty persons, and must consist of one or more persons called general partners, who shall be liable for all debts and obligations of the firm, and one or more persons to be called limited partners, who shall at the time of entering into such partnership contribute thereto a sum or sums as capital or property valued at a stated amount, and who shall not be liable for the debts or obligations of the firm beyond the amount so contributed.

(3) A limited partner shall not during the continuance of the partnership, either directly or indirectly, draw out or receive back any part of his contribution, and if he does so draw out or receive back any such part shall be liable for the debts and obligations of the firm up to the amount so drawn out or received back.

(4) A body corporate may be a limited partner.

5 Registration of limited partnership required

Every limited partnership must be registered as such in accordance with the provisions of this Act, or in default thereof it shall be deemed to be a general partnership, and every limited partner shall be deemed to be a general partner.

6 Modifications of general law in case of limited partnerships

(1) A limited partner shall not take part in the management of the partnership business, and shall not have power to bind the firm:

Provided that a limited partner may by himself or his agent at any time inspect the books of the firm and examine into the state and prospects of the partnership business, and may advise with the partners thereon.

If a limited partner takes part in the management of the partnership business he shall be liable for all debts and obligations of the firm incurred while he so takes part in the management as though he were a general partner.

(2) A limited partnership shall not be dissolved by the death or bankruptcy of a limited partner, and the lunacy of a limited partner shall not be a ground for dissolution of the partnership by the court unless the lunatic's share cannot be otherwise ascertained and realised.

(3) In the event of the dissolution of a limited partnership its affairs shall be wound up by the general partners unless the court otherwise orders.

(4) ...

(5) Subject to any agreement expressed or implied between the partners—

(a) Any difference arising as to ordinary matters connected with the partnership business may be decided by a majority of the general partners;

(b) A limited partner may, with the consent of the general partners, assign his share in the partnership, and upon such an assignment the assignee shall become a limited partner with all the rights of the assignor;

(c) The other partners shall not be entitled to dissolve the partnership by reason of any limited partner suffering his share to be charged for his separate debt;

(d) A person may be introduced as a partner without the consent of the existing limited partners;

(e) A limited partner shall not be entitled to dissolve the partnership by notice.

7 Law as to private partnerships to apply where not excluded by this Act

Subject to the provisions of this Act, the Partnership Act 1890 and the rules of equity and of common law applicable to partnerships, except so far as they are inconsistent with the express provisions of the last-mentioned Act, shall apply to limited partnerships.

8 Manner and particulars of registration

The registration of a limited partnership shall be effected by sending by post or delivering to the registrar at the register office in that part of the United Kingdom in which the principal place of business of the limited partnership is situated or proposed to be situated a statement signed by the partners containing the following particulars—

(a) The firm name;
(b) The general nature of the business;
(c) The principal place of business;
(d) The full name of each of the partners;
(e) The term, if any, for which the partnership is entered into, and the date of its commencement;
(f) A statement that the partnership is limited, and the description of every limited partner as such;
(g) The sum contributed by each limited partner, and whether paid in cash or how otherwise.

9 Registration of changes in partnerships

(1) If during the continuance of a limited partnership any change is made or occurs in—

(a) the firm name,
(b) the general nature of the business,
(c) the principal place of business,
(d) the partners or the name of any partner,
(e) the term or character of the partnership,
(f) the sum contributed by any limited partner,
(g) the liability of any partner by reason of his becoming a limited instead of a general partner or a general instead of a limited partner,

a statement, signed by the firm, specifying the nature of the change shall within seven days be sent by post or delivered to the registrar at the register office in that part of the United Kingdom in which the partnership is registered.

(2) If default is made in compliance with the requirements of this section each of the general partners shall, on conviction under the Summary Jurisdiction Acts, be liable to a fine not exceeding one pound for each day during which the default continues.

10 Advertisement in Gazette of statement of general partner becoming a limited partner and of assignment of share of limited partner

(1) Notice of any arrangement or transaction under which any person will cease to be a general partner in any firm, and will become a limited partner in that firm, or under which the share of a limited partner in a firm will be assigned to any person, shall be forthwith advertised in the Gazette, and until notice of the arrangement or transaction is so advertised the arrangement or transaction shall, for the purposes of this Act, be deemed to be of no effect.

(2) For the purposes of this section, the expression "the Gazette" means—

In the case of a limited partnership registered in England, the London Gazette.
In the case of a limited partnership registered in Scotland, the Edinburgh Gazette.
In the case of a limited partnership registered in Ireland, the Dublin Gazette.

11, 12 (*Repealed*)

13 Registrar to file statement and issue certificate of registration

On receiving any statement made in pursuance of this Act the registrar shall cause the same to be filed, and he shall send by post to the firm from whom such statement shall have been received a certificate of the registration thereof.

14 Register and index to be kept

At each of the register offices herein-after referred to the registrar shall keep, in proper books to be provided for the purpose, or register and an index of all the limited partnerships registered as aforesaid, and of all the statements registered in relation to such partnerships.

15 Registrar of joint stock companies to be registrar under Act

The registrar of joint stock companies shall be the registrar of limited partnerships, and the several offices for the registration of joint stock companies in London, Edinburgh, and Dublin shall be the offices for the registration of limited partnerships carrying on business within those parts of the United Kingdom in which they are respectively situated.

16 Inspection of statements registered

(1) Any person may inspect the statements filed by the registrar in the register offices aforesaid, and there shall be paid for such inspection such fees as may be appointed by the Board of Trade, not exceeding [5p] for each inspection; and any person may require a certificate of the registration of any limited partnership, or a copy of or extract from any registered statement, to be certified by the registrar, and there shall be paid for such certificate of registration, certified copy, or extract such fees as the Board of Trade may appoint, not exceeding [10p] for the certificate of registration, and not exceeding [2p] for each folio of seventy-two words, or in Scotland for each sheet of two hundred words.

(2) A certificate of registration or a copy of or extract from any statement registered under this Act, if duly certified to be a true copy under the hand of the registrar or one of the assistant registrars (whom it shall not be necessary to prove to be the registrar or assistant registrar) shall, in all legal proceedings, civil or criminal, and in all cases whatsoever be received in evidence.

17 Power to Board of Trade to make rules

The Board of Trade may make rules (but as to fees with the concurrence of the Treasury) concerning any of the following matters—

(a) The fees to be paid to the registrar under this Act, so that they do not exceed in the case of the original registration of a limited partnership the sum of two pounds, and in any other case the sum of [25p];
(b) The duties of additional duties to be performed by the registrar for the purposes of this Act;
(c) The performance by assistant registrars and other officers of acts by this Act required to be done by the registrar;
(d) The forms to be used for the purposes of this Act;
(e) Generally, the conduct and regulation of registration under this Act and any matters incidental thereto.

Company Directors Disqualification Act 1986

[There are reproduced below those sections of the Company Directors Disqualification Act 1986 which are applied to insolvent partnerships by art 16 of the Insolvent Partnerships Order 1994. Sections 6 to 9 of and Sch 1 to the Act are modified by art 16 of and Sch 8 to the Order and are reproduced in their modified form.]

6 Duty of court to disqualify unfit officers of insolvent partnerships

(1) The court shall make a disqualification order against a person in any case where, on an application under this section, it is satisfied—

- (a) that he is or has been an officer of a partnership which has at any time become insolvent (whether while he was an officer or subsequently), and
- (b) that his conduct as an officer of that partnership (either taken alone or taken together with his conduct as an officer of any other partnership or partnerships, or as a director of any company or companies) makes him unfit to be concerned in the management of a company.

(2) For the purposes of this section and the next—

- (a) a partnership becomes insolvent if—
  - (i) the court makes an order for it to be wound up as an unregistered company at a time when its assets are insufficient for the payment of its debts and other liabilities and the expenses of the winding up; or
  - (ii) an administration order is made in relation to the partnership; and
- (b) a company becomes insolvent if—
  - (i) the company goes into liquidation at a time when its assets are insufficient for the payment of its debts and other liabilities and the expenses of the winding up,
  - (ii) an administration order is made in relation to the company, or
  - (iii) an administrative receiver of the company is appointed.

(3) For the purposes of this section and the next, references to a person's conduct as an officer of any partnership or partnerships, or as a director of any company or companies, include, where the partnership or company concerned or any of the partnerships or companies concerned has become insolvent, that person's conduct in relation to any matter connected with or arising out of the insolvency of that partnership or company.

(4) In this section and the next "the court" means—

- (a) in the case of a person who is or has been an officer of a partnership which is being wound up as an unregistered company by the court, the court by which the partnership is being wound up,
- (b) in the case of a person who is or has been an officer of a partnership in relation to which an administration order is in force, the court by which that order was made, and
- (c) in any other case, the High Court;

and in both sections "director" includes a shadow director.

(5) Under this section the minimum period of disqualification is 2 years, and the maximum period is 15 years.

7 Applications to court under s 6; reporting provisions

(1) If it appears to the Secretary of State that it is expedient in the public interest that a disqualification order under section 6 should be made against any person, an application for the making of such an order against that person may be made—

    (a) by the Secretary of State, or

    (b) if the Secretary of State so directs in the case of a person who is or has been an officer of a partnership which is being wound up by the court as an unregistered company, by the official receiver.

(2) Except with the leave of the court, an application for the making under that section of a disqualification order against any person shall not be made after the end of the period of 2 years beginning with the day on which the partnership of which that person is or has been an officer became insolvent.

(3) If it appears to the office-holder responsible under this section, that is to say—

    (a) in the case of the partnership which is being wound up by the court as an unregistered company, the official receiver, or

    (b) in the case of a partnership in relation to which an administration order is in force, the administrator,

that the conditions mentioned in section 6(1) are satisfied as respects a person who is or has been an officer of that partnership, the office-holder shall forthwith report the matter to the Secretary of State.

(4) The Secretary of State or the official receiver may require any of the persons mentioned in subsection (5) below—

    (a) to furnish him with such information with respect to any person's conduct as an officer of a partnership or as a director of a company, and

    (b) to produce and permit inspection of such books, papers and other records relevant to that person's conduct as such an officer or director,

as the Secretary of State or the official receiver may reasonably require for the purpose of determining whether to exercise, or of exercising, any function of his under this section.

(5) The persons referred to in subsection (4) are—

    (a) the liquidator or administrator, or former liquidator or administrator of the partnership,

    (b) the liquidator, administrator or administrative receiver, or former liquidator, administrator or administrative receiver, of the company.

8 Section 8: Disqualification after investigation

(1) If it appears to the Secretary of State from a report made by inspectors under section 437 of the Companies Act or section 94 or 177 of the Financial Services Act 1986, or from information or documents obtained under—

    (a) section 447 or 448 of the Companies Act,

    (b) section 105 of the Financial Services Act 1986,

    (c) section 2 of the Criminal Justice Act 1987,

    (d) section 52 of the Criminal Justice (Scotland) Act 1987, or

    (e) section 83 of the Companies Act 1989,

that it is expedient in the public interest that a disqualification order should be made against any person who is or has been an officer of any insolvent partnership, he may apply to the court for such an order to be made against that person.

(2) The court may make a disqualification order against a person where, on an application under this section, it is satisfied that his conduct in relation to the partnership makes him unfit to be concerned in the management of a company.

(3) In this section "the court" means the High Court.

(4) The maximum period of disqualification under this section is 15 years.

9 Matters for determining unfitness of officers of partnerships

(1) This section applies where it falls to a court to determine whether a person's conduct as an officer of a partnership (either taken alone or taken together with his conduct as an officer of any other partnership or partnerships or as a director or shadow director of any company or companies) makes him unfit to be concerned in the management of a company.

(2) The court shall, as respects that person's conduct as an officer of that partnership or each of those partnerships or as a director of that company or each of those companies, have regard in particular—

    (a) to the matters mentioned in Part I of Schedule 1 to this Act, and

    (b) where the partnership or company (as the case may be) has become insolvent, to the matters mentioned in Part II of that Schedule;

the references in that Schedule to the officer and the partnership or, as the case may be, to the director and the company, are to be read accordingly.

(3) Subsections (2) and (3) of section 6 apply for the purposes of this section and Schedule 1 as they apply for the purposes of sections 6 and 7.

(4) Subject to the next subsection, any reference in Schedule 1 to an enactment contained in the Companies Act or the Insolvency Act includes, in relation to any time before the coming into force of that enactment, the corresponding enactment in force at that time.

(5) The Secretary of State may by order modify any of the provisions of Schedule 1; and such an order may contain such transitional provisions as may appear to the Secretary of State necessary or expedient.

(6) The power to make orders under this section is exercisable by statutory instrument subject to annulment in pursuance of a resolution of either House of Parliament.

Other cases of disqualification

10 Participation in wrongful trading

(1) Where the court makes a declaration under section 213 or 214 of the Insolvency Act that a person is liable to make a contribution to a company's assets, then, whether or not an application for such an order is made by any person, the court may, if it thinks fit, also make a disqualification order against the person to whom the declaration relates.

(2) The maximum period of disqualification under this section is 15 years.

15 Personal liability for company's debts where person acts while disqualified

(1) A person is personally responsible for all the relevant debts of a company if at any time—

    (a) in contravention of a disqualification order or of section 11 of this Act he is involved in the management of the company, or

    (b) as a person who is involved in the management of the company, he acts or is willing to act on instructions given without the leave of the court by a person whom he knows at that time to be the subject of a disqualification order or to be an undischarged bankrupt.

(2) Where a person is personally responsible under this section for the relevant debts of a company, he is jointly and severally liable in respect of those debts with the company and any other person who, whether under this section or otherwise, is so liable.

(3) For the purposes of this section the relevant debts of a company are—

    (a) in relation to a person who is personally responsible under paragraph (a) of subsection (1), such debts and other liabilities of the company as are incurred at a time when that person was involved in the management of the company, and

    (b) in relation to a person who is personally responsible under paragraph (b) of that subsection, such debts and other liabilities of the company as are incurred at a time when that person was acting or was willing to act on instructions given as mentioned in that paragraph.

(4) For the purposes of this section, a person is involved in the management of a company if he is a director of the company or if he is concerned, whether directly or indirectly, or takes part, in the management of the company.

(5) For the purposes of this section a person who, as a person involved in the management of a company, has at any time acted on instructions given without the leave of the court by a person whom he knew at that time to be the subject of a disqualification order or to be an undischarged bankrupt is presumed, unless the contrary is shown, to have been willing at any time thereafter to act on any instructions given by that person.

19 Special savings from repealed enactments

Schedule 2 to this Act has effect—

    (a) in connection with certain transitional cases arising under sections 93 and 94 of the Companies Act 1981, so as to limit the power to make a disqualification order, or to restrict the duration of an order, by reference to events occurring or things done before those sections came into force,

    (b) to preserve orders made under section 28 of the Companies Act 1976 (repealed by the Act of 1981), and

    (c) to preclude any applications for a disqualification order under section 6 or 8, where the relevant company went into liquidation before 28th April 1986.

Miscellaneous and general

20 Admissibility in evidence of statements

In any proceedings (whether or not under this Act), any statement made in pursuance of a requirement imposed by or under sections 6 to 10, 15 or 19(c) of, or Schedule 1 to, this Act, or by or under rules made for the purposes of this Act under the Insolvency Act, may be used in evidence against any person making or concurring in making the statement.

SCHEDULE 1
MATTERS FOR DETERMINING UNFITNESS OF OFFICERS OF PARTNERSHIPS

PART I
MATTERS APPLICABLE IN ALL CASES

1 Any misfeasance or breach of any fiduciary or other duty by the officer in relation to the partnership or, as the case may be, by the director in relation to the company.

2 Any misapplication or retention by the officer or the director of, or any conduct by the officer or the director giving rise to an obligation to account for, any money or other property of the partnership or, as the case may be, of the company.

3 The extent of the officer's or the director's responsibility for the partnership or, as the case may be, the company entering into any transaction liable to be set aside under Part XVI of the Insolvency Act (provisions against debt avoidance).

4 The extent of the director's responsibility for any failure by the company to comply with any of the following provisions of the Companies Act, namely—

- (a) section 221 (companies to keep accounting records);
- (b) section 222 (where and for how long records to be kept);
- (c) section 288 (register of directors and secretaries);
- (d) section 352 (obligation to keep and enter up register of members);
- (e) section 353 (location of register of members);
- (f) section 363 (duty of company to make annual returns); and
- (g) sections 399 and 415 (company's duty to register charges it creates).

5 The extent of the director's responsibility for any failure by the directors of the company to comply with—

- (a) section 226 or 227 of the Companies Act (duty to prepare annual accounts), or
- (b) section 233 of that Act (approval and signature of accounts).

6 Any failure by the officer to comply with any obligation imposed on him by or under any of the following provisions of the Limited Partnerships Act 1907—

- (a) section 8 (registration of particulars of limited partnership);
- (b) section 9 (registration of changes in particulars);
- (c) section 10 (advertisement of general partner becoming limited partner and of assignment of share of limited partner).

PART II
MATTERS APPLICABLE WHERE PARTNERSHIP OR COMPANY HAS BECOME INSOLVENT

7 The extent of the officer's or the director's responsibility for the causes of the partnership or (as the case may be) the company becoming insolvent.

8 The extent of the officer's or the director's responsibility for any failure by the partnership or (as the case may be) the company to supply any goods or services which have been paid for (in whole or in part).

9 The extent of the officer's or the director's responsibility for the partnership or (as the case may be) the company entering into any transaction or giving any preference, being a transaction or preference—

    (a) liable to be set aside under section 127 or sections 238 to 240 of the Insolvency Act, or

    (b) challengeable under section 242 or 243 of that Act or under any rule of law in Scotland.

10 The extent of the director's responsibility for any failure by the directors of the company to comply with section 98 of the Insolvency Act (duty to call creditors' meeting in creditors' voluntary winding up).

11 Any failure by the director to comply with any obligation imposed on him by or under any of the following provisions of the Insolvency Act—

    (a) section 47 (statement of affairs to administrative receiver);

    (b) section 66 (statement of affairs in Scottish receivership);

    (c) section 99 (directors' duty to attend meeting; statement of affairs in creditors' voluntary winding up).

12 Any failure by the officer or the director to comply with any obligation imposed on him by or under any of the following provisions of the Insolvency Act (both as they apply in relation to companies and as they apply in relation to insolvent partnerships by virtue of the provisions of the Insolvent Partnerships Order 1994)—

    (a) section 22 (statement of affairs in administration);

    (b) section 133 (statement of affairs in winding up by the court);

    (c) section 234 (duty of any one with property to deliver it up);

    (d) section 235 (duty of co-operate with liquidator, etc.).

Rules of the Supreme Court 1965

ORDER 81

PARTNERS

1 Actions by and against firms within jurisdiction

Subject to the provisions of any enactment, any two or more persons claiming to be entitled, or alleged to be liable, as partners in respect of a cause of action and carrying on business within the jurisdiction may sue, or be sued, in the name of the firm (if any) of which they were partners at the time when the cause of action accrued.

2 Disclosure of partners' names

(1) Any defendant to an action brought by partners in the name of a firm may serve on the plaintiffs or their solicitor a notice requiring them or him forthwith to furnish the defendant with a written statement of the names and places of residence of all the persons who were partners in the firm at the time when the cause of action accrued; and if the notice is not complied with the Court may order the plaintiffs or their solicitor to furnish the defendant with such a statement and to verify it on oath or otherwise as may be specified in the order, or may order that further proceedings in the action be stayed on such terms as the Court may direct.

(2) When the names of the partners have been declared in compliance with a notice or order given or made under paragraph (1) the proceedings shall continue in the name of the firm but with the same consequences as would have ensued if the persons whose names have been so declared had been named as plaintiffs in the writ.

(3) Paragraph (1) shall have effect in relation to an action brought against partners in the name of a firm as it has effect in relation to an action brought by partners in the name of a firm but with the substitution, for references to the defendant and the plaintiffs, of references to the plaintiff and the defendants respectively, and with the omission of the words "or may order" to the end.

3 Service of writ

(1) Where by virtue of rule 1 partners are sued in the name of a firm, the writ may, except in the case mentioned in paragraph (3) be served—

(a) on any one or more of the partners, or
(b) at the principal place of business of the partnership within the jurisdiction, on any person having at the time of service the control or management of the partnership business there; or
(c) by sending a copy of the writ by ordinary first-class post (as defined in Order 10, rule 1(2)) to the firm at the principal place of business of the partnership within the jurisdiction

and subject to paragraph (2) where service of the writ is effected in accordance with this paragraph, the writ shall be deemed to have been duly served on the firm, whether or not any member of the firm is out of the jurisdiction.

(2) Where a writ is served on a firm in accordance with sub-paragraph (1)(c)—

(a) the date of service shall, unless the contrary is shown, be deemed to be the seventh day (ignoring Order 3, rule 2(5)) after the date on which the copy was sent to the firm; and

(b) any affidavit proving due service of the writ must contain a statement to the effect that—

(i) in the opinion of a deponent (or, if the deponent is the plaintiff's solicitor or an employee of that solicitor, in the opinion of the plaintiff) the copy of the writ, if sent to the firm at the address in question, will have come to the knowledge of one of the persons mentioned in paragraph (1)(a) or (b) within 7 days thereafter, and

(ii) the copy of the writ has not been returned to the plaintiff through the post undelivered to the addressee.

(3) Where a partnership has, to the knowledge of the plaintiff, been dissolved before an action against the firm is begun, the writ by which the action is begun must be served on every person within the jurisdiction sought to be made liable in the action.

(4) Every person on whom a writ is served under paragraph (1)(a) or (b) must at the time of service be given a written notice stating whether he is served as a partner or as a person having the control or management of the partnership business or both as a partner and as such a person; and any person on whom a writ is so served but to whom no such notice is given shall be deemed to be served as a partner.

4 Acknowledgment of service in action against firm

(1) Where persons are sued as partners in the name of their firm, service may not be acknowledged in the name of the firm but only by the partners thereof in their own names, but the action shall nevertheless continue in the name of the firm.

(2) Where in an action against a firm the writ by which the action is begun is served on a person as a partner, that person, if he denies that he was a partner or liable as such at any material time, may acknowledge service of the writ and state in his acknowledgment that he does so as a person served as a partner in the defendant firm but who denies that he was a partner at any material time.

An acknowledgment of service given in accordance with this paragraph shall, unless and until it is set aside, be treated as an acknowledgment by the defendant firm.

(3) Where an acknowledgment of service has been given by a defendant in accordance with paragraph (2) then—

(a) the plaintiff may either apply to the Court to set it aside on the ground that the defendant was a partner or liable as such at a material time or may leave that question to be determined at a later stage of the proceedings;

(b) the defendant may either apply to the Court to set aside the service of the writ on him on the ground that he was not a partner or liable as such at a material time or may at the proper time serve a defence on the plaintiff denying in respect of the plaintiff's claim either his liability as a partner or the liability of the defendant firm or both.

(4) The Court may at any stage of the proceedings in an action in which a defendant has acknowledged service in accordance with paragraph (2) on the application of the plaintiff or of that defendant, order that any question as to the liability of that defendant

or as to the liability of the defendant firm be tried in such manner and at such time as the Court directs.

(5) Where in an action against a firm the writ by which the action is begun is served on a person as a person having the control or management of the partnership business, that person may not acknowledge service in the action unless he is a member of the firm sued.

5 Enforcing judgment or order against firm

(1) Where a judgment is given or order made against a firm, execution to enforce the judgment or order may, subject to rule 6, issue against any property of the firm within the jurisdiction.

(2) Where a judgment is given or order made against a firm, execution to enforce the judgment or order may, subject to rule 6 and to the next following paragraph, issue against any person who—

(a) acknowledged service of the writ in the action as a partner, or
(b) having been served as a partner with the writ of summons, failed to acknowledge service of it in the action, or
(c) admitted in his pleading that he is a partner, or
(d) was adjudged to be a partner.

(3) Execution to enforce a judgment or order given or made against a firm may not issue against a member of the firm who was out of the jurisdiction when the writ of summons was issued unless he—

(a) acknowledged service of the writ in the action as a partner, or
(b) was served within the jurisdiction with the writ as a partner, or
(c) was, with the leave of the Court given under Order 11, served out of the jurisdiction with the writ, as a partner;

and, except as provided by paragraph (1) and by the foregoing provisions of this paragraph, a judgment or order given or made against a firm shall not render liable, release or otherwise affect a member of the firm who was out of the jurisdiction when the writ was issued.

(4) Where a party who has obtained a judgment or order against a firm claims that a person is liable to satisfy the judgment or order as being a member of the firm, and the foregoing provisions of this rule do not apply in relation to that person, that party may apply to the Court for leave to issue execution against that person, the application to be made by summons which must be served personally on that person.

(5) Where the person against whom an application under paragraph (4) is made does not dispute his liability, the Court hearing the application may, subject to paragraph (3) give leave to issue execution against that person, and, where that person disputes his liability, the Court may order that the liability of that person be tried and determined in any manner in which any issue or question in an action may be tried and determined.

6 Enforcing judgment or order in actions between partners, etc

(1) Execution to enforce a judgment or order given or made in—

(a) an action by or against a firm in the name of the firm against or by a member of the firm, or
(b) an action by a firm in the name of the firm against a firm in the name of the firm where those firms have one or more members in common,

shall not issue except with the leave of the Court.

(2) The Court hearing an application under this rule may give such directions, including directions as to the taking of accounts and the making of inquiries, as may be just.

7 Attachment of debts owed by firm

(1) An order may be made under Order 49, rule 1, in relation to debts due or accruing due from a firm carrying on business within the jurisdiction notwithstanding that one or more members of the firm is resident out of the jurisdiction.

(2) An order to show cause under the said rule 1 relating to such debts as aforesaid must be served on a member of the firm within the jurisdiction or on some other person having the control or management of the partnership business.

(3) Where an order made under the said rule 1 requires a firm to appear before the Court, an appearance by a member of the firm constitutes a sufficient compliance with the order.

8 Actions begun by originating summons

Rules 2–7 shall, with the necessary modifications, apply in relation to an action by or against partners in the name of their firm begun by originating summons as they apply in relation to such an action begun by writ.

9 Application to person carrying on business in another name

An individual carrying on business within the jurisdiction in a name or style other than his own name, may whether or not he is within the jurisdiction be sued in that name or style as if it were the name of a firm, and rules 2 to 8 shall, so far as applicable, apply as if he were a partner and the name in which he carries on business were the name of his firm.

10 Applications for orders charging partner's interest in partnership property, etc

(1) Every application to the Court by a judgment creditor of a partner for an order under section 23 of the Partnership Act 1890 (which authorises the High Court or a judge thereof to make certain orders on the application of a judgment creditor of a partner, including an order charging the partner's interest in the partnership property) and every application to the Court by a partner of the judgment debtor made in consequence of the first-mentioned application must be made by summons.

(2) A master or the Admiralty Registrar or a district registrar may exercise the powers conferred on a judge by the said section 23.

(3) Every summons issued by a judgment creditor under this rule, and every order made on such a summons, must be served on the judgment debtor and on such of his partners as are within the jurisdiction or, if the partnership is a cost book company, on the judgment debtor and the purser of the company.

(4) Every summons issued by a partner of a judgment debtor under this rule, and every order made on such a summons, must be served—

    (a) on the judgment creditor, and
    (b) on the judgment debtor, and
    (c) on such of the other partners of the judgment debtor as do not join in the application and are within the jurisdiction or, if the partnership is a cost book company, on the purser of the company.

(5) A summons or order served in accordance with this rule on the purser of a cost book company or, in the case of a partnership not being such a company, on some only of the partners thereof, shall be deemed to have been served on that company or on all the partners of that partnership, as the case may be.

County Court Rules 1981

ORDER 4, RULE 5

5 Partnership proceedings

Proceedings for the dissolution or winding up of a partnership shall be commenced in the court for the district or one of the districts in which the partnership business was or is carried on.

ORDER 5, RULE 9

9 Partners may sue and be sued in firm name

(1) Subject to the provisions of any enactment, any two or more persons claiming to be entitled, or alleged to be liable, as partners in respect of a cause of action and carrying on business within England or Wales may sue or be sued in the name of the firm of which they were partners when the cause of action arose.

(2) Where partners sue or are sued in the name of the firm, the partners shall, on demand made in writing by any other party, forthwith deliver to the party making the demand and file a statement of the names and places of residence of all the persons who were partners in the firm when the cause of action arose.

(3) If the partners fail to comply with such a demand, the court, on application by any other party, may order the partners to furnish him with such a statement and to verify it on oath and may direct that in default—

 (a) if the partners are plaintiffs, the proceedings be stayed on such terms as the court thinks fit, or
 (b) if the partners are defendants, they be debarred from defending the action.

(4) When the names and places of residence of the partners have been stated in compliance with a demand or order under this rule, the proceedings shall continue in the name of the firm.

ORDER 7, RULE 13

13 Partners

(1) Subject to the following paragraphs of this rule, where partners are sued in the name of their firm, service of a summons shall be good service on all the partners, whether any of them is out of England and Wales or not, if the summons is—

 (a) delivered by the plaintiff to a partner personally, or
 (b) served by an officer of the court sending it by first-class post to the firm at the address stated in the request for the summons.

(2) Where the partnership has to the knowledge of the plaintiff been dissolved before the commencement of the action, the summons shall be served upon every person within England and Wales sought to be made liable.

(3) Rule 10(2) and (3) shall apply in relation to service by post under paragraph (1)(b) as they apply in relation to service under rule 10.

(4) Rule 10(4) shall apply in relation to service under this rule as it applies to service under rule 10, but with the reference to paragraph (1)(b) being read as a reference to the same paragraph in this rule and with the substitution for paragraphs (b) and (c) of the following paragraphs—

"(b) delivering the summons at the principal place of the partnership business within the district within which the summons is to be served to any person having, or appearing to have, at the time of service, the control or management of the business there, or

(c) delivering the summons to a partner personally.".

ORDER 25, RULE 11

11 Enforcement of High Court judgment

(1) A judgment creditor who desires to enforce a judgment or order of the High Court, or a judgment, order, decree or award of any court or arbitrator which is or has become enforceable as if it were a judgment or order of the High Court, shall file in the appropriate court (with such documents as are required to be filed for the purpose of enforcing a judgment or order of a county court)—

(a) an office copy of the judgment or order or, in the case of a judgment, order, decree or award of a court other than the High Court or an arbitrator, such evidence of the judgment, order, decree or award and of its enforceability as a judgment of the High Court as the registrar [district judge] may require;

(b) an affidavit verifying the amount due under the judgment, order, decree or award, and

(c) where a writ of execution has been issued to enforce it, a copy of the sheriff's return to the writ.

(2) In this rule the "appropriate court" means the county court in which the relevant enforcement proceedings might, by virtue of these rules, be brought if the judgment or order had been obtained in proceedings commenced in a county court.

Provided that if under these rules the court in which the relevant enforcement proceedings might be brought is identified by reference to the court in which the judgment or order has been obtained the appropriate court shall be the court for the district in which the debtor resides or carries on business.

(3) The provisions of this rule are without prejudice to Order 26, rule 2.

INDEX

References are to paragraph numbers.